Perfectly Prep ∷

CHILD DEVELOPMENT IN CULTURAL CONTEXT

Series Editors

Cynthia Garcia Coll   Peggy Miller

Advisory Board

Jerome Kagan   Carol Worthman   Barrie Thorne

Perfectly Prep: Gender Extremes at a New England Prep School
Sarah A. Chase

Forthcoming Books in the Series

Children of Immigrants: Academic Attitudes and Pathways During Middle Childhood
Cynthia Garcia Coll and Amy Marks

Academic Motivation and the Culture of Schooling
Cynthia Hudley and Adele Gottfried

Literacy and Mothering: Women's Schooling, Families, and Child Development
Robert LeVine and the Harvard Project on Maternal Schooling

Perfectly Prep ::

Gender Extremes at a New England Prep School

Sarah A. Chase

OXFORD
UNIVERSITY PRESS

2008

OXFORD
UNIVERSITY PRESS

Oxford University Press, Inc., publishes works that further
Oxford University's objective of excellence
in research, scholarship, and education.

Oxford   New York
Auckland   Cape Town   Dar es Salaam   Hong Kong   Karachi
Kuala Lumpur   Madrid   Melbourne   Mexico City   Nairobi
New Delhi   Shanghai   Taipei   Toronto

With offices in
Argentina   Austria   Brazil   Chile   Czech Republic   France   Greece
Guatemala   Hungary   Italy   Japan   Poland   Portugal   Singapore
South Korea   Switzerland   Thailand   Turkey   Ukraine   Vietnam

Copyright © 2008 by Oxford University Press, Inc.

Published by Oxford University Press, Inc.
198 Madison Avenue, New York NY 10016
www.oup.com

Oxford is a registered trademark of Oxford University Press

Library of Congress Cataloguing-in-Publication Data is available
ISBN 978-0-19-530881-5

Photographs by Lindsay Lehmann

9 8 7 6 5 4 3 2
Printed in the United States of America
on acid-free paper

To my husband and our sons

ACKNOWLEDGMENTS ⠿

There are many people whom I would like to thank for their help and support in this endeavor and without whom this book would not have been completed. I owe an enormous debt to my intellectual mentors, William Beeman, Phil Leis, and especially Cynthia Garcia Coll and Marida Hollos, for their instruction, guidance, encouragement, and invaluable suggestions. I am sincerely grateful to the editors of this series for their encouragement, help, and belief in this project and to Steve Holtje for his help in editing the work. I would also like to thank Chris for his technical help and Kathe for her efforts on my behalf in procuring materials through interlibrary loan. I would like to thank the faculty and administrators at the school here called Bolton Academy for allowing me to conduct my research there and being so supportive and helpful during the work in progress. I am profoundly and everlastingly grateful to the students of Bolton Academy for their openness, enthusiasm, participation, and friendship, which made this research possible.

Lastly, I would like to thank my family and friends for their patience and support. To all of "the posse" and our angels, Sharon and Judy, I am eternally grateful for your friendship and support. I owe a special debt to my parents, Paul and Molly, and my in-laws, Monie and Stuart. To my sons, I am grateful for your patience when "I'm busy!" became a constant refrain. I hope that they will agree my efforts were worthwhile and that they will find this research meaningful when they approach adolescence. Mostly, however, I would like to thank my husband, whose blood, sweat, and almost tears went into countless editings and revisions of this work.

CONTENTS ⸬

1 ::

Gender Ideologies at Prep School

On opening day in early September, the new students of Bolton Academy begin to arrive on campus and settle into this small New England boarding school.[1] Many drive from the wealthy suburbs of cities such as New York, Boston, and Washington, D.C., along the way passing both picturesque dairy farms and poor mill towns. Suddenly they arrive at the elegant stone walls, groomed playing fields, manicured lawns, and ivy-covered brick school buildings and dormitories of Bolton Academy. Passing through the majestic cast-iron gates, they enter the "bubble" of boarding school life.

The boys and girls are clean-cut and attractive, sporting summer tans and wearing casual, preppy clothes from J. Crew, Lilly, Vineyard Vines, Polo, and Abercrombie and Fitch. The girls are fastidious about their outfits, many wearing short skirts showing their well-tanned legs. The boys are more relaxed and casual in their attire, sporting khaki shorts or jeans and a polo shirt or T-shirt. Pink and pastels are popular colors for both sexes, and the collars of many polo shirts are "popped," sticking straight up in distinctly preppy fashion. The African Americans, international students, hockey players, and a handful of others deviate from the preppy look. While the international students usually are more dressy, sometimes coats and ties for the boys, the other groups tend to wear clothes that are darker in color and either tighter (girls) or looser (boys), such as black jeans, sport jerseys, and matching long, baggy shorts.

While the new students meet their dorm parents and unpack their belongings in their small and sparsely furnished rooms, their parents meet with the headmaster, who ends his welcome speech by politely telling them it is time to leave so that their sons and daughters can start adjusting to their new environs.

One by one the cars drive away until only a tag for a $350 Brooks Brothers blue blazer lies on the main driveway.

For the last fourteen years I have lived the boarding school life, observing the daily rituals of prep school students and witnessing one of the rites of passage for the wealthy and powerful in America. When I first arrived as a newlywed on the campus of Bolton Academy, a college preparatory school for grades nine through twelve, I lived in a senior boys' dormitory with my husband, who served as a teacher, dorm parent, and coach. Although my mother had attended a New England preparatory day school, she and my father moved to an economically struggling small town in Colorado, where my sisters and I attended public schools and had no exposure to private schools. I thus had no idea of what life at a boarding school would be like.

As we started our new life living with hundreds of adolescents, I was struck by how differently the boys and girls behaved and how different their lives seemed. The class, ethnic, and individual differences in how the students seemed to define masculinity and femininity surprised me. I was intrigued by the intensity of the contradictory pressures the boys and girls felt and how these affected their social lives and academic performances. I puzzled, along with the school's administration and faculty, about why the girls consistently outperformed the boys academically. I marveled at the inner workings of the students' peer groups, the strength of their culture, and how often that culture was at odds with the intentions of the school and their parents.[2] I noticed how the pristine campus, attractive students, and luxuries of wealth contrasted with the stress, inner turmoil, apathy, low self-esteem, and substance abuse described by many of the students. Expecting an Eden free of all the teenage problems and educational hindrances of public high schools, I was surprised by the hidden price of privilege.

Curious about the largely unstudied lives of the upper class and the inner workings of the institutional and social perpetuation of power, I wanted to see if I could find some answers to the often-heard exclamations of frustrated teachers and parents: "What are they thinking?" "Why do they act this way?" "I wish we knew what their lives were really like!" I thus set out to try to penetrate the peer cultures of these teenagers in order to better understand their privileged and highly gendered lives and gain insight into their paths of development.

I am an anthropologist, and so my research takes the form of an ethnography, based on fieldwork within a particular culture or subculture and involving long-term, firsthand contact. My background combined with my open personality, my status as a known figure on the campus but not someone with authority, and the students' acquaintance with my husband and sons made me a true insider-outsider, enabling me to secure their trust and gain access to their lives. From my unique vantage point, I observed the collision of adolescence,[3] American culture, gender, socioeconomic class, ethnicity,[4] sexuality, the prep school experience, and institutional and parental expectations.

Despite the similar circumstances of preparatory school, I found the differences in behavior of the boys and girls at Bolton startling. During exam periods, most of the girls worked themselves into a state of sleep deprivation and despair, while the boys appeared unconcerned and relaxed. While the girls tried to be "cute" and "perfect," the boys tried to be "bad-ass" and the "best" at everything. Both genders hung pictures of beautiful women on their walls. The boys competed to see who could hold the most liquor, while the girls often faked being drunk. The girls were covert about their sexual needs, desires, and experiences, while the boys were open and even boastful about theirs. Both genders said the girls were more competitive and had more problematic relationships with each other. On the eve of graduation, many boys regretted not having worked hard enough, but many girls regretted having worked too much. Finally, the boys exclaimed that "it would suck" to be a girl, while more than one-third of the girls would opt to be male if given the chance.

As I became more involved in the students' lives, I became aware of three significant aspects of their gendered behavior. First, I noticed definite class and ethnic differences among the behaviors of the boys and girls. Second, I realized that these behaviors were often performances that masked the students' true tendencies, needs, or desires. And third, I discovered that both boys and girls achieved status and relationships by excelling at stereotypically gendered behaviors. This study attempts to demystify the highly gendered and seemingly incongruous nature of these adolescents' lives.

:: CULTURE AND DEVELOPMENT

Traditional theories of human development in psychology evolved from research based on middle-class Western white males. These theories viewed biology as setting a universal path of development and conflict (Freud, 1934, 1959; Erikson, 1963; Piaget, 1972).[5] Parents influenced children by controlling the children's biologically determined impulses and teaching appropriate behavior. These theories ignored both larger cultural contexts and power structures as well as individuals' own immediate environment.

Even as theorists began to acknowledge the impact of culture on development, they often treated the individual as separate from the cultural process and existing independently of his or her cultural community, thinking that a static culture molded the individual (Piaget, 1972; Kohlberg, 1976). Thus, they viewed the process of socialization as one-directional and coming mainly from a single source, parents. Prominent developmental theorists and texts continue to portray biology and culture in a deterministic manner as programming individuals to feel and act in certain ways.

Recently researchers have begun to recognize the great complexity and diversity of development. Challenging the limited traditional analytical spectrum, researchers have argued for a more active role for the individual in the development process and have added gender, culture, class, ethnic, and power differences to these models (Bronfenbrenner, 1979; Weisner, Gallimore, & Jordan, 1988; Garcia Coll et al., 1996; Garcia Coll & Marks, in press; Bussey & Bandura, 1999; Rogoff, 2003; Ferguson, 2000; Way & Chu, 2004; Wang & Taylor, 2000; Leaper, 2000).

This work follows this paradigm shift in theories of human development arguing that culture and development are closely linked and are mutually constructed in a dynamic fashion through the power of human agency. Like Ortner (1996, p. 12), I examine how the Bolton students "'enact,' 'resist,' or 'negotiate' the world as given, and in so doing 'make' the world." Like Rogoff (2003), I regard human development as a "cultural process" in which children participate and where children not only are products of socialization but also effectively produce their environment. Children are "active contributors" (Engfer, Walper, & Rutter, 1994), influencing their environment as they are influenced by it and thus becoming co-creators of their environments (Rogoff, 1990b; Collins & Luebker, 1994; Kuczynski, 1997; Shweder, 1990; Packer, 1993; Cole, 1985).

:: THE MYSTERIES OF GENDER

Humans have long strived to understand just how and why males and females differ. Anthropologists have contributed a great deal to the study of gender differences by revealing widely varying and often opposing behaviors and traits among men and women in different cultures.

M. Mead introduced the idea that children learn gender identity and roles through socialization with her descriptions in *Sex and Temperament in Three Primitive Societies* (1935) of cultures where men were mild and nurturing and others in which women were aggressive and fierce. Although some of the specifics of Mead's descriptions have since been questioned (Errington & Gewertz, 1987; Freeman, 1983), her work paved the way for the recognition of the malleability of gendered traits.

The study of gender in anthropology rests on the principle that although biology may provide the raw materials for sex differences, gendered behaviors and meanings are cultural and historical creations (M. Mead, 1935). This cultural construction of male and female is labeled *gender*. Ideas concerning what it means to be male and female have been found to differ greatly from culture to culture and include *gender roles* (the normative behavior assigned to each sex), *gender status* (how one gender is valued vis-à-vis the other), *gender ideals* (how a culture defines what is masculine and feminine), and *sex stereotypes* (the characteristics each gender is believed to possess), as well as sex-related practices and beliefs.[6]

As with development as a whole, it is now widely acknowledged that individual, environmental, and biological factors contribute to the complexity and subtleties of gender development (Martin, Ruble, & Szkrybalo, 2002). Often, however, gender theories continue to be largely deterministic, based on biological differences, gendered personalities, or belief in a static culture.

Psychologists have historically attributed the behavior and developmental differences of boys and girls to biology or socialization. Starting with Freud's castration theories (1962), early gender theory rested on the psychoanalytic basis for gender development. According to Erikson (1968, p. 266), women's identity formation is different from men's because their "somatic design harbors an 'inner space' destined to bear the offspring of chosen men and, with it, a biological, psychological and ethical commitment to take care of human infancy." He adds, "Something in the young woman's identity must keep itself open for the peculiarities of the man to be joined and the children to be brought up" (p. 283).

The existence of gendered personalities was, and often remains, a recurring theme in psychological research. Chodorow (1978, p. 7) argues for universal gendered personalities resulting from differences in early socialization patterns, especially interaction with the mother:

> The sexual and familial division of labor in which women and
> mothers are more involved in interpersonal, affective relationships

than men produces in daughters and sons a division of psychological capacities which leads them to reproduce this sexual and
familial division of labor.

Gilligan (1982) claims that women's development of identity and
morality differs from men's, and that identity development in adolescent girls is a struggle not so much for autonomy, as it is in boys, as
for relationships and connections, resulting in different motives, moral
commitments, and worldview. Gilligan's later works (Gilligan, Lyons, &
Hanmer, 1990; Brown & Gilligan, 1992) expand on this argument that an
"inner sense of connection with others" is a "central organizing feature"
in women's development and that psychological crises (including eating disorders) in women's lives stem from disconnections.

Other theories are equally deterministic, with culture, socialization,
or biology seen as dictating behavior. Gray (1992), for example, posits a
biological model where large differences in aggression and competitiveness between males and females are due to testosterone. Evolutionary
theorists view gender differences as the result of evolution (Low, 2000;
Weisfeld, 1999; Buss, 1995; Buss & Schmitt, 1993), resulting in biological
predispositions or constraints on gendered behavior.

Ideas concerning the similarity or difference between males and
females have waxed and waned over time. Since Gilligan's (1982) theories of fundamental gender differences in development became well
known, much research (see Belenky, Clinchy, Goldberger, & Tarule, 1986;
Jordan, Kaplan, Miller, Stiver, & Surrey, 1991; Ashmore, 1990) as well as
popular opinion tends to maximize gender differences.

I highlight the importance of the "active and constructive" cognitive
processes involved in gender development (Martin, Ruble, & Szkrybalo,
2002) and focus on the considerable but hidden similarity in needs and
desires between boys and girls as well as the differences between individuals in each gender. Like other researchers who view gender as performative (Garfinkel, 1967; Newton, 1979; Butler, 1990; Ortner, 1996; West
& Zimmerman, 1987; Shields, 2002), I question any static explanation
for gender differences in behavior as well as the existence of gendered
personalities. Instead, I highlight the importance of individual intent or
agency (Ortner, 1996) on behavior by revealing the performative nature
of much gendered behavior. In this view, social life consists of "serious
games" dependent on "webs of relationships and interaction" where
actors play with "skill, intention, wit, knowledge, [and] intelligence"
(Ortner, 1996, p. 12).

Performance theory recognizes a separation of the material world from the viewer's perception of it. Meanings are social, as the viewer ascribes meanings to the world and its objects through *signs* (Counsell & Wolf, 2001). Performance theory utilizes Saussure's (1959) ideas that signs do not merely express existing meanings but rather are the mechanisms by which meanings are made. Thus, performers use signs to generate meanings within cultural systems of knowledge. The behavior of the Bolton boys and girls is not determined by an existing culture and does not stand in the same relation to biological reality that a shadow has to a shape or a footprint to a foot; rather, the students "conduct," "portray," or "display" (Goffman, 1969) gendered behavior to fit the context, the expectations of the audience, and their own conceptions of masculinity and femininity.

Applying ideas of strategic interaction (Blumer, 1969; Hewitt, 1976; Goffman, 1959, 1967, 1969; Rosenberg, 1979), I view the construction of gender as similar to a theatrical performance or the playing of a game.[7] Without discounting other influences, I show that these students act and present themselves to others in an attempt to guide and control the impressions others form of them. Similar to the way they would play a game of chess, they make strategic moves within the confines of socially constructed gender meanings.

Through daily rituals, the Bolton boys and girls debate, construct, and revise their expressions of masculinity and femininity (Thorne, 1993; Connell, 2000) and accept, adjust, or rebel against (L. M. Brown, 1998; Chu, 2004) the accepted gender ideals on their own terms. The Bolton students "make" (de Beauvoir, 1953; Ortner, 1996), "do" (West & Zimmerman, 1987), or "play" (Thorne, 1993) gender through their social interactions (West & Fenstermaker, 1995; Deaux & Major, 1987).[8] As they strategically conform to or resist these gender ideals, they influence and create their own culture.

The students also internalize their gendered performances. By continuously acting in gendered ways, the students as well as those around them "come to believe and perform in the mode of belief" (Butler, 1990, p. 179). The internalization of gendered traits and the relative value society places on them play out in the students' self-concept, self-identity, and self-esteem.

While recognizing current research pointing to some biological differences that could affect behavior, I postulate a fundamental similarity between males and females. At the same time that new cognitive and social-cultural effects on development are becoming understood, so again is the importance of biology. This new biological emphasis differs from historical biological perspectives, however, in that biological differences and environmental factors are viewed as interacting in complex and continuous processes (see Bugental & Goodnow, 1998; Bandura, 1989). Researchers are focusing on how individual differences in biology and constitution influence social, emotional, and personality development, how humans are uniquely "wired" to be able to create culture (Nagell, Olguin, & Tomasello, 1993), and how genes and hormones affect brain structure (Halpern, 1992; Shaywitz, Shaywitz, Pugh, & Constable, 1995) and behavior (Finegan, Niccols, & Sitarenios, 1992; Buchanan, Eccles, & Becker, 1992), including aggression (Coie & Dodge, 1998; Radke-Yarrow & Kochanska, 1990) and empathy (Eisenberg & Fabes, 1998; Davis, Luce, & Kraus, 1994).

This work reveals clearly how biology can influence gender indirectly. Factors such as temperament, early or late onset of puberty in relation to peers (Buchanan, Eccles, & Becker, 1992), height, and physical attractiveness (Unger, 1993) elicit varied responses from the individuals who constitute the social environment. The students at Bolton who are considered attractive, athletic, tall, or thin are treated much differently than those considered unattractive, unathletic, short, or overweight.

At the same time, however, this research reveals that cultural aspects of gender development are particularly significant. The needs and desires of males and females are largely similar, and the differences between the genders are much less than they appear to be. In particular, both genders demonstrate similar needs for status and human bonds. Like Baumeister and Sommer (1997), I propose that men and women are equally social but direct their sociality differently.

It is by excelling at performing the upper-class ideal of gender that the Bolton students are best able to fulfill their needs for both status and human bonds. A system of opposing class-based symbols and behavior (Eckert, 1989) represents masculinity and femininity, with anything associated with one gender being heartily embraced by that gender but emphatically rejected by the opposing gender. This symbolic system is expansive and comprehensive, marking almost all behaviors, values, and interests (including such far-reaching elements as academic effort and pursuits and career goals) as either "masculine" or "feminine." It is these personal and social expectations that serve to perpetuate the class-based ideals of masculinity and femininity. This work examines the students' own ideals as well as how they are influenced by the inner workings of peer groups, their parents, and the practices and traditions of the school itself.

The recognition of the multiple influences on development has increased the attention paid to sources of socialization other than parents, especially the peer group. Peer groups are recognized as both the product of and contributing producers of gender differentiation (Bussey & Bandura, 1999), leaving permanent marks on individuals' personalities (Harris, 1995; Birch, 1987). The separate and differing natures of male and female peer groups are seen as resulting in different cultures and therefore having different developmental processes, with their resultant different styles of interaction, values, and goals (Maccoby, 1998). Individuals internalize group norms as their own preferences and behave accordingly (Bussey & Bandura, 1992).

In recognizing the complexity and diversity of development, developmental psychologists are coming to understand the value of methodologies offered by disciplines such as anthropology and sociology.[9] Critics have pointed out that the methodologies of traditional psychological studies on which most developmental theories rest are limited because the research is conducted primarily in laboratory settings.[10] Our understanding of the paths of human development rests primarily on research on middle-class white males that is generally conducted on strangers in artificial settings for short-term studies or interviews. The shallowness of most data, the failure of the data to reveal a coherent, broadly applicable, and permanent representation, the lack of context for the research findings, the inability to account for subjectivity, and the impersonal nature of these data with the corresponding inability to reconstruct the individual limit the current research on development (Jessor, Colby, & Shweder, 1996). Consequently, researchers urge that studies include various approaches and be conducted in natural settings (Jessor, Colby, & Shweder, 1996; Sherif, Harvey, White, Hood, & Sherif, 1961; Parlee, 1979; Eagly, 1987; Block, 1976).

A few significant works, primarily by linguistic anthropologists and sociologists, have begun to explore exactly how peer groups operate and exert their influence in a natural setting. Through ethnographies conducted primarily on the playgrounds and in the cafeterias and hallways of public elementary and middle schools, these studies document the language and everyday interaction of peer groups and their effects on the formation of gender and social identities (see Eckert, 1989; Adler & Adler, 1998; Eder, 1995; Goodwin, 1990, 2006; Thorne, 1993).

The variety of methodologies utilized, the breadth of the research, and the focus on the lives of upper-class adolescents set the present work apart. This is an ethnographic account based on long-term participant observation of high school students in a privileged and relatively closed community. It compares the different experiences and attitudes of a diverse group of teenagers in the same natural setting over a two-year period and includes a sample size of more than 75% of the student body at Bolton Academy. Not only does this research provide a unique, in-depth account of peer groups, but it also addresses issues of gender, social class, race/ethnicity, and sexuality.

∷ PERPETUATING POWER

Power structures and hierarchies enmeshed in the institutions and practices of society are part of the larger culture that shapes individuals' environments and thus their development (Garcia Coll et al., 1996.) The divergent opportunities available to individuals because of gender, socioeconomic class, and ethnicity/race are incorporated by socializing agents such as parents (Ogbu, 1981), peer groups, and schools, so children's development is largely an adaptation to their existing opportunities (Leaper, 2000).

Schools reflect and affect larger cultural patterns and beliefs (Tobin, Wu, & Davidson, 1989) and act as co-expressors of masculinity and femininity (Heward, 1988; Connell, 2000; Ferguson, 2000; Martino & Meyenn, 2001). Preparatory schools along with other American institutions are historically a man's world, a world based on hierarchy (Peshkin, 2001), excellence, political conservatism, cutthroat achievement, competition, toughness, pursuit of individual success, and survival of the fittest. Through its disciplinary system, supervision, policies, dress code, social events, sports, academic competition, social hierarchy, academic curriculum, gendered subjects, and selective admission, Bolton Academy sustains these values and tacitly encourages extreme gendered behaviors.

Females attending these schools or entering the professional world may adopt the manly ideals but are burdened by prevalent gender ideals and their inequality as women. Like the middle-class and working-class girls in L. M. Brown's study (1998) who accept the dichotomization of gender, admire "masculine" characteristics, distance themselves from more "feminine" qualities, and use misogynistic and homophobic language, these prep school girls, our country's most privileged, well-educated young women and those who have the greatest chance of becoming leaders, adopt the voices and accents of patriarchy and women's oppression. Likewise, prep school boys also learn that success is based on their ability to embrace masculinity fully, and to devalue and separate themselves from things feminine.

Several recent works illustrate that the interplay of gender, class, sexuality, and racial/ethnic structures and hierarchies results in multiple and often opposing masculinities and femininities (Connell, 2000; Bettie, 2003; Ortner, 2003; Way & Chu, 2004), demonstrating the complex ways that these social categories are created through social interaction rather than simply being natural entities. Race and class are political, historical, and situational constructs (and performances) in relationship to gender (Bettie, 2003, p. 35). In this view, class is learned (Steedman, 1987) through relationships with family and peers and in social institutions such as schools. Individuals perform class through class-specific styles of speech such as accents or nonstandard grammar (Labov, 1964, 1972), dress, mannerisms, and symbolically significant material possessions.

Calling for an expansion from the white middle-class subjects of traditional research, these previous works focus on minorities and the lower class. Researchers have largely ignored the upper class, despite the uniqueness of that class's experiences and the insights it provides. Notwithstanding the individuality among the students (see also Briggs, 1998) and the importance of personal psyche in creating a sense of gender (Chodorow, 1999), the importance of social class in relation to gender becomes clear. Distinct patterns emerge among the different social classes and ethnic/racial groups at Bolton as the students negotiate aspects of gender such as gender ideals, sexual practices, body image, and appearance.

Although institutions perpetuate collective definitions of masculinity and femininity, the players make strategic decisions to follow the rules more or less closely depending on the context. Observing these students as they live their everyday lives together at a boarding school, a hub of power and prestige in America, makes it clear that the path to acceptance for these students is based on excelling at difference. By excelling at the categories of in-group membership and the appropriate, gender-associated behaviors and thereby distancing themselves from those outside the group, these students gain both status and popularity in the hierarchy of the school.

This journey into the lives of prep school students is an attempt to understand the pressures and consequences of these prescribed gender ideals from their own perspectives and through their own words. The chapters of this book are organized around the symbolic opposition these adolescents create as they live, eat, study, and play among their peers and teachers at Bolton Academy. Although this work is limited to one very select group of American adolescents, these findings have broader implications. The class, ethnic, and individual differences in the performance of gender reveal how culture and development are inter-related and necessarily fused through the power of agency. Oppositions and hierarchies based on gender, class, ethnicity, sexual orientation, and social hierarchy may be augmented in this setting but remain revealing of American cultural patterns. A culture's underlying values and beliefs are revealed in its traditions and customs as well as in the small rituals of everyday life, and so this inside look at the everyday social interactions of this group of adolescents reveals how institutions and groups in power incorporate and perpetuate hierarchies and power structures, which in turn serve to form American character.

2 ::

Prep Schools and Bolton Academy

The mystique of prep schools and their mostly elite student body has captured popular imagination and drawn national attention in recent years. Over the past few years networks have aired several different TV series about prep school life, including *Young Americans*, about a poor but brilliant boy who attends a prep school in Connecticut; *Gossip Girl*, about prep school privilege and delinquency in New York City; and *Zoey 101*, about a creative and spunky girl who attends a previously all-boys prep school in California. Recently a film depicting prep drama was shot on a prep school campus and was slated to appear at the Cannes film festival. *Prep*, a novel about prep school, became a best seller (Sittenfeld, 2005), while a book sensationalizing the sexual exploits of a prep school's students (Jones & Miley, 2007) is the subject of talk shows and hushed discussions on the summer cocktail party circuit and in faculty rooms at prep schools across New England. Despite this increased focus on prep schools, few scholarly accounts examine either the prep schools themselves or the elite society from which most of their students come.

:: PREP SCHOOLS AND POWER IN THE UNITED STATES

Because access to the elite is strictly limited, the powerful and the power structure in complex societies have rarely been scrutinized. Social scientists have tended to study the more accessible middle classes or endeavored to make visible the invisible, downtrodden, or marginalized of society. To understand any society, however, it is vital to study "up," as the individuals who occupy the upper echelons of society serve as the leaders and trendsetters.

The American elite influence not only their own country but also the world. The wealthy hold political power in America, epitomized by the pictures of the Kennedys at their Hyannis compound or the Bushes at their Kennebunkport estate. An extensive study of corporate executives (Dye, 1995) estimated that based on parental occupation, listing in the Social Register, and attendance at a prestigious prep school, 30 percent of American corporate directors came from the top 1 percent in regard to wealth. Socially, the wealthy set the fashions and trends, are the gate-keepers for what is in and what is out, and guide the nation's sensibili-ties through images of their lives and material trappings as featured in glossy magazines or on TV. Current examples include the attention given to the exploits of Paris Hilton and the popularity of teen books about the lives of rich teenagers such as *The Clique* series (Harrison, 2005).

Logistical and ethical concerns are causing anthropologists to bring their methods, developed on the tradition of studying the non-powerful in non-Western societies, to the study of their own societies (Hymes, 1972; Messerschmidt, 1981). Due to limited access to the elite, however, few studies have examined the lives of the upper-class. Prep schools in particular are difficult to study. Weinberg (1968) describes these dif-ficulties as "the general difficulties of studying elites, the omnipotence of the principal or headmaster, and the problem of data collection in a student subculture located in a total institutional setting" (p. 141). Anthropology is particularly suited for a study of the culture of prep schools and the unique issues and concerns of elites in America who continue to dominate the rest of society both economically and socially (Wolfe, 1991).

Institutions such as schools promote cultural themes and power structures (Whiting & Edwards, 1988; Tobin, Wu, & Davidson, 1989; Ortner, 2003). American boarding schools were designed to perpetuate privilege (Cookson & Persell, 1985), enmeshing the values of the Ameri-can white upper class in its foundations.[1] Prep schools have been called the initiation rite for the upper classes in America (Gilmore, 1990; Chan-dos, 1984; Heward, 1988; Cookson & Persell, 1985; Mills, 1959).[2] Cookson and Persell state, "The philosophies, programs, and life-styles of board-ing schools help transmit power and privilege and . . . elite families use the schools to maintain their social class" (1985, p. 4). Domhoff (2002) describes boarding schools as "linchpins" in the upper-class educational system that serve, along with other exclusive social institutions such as private clubs and exclusive retreats and resorts, to build upper-class social cohesion. Weinberg (1968) notes that prep schools play a primary role in "group formation among elites" (p. 141).

That these schools separate and isolate the children of the upper class is in itself evidence of institutional perpetuation of power and belief in a social hierarchy. Further, the beauty and grandeur of the grounds, chapels and other buildings, and furnishings; the emphasis on tradition and excellence; the classical and conservative nature of the curriculum (Latin and Greek classes); the importance placed on sports, sportsmanship, and the arts; and the formal dress code promote upper-class values and a social hierarchy.

Although prep schools in America have changed since their conception, in many ways they have remained the same. The demographics of private education have shifted as Ivy League and top-tier colleges are able to draw from a larger pool, and prep school students and legacies (the children of alumni) are no longer shoo-ins for admission. Since it is now harder for all students to gain entrance to the top colleges, preparatory schools must sell other qualities to attract prospective students and their parents.

Prep schools continue to offer the wealthy a wide range of educational advantages that serve to perpetuate wealth and status. They provide academic, artistic, and athletic opportunities that public schools with squeezed budgets cannot offer. Preparatory schools still offer a better chance for college acceptance than most public schools, which cannot offer advanced-level courses, access to SAT prep classes (some prep schools even require them), and aggressive college counseling services. They offer individual attention almost beyond belief. For $45 an hour, students can hire a private tutor (often a faculty member's wife who is a former teacher now staying home with her small children) to help them with a particular subject or just help them to get organized. In a valiant effort to keep students enrolled, especially the very wealthy who may be potential big donors, the schools bend over backward to help students achieve. At Bolton teachers have gone to students' rooms every morning to wake them so they are not late for class, they have had students come to their houses every night to do their homework, and they give extra help virtually on demand. Everything possible is done to help the students succeed.

Parents also continue to send their children to private prep schools for the "right" social connections and influences. Prep schools sell the safety of their campuses and the "quality" of the peer groups of which students will become part. They offer an environment where students will be surrounded by the "right" kind of people and will be apt to make lifelong friendships. The status of having attended prep school will also help them both socially and in business. In some ways, these schools sell entrance into the upper social class.

Survival of the fittest is an integral part of boarding school. Although the physical life at boarding school has softened over the years, "emotionally and intellectually the prep rite of passage is still meant to inflict a certain amount of pain—for without pain there can be no transformation and legitimation" (Cookson & Persell, 1985, p. 29). These values and ideals are played out in the stress and pressure the Bolton students feel to be "perfect" and the "best at everything," the awards and prizes for excellence, the social hierarchy between faculty and students and between the different forms (grades), and the athletic, social, and academic competition.

Definitions of masculinity and femininity are also enmeshed in the history of institutions and economic structures (Connell, 1995). Boarding schools promote a definition of masculinity based on occupational and class values of toughness and individual success, which are antithetical to "feminine" characteristics of caring and nurturing (Heward, 1988, p. 195). Because masculinity is something that needs to be achieved, preparatory schools provide a way for upper-class youth to earn their manhood through hardship, self-direction, discipline, and absolute self-reliance (Gilmore, 1990; Chandos, 1984).

Given the dominant masculine traditions of competition, toughness, and pursuit of individual success at boarding schools, conflicting gender ideals intensify. When boarding schools admitted girls, they subjected the girls to the prevalent value system and judged them by it. Their parents were spending much money on their education, apparently endorsing the pursuit of academic excellence as well as occupational status for their daughters. Despite the entrance of girls into institutions of status and power, this book demonstrates that they are still strictly held to their traditional gender ideals, which are the antithesis of male ideals and cultural values. The high value placed on success, individuality, and excellence in these institutions encourages extremes in gender differentiation as well as the devaluation of sensitivity, caring, and other stereotypical female traits and ultimately female lives and females themselves.

:: THE PRICE OF PRIVILEGE

Adolescents from elite families pay a price for their privileged childhood and have unique developmental concerns. Psychologists have asserted that the "culture of affluence" adversely affects adolescents' well-being due to an "over-emphasis on achievement and isolation from parents" Luthar (2003). One of the consequences of the tough admissions policies at top colleges is that prep school students are under incredible pressure to succeed. In order to attend the same colleges that their parents or grandparents did, today's high school students must be of a much higher caliber. The intensity and pressure these students face are greater than ever before.

The most affluent youths report being the least happy, while the least wealthy report being the happiest (Csikszentmihalyi & Schneider, 2000). Affluent adolescents use the highest amount of certain drugs, including marijuana, inhalants, and tranquilizers (Johnston, O'Malley, & Bachman, 1999). Unlike inner-city youth, they often use substances in an effort to alleviate emotional distress (Way, Stauber, Nakkula, & London, 1994; Luthar & D'Avanzo, 1999). Popularity is more closely tied to substance use among affluent teens than it is among their less affluent counterparts (Cooper, 1994; Feldman, Rosenthal, Brown, & Canning, 1995).

Researchers have described the lives of the rich as an endless pursuit of perfection and excellence: being average is tantamount to failure (Luthar, 2003). The wealthy have stressful and competitive lifestyles, seeking to acquire material possessions. Their children develop stress-related symptoms due to extreme pressures to excel (Pittman, 1985), some not connected to anything meaningful other than "the raw and relentless pursuit of pleasure" (Resnick [1999], cited in Luthar, 2003, p. 1584).

Because of the upper-class emphasis on appearance, personal appearance becomes a primary objective even for children (Coles, 1977). Upper-class women long to be thinner (McLaren, 2002) in order to enhance their class distinctions in attractiveness and desirability based on weight and lack of exceptional cleavage (Jefferson, 2000). This preoccupation with wealth and appearance explains the famous upper-class women's motto I have seen needlepointed into pillows: "You can never be too rich or too thin." Upper-class women also appear to focus less on careers and more on social avenues to status.[3]

Eating disorders are prevalent in white upper-middle-class and upper-class adolescent girls, who attempt to be perfect (Bruch, 1973, 1978). Most anorexics come from homes where pressure for social position, appearance, and academic achievement are high, with girls often being sent to the "best" schools (Bruch, 1978, p. 35). Many of these girls consider themselves not worthy of all the privileges and benefits their families offer them. In order to live up to the expectations of their families, the girls strive to be "brilliant, athletic stars and beautiful (thin)" but feel like "disappointing failures" because they were "not good enough in comparison with others" (p. 24). Upper-class girls often feel like they have to "have it all" by being thin, beautiful, and successful (Gordon, 1990).

Male binge drinking can also be linked to upper-class values and the culture of affluence. Despite their wealth, upper-class boys often experience unhappiness because of the pressures to work and acquire material goods, competition, hierarchy, the lack of time for relationships, the lack of value placed on internal rewards, high levels of stress, and the potential for much self-doubt and insecurity (Luthar, 2003). At Bolton, the students feel intense parental pressure to surpass or at least equal their parents' high social and professional status, to make it into the family alma mater, and to be perfect. The unique associations among affluent youth between popularity, depression, anxiety, and pressure to excel account for much of the substance abuse seen in this group.

:: PREP SCHOOLS AS A SITE OF STUDY

Studying elite adolescents in a New England preparatory school setting is advantageous for several reasons. First, anthropology can add to our understanding of young-adult development a new perspective based on in-depth participant observation with "manageable" sets of people who "represent a distinct social sector or scene" (Caughey, 1986). The students at a preparatory boarding school fit the criterion of "manageable" because they are uniquely accessible. A few hundred students take classes, play sports, eat, study, have relationships, party, and sleep all in one location. The dorms provide a valuable site for research because there the students live and spend most of their evening hours together and are used to having adults in their midst as dorm parents, advisors, or faculty on duty.

Second, preparatory schools fit Goffman's (1961) definition of "total institutions" as "places of residence and work where a large number of like-situated individuals, cut off from wider society for an appreciable period of time, lead together an enclosed, formally administered round of life" (p. xiii).[4] The Bolton students speak of it as being in a "bubble." This provides unique opportunities for the researcher to penetrate their lives somewhat unnoticed, conduct group interviews in their "homes," and study their dorm room decorations.

Third, because of the intensity of preparatory school and the parental and administrative pressures for success (the first because of the cost of their education, the second because the school's reputation hinges on its students gaining admission to prestigious schools), the issues faced by high-achieving adolescents in the United States are exacerbated in this setting. Many elite high schools and colleges have reported a high level of stress and burnout among this population and a corresponding increase in suicide, binge drinking, and eating disorders on their campuses (Zernike, 2000; Healy, 2001; Frahm & Puleo, 2000). Although pressure is not new, the director of admissions at Harvard sees "more of this clearly articulated stress, pressure, feelings of inadequacy, comparing oneself to all these other extraordinary people" (Zernike, 2000). An MIT task force on mental health, which was established after six students committed suicide in the four-year period from 1998 to 2001, convinced the highly competitive college to expand its mental health services in order to "relieve the emotional and academic stresses felt by many students" (Healy, 2001).

:: PREP SCHOOLS: THEN AND NOW

American boarding schools originated in New England in the late eighteenth century, modeled on the British public schools. Their original mission was to educate "an unselfish and virtuous elite for positions of influence and leadership" (Hicks, 1996, p. 527). Their primary objectives were "the discouragement of self-centeredness" and the formation of "unselfish and wise habits in the sons of the rich" in order to make "natural" aristocrats out of "artificial" ones. To do so, the early founders thought, required the "isolation of a rural setting and the rigor of a strenuous and well-ordered life" (Hicks, 1996, p. 531). Promoting a Spartan existence and trials that would counteract parents' overindulgence and the soft life of the rich, the schools sought to instill "intellectual, moral and physical fiber." In the 1960s, prep schools "broadened their relevance by making room for a 'natural' aristocracy of all races, colors, creeds and classes" (Hicks, 1996, p. 534).

Serving as the initiation rite for the power elite in America (Cookson & Persell, 1985; Mills, 1959), prep schools provide "a selection and training place of the upper classes," "a unifying influence or a force for the nationalization of the upper classes," and "the characterizing point in the upper-class experience" (Mills, 1959, pp. 64–65). At the same time that they perpetuate class position, they cream off the best and brightest of the non-WASP students to help forge a new "ethnic aristocracy of talented and ambitious young people" (Baltzell, 1964, p. 344). Studies have demonstrated the influence of preparatory schools, revealing that alumni of thirteen elite boarding schools accounted for 10% of the members of the boards of directors of large American business organizations even though they constituted less than 1% of the population at large. Furthermore, 17% of individuals who are top officers of two large companies and 15% of those who are top officers of three large companies also attended these thirteen elite barding schools (Useem, 1984, p. 67).

On paper, many of the prep schools share similar mission statements: to develop each student's mind, body, and spirit to the fullest potential, to build character, and to prepare students for college and the real world. Most of the schools maintain groomed campuses, have state-of-the-art academic, athletic, and arts facilities, and hire capable and attractive faculty and staff. Despite these similarities, each prep school has its own personality and sells a particular image to prospective parents and students. Some schools promote their distinguished heritage and convey an aura of academic excellence and affluent exclusivity, while others offer special ESL or learning skills programs, work with students with learning disabilities, or base their curriculum on character development. Many schools cater to the notion that a strong school must have a strong athletic program and recruit athletes to boost the soccer, football, basketball, hockey, lacrosse, and wrestling teams. Some schools have large endowments that allow them to offer generous scholarships to attract the student body they desire, while others must admit a critical number of full-pay students who do not always meet the school's desired admissions criteria. Some schools encourage student independence by easing curfew, intervisitation (visiting the dorm room of a member of the opposite sex), and study hall rules, while others regulate student free time around the clock. Some schools promote a family atmosphere through small living units and frequent meetings between students and their faculty advisors, while others rely on rituals and traditions (school meetings, sit-down dinners, senior chapel speeches, and religious services) to promote community and moral values.[5]

Admissions officers orchestrate the diversity of preparatory schools, carefully choosing the makeup of each class:

A school filled with "brains" stands the risk of driving away the less brainy but wealthier families. A school that is entirely "prepped out" may find its reputation among college admissions officers slipping. Too many "jocks" make teachers unhappy, too few jocks make students and alumni unhappy. Moreover, the picture is complicated by the search for diversity. (Cookson & Persell, 1985, pp. 54–55)

Appearance is important both to the schools and to their wealthy patrons. Parents and students expect prep schools to look old, elegant, and traditional but at the same time to have the finest state-of-the-art athletic and recreation facilities. Resembling country clubs with school buildings, they project an aura of exclusiveness from the manicured lawns to the elegant furnishings in the alumni offices and the spectacular chapels full of marble and stained glass. This image extends even to the appearance of the student body: "It is not by chance that most prep school students have shiny, well-combed hair, are trim, healthy, and at least reasonably attractive. . . . Part of the screening process is to weed out those who will not fit in" (Cookson & Persell, 1985, pp. 54–55).

One aspect that makes the prep school experience so significant and memorable to these students is their common survival of pressures coming "from three different directions in a triangle of tension":

Families are anxious that their children succeed, which often runs counter to their schools' public insistence on "morality," which is directly opposite to the student culture's message of eat, drink and be merry for tomorrow you graduate. These competing values create a psychic gauntlet through which the elite student must pass—the prep rite of passage. (Cookson & Persell, 1985, p. 20)

Despite these schools' efforts to control their privileged environments, the students create their own culture. The pressures they feel, their often unlimited funds, their constant interaction with their peers, and the strong influence of the larger adolescent culture all influence the student culture, within which sexual activity, drug use, binge drinking, eating disorders, racism, and cheating occur. Notwithstanding this "hidden curriculum" of prep schools (Crosier, 1991), the students rarely encounter the problems that plague the nation's public high schools: crime (other than stealing), overcrowding, no individual attention, lack of enrichment programs (music, arts, sports, and so on) due to budget cuts, violence (other than hazing), truancy, fear, overt racism, and many other social ills reported on the nightly news.

:: BOLTON ACADEMY

Bolton Academy is a small New England coeducational boarding and day school, grades 9–12. Although not one of the "top tier" boarding schools, it is prestigious and one of the most expensive to attend. According to an article in *Boston* magazine entitled "The Ultimate Guide to New England's Private Schools," Bolton competes with approximately 120 other private schools in neighboring states (J. Marcus, 2002, p. 75).

In the year this study was conducted, 75% of Bolton's students were boarders, with the rest day students. The student body had a 55-to-45 male/female ratio and a 5-to-1 student/faculty ratio. Students of color and international students comprised 11% and 12% of the student body, respectively. Twenty-seven percent of the students receive need-based financial aid.

The campus displays majestic brick buildings covered in ivy, manicured lawns, and playing fields, all surrounded by lush woods, streams, and ponds. People often pull their cars over to the side of the road to take pictures of the beautiful buildings and groomed lawns (the school maintains its grounds with an annual budget of well over $150,000), especially in the fall, when the foliage is at its peak. An Old English–style chapel complete with grand stained-glass windows adorns the main green, and majestic gates guard the entrance. The school's physical plant—student run radio station; magnificent student center with games, large-screen TV, and snack bar; performing arts studio; and extensive state-of-the-art sports facilities, including an Olympic-size swimming pool (complete with teak benches), boat house, two ice hockey rinks, and an Astroturf field—would rival that of any college. In the gym, pictures of sports teams from past years hang next to mahogany plaques engraved with the names of the captains of each sport.

The students complain about the academic rigor and intensity at Bolton, considering the academics to be far superior to and more difficult than those at a public school. Students must take a demanding schedule of English, science, math, foreign language, arts, history, computer, and religion courses, as well as mandatory sports and/or extracurricular activities. Advanced placement courses are offered in numerous subject areas.

Like all private schools, Bolton depends on its image in order to sell itself to prospective students and their parents, spending time and money to present the school in the best possible light in order to attract the most qualified candidates. The admissions building, where prospective students meet with admissions officers, is traditionally and elegantly decorated with oriental rugs and leather furniture. The admissions officers themselves are among the most attractive and impeccably dressed adults on campus.

The sleek and tasteful school catalogue contains many glossy pictures of smiling students, teachers, and the facilities. The catalogue lists the colleges to which Bolton students were accepted. An elite professional team prepares much of the school's printed and electronic promotional materials and spends several days each season on campus carefully composing shots. When they photograph the headmaster and his wife on the front green, they set up an intricate lighting system to create the right look and orchestrate every detail, even to the point of having the headmaster remove his keys from his pocket to avoid any break in the line of his pants. Everything looks perfect.

The alumni and development office, an important group on campus, organizes reunions, publishes an alumni magazine, and raises funds.[6] The office pays special attention to wealthy students whose parents may reward the school with monetary gifts, referring to them as "their kids." Every other year the alumni and development office organizes an auction to raise money for scholarships during a spring parents' weekend. During the year of this study a group of loyal volunteers transformed the indoor multipurpose athletic center into a beautiful and elaborate re-creation of an Italian town. The auction raised more than $100,000. The auctioned items and the amounts raised included: to be headmaster for a day, $1,000; dinner with the headmaster and his wife, $550; first pick of dorms for the next year, $2,400 (juniors), $1,200 (sophomores), $800 (freshmen); and front-row seats at graduation, $1,550. Parents and alumni also donated vacations in their villas or trips aboard their yachts for auction to the highest bidder.

The students at Bolton are, with very few exceptions, remarkably clean-cut, dressed in designer clothes whenever possible, thin, and attractive. The boys generally wear their hair short and the girls wear theirs long. They wear tailored clothes, not the loosely hanging or low-riding styles popular among some adolescents.

The school administration struggles to keep the girls covered to a degree they deem appropriate, banning bare bellies and implementing a rule to keep skirts at least as long as the girl's fingertips when her arms are at her sides. Even on frigid winter days, girls have bare legs under skirts so short they must hold them down when they walk for fear a breeze will reveal their undergarments. After spring break most of the faces return tanned from trips to sunny locales such as Florida or the Bahamas.

Although Bolton has its own traditions and rituals, many aspects of the typical high school experience in America are not part of the Bolton experience. For boarders, there are no cars. There is no homecoming king or queen, no homecoming parade, no limousines, and no after-prom parties. There are no powder puff football games and no cheerleaders.

One afternoon when Bolton plays a soccer game against a local high school that brings cheerleaders, groups of boys and girls from Bolton snicker and laugh as the cheerleaders perform with pompoms on the field. Every so often, a random cry of "Oh my God!" or laughter erupts. A Bolton girl exclaims, "It's so degrading." Boys and girls alike mock the visiting cheerleaders.

As the students themselves frequently observe, there is both more diversity at Bolton than at public schools and less. At Bolton, there are more international students and students of color than at the public schools in the towns where the majority of the wealthy students are from. Because of Bolton's financial aid program, the class status of the student body is diverse, ranging from the extremely wealthy to the very poor. However, the visual homogeneity of the student body is striking, as the majority of the students embrace preppy styles of clothes and grooming.

For most of Bolton's students, boarding school turned out to be different from how they thought it was going to be. They commonly say, "I thought it would be a *lot* different" or "This was just a big shock to my system. Oh man! I don't know what I thought it would be, but not this." The boys and girls cite similar reasons for the disparity between their expectations and the reality of their experiences: lack of freedom, an intense schedule, and the closeness of relationships with faculty and peers.

Many of the students expected a stereotype, everyone "preppy and smart" or "snobby," but found a different reality. One girl observes, "I thought everyone was going to be gifted and talented kids, and then

I get here and I see people . . ." She pauses, groping for words, and another girl interjects, "That are dumber than dogs!" A boy didn't expect "as many people who got in maybe because they had money or something," noting, "They are stupid. I didn't think they'd be here." With a locked jaw, another boy says, "I thought we'd be yachting. I thought we'd be like, 'Hey, Buffy.'"

In one dorm, a boy states:

> I knew nothing about prep schools and . . . I was shocked. Like
> I thought it was going to be a bunch of completely stuck-up prep
> kids who studied their asses off . . . and I was like, "Wow, this is a
> lot better than I thought." And then when I was here longer, I was
> like, "Wow! This sucks."

Arriving at Bolton with a negative view of "rich white people" as "stuck up and idiots," an African American scholarship student discovered that "rich white people are cool."

Others, particularly the African American scholarship students, were surprised at the amount of drugs at Bolton, something they don't see among their friends at home. A New York City girl says, "I see regular crackheads at home, but here I see it, and it's my friend doing something bad." A boy reflects, "I didn't think there'd be that much of a drug problem. . . . I didn't think it would be that severe, that that many kids would be doing it."

The scholarship students also frequently cite the "negativism" on campus, surprised that so many students do not want to be at Bolton and do not appreciate what an opportunity it is. One girl notes, "I value being here. I value it a *lot*, and a lot of people don't. They just don't want to be here at all. From the day they came they're like, 'I want to go home.' They don't look at it as such a privilege."

Past the manicured lawns, the majestic chapel, the ivy-covered school buildings, and the clean-cut boys in coats and ties and girls in dresses lies the brick building that houses the cafeteria, post office, health center, and business office. In a little office next to the cafeteria, the harried school counselor meets with students, some who come voluntarily and others who are forced to see her because they are having problems. When one of the students who is required to visit her doesn't show up, she squeezes me into her busy day to describe the special concerns and issues she sees among the Bolton students.

She describes freshmen as "adjusting, being away from home." Sophomores are "trying to adjust to increased expectations," and this is when "sex and social decisions hit" the hardest. Juniors are "focusing on results" because this is the year colleges look at most closely, but due to the "high intensity" they experience "lots of problems." Seniors have "many demands" that involve either "letting go" of Bolton or fear about the next stage in their lives.

The biggest issues the students at Bolton face are parental pressures and the stress and fast pace of life at Bolton. The counselor notes:

> The pace here for most people is so quick that there's no time for reflection . . . and it's gotten faster. Almost every moment is taken. . . . For these kids every moment is committed until about 10:00 P.M., when the supervision starts to dwindle, and I think the kids kind of engage in their own kid culture late at night because that's when they have time to do it.

The counselor believes the pace is getting faster, and she hears more about the abuse of performance drugs. She explains that about one-sixth of the students at Bolton are on Ritalin or antidepressants, a greater proportion than one would find in the public schools but less than at the more competitive prep schools, because "any issue they have, . . . any learning disability, any kind of mood blip, . . . any kind of base anxiety is exacerbated because of the demands that are put on them."

She views this extensive use of medications as unique to prep schools because the financial and social status of the parents often increases the pressures they put on their children to succeed: "Parents are assuming that their kids will go to college. That's not a yes-or-no question. Their kids will go to college and they would like to place their kid at the most competitive college that they can." She adds that parents push their kids "to perform, perform, perform so that their lives will sort of mimic the lives of their parents, their social group will mimic the social group of their parents."

She notices that because students "are under so much stress," they don't know how to have fun:

> It surprises and saddens me that more of these kids don't just have good clean kid fun. . . . They're serious. They respond to the multiple demands placed on them. Really, they're small adults and they're adults that you can feel are getting ready to go out into the corporate world. . . . It surprises me that as many kids make it as they do. . . . I feel that we are asking too much of these kids.

She concludes, "These kids are balancing so much. It's hard here, and by the time many of the students get to their goal they are burnt out. They don't want to do it anymore."

Since Bolton is less competitive than some other schools, the students generally face less pressure and have fewer problems. She explains, "All problems increase as you go up to higher-level prep schools." When she and counselors at other schools compare the problems of their students, the "one thing that stands out is that the expectations of the parents are so much more" at the most competitive schools. She concludes, "Prep school facilitates giving up childhood."

Confirming the counselor's viewpoint, the students describe Bolton as kinder and gentler than many other preparatory schools. Numerous times during my research, students who transferred from other prep schools, often more prestigious ones, exclaim enthusiastically that the issues at Bolton are minor because Bolton is "less competitive" and the intensity level and competition are not as fierce. Parental pressure is also less intense than at the "higher-level" schools.

Students credit Bolton's strict policy against hazing and the fact that Bolton is "not an athletic powerhouse" for the lack of violence and hazing. Some of the boys were surprised at the lack of hazing, claiming that Bolton is "different than a lot of other boarding schools just because there's a strict no-hazing rule." A boy who came from an all boys' school found "a lot more violence and hazing there." Another boy states:

> My brother went to [another prep school] and he said he was lucky to make it through his sophomore and junior year because there was such hazing, that coupled with the amount of work he had. Like he'd be up until 3 every night doing his work and then he'd be hazed till 5, then he'd go to bed. But here, because there's no hazing, it's a completely different dynamic.

Girls also describe Bolton as socially less competitive and intimidating because they feel less pressure to conform in appearance and to wear the right label of designer clothes than at some other prep schools. The students also praise the faculty advisor system at Bolton as improving student/faculty relationships and contact.

Although it has its own personality, Bolton is a typical small New England prep school. As they did at their conception, prep schools continue to offer entrance into upper-class culture and social networks of wealth even if they fail to deliver the same certainty of acceptance into

Ivy League colleges. These upper-class students receive the benefits but also must pay the costs of privileged lives.

:: GETTING BEHIND THE SCENES

The value of an anthropologist rests not in bringing home mere facts but "on the degree to which he is able to clarify what goes on in such places, to reduce the puzzlement—what manner of men are these" (Geertz, 1973, p. 16). As Geertz explains, anthropology is "not an experimental science in search of law but an interpretive one in search of meaning." Thus, this work is very different from the sociological and psychological research based on the statistical analysis of surveys, lab tests, or interviews. Anthropology is different from other disciplines because it attempts to be holistic, examining whole functioning communities and all aspects of life. It is also comparative and cross-cultural because anthropologists compare data from different areas and from different time periods. Anthropological methods are unique because they are based on long-term fieldwork (usually around one year) during which the anthropologist participates as much as possible in the daily lives of the locals. Using participant-observation techniques, along with written questionnaires and some statistical data, I observed the daily lives of these adolescents to examine the interplay of culture and development. As anthropological research depends to a large degree on the interpretation of the researcher, a detailed account of the methodologies used is vital in order for the reader to determine the validity of the work.

I first approached the headmaster of the school to ask permission to conduct my research at Bolton, explaining what I wanted to study and how I would go about it. I explained how my findings might help high school teachers and administrators understand their students better and thus be more able to help the students reach their full potential. I stressed that I needed to be able to maintain complete confidentiality in order to get the students to open up and tell me any useful information. In line with his progressive and proactive leadership style, he granted me full access to school life. I then addressed the students and faculty at Bolton Academy during a school meeting in the chapel, introducing myself and explaining my research as well as my obligations and restrictions as an anthropologist. I assured the students of complete confidentiality and stressed that I was under no obligation to or contract with the school. I took great care to let the students know the range of my research, detailing the types of events and data I would be observing (including the public files of the school Internet service). When the data seemed especially personal, I asked the participants directly for permission to use the information. At the end of the research, I made public offers to remove any information that they regretted sharing with me or felt might have negative repercussions for them or other students. No students made any such requests. To protect the students' identities, I have changed the name of the school—as well as competitor schools—and not only changed the students' names but also turned them into composite characters. Although all the events described here actually occurred during the course of this research, not all the incidents attributed to a particular composite character happened in the life of any one real-life individual. I also postponed publication of this book until all individuals involved were 18 years old and had left Bolton.

Hot double-fudge brownies formed the cornerstone of this research. Homemade goodies are a prized commodity at Bolton Academy due to the institutional-style food served in the dining hall and the well-known teenage desire for snacks. I used brownies and other snacks in my research both as a lure and as a small way of giving something back to the students for taking the time to talk with me. Gathering around some pints of Ben and Jerry's ice cream, milk, fruit, and brownies provided a relaxed atmosphere in which to chat. I provided snacks during all dorm interviews, on the senior trip, in exchange for senior speeches, and as a special thank-you when a group let me observe them doing a particular activity.

My research consisted of two phases, my preliminary research and the main research. The preliminary research included two types of research: long-term casual participant-observation and then intensive data collection. After the preliminary research was completed, a hypothesis was developed, and then the main research project took place during the 2000–2001 school year to test the assertions in my hypothesis. I chose to conduct the research over one academic year because dorm assignments change every year, and I wanted to achieve the broadest possible coverage.

I used a wide variety of methods in my attempt to penetrate the world of these adolescents. The primary sources of data were written texts, oral texts, participant observation, room tours, terminology surveys, and statistical data. The written texts include disciplinary committee platforms (statements by those individuals hoping to be elected to the disciplinary committee), notes to me from the students, school newspapers, senior pages in the yearbook, and postings by students on the school Web page. I gathered these either from the students themselves or from the location where they were posted or distributed. I also collected anonymous written surveys on a variety of topics with the help of the school's English teachers, who passed them out in class and then collected them; the only identifying characteristics collected on these surveys were age, sex, and nationality.

The oral texts include group interviews conducted by me in the dorms, group interviews conducted by the students themselves on sexuality and deviance, private interviews with particular students, chapel speeches (every senior is required to present a chapel speech passing on advice to younger students), student speeches at graduation, platform speeches by candidates for student body president, and student meetings. I also interviewed administrators, teachers, and the school counselor. All group interviews were recorded and then transcribed in full. The transcripts for all speeches were obtained from the student giving the speech. Detailed notes were taken for the other events, either while it was occurring or shortly thereafter.

Participant-observation is central to this study. While conducting the research I lived on campus with my husband and had constant contact with the students. I ate in the dining hall and attended picnics, plays, sports events, graduations, convocations, award banquets, and graduation parties. I hosted advisee dinners and sports banquets. I provided birthday cakes for celebrations in the dorms, drove kids to local stores, and drove an advisee to the psychologist for help with an eating disorder. I spent time with students talking about things as varied as anorexia, older boyfriends, lives falling apart due to drugs, and pressures from a demanding father who wanted to control his son's future. I took them shopping for prom dresses, observed them in the dressing room before a dance performance and backstage during a Mr. Bolton contest, and hung out in the dorms during final exams, the day of the Super Bowl, and when Valentine flowers were delivered. I watched them perform senior pranks, sat in the back of the football bus and the field hockey van on the way to games, attended foam dances (where students dance in mounds of bubbles), and joined the seniors on their whitewater rafting trip. We discussed, and in some cases read together, the magazines they read, and I then analyzed the content of the most popular ones. In short, I participated as fully as possible in the daily lives of the students at Bolton.

I gathered other types of data as well. Students in the dorms gave me tours of their rooms that consisted of showing and describing to me the items displayed there. At the end of the tours, I asked what the most meaningful item in their room was and why. Three different terminology surveys were conducted. These include personal maps of where the different cliques ate in the dining hall, appearance terminology, and sexual terminology. I collected statistical data from the school newspaper and archives, academic dean, school counselor, alumni office, and business office.

Group interviews took place in the dorms usually from 9:30 to 10:30 P.M. This time was chosen because it is at the end of study hall (8:00 to 10:00) and before lights-out, 10:30 for the underformers (freshmen and sophomores) and 11:00 for upperformers (juniors and seniors). From 10:00 to 10:30 the students had to be in their dorms, and most were relaxing before bed, making this a good time to approach them for interviews. The dean of students at Bolton Academy gave me permission to go into the dorms at 9:30 P.M. (before the end of study hall) as an added incentive for kids to talk to me, provided I work with the dorm parent to make sure that those students whose grades were suffering waited until study hall was over.

I visited each dorm about four times during the school year. The first two visits were generally group interviews, the third was a self-interview, and on the fourth I collected personal maps of the dining hall and conducted the room surveys. I generally conducted interviews on nights when there was study hall, saving weekends for participant observation. Although one might think that when there was no study hall and the kids would have more free time it would be a good time to snag them for interviews, it did not work that way. Life at a prep school is so intense during the week that weekends are sacred for just relaxing. This is the students' time, and because it is so rare and precious, I had little opportunity (or desire) to impose on it.

I learned this reality during my preliminary research when a dorm parent insisted that I come to his dorm on a Friday night, when there was no study hall. I arrived with snacks in hand to find the lights off in the common room and several students lying down on couches in front of the TV with open pizza boxes, sodas, and cookies strewn on the table before them. I immediately sensed that the kids, half asleep and engrossed in a very bloody Arnold Schwarzenegger movie, were not the least interested in being interviewed or even in my snacks (this had never happened before or since). So, despite being urged to proceed by a dorm parent who was sure that this was a good time, I simply sat down nearby and watched the rest of the movie with them.

When I arrived at a dorm, I would ask the prefect (the student leader assigned to the dorm) or a student that I knew to help me round up students who would be willing to talk to me. While the students were gathering, I set up my very large microphone right in the center of where we would gather. I did this purposely so that the students would have no doubt that what they were saying was being tape-recorded, and would be constantly reminded of it. I had an open-ended questionnaire, but the interviews were informal in nature and the tangents the students took or their own questions were always interesting and revealing, thus highly encouraged. During the group interviews, I would ask the students questions regarding their thoughts on the experience of prep school, their concerns, pressures in their daily lives, their opinions about males and females, how their peer groups work, how they view race and class issues in their lives, the types of rule breaking that occur and how they feel about it, and their sexuality (by far their favorite topic).

In an effort to avoid having my age and gender affect how students answered some of the most sensitive questions, those involving sexuality and deviance, in most instances I had the students conduct self-interviews on those topics. I would arrive at the dorm with a variety of snacks, set up the recording equipment, hand the students a list of questions but encourage them to ask their own questions (which they often did), and then leave. Then student volunteers (often I would ask ahead of time a student who had been involved in the study and whom the other kids seemed to like) would conduct these interviews, and then I would return at the end of the interview. Other than perhaps more vulgarity among the male students, my presence or absence did not seem to alter the content or tone of the interviews.

At the end of my research I had interviewed either individually or in the group settings more than 75% of the student body in the interviews alone. The anonymous surveys and participant observation only increased my coverage, and I feel confident that my material is representative of the vast majority of the student body of Bolton Academy. Least represented in my research are: students from Asian countries (because they did not come out for the treats and interviews), children of faculty (because they did not often frequent the dorms or dayrooms), and day students (because although I did visit the dayrooms numerous times, they were largely only on campus during the day and the opportunity to question them in depth and to observe their behavior was more limited than with the boarding students). I do not view these limitations to be of great consequence, however, because my goal was to uncover the predominant culture at Bolton, which I believe I was able to achieve.

During the 2000–2001 school year, 12% of the student body was foreign, and I attempted to compare their responses to their American counterparts' in order to demonstrate more clearly what might be uniquely American. It was usually easy to identify the international students' responses. The students were asked to list their nationality on all surveys, all students' home addresses are listed in the face book (a booklet that has pictures of all students, faculty, and staff), and international students often self-identified when they learned that this was a study on American culture (i.e., "I'm from France but . . ."). Many times I asked the international students directly to compare adolescence in their own culture to what they were experiencing at Bolton. These data added a cross-cultural view to this work.

Finding Patterns

The data for each dorm were compiled and organized in a consistent order. The responses for each dorm were then closely read against the transcripts of the students' discourse and compared for content and patterns. No computer program was used for fear of losing the intricacies of the data. The answers to the written questionnaires were similarly compiled and compared. Numerical data were analyzed by using simple percentages of the given number of responses. The number of responses varied depending on how the information was gathered, and in each case the total number of responses is given.

Doing the Right Thing

Ethical concerns are of the utmost importance in anthropology. Because of the personal nature of anthropological techniques and the closeness of the researcher to the people studied, the potential for ethical dilemmas is great. The American Anthropological Association (1998) has created a code of ethics that guides anthropologists in making decisions about ethics and values. The code of ethics describes the anthropologist as having an obligation to the discipline of anthropology, the wider society and culture, the human species, other species, and the environment.

Anthropologists' primary obligation is their responsibility to the people, animals, and material studied. This concern should take priority over all else, including the ability to conduct the research at all. In order to ensure that their research does not harm or wrong the informants, anthropologists must do all they can to preserve the safety, dignity, and privacy of the people with whom they work. The researcher must obtain informed consent from the people studied, meaning that they must understand the purpose, nature, and procedures of the research and its potential impact on them. Anthropologists should recognize their debt to the communities studied and the people with whom they work, and reciprocate in appropriate ways.

It was sometimes hard for the teachers and administrators at the school to understand my need to be able to offer complete confidentiality to the students. The dean of students called me into his office once and said that some of the teachers were having difficulty understanding how I could be an adult interacting with these students and not "do something" if I saw them breaking the rules. I had to explain that first and foremost an anthropologist has a responsibility to protect and not cause harm to the individuals he or she befriends and studies, and that if I had to turn any student in, I could not and would not do this study at all. I also explained that the role of the anthropologist is to describe impartially, to analyze behavior, and not to make judgments about others' behavior, whether it be crack addiction in Spanish Harlem (Bourgois, 1995), prostitution in the era of AIDS (Sterk, 2000), or rule breaking at a prep school. Anthropologists' work can ultimately serve to bring about desired change in behavior or circumstances by providing documentation and understanding of others' lives and behaviors that might enable or encourage individuals in power to facilitate change.

I was an adult like the teachers and administrators, but my role was different from theirs. Although I was prepared to leave if the students ever started to break school rules or the law in my presence, none ever did. I dreaded some large ethical dilemma where I would witness or hear of something so bad that I would feel that I had to report it in order to save a student and would thus have to abandon my research on ethical grounds. Luckily, this never happened. The worst thing I witnessed was when one girl showed me the small mouse she was keeping as a pet in her room, which was against school rules. She asked me not to tell and I didn't.

Although I didn't witness any illicit activities during my research, I did get to experience the thrill of being busted. One night when I was in a boys' dorm, a meeting was taking place in the common room, so I conducted the interview in one boy's dorm room. While I was interviewing five or six boys about their relationships with their parents, the door suddenly flew open and the dean of students rushed in. We all jumped. When the dean saw me, he stopped and laughed, explaining that he had heard a girl's voice from behind the closed door and had feared the worst.

That I did not judge the students' behavior or turn them in does not mean that I endorsed everything they did. Although sometimes joining in the students' lives was fun and highly entertaining, it was also at times disturbing or depressing, and often uncomfortable. I would frequently come home from my late-night forays into the students' world with knots in my stomach and depressed about the reality I was witnessing. I would think about my own young sons and hope that what I was doing would help them someday when they reached adolescence and would have to face the same challenges and pressures that these students were facing. "If they could only understand it and see what was going on," I would say to myself, "that would help so much."

Although many of my experiences venturing into their world were uncomfortable, the one that sticks in my mind as the worst is also the one that helped me to understand it the most. During one session in a boys' dorm, the boys started talking about the male faculty members' wives, all of whom I knew. After they had talked about all of my friends, describing them as either "so hot" or "heinous" or "she might have been hot 20 years ago," one of the boys turned to me and added, "And you, you're built like a tank." He quickly realized what he had said and mumbled, "Just kidding." I just smiled, pretending it hadn't bothered me. As an athletic 38-year-old who takes great pride in her comfort with her body and her lack of the "body issues" I had seen in so many other women, I was ashamed of the effect it had on me. I went home and scrutinized myself in the mirror, becoming unhappy with what I saw. I now fully understand the intensity of the pressures students of both sexes feel when faced with the scrutiny of their peers and the strength needed to ignore it.

What's Missing

It is undeniable that a limitation to my being able to gain full access to the prep school world is my age and gender. Although I was extremely surprised and delighted by the responsiveness and apparent openness of both the boys and the girls (I think they liked the food), my access to the boys was more limited than it was to the girls. Despite what

I considered my extremely good rapport with the boys and my inclusion of several student-run interviews and taped "rap sessions," it would be unreasonable to think that my being a woman did not somehow affect the responses of the boys (see Canaan, 1986). I do, however, believe my research on the male students remains sound (see Jankowaik, 1993).

As one means of determining the effect my presence might have on both the male and female students, one of the questions in the self-interview concerned what aspects of their lives they would have a hard time talking about to me. The responses of the males and females were very similar, and most stated that they felt free to respond to the general questions I was asking on almost any subject. A few students mentioned that they would hesitate to discuss "the extremely personal aspects" of their lives, such as their sex life, if I were to ask those questions. Most of the male and female students said that there was nothing that they would hesitate to share with me: "Nothing at all," "Seriously nothing," or "Nothing. She's totally cool." One boy went so far as to state:

> I think because of the confidentiality, I could pretty much talk about anything, but with Mrs. Chase, not with other people. The fact that I have confidentiality doesn't mean *anything*. It doesn't mean dick to me, in fact. I don't know why, but I just trust Mrs. Chase.

Others commented on how much truth came out in the interviews. One boy laughingly said, "I, like, tell her, like, everything about my life." Another male wrote me, "When you come to the guys' dorms, we try to be pretty blunt and open. So tackle the girls and you've got Bolton."

Another assumption of this work is that individuals have shared their true thoughts and ideas and have described factual events accurately. In no type of research, however, can the researcher be sure that the informants are being truthful. Also, the events described are neither verifiable nor necessarily factual, but rather they are simply the students' opinions and ideas. The importance of the information lies in what it reveals as meaningful in the students' lives and how they talk about it, so I do not regard this inability to validate beliefs or events as a limitation of this work. Rather, their limited, highly exaggerated, or widely fluctuating responses clearly demonstrate gender ideals. Furthermore, what the students do not say is equally revealing. One boy confides:

> Some of the questions that were asked even tonight I didn't answer normally because there are a lot of guys in the room, but if it was

just me and Mrs. Chase I would have answered more fully because there are some responses from the guys that I wouldn't have liked.

Others agree, and one boy adds that males are hesitant to share things in a group setting "if you think it's going to make you look like less of a bad-ass, if it will fuck with your image at all."

The spring after I completed my research, I presented an outline of my findings and analysis to interested students, administrators, and faculty and asked for feedback to confirm the accuracy of my data from the students' perspective. Although several faculty and administrators questioned my portrayal of the students' lives, the students unanimously supported and defended my findings to the faculty, saying, "She's got it right. That's the way it is!" After the presentation, one boy wrote to me, "I don't think there is anything that I from a student's perspective can correct you on." Another girl wrote:

> Your presentation was incredibly accurate and on target. All the conclusions you made were so right, and I know the students present felt the same way I do. There was not one thing you said that I felt was not truthful about our society . . . but I think some of it is hard for the faculty to hear.

3 ::

Social Worlds: How Girls and Guys
Do It Differently

Although the desire to belong is strong among all groups of adolescents, how individuals need to act in order to fit in is unique to each cultural and social context. As early as the 1830s, Tocqueville cited independence, along with equality and democracy, as the basis of what he considered "the American cultural dialogue" (Tocqueville, 1945). Since then, researchers of American culture have described an American symbolic system based on the principles of freedom, equality, democracy, self-reliance, and individuality.[1]

The American value system and power structure, coupled with upper-class ideals and the particular experience of attending a New England boarding school, create a unique environment in which the students "do" gender, class, ethnicity, and sexuality. While exploring the issues the Bolton students wrestled with and anguished over, I discovered that their concerns revolved around the need for perfection, excellence, and superiority in order to fit in and be popular and not be seen as a "loser" and left out. These concerns, along with the special circumstances of attending a prep school, influence how they negotiate cultural oppositions such as equality and inequality, individuality and conformity, freedom and constraint, excellence and fun, and especially the overarching expectation of a male focus on "self" and autonomy and a female focus on "other" and caring about what others think.

:: MORE SIMILARITIES THAN DIFFERENCES

Based on a dichotomy between the self-concepts of "independent" and "interdependent," many researchers describe a fundamental difference in the needs and desires of men and women. Women are represented as valuing relationships (Chodorow, 1978; Gilligan, 1982; Miller, 1976; Belenky, Clinchy, Goldberger, & Tarule, 1986; Cross & Madson, 1997; Jordan & Surrey 1986; Sampson, 1988; Stewart & Lykes, 1985), while men value autonomy and status. Women are described as "interdependent," "collectivist," "sociocentric," "ensembled," "communal," or "connected," while males are viewed as "independent," "individualist," "egocentric," "separate," or "autonomous." These theories have become popular, and consequently a large-scale division between the self-concepts, motives, and values of the genders has become generally accepted.

Researchers have begun to view the general idea of individualism/collectivism dualisms as too broad, static, extreme, limiting, one-dimensional, and irrelevant to real life (see Killen & Wainryb, 2000; Rosenberg, 1992; Lebra, 1976; Harkness, 2001; Hollos & Leis, 2001; Hollan, 1992; Holland & Kipnis, 1994; Spiro, 1993; Kuwayama, 1992; Strauss, 2000; Plumwood, 1993).[2] Current research critiques such dichotomies because they render invisible interdependencies and the coexistence of such dualities as well as multidimensional levels of conformity. This work similarly argues against the notion that there is an actual gender dichotomy of self and other by demonstrating how differences in behavior are often simply performances.

The opposition between the ideals of self and other for the Bolton boys and girls is so significant that it differentiates the performances of masculinity and femininity as a whole. The performance of femininity revolves around a focus on other and relationships. Girls make time in their busy schedules to help friends and to wake up early in order to look good for class. One girl spends an hour straightening her hair every day because her boyfriend says she looks "like a model" with her hair straight, and another girl makes an emergency trip to Wal-Mart during the middle of final exams in order to buy hair dye. Many of the girls' behaviors can be regarded as a struggle between the culturally encouraged other (and relationships) and the culturally discouraged self (and achievement), with other most often winning out.

Similarly, the performance of masculinity revolves around a focus on self. The boys engage in one-upmanship, struggling for status and overtly displaying self-confidence, self-interest, and self-reliance. Succumbing to pressure to suppress their emotions, needs, and connections with others, the boys often feel lonely and isolated because they deny or downplay any mental or physical hardships and refuse to express their feelings with their male friends. The pressure they feel to appear self-sufficient and self-driven plays out as a constant struggle between the culturally sanctioned self and the culturally discouraged other, with self the undisputed winner.

The Bolton students face the pressures of this self/other dichotomy early. Best (1983) describes a strict "gender role curriculum" that elementary school students learn from their peers by second grade. Girls should be helpful and nurturing, while boys should look down on and distance themselves from girls. Definite hierarchies arise for each gender, with the male standard being machoism, athleticism, and intelligence, while the female standard is based on beauty.

The gendered performances of self and other exist among the students at Bolton largely because the boys and girls are striving to attain social success, not because of any significant differences in biology or development and not because they are simply programmed by socialization. If the Bolton students deviate from these gender ideals, they are often chastised by the other students and suffer a loss of social status and connections. These cultural rewards and punishments serve to maintain and enhance the gender differences in behavior.

:: BONDS AND STATUS

Despite popular theories to the contrary (Chodorow, 1978; Gilligan, 1982; Miller, 1976; Cross & Madson, 1997), this book reveals that both genders desire bonds and connections as well as autonomy and status. Relationships and fitting in are extremely important for both genders (Baumeister & Somer, 1997; Gabriel & Gardner, 1999).[3] The difference lies in males' focus on larger groups and females' concentration on one-on-one relationships. Research supports a strong (although often covert) male focus on human bonds. Males describe themselves more in terms of membership in groups than females do (McGuire & McGuire, 1982), have more cohesive friendship groups than those of females (Stokes & Levin, 1986), are more likely to congregate in larger groups than females (Maccoby, 1998), have larger social networks than females (Belle, 1989; Berndt & Hoyle, 1985), have more coordinated group activities (Benenson, Apostoleris, & Parnass, 1997), and have lower reading achievement if they are not accepted as part of the "in" group by their peers (Best, 1983).[4]

Research also confirms the values and traits of females as individualistic and independent. Girls have proven to be as aggressive as boys, but they hide these tendencies (Bjorkqvist, 1994; Crick et al., 1999). Although boys engage in more aggressive behavior than girls (Maccoby & Jacklin, 1974), girls are more apt to engage in relational aggression and view this type of aggression as a common anger response for girls (Crick & Grotpeter, 1995; Crick, Bigbee, & Howes, 1996). Examining group conformity, Eagly, Wood, and Fishbaugh (1981) demonstrate that females make no more of an effort to maintain group harmony by changing their opinions to match those of others than do males and that males conform less only when others are watching (indicating the desire to put forth the image of strength and nonconformity). Also, women are more likely than men to initiate breakups, and men often suffer greater distress than women after a breakup (Rubin, Peplau, & Hill, 1981). Women also initiate divorce more often than men, but men remarry more often and more quickly than women (Albrecht, Bahr, & Goodman, 1983).

Because of social pressures and the expectations of others, boys and girls behave in ways that conceal many of their true feelings and emotions. Shields (2002) reveals that because of the stereotypes concerning the appropriate way males and females should show emotion, how individuals "do emotion" is pivotal in how they "do gender."[5] The demonstration of emotions (with exceptions such as anger) is regarded as feminine. Girls are socialized to such a degree to be nice that instead of showing anger openly, they turn to social aggression (rumors, teasing, backstabbing) as a way to solve the dilemma of feeling angry and wanting to be honest yet also wanting to be nice (Underwood, 2003; Galen & Underwood, 1997; Kring, 2000).[6] For boys, it is not uncommon to see a father admonish his four-year-old son who has injured himself to "be a man" and not to cry.

Despite this socialization, boys covertly value other and girls covertly value self in their everyday lives. Recent research describes how boys desire to show emotions and need connections (Way, 1998; Chu, 2000, 2004; Tolman, Spencer, Harmon, Rosen-Reynoso, & Striep, 2004), whereas girls reveal their individuality and need for autonomy and status through their competition, cruelty, and hidden fighting (Simmons, 2002; Shields, 2002; Underwood, 2003; L. M. Brown, 2003). At Bolton the boys privately bemoan the need to act strong, tough, and cool as well as their inability to show emotion and share feelings. The Bolton girls complain that they are constrained because they need to care so much about what others think about their appearance and behavior. Girls' difficult relationships, competition, meanness, and gossiping about each other also reveal their quest for status and self-aggrandizement.

:: THE OVERT VALUE OF OTHER

Publicly both the boys and the girls focus on others or relationships, espousing community, helping others, and being selfless rather than selfish. In many of the platform speeches by candidates for student body president, the students either promise or focus on better relationships within the school community or their own selflessness. One Bolton boy who was a presidential hopeful contends:

> I spend more time engulfed in helping friends with their home-
> work than spending time on my own studies. I even helped two
> of the other presidential candidates with their speeches. I have
> a passion for helping others . . . I am simply not as interested in
> helping myself than I am in helping others around me.

In their chapel speeches, the boys are just as likely as the girls to talk about the importance of others. One boy, describing how much he misses his dad, whom he has not seen in four years, says, "Cherish those special relationships you have because you are never gonna know when those phone calls are going to stop." In another chapel speech, which the administration delayed one week because of its fear about how the speech would be taken by visitors who would be attending chapel, a girl describes her discovery that she was pregnant and her first impulse to have an abortion:

> Through a combination of lack of thought and consideration, fear,
> and other *selfish* reasons, I decided that the only way out of my
> "problem" was forcing myself to go through having an abortion.
> (Emphasis in original)

Overcoming her "selfish" motives, she decided to have the baby.

:: THE COVERT VALUE OF SELF

Even though both the boys and girls publicly focus on other, they covertly value self more, with its consequences of academic, athletic, and career and financial success. How much self-orientation and other-orientation they are expected to display is gender-dependent. The ideals of masculinity revolve around the more highly valued self, while the ideals of femininity revolve around the less valued other. Although the boys and girls have similar needs and desires, they face different expectations and pressures as they negotiate and manipulate self and other.

:: RELATIONSHIPS—THE DOMAIN OF GIRLS

The Bolton students regard relationships, both good and bad, to be the domain of girls and the essence of femininity. Although the girls focus on relationships, their backstabbing, "ratting," spreading rumors, cruelty, and "being two-faced" are anti-relational. Both genders describe girls as much more competitive and having more problematic relationships with each other than males. While the girls present themselves as being concerned with establishing close connections and relationships, they covertly desire status and independence and act in ways that disrupt their relationships. Like the boys, their drive for status and power is ultimately a desire for bonds, but both genders achieve their desired connections at a price. Whereas the boys jockey for social status openly, the girls destroy relationships covertly while maintaining the overt appearance of caring and being nice.

:: THE PLACES YOU WILL GO, THE PEOPLE YOU WILL MEET

Despite the problematic relationships of the girls and the relational costs of "coolness" for the boys, the students base the essence and benefits of their preparatory school experience on gender ideals. Although the students agree on some aspects of what it means to be attending a preparatory school, the girls focus more on close relationships and the boys emphasize group connections through success, status, excellence, sports, achievement, restrictions, and business advantages.

Some of the reasons the boys and girls give for attending boarding school are similar: it offers preparation for college, a better education, small class size, sports, an opportunity to mature, and independence. Many say, "It was expected" or "My parents dumped me" (meaning they were forced to come to Bolton). When they expand on their reasons, the girls focus more on the intensity of interpersonal relationships, while the boys focus more on issues of status, freedom and constraint, and "fun."

What the girls enjoy most about the prep school experience is the intensity and closeness of the relationships with their peers:

-It's like living with all your friends. It's so much fun.

-We borrow each other's clothes, we all like—

-We have like, a slumber party all the time.

-It's like a permanent sleepover.

The girls also appreciate the exposure they have to faculty and the more substantial relationships that result: "You make a lot of lasting relationship with teachers because they're not just your teacher, they're your coach, they're your advisor," and "Some of them are your best friends." Many girls applied to Bolton because of these relationships or because the admissions officer who showed them around "seemed like such a sweet guy."

What the girls dislike about prep school are the negative aspects of relationships. Some girls explain: "Since relationships are so important, having to deal with those people every day" becomes oppressive. "We're so close, people know everything about you, even things you don't want them to know." Other girls reveal, "We even get our periods around the same time" and "We all start bitching at each other." One of the girls hates "how you can develop, like, a huge reputation." The girls also criticize faculty who are "always expecting you to do something bad" and male students who are "jerks" and "have no idea what a woman wants."

One girl notes the important but consuming nature of relationships: "We are dealing with relationships mostly. Relationships with our peers and our parents and with our teachers, etc. We deal with these in addition to our schoolwork, our extracurricular activities, and our sports, and at times it becomes overwhelming." Another claims, "The worst thing here is the backstabbing and gossiping with no truth at all." Another comments, "Things between girls are always competitive, and most girls are two-faced."

Unlike the girls, the boys do not glow about the closeness of relationships with faculty and their peers, and their relationship issues and problems are not as intense. They focus more on group connections such as sports, status, success, and contacts as well as freedom and constraint issues. One boy says, "A lot, a lot of people come for sports, better sports, 'cause they want to play in college." Many boys say they came to Bolton for one reason: "hockey" or "the hockey coach." Typically, the boys have a hard time thinking of the best thing about boarding school, but eventually they mention "getting away from your parents," "independence," and "freedom to make your own choices." Unlike the glowing accounts of the girls, the boys assert:

-The guys are fun. The girls really suck.

-They're annoying and stupid.

-They always scream and act cute, and it's really pissing me off.

The boys think that the contacts they will gain and the status of having attended Bolton will help them in their future lives. One boy declares, "Seriously, it's all about who you know . . . rubbing elbows, you know." Another adds, "Even if the person went to a different prep school, you can talk: 'Oh yeah, the hockey team played that team,' and you're like, 'Oh,' and automatically you sort of know this guy already."

The only group of male dorm residents that enthusiastically describes the best thing about boarding school are those in the socially lower-ranking (or less "bad-ass") freshman dorm; these boys focus on relationships and opportunities. One of the boys, Jeff, who consistently resists the prescribed gender parameters on behavior, unabashedly states that the best thing about Bolton is "the relationships between the people in the dorms." Others add similar relationship-centered issues: "I'm not afraid of the seniors" and "There's no hazing here."

When describing the worst thing about boarding school, the boys give fast and heartfelt answers about how they detest the rules, restrictions, and lack of fun. Unlike the girls, they do not mention any negative aspects of relationships.

∷ ISSUES AND PRESSURES

In the anonymous surveys they filled out in their English classes, the students reveal the pressure they feel to fit into the "appropriate" category of self-directedness for boys and other-directedness for girls as well as the desire to act otherwise.

The girls typically bemoan the pressures they feel to focus on others. One girl states, "I don't think guys take their girlfriends or girls as seriously as girls [take guys]. I don't believe that boys here are starving themselves because of a girl." Another writes, "Girls feel more pressure to please everyone, fit in, be popular. Boys just roll out of bed, maybe shower, and deal with classes until sports." One writes:

> Just being in the presence of a girl who's prettier than me makes me feel ugly and uncomfortable. . . . I pressure myself to be perfect—at school, in sports, and physically. (I hate my nose!) When I can't achieve perfection, it's depressing and hard to come to grips with.

In contrast, the boys' issues are more self-directed and involve group connections as they strive to succeed academically and athletically, to "get girls," and to rank socially. Unlike the girls, the boys do not report significant relational problems.

In stark contrast to what they say in public, the boys repeatedly write about how relationships and "fitting in" are major concerns in their lives, often revealing the desire for closer relationships with each other, girls, parents, and teachers. One boy regrets the lack of relationships in his life:

> Right now in my life, I am dealing with loneliness. . . . Basically, I have no friends. I made high honors, but feel that I have no one to talk to.

Many boys write about the importance of their relationships. One boy comments:

> I believe that dorm life would be the hardest for you to understand. In the dorm there is a certain feeling that we have towards each other and these feelings are sometimes shown in ways that are hard for adults to understand.

Another student writes,

> It would probably be the hardest . . . to uncover the way one's parents still affect them, even though they are miles away.

This hidden focus on relationships by the boys indicates that relationships are not an acceptable topic of discussion for males as well as that their self-directedness is forced upon them by the cultural ideals of masculinity.

The students agree that the girls have more intense and intimate relationships with each other, parents, and faculty but that the boys are more
inclusive and flexible in their groupings and have fewer relationship
problems. The boys' joking or buddy-buddy relationships with coaches
and certain dorm parents are usually not considered as close as the girls'
relationships with adults.

The girls contend that the special circumstances of boarding school
result in more intense relationships "in all ways." One girl explains, "I
mean, if you're living, sharing a bathroom, sharing living space with
people . . . you know you have a closer relationship. Just 'cause you
spend every moment with them." Thrown together with others whom
they normally would have little or no contact with, many become friends
with individuals of different ethnic groups, classes, and nationalities
who are "from completely different worlds." The girls' relationships
with the opposite sex also move quicker due to the greater amount of
contact they have with boyfriends at Bolton than they would have at
a public high school. One girl explains: "I mean, I'd walk to breakfast
and I'd see him . . . and, you know, there's no real getting away. . . .
It's not that I could do something about it." Another girl claims that
the students at Bolton often think that the girls at the poor local high
schools might be "like, skanky or something, when you actually start
talking to them about relationships with guys, it's much more intense
here."

The girls also have stronger feelings for individuals whom they do
not like because of the forced proximity of boarding school. One girl
explains, "You also fight with people a lot." Another says, "You get sick
of people."

The boys claim not to need the same intensity of relationships as
the girls and that "guys are much more self-involved than girls." One
boy quips, "It makes them [males] smarter. They know more about
themselves." Others believe that boys just don't show their emotions.
Jeff, the sensitive freshman, says he feels "more like a girl sometimes"
because he needs "good friendships." His friends snicker and hoot. He
continues:

> But like a lot of guys, like the traditional guy [begins speaking in
> deep voice] *needs no one. Goes alone.* [In his regular voice] You know

what I mean? Like [a] cowboy riding off into the sunset. They're more independent, and they're more confident on their own, whereas girls need the friends, the support.

Sharing among the girls demonstrates both status and the boundaries of connections. To have people borrow from you and let you borrow from them means you are considered part of a group. They share clothes, food, music, and makeup. They share clothes ("Oh my God! All the time!") and see it as an important part of their friendships: "It's amazing. You should see my borrowed list. I make a list of people who have borrowed stuff from me because otherwise I'll forget and then I won't get it back." Although boys borrow things from each other, such as sweaters, ties, or socks, it is nothing compared to the girls, who borrow "whole outfits" and "everything . . . except for, like, underwear."

Sharing is not egalitarian, and certain girls have sharing rites with other girls. The "senior princesses" do not share with anyone who is not part of their clique. Because these high-status girls place importance on looks, the sharing of clothes (and the ability to fit into each other's clothes) is an important aspect of their friendship and delineates who is "in" and who is not. These girls exclaim:

-Oh my God! I am never wearing my own clothes, ever.

-We're relatively the same size. Even if it doesn't fit, we'll squeeze into each other's clothes and be like, "Look, it fits! It fits!"

The girls also describe the camaraderie and emotional support that they provide for each other. If a friend has personal problems, "everybody is affected by it" and "you'll get like 17 hugs." One girl adds, "You don't have to knock when we go into each other's rooms. We, like, go in at three in the morning, wake them up, and sit down and start talking." The girls relate how the dorms are "like a family" with everyone "pulling together" to help each other out or to "meet the dress code."

For girls, organized and unorganized acts of camaraderie are central to the performance of femininity and symbolic of their status among their peers. The girls give "secret psychs" to each other before sport matches. A prefect gives little packets of Halloween candy to her dorm mates. Girls rush to the bathroom in a group to comfort a friend who is crying. Girls cry together and comfort each other when one of their friends is expelled for breaking a major school rule. In a phenomenon that appears unique to the girls, they walk to the dining hall in "packs," rarely alone. Both males and females also describe going to the bathroom as a group activity for girls, and I observe this in the dining hall, at weekend events, and at prom.

The boys also describe the special circumstances of boarding school as making relationships more intense in both positive and negative ways. One boy comments, "You either start liking everybody more or you start hating everybody." Others agree: "Everything is elevated to a higher degree." Unlike the close relationships the girls develop, the boys talk almost exclusively about how living together forces everyone to know each other's habits. One boy reports, "You know whether or not people shower," grumbling that his roommate only showers "once every 60 days." Another boy asserts, "You definitely find out things you don't want to know about your roommate and his . . . habits, in terms of his self-gratification." The others agree.

Unlike the girls, the boys have difficulty describing much dorm unity and do not describe the same type or degree of camaraderie as the girls do. The boys say they bond differently than the girls: "Nothing is planned. We'll all watch a movie or eat dinner with who's around or something like that." Exceptions include when an entire male dorm "bleached their pubic hair. It was like a bonding thing," and when friends allow each other to masturbate in their rooms.

Focusing on relationships and closeness is the essence of performing femininity at Bolton and is a sign of popularity among the girls. They often seem to try to outdo each other in their descriptions of caring and sentiment, as if they are putting on an emotion show. This is not to say that they do not feel intensely, but rather that the demonstration of feelings builds on itself in a snowball effect.

An example of this phenomenon occurs when some girls describe how they reacted when one of their dorm mates, along with a male student, was kicked out. Contrasting the reactions of the boys and girls to illustrate how the intensity of their relationships differs, one girl states, "Guys are like, 'Oh well,' cross them off in the face book, and don't think about them again," but the girls put themselves on the line in order to have their friend stay, threatening to leave the school because of their anger. One girl petitioned the headmaster to allow her friend to stay at Bolton, promising that she would "personally guarantee" that her friend would not get into any more trouble and if she did, she would leave as well.

When their friend was kicked out, the girls were "flipping out," "hitting the wall," and "in hysterics." One girl explains:

> When someone gets kicked out in your dorm, it's not just your feelings you have to deal with and your shock that it happened but the entire dorm and it accumulates so it's like multiplied. It's like twenty girls all on the brink of crises. It sort of feeds off of itself because when you see other people upset, you get more upset and there's no one you can talk to and you're in the environment in the dorm where everyone is upset.

The girls end up talking about turning the expelled girl's room into a shrine.

When the girls do not place a high value on relationships, other students question or chastise them. In one case, after a girl relates how she and her roommate had not gotten along last year, the girls are incredulous, one of them asking, "Was it hard when you and Mary weren't speaking?" She answers in an exasperated tone, "No, I didn't think it was hard. I don't know why *everyone* thinks it's *so* hard not to talk to your roommate!"

A likely reason why the boys and girls differ in their display of emotion and closeness is that the boys feel less free to show their emotions because it is not part of the performance of masculinity. Although the boys have real feelings, they say it is not acceptable for them to express or discuss their emotions. The boys illustrate this difference by contrasting how they and girls react when friends get expelled. While the girls grieve together and are emotive with each other, the boys grieve alone and do not show their emotions. One of the boys contends:

> Girls might just gather up and cry. Whereas guys just go into their rooms. They do talk about it with their friends. It makes it better, but they find their own time to be in their room to think about it and be by themselves.

Another adds, "Or if they do cry when the person is leaving, it's more like a one-on-one thing, and it's like an embarrassing, uncomfortable quick thing." Because of the rarity of boys' expressing emotions, they agree, "it means more."

This lack of display of emotions includes happy emotions as well. One boy asserts, "When girls are happy, it's like, 'Oh! Da!' [He makes a goofy face indicating hysterics] And when guys are happy, they're just like . . . [He smiles only slightly] Everything is more individual. Every emotion is more individual."

:: RELATIONSHIPS GONE BAD

The flip side to girls' closeness and emphasis on relationships is that their relationships are more difficult, complicated, and tumultuous. Their problems with each other are rooted in competition, signaling their quest for autonomy and status.

Fighting, gossiping, and rumors take up a large amount of the girls' time. Unlike anything seen among the boys, a status-driven feud between the senior girls' clique and another group comprising two attractive girls, Katherine and Elizabeth, and their friends takes place throughout the year. Describing a different "set of rules" for relationships among boys and girls, the girls claim that they are "so mean" to each other because of the competition between them. One girl explains, "Girls are cruel . . . like, we are. I mean, since we were, like, eight years old we were talking about each other." One adds, "I've had so many fights, like, tears, just verbal fights." Others describe "melodrama," saying, "With girls it's just a big soap opera." Still others mention, "It's all emotional, dramatic" because girls always make "a big deal out of little things."

Unlike the boys, who openly are mean and pick on others, the girls hide their drama and feuding, usually not confronting each other openly but rather mocking or disparaging girls who are not present. They contrast this with how boys handle disagreements: "The boys will punch each other, you know, and then they're buddies."

Both the boys and girls note how viciously and quickly rumors spread on campus. The rumors, which can damage the girls' reputations, often are started by other girls. The students attribute the viciousness of the rumor mill to the smallness and closeness of the student body: "Everybody knows everybody and are always in each other's business."

The girls say that so many rumors arise because "people have nothing else to do," "they're jealous," "it's fun," and "people make up rumors just for the sake of making up rumors." Most of the rumors are about "hook-ups" and involve sexual behaviors that are damaging to their reputations. One girl explains, "You can just be walking around with a guy who's a friend and the next day it's like, 'Oh, I heard you had sex with him.' You're like, 'Ahhh! What?'"

One boy, Matt, illustrates how easily rumors spread, telling how "everyone" called him "uni-nut" or "uni-ball" the year before because of a rumor that he only had one testicle:

> We were sitting around the room one day and talking about injuries and I was like, "You think that's bad, I only got one nut." John's like, "Ha, ha." I was like, "Dude, I was only kidding." He's like, "Yeah, I know." He ran out into the hall and was like [he yells], "Matt only has one nut." And fucking Liz was on the hall. And then the whole school knew the next day. So everyone was like, "You only have one nut?" So I had to prove it right and left every weekend. "Ahhh, here you go." [Makes the motion of pulling his pants down]. It got *so* old showing people my balls.

Although a few of the boys mention damaging rumors, the rumors do not seem to affect them as much as the girls. One boy is taunted by another about a rumor about him being caught "with your finger up your butt hole," but most rumors are humorous in nature or involve hook-ups, which often improve a male's reputation rather than damage it.

:: OPPOSITE-SEX FRIENDS

The students conform to stereotypical gendered behavior in differing degrees depending on whom they are with, revealing the performative nature of gender as well as their covert needs. This coincides with Maccoby's (1998) assertions that individuals act more stereotypically among same-sex peers, as "the gendered aspects of an individual's behavior are brought into play by the gender of others" (p. 9). When boys are with boys, they tend to act more stereotypically masculine, but when they are with girls they feel freer to show their emotions and be more caring. When girls are with girls, they act more stereotypically feminine, but when they are with boys they sometimes do not have to control their bodily functions or try to be so perfect. Given this tendency to act more stereotypically with members of one's own sex, the gendered performances of the students are undoubtedly exacerbated in the boarding school environment, where they are always surrounded by their same-sex peers.

Some students prefer the increased comfort level of same-sex friends. Typical is one boy's response: "You can relate to them more. When you're around girls, you always have to be on." A boy says he feels "more comfortable" with other males because "I like to sit around them with my hands down my pants and I fart in front of them."

Many others, however, prefer opposite-sex friends because they can act less stereotypically around them; there is less competition and one-upmanship forcing them to behave that way. The main reason girls prefer opposite-sex friends is to avoid the hidden competition between girls. One girl observes that a lot of girls, "the second they meet you, will stare you up and down and check out what you're wearing, and it's so competitive." Others agree: "Girls are just naturally competitive with each other." One group of girls says how much they "love hanging out with the guys" because "they're a lot more honest," including how open they are about "bodily functions" like burping and how they all line up together to pee. They laugh about how one of the girls "gets right up there with them."

Many girls find stereotypical female behavior irritating. One girl comments, "They cry and complain. Oh my gosh. It's like a headache. They cry over *nothing*! I think guys are so much easier to get along with 'cause girls bicker." Another adds, "Because they don't really have a standard for who they can be friends with. Girls are like, 'Well, she looks tacky, so we can't talk to her.'" They agree that "girls are a lot more superficial."

Frequently the girls prefer opposite-sex friends because they like how boys deal with conflicts. The girls say that boys are forgiving in their conflicts, while girls are covertly hostile and hold grudges. Both genders view boys as confronting more and being more honest, open, and forgiving in their relationships with their same-sex peers. As one girls' dorm explains, "Girls are more catty and talk behind people's backs, like most of them. And guys are more open about their dislikes for people." An attractive girl notes, "Girls really get jealous. . . . Most of my best friends are guys. Girls to me are very sleazy and they scheme a lot." Others agree, "Guys will bitch you out to your face. Girls will go through 20 other girls before you can hear what you did wrong."

Boys also prefer opposite-sex friends because they are allowed to express feelings and do not to have to act cool and compete with other males. One group commented on how "you can be more honest" with girls because of the lack of competition. When one boy confides that he feels more comfortable with girls because he can cry and not be made fun of, the other boys make fun of him, exemplifying the pressure to conform:

-Like, if another guy, like, cries in front of another guy, it's like, "What the hell? Are you kidding?" You know, but, like, if a—

-Yeah, no kidding. [Lots of laughter]

-Hey, whatever, you know. I'm being honest. Shut up. Everyone cries.

Others feel more comfortable with girls because with them the boys can show weakness or caring as well as receive empathy:

-Girls are so much more open if you ever have a serious problem. Girls are better listeners. They care more, they really do. If you have a serious problem, they'll listen. Guys don't take you seriously.

-Yeah, they'll be like, "Stop acting like a bitch. Be a man and stop acting like a bitch."

-We know guys don't care, so we don't come to guys with our problems.

:: ROMANCE

The students agree that the boys generally want sex while the girls want a relationship. In the girls' dorms, I often hear the girls say "I want a boyfriend!" but never "I want sex." In the boys' dorms, I hear the boys say "I want sex" but not "I want a girlfriend." Undoubtedly many girls want sex and many boys want a relationship, but that is not part of the acceptable verbal behavior for their gender.

The pain for girls not to have a boyfriend is evident at Valentine's Day. When Valentine's Day carnations are delivered to the dorms, the girls become giddy and nervous as soon as the boy delivering the flowers walks through the door, even more so when he begins to hand them out. Some girls look expectant and thrilled, others despondent. Some girls leave. I hear one girl shout, "Audrey [a very popular girl] is going to get the most, you know it." Another states, "I'm going to get, like, one." One depressed-sounding girl says to no one in particular, "Valentine's Day sucks," and another replies, "I hate it." Neither girl receives a carnation.

Instead of looking for a relationship, the boys say they primarily look for sex with girls. One boy says he will tell a girl, "'I'll still care about you. Nothing will change.' These are the bullshit lines we use. And they work!" He adds, "We just care about having sex. Girls care about relationships." He continues, "When you want it so badly, you will tell her anything. At the time she is the only one you want."

:: GOALS AND PRIORITIES

The girls at Bolton place relationships with friends and family (not with boyfriends) along with school, health, and athletics high on their list of goals and priorities. How high boys are on their list varies greatly depending on the circumstances, but the girls admit that when they are in a relationship, they usually want "more out of it" in the sense of "commitment and togetherness" and will devote more time to it.

Only one girl in the sophomore dorm says that "a love life" is a top priority. The other girls in that dorm place boys at the bottom of their lists, explaining:

-They don't even make the top five.

-I'm really down on boys right now.

-Food is before boys.

Because girls often put friends as their "number one priority, always have been," they are willing to sacrifice more for their relationships than guys are, including academic success. One girl explains:

Yeah, because we will sit on the phone for a long time talking to a friend, you know. Like, I may have craploads of homework, but if I feel like I need to sort out something with my friend, I will talk to her for like three hours.

Although the girls acknowledge that their priorities, "school and friends," differ from those of the boys, who only care about "sports and themselves," they also recognize that their underlying priority—to belong—is the same. While good looks and being "feminine" increase a girl's popularity, for boys "it's so important to be athletic, to be the big man on campus." Desiring to fit the popular mold, one accomplished girl athlete says, "I'd do anything just to be the person who doesn't play sports and, like, dances or does drama." Ultimately the girls conclude that both boys and girls strive to be accepted and popular. One girl notices:

> I think that we have really similar goals, actually. I think we both have to meet a physical standard. I think we have to make a social standard, like in terms of having friends and being in the right group. In those terms, I think we have the same goals.

The top goals and priorities of the boys are college, grades, sports, having fun, and girls. Their responses are more varied than those of the girls, and range from "getting into a good college" and "winning the hockey game tomorrow" to "not flunking out." The boys also mention girls as a priority much more than girls mention boys. "Getting some" is more important to them than a relationship. Typically absent are references to relationships with friends or family.

Unlike the girls, many boys list trivial priorities as goals: "Watching a movie tonight" or "My number one priority is waking up in the morning, going to breakfast, taking a shower." Admitting to lofty goals or hard work is not cool. Instead, many of the boys say that their goal is not to work too hard or to do just enough to get by: "I just want to make it through the year," doing "just good enough to keep them off your ass," and "staying off ac-pro [academic probation] while being as lazy as possible."

Many of the boys focus on fun as a goal. One boy says, "Having fun would definitely be on a lot of guys' lists." In the freshman dorm, after the boys have trouble coming up with any goals, one boy says, "I'm just having fun right now." Also unlike the girls, the boys often list athletics among their top priorities. Although some list sports as their number one priority, such as one boy who said, "Hockey is life, damn it!" most list sports as second after grades.

While having sex is a top male priority, it is not on any girl's list. When one boy lists "gettin' some 'cause there's been a rather long dry spell for me," the others enthusiastically agree. One boy explains the differences in how boys and girls prioritize sex and relationships: "Guys are just like, 'I want to get some play.' Girls are like, 'Oh my God! I'm in a relationship. Blah, blah, blah . . .'" Only a few boys focus on relationships, such as one boy who lists his priorities as: "Dad (I always have to impress him), friends (you don't want to let them down), the woman (that's definitely a priority, I don't care what you say), success, happ[iness]."

In general, the boys view the goals and priorities of boys and girls as falling along the lines of a focus on self and other, describing boys' primary concern as "guys just wanna get ass!" while for girls, "everything is social life."

∷ LIFE WHEN YOU'RE FORTY

Most of the girls center their goals for adulthood around close relationships, mainly a husband and children, placing these relationships before their careers. Typically the girls say, "I want kids," "Have a family, settle down," or "I'd be like a housewife. Four kids. Not work."

Many prefer not to work at all or at least not until after their children grow up because they did not like how "stressed" their mothers were from work or how little they saw them when they were growing up:

-I don't want to be my mom, who's . . . you know, comes home at nine o'clock every night—

-Stressed out.

-Yes, and has heart problems because she stresses out and work is her life.

Others don't want their children to be raised by nannies the way they were. One girl explains, "I don't want a career when I have kids, just because my mom has worked my whole life and I've had nannies after nannies after nannies." Instead, many of the girls hope to have a "hobby" and be "an artist or something creative on the side. And taking like classes in sewing or something. Doing like what my mom does, taking tennis or something." Others agree, thinking that they might get some type of a job but not wanting to be "a career woman." The African American girls on scholarship stand out for their focus on career, many saying they want to become lawyers.

Only a few focus on money, seeking financial security and independence. One of the girls wants to be "comfortably independent" because her parents are divorced and she just wants "to be prepared." Others agree that "being able to support yourself" is important. The only girl who focuses openly on wealth is an African American on financial aid who is having trouble meeting her tuition. Even though she craves "financial security," her main focus is relationships because she wants security for her children:

> Not, like, necessarily rich or wealthy or anything, but financially secure because I don't want my kids to have to worry about, you know, this and that, things that kids shouldn't have to worry about, you know what I mean. A child should not have to be stressed out about their tuition. It's the parents' job to be stressed out about it, you know. . . . And I want to have seven kids.

She then tells the other girls the names that she has already picked out for her seven children.

A few others focus on money indirectly by desiring a luxurious lifestyle. One girl wants "to be living in Virginia, have a big house, and not having to work." Another girl desires "a cattle ranch in Montana and a husband who drives a diesel truck and, uh, a Porsche."

On the infrequent occasions when girls do not focus on relationships, their responses jolt the other girls to question their goals. One girl states:

> At this point in time I'm not sure if I want to get married or have kids, but what I've always wanted to do is, I've never really cared about financial standings, you know. I'm even considering kind of like wandering for a while, you know. Kind of like going from place to place.

Because this girl in her chapel speech has publicly exposed her difficult family situation filled with alcoholism and violence, the other girls do not question her. However, when a girl from Germany gives a self-focused response similar to that of many of the boys, saying that her goals are to "never marry, never have kids, travel a lot, having lovers everywhere, having a lot of money, a lot of fun and a good job and a lot of party," the other girls are incredulous, saying how "lonely" she will be without a husband and kids and what an "empty" life it would be.

Wanting better relationships and more excitement than their parents, many girls confide that divorce is their "greatest fear." Whether or not the girls want to duplicate the lives of their parents depends on how successful their relationships are. Thus girls who say they would want their parents' life, as well as those who say they do not, primarily cite relationships as the reason.

The boys' emphasis on fun and wealth as future goals demonstrates the importance of these traits in the social hierarchy and for group membership. Instead of desiring close relationships, they want the status of being "rich" and "retired" and "having fun" and having great athletes for sons. Although many boys mention family, it is low on their lists and the focus is on "a hot wife."

The number one goal of many of the boys is early retirement. Although a few of the boys mention what type of career they would like to have, many say that whatever they do, they want to be "still havin' fun, still havin' fun." In almost every dorm, most of the boys desire "early retirement," often at 30 or 35, because "I don't want to have to be working when I'm old." One boy says, "I want to be able to golf every day, never have to work, because I already work too much." Another comments, "I want to be retired. I want to be a senior PGA player. And I want to bang like rabbits. And I don't want to work." Many desire "a young trophy wife and a wife who's willing to do everything."

Most of the boys agree that having "a lot of money" is "absolutely" important to them. Many desire to be "stinking rich" and "a million-aire." One boy desires "the [TV] sitcom life":

> I'll have a hot wife. I'm going to have a four-car garage, a big-ass house, at least one Porsche. I'm going to be stinking rich because . . . I'm smart, that's all there is to it. I'm going to get rich early, and I'm not going to work that hard when I'm 40. I'm going to have a beach house and I also want a house on the lake. I'm going to have two kids. I'm going to live right next to my best friends now. They're gonna have kids. We're gonna be all in a row with our hot wives, our four-car garages. We're gonna have poker night a lot, drinkin' the beer, smoking the cigars.

The few who do not desire great wealth stand out from the rest. When an African American boy objects to the primary value the others are placing on wealth, pointing out, "It isn't all about money," the others retort, "Yeah, it is." When he argues, "Money isn't everything in the world. It helps, but it isn't everything," the others reply, "People who say money isn't everything in the world don't have any."

Although some of the boys mention family as an important element in their vision of their futures, others do not; it is not a central theme, as it is with the girls. When one boy states that he "definitely" does not want a family, the other boys do not question his goals:

> I haven't decided exactly what I want to be like when I'm 40, but I definitely do *not* want to be married, have children or be settled in any way. I still have the stars in my eyes and I want to be

famous but that's probably not going to happen. . . . I'll probably just be old man Hunter who lives on the hill and chases kids away with a broom.

When another boy bashes children, saying that he does not want kids " 'cause they're so overrated" and "all kids do is shit and eat. They can't walk, they can't talk. They're fucking useless," the others do not condemn his remarks. Instead, another boy whose ambitions are different simply remarks, "I definitely want kids. I want to be a 35-year-old grandfather."

Placing importance on athletics for group membership and status (both theirs and their child's), the boys desire sons who are "really good athletes." Although the boys themselves often complain that they feel too much pressure to be good at sports, they insist, "I'm going to be that dad who makes his son play sports—football and basketball and baseball" and "My kid's going to be a three-star all-state athlete by his sophomore year."

Only a few of the boys (usually not great athletes themselves) say that they don't care whether or not their kids are good at sports. One boy says that he doesn't "give a shit" if his son is a standout athlete "as long as my kid's not a dork." Another adds, "All I care about is my kid being happy."

When describing why they do not want the lives of their parents, boys focus on how hard their parents work, how stressed out they are, how little fun they have, and their financial worries. Many boys say that their parents "work too much," "aren't lazy enough," or "don't have enough fun." One boy declares, "My parents are still working and they're 40, and that's not what I want to do." In another dorm, a boy notes, "There's too much struggle there, financially, and they don't seem to be happy." Another boy proclaims, "I don't ever want to work."

Some boys focus on relationships, both good and bad, when deciding if they want to duplicate their fathers' lives. Citing their fathers' marital failures or how little time they have for their children, some boys say they would do things differently, while others would like the same life because their fathers were able to devote time to their family. Usually the boys agree that playing sports with their children and spending time with them are important. One boy, wanting to do things differently than his dad, says, "I mean, he'd go out and play catch with us, but you could tell he hated it the whole time. . . . It wasn't something he enjoyed." Another counters, "I want to be somewhat like my dad. I mean, just always involved in my kid's life."

∷ GIRL TALK/BOY TALK

The gendered performances in girls' and boys' talk further illuminates how social pressures to fit gender ideals mask similarities in needs and quests for status. Sociolinguists have described gender differences in phonology (for politeness Japanese women adopt an artificially high voice), grammar (women are more careful about using correct grammar), and vocabulary ("Oh fudge!" or "Goodness!" instead of the more forceful expletives men would use), as well as body stances and movement while speaking. The essence of these gender differences lies in the idea that girls organize their talk cooperatively while boys organize theirs competitively (Coates, 1986, 1996, 2003; Lakoff, 1975, 1990; Tannen, 1990, 1993, 1994). Similarly, Tannen (1990, 1993) uses the terms "rapport" and "report" to contrast how women tend to use language and body movements to build social connections with others, while men focus their language and body movements on establishing a social hierarchy. Coates (1986) describes women as discussing one topic for longer, sharing more information about themselves, talking about feelings and relationships more, asking more questions (often to keep the conversation going), using tag questions ("Isn't it?"), making more links between speaker turns, respecting each other's turns and disliking any one person to dominate the conversation, and listening more than men. Men, on the other hand, vie to tell anecdotes that center around themes of superiority and aggression, ask few questions (interpreting questions as only requests for information), make more abrupt topic shifts, interrupt more, enjoy loud and aggressive arguments often over trivial topics, and tend to establish a hierarchy more than women (with some men dominating the conversation, while others talk very little).

The theory of contrasting cooperative and competitive linguistic styles for men and women has recently come under fire as a continuation of the view of binary (and thus limiting) differences in male and female personalities (see Goodwin, 2006). Instead, current researchers contend that girls are often direct in their confrontations, which include direct verbal aggression, such as name-calling and threats, and nonverbal aggression, such as stares (Goodwin, 2006, 1990; Underwood

2003). Although I witness both direct and indirect types of confrontation between the Bolton girls, it is clear the girls feel pressure to *appear* harmonious and cooperative in their relationships with others, and both genders view girls as usually doing so and then engaging in backstabbing on the sly.

Admitting to direct conflict, the girls tell tales of stares, eye rolling, insulting comments such as "I can't believe she's wearing *that!*" that are whispered but meant to be overheard, or snide comments from other girls insinuating that they are fat, ugly, or dressed inappropriately. The senior girls unabashedly acknowledge that they always sit near the entrance of the dining hall so that they can "give everybody coming in or out a once-over." Despite these tales and the large amount of hidden infighting among the girls, they remain generally harmonious and act decorously in public settings. Caring about what others think, the girls largely engage in conversation that is conducive to building relationships or at least the *appearance* of relationships. Although conflict does occur occasionally, I rarely see open conflict, as they gloss over any disagreements or differences in opinion. Feeling inhibited about speaking their minds, the girls commonly say, "I'm not good at confrontation" when explaining why they did not speak out.

The talk of the boys, on the other hand, is markedly different and focuses on a *lack* of concern for others or what others think, humor (often at the expense of others), and establishing a pecking order. The boys engage in one-upmanship and seek status by insulting and making fun of each other or by outdoing each other with indecorous acts (such as who can burp or fart the loudest into the microphone), and there is often open verbal and physical conflict.

Despite the belief that overt conflict occurs among the boys and covert conflict occurs among the girls, both genders regard the girls as having more hostility toward each other. During our interviews, the boys are openly aggressive to other boys around them and rarely talk about boys who are not present. Girls, on the other hand, are not usually aggressive when they talk face-to-face, but they frequently talk about girls not present. When the girls criticize another girl, they usually demean her appearance and personality. In one instance, Chelsea and Katelyn, two pretty girls, are outraged because the "bitch squad" (a clique of wealthy senior girls) is reported to have called them "bitches" who "think they own the whole damn school and can get any boy they want." In their own conversation, Chelsea, Katelyn, and their friends retaliate, criticizing a member of the bitch squad as "flat" and "the fakest person I've ever met. She is like a 30 minus-A" and wears "pop-in boobs."

The boys, on the other hand, rarely criticize other boys who are not present but enjoy making fun of or belittling the boys around them. Typically, they make fun of a boy's sexual inexperience or inadequacies, athletic ability, or muscle size and strength.

As a result, peer groups of both genders often talk negatively about girls. Girls talk unfavorably about other girls' behavior. Boys talk both favorably and unfavorably about girls' appearance, wanting to have sex with them if they are "hot" or making fun of them if they are "ugly" or "fat."

When talking with each other, the girls frequently use demonstrative terms and proclamations of endearment, especially at times of parting such as near graduation or after a friend's expulsion. The girls are also much more physically demonstrative with each other. During the interviews (and on other visits to the dorms) I see scantily clothed girls in boxers with tank tops, lounging on each other, massaging each other, and giving each other back rubs. The girls also give each other support and hugs when they need them and hold each other when they cry.

I witness little of and hear little about this type of emotionally supportive and demonstrative behavior among the boys. The boys are usually fully clothed and do not touch one another except to give each other high fives or to punch each other. During the few times they express serious or deep feelings, it is uncomfortable for them and usually framed as joking.[7] In one dorm where the boys became close despite initial racial difficulties, they talk about how much they have grown to like each other:

-I appreciate you all and I'm gonna miss you all. [The others joke and make crying noises]

-I love you too. [Said sarcastically]

-All right, that's too much love.

-How about that Lakers game?

Although these boys feel strongly about each other, they joke and make fun of demonstrative behavior. Such behavior is not part of the masculine ideal and is cut short with the forced mention of a manlier topic, basketball, in order to restore the masculine ideal in their relationship.

The content of the students' discourse, which I observe directly and which they self-report, often differs along the lines of the amount of focus on relationships and people. The girls report talking mainly about "other people," "people you hate," "boys," "sex is big," "sex is brought up in every conversation I have," "rumors," "gossip," and "who likes who." I observed this talk about other people in many different situations. In one instance, a freshman, Jen, has been asked to the prom only days before the event. I take her and two older girls on a rush trip to a shopping mall for a dress. The girls' conversation is typical, as it is other-directed. The girls talk about prom, appearances ("I didn't even put gel in my hair today" and "The other day when we had SATs I didn't even blow-dry my hair!"), how a girl was mean and told Jen she was fat, boys they like, girls they don't like, music, feelings, relationships, how a popular upperformer had called one of the freshman girls the night before and said, "I just broke up with Lilly. Do you want to give me head?" and the sexual mores of the girl, who, they report, was "flattered" because "she thinks he's so hot."

The boys, on the other hand, mainly discuss sex, "the girls I'd like to fuck," "girls, like, who's hottest," "money," "drugs and alcohol," "sports," "how much this place sucks," and "how much I wish I was home having sex, doing drugs." They also complain about the restrictions on their freedom due to the rules at Bolton. In one dorm, the boys first answer that their main topics of conversation are "drugs and sex," "booty," and "alcohol." They then all start to chant over and over again, "Wet, hot, tight, ball pussy!"

Much of the boys' talk is an open attempt to establish a ranking or status order between them. On numerous occasions, I witnessed the boys in the dorms picking on one another or trying to outdo each other in their tales of toughness or athletic or sexual conquests. This status-seeking behavior is evident in the weekly event of an all-male advisee group dinner. As the boys, all upperclassmen, munch hot dogs, hamburgers, and chips, they have an impromptu spelling bee, trying to outspell each other. They ridicule Harrison, a wealthy boy known not to be smart, even though he is their friend. They announce that the advisor's six-year-old son can spell better than he can, and it becomes quite a sport as the six-year-old takes him on. The other boys tease Harrison mercilessly. They discuss who got in a fight, who could "pound" whom, and what fight they'd like to see. They discuss how the school's sports teams are doing. They talk about how they fall asleep in class. The boys talk about who lifted weights this summer. Then one boy laughs and says to another, "You just got titties, man, I'm sorry!" Since this is the first time the advisee group has met after grades came out, the students badger the advisor to tell them who has "won," as they phrase it: "Who did the best?" "Who was the standout advisee?" "Who got the best grades overall?"

This account illustrates how competitive talk is part of the performance of masculinity, as the boys try to outdo each other in both spelling and having the best grades. It illustrates how boys are allowed to be mean and to make fun of both friends and nonfriends in face-to-face interactions. It also reveals how humor is an essential part of their conversation and is a path to status. Not only do boys relate through humor, but they often try to outdo each other as well. Group bonding among these boys is obvious, and it appears to be largely achieved through status acquisition and jockeying for power.

Thus, while the performance of femininity includes discussions of particular people, emotions, and relationships, the performance of masculinity includes discussions of places or things as well as fun or self-focused topics.

:: THE SAGA OF PROM

The saga of prom at Bolton encapsulates the performances of masculinity and femininity, illustrating the desires of both genders to stand out and be special yet to fit into the group. The performance of femininity centers around looking "perfect" for the big event. For the girls, the shopping, preparations, and prom itself are full-blown events of drama, camaraderie, tears, and heartache. The boys, although they want to look good, do not appear to feel this same pressure, nor do they show it. While the girls collaborate and prepare for prom together, for the boys the preparations and the prom itself are more individual activities.

Prom Shopping

One Saturday morning I drive five girls (a freshman, three sophomores, a junior, and a senior) to a city about an hour away to shop for prom. Once at the mall, I join the sophomores as they shop at a fancy department store for shoes and makeup. One wealthy and popular girl, Elizabeth, is obviously an experienced shopper. The other girls look to her for guidance and as a measure of good taste. "This is not a shoe. It is an incredible work of art," Elizabeth declares in the shoe department. Another girl tries on shoes with high heels. "I won't be able to dance in these," she exclaims, tottering around the store. The others reply, "You don't need to. You only have to wear them for an hour or so. Then you can change into Reefs for dancing. Everyone does." One girl adds, "I'm going to have trouble getting on the bus with my dress and shoes."

In the makeup department Elizabeth buys lip gloss, blush, sparkle, and two blue eye shadows to match her blue dress. "I want to sparkle all over," she explains. "Here, smell this," another girl cries as she sprays me with perfume. Another girl wants to try the sample of pink nail polish, but her nails already have polish on them. I offer my own. "Oh! We'll give you a manicure," she squeals. I come home with one pink nail and smelling of several types of perfume.

The sophomores report that most dresses cost between $150 and $300. Elizabeth says, "My dress only cost $160, but I want to get something really beautiful when I'm a senior so I bought something pretty inexpensive this year." Describing her dress to the others, she says, "It's very prommy. I mean, it's over the top, but I like it."

Tux Rental

The boys rent rather than buy their tuxes. In the common room outside the dining hall, a table is set up for the rental process. Two women assist the boys as they mill around flipping through books that display the choices. Downplaying his desire to look good, one of the boys says, "I don't know how to do this pretty-boy stuff." Another, looking for an inexpensive option, states, "I don't care how it looks. It's all about the price." Several girlfriends take charge and tell their dates what to get: "I'll show you what I like." Some girls pass by and take pity on a boy who is having difficulties: "Oh, we'll help you." A boy says to his girlfriend, "You're going to have to help me because I don't know how to pick out tuxes."

Although the boys should look good for prom, it is expected that they should not know about clothes or care how they look. Despite putting on a front, some boys care greatly about their appearance. Two boys look through the books together when no girls are around. One says, "I want something classic." The other advises, "White makes you look more tan." A boy overhearing adds, "That's why I only wear white in the summertime. It makes you look tan." The boy giving advice adds, "If you get it tight, it makes you look bigger."

Will, a wealthy boy, agonizes over the choices. His friend Jack, another very wealthy boy, advises, "Get cummerbunds. Vests are tacky. Here, I'll pick one out for you." When Will hesitates, Jack says in disgust, "You are *not* getting a vest, Will." Will reassures his friend, "I don't want a vest." Jack points to one tux, saying, "That is the worst thing I have ever seen." Will interjects, "I want Ralph Lauren." Jack nods approvingly and says, "Refined man." The saleslady tells them that nobody rents cummerbunds anymore, that everyone wears vests. Jack retorts, "That is because America is trashy."

Two pretty and highly sought-after African American girls, Tamara and Kara, who are fastidious about their own appearance, spend an inordinate amount of time choosing the tuxes for their dates. Bobby, a muscular African American football player, is going with Kara and sits back in seeming total helplessness as she fills out his name, room number, and telephone number on the rental form. After she deliberates for what seems like hours, Bobby tries to move the process along by letting her know what he likes. Tamara exclaims, "Stop. Stop. We should just not have the guys here." The selection process takes so long it becomes painful. At one point Kara points across the room and tells Bobby, "Go sit at that table." He responds weakly, "Can't I just sit here? I want to feel as if I'm part of this. I'll say if I don't like something." When Kara and Tamara finally make up their minds, I think Bobby, Tamara's date, the saleswomen, and any of us watching feel as though we have been through a battle. As a postscript to this story, Kara broke up with Bobby a week before the prom; he went in his very nice outfit with a friend and looked miserable the whole time.

Getting "Fit" for Prom

Five days before prom, the girls are discussing prom in the dorm. Britney has decided to go to prom after all. "So if I'm going to prom, that means I can't eat till Saturday," she announces. Although Saturday is five days away, a close friend replies, "That's okay. I'll do it with you." The other girls urge Britney to eat because she is quite thin already. Britney squeezes her stomach and complains, "But if I eat, I get a little . . . this thing. [Not eating is] what gets it the flattest the fastest. It makes you feel so much better." When one girl tells her it's "unhealthy" to fast for such a long time and another says, "You're going to pass out dancing." Britney replies, "No, if you stay on juices and stuff. I lasted for a month with just liquids. It was fine."

Prom Dates

On Thursday night at our house a few weeks before prom, a group of boys is sitting around the table chatting over dessert. It comes up that one of the boys, Kei, does not have a date for prom. Much to his dismay, the other boys give him a hard time and start suggesting possible dates for him. Amid merriment and laughter, one boy shouts that they need a face book in order to do this properly. I promptly produce one, and they huddle around flipping through the pages, covering the entire book from freshmen ("we have to start low") to the kitchen staff at the end. When they mention the names of unattractive girls, they break into peals of laughter:

-I hate her.

-She's not too bad.

-She's way out of his league.

-I hear she's a good dancer.

-She has *major* issues.

-She has man shoulders.

Everyone laughs when an older, unattractive office staff member is suggested. Eventually, Kei asks a popular, social girl. At prom, she flutters here and there socializing while he tags along behind looking miserable.

The girls, on the other hand, place more importance on their date being "fun" or "funny" rather than good-looking. Although some girls say that having someone who "looks good in prom photos" or "somebody who will decorate your arm" is the ideal prom date, most of the girls want to go with someone fun. The characteristics listed most are "someone who will dance," "someone who is funny as hell and will keep talking," "someone who likes to dance, knows how to enjoy himself, and is very funny," "an entertainer," and "your buddy, a good friend." Many declare, "Prom dates are mostly personality and not looks." A girl notes, "I don't care if they're ugly as long as they're funny." Kara agrees, "I'd go with the ugliest guy in the world if he could make me laugh for two hours."

That putting personality before looks is expected by the girls is demonstrated when Mercedes views an ideal prom date as not someone with a great personality but rather someone who is "really great-looking and a really great personality." One of the other girls who is not a member of the bitch squad chides her, "See, that's shallow." She replies, "I'm sorry, I'm just being honest."

Getting Ready

Girls

Prom is held on a Saturday evening at end of May. The afternoon is hot, and the girls' dorms bustle with activity. Returning late from their Saturday games, the girls race around to change out of their uniforms, shower, dress, and get ready in time. Others who have had all afternoon to get ready are more relaxed. The dorm bathrooms are filled with girls showering, blow-drying their hair, and doing each other's hair. The girls scurry about in the halls in various states of undress. Long dresses hang from doors or in open closets. Girls with extra-big closets have been keeping the dresses of their friends.

In one dorm, Kristin and Elizabeth, known for their good taste and love of makeup and clothes, have a room full of girls and their dresses. Their door is open, and a constant stream of traffic flows in and out. They giddily tell me that they have rearranged their whole room just for prom preparations. Five girls huddle around two huge tubs and one professional case of makeup on the floor, applying makeup in front of a large mirror. Music is blaring, and the girls chatter nervously. Kristin, well known for her expertise in applying makeup, puts makeup on one girl after another. When Lily, who does not usually wear makeup, asks Kristin if she should wear some for prom, Kristin shrieks, "Lily, you ask that question!" As Kristin is putting eye makeup on Lily, she protests, "I look like a raccoon!"

As the time to board the bus grows closer, the tension starts to mount. In Kristin and Elizabeth's room girls discuss how much pressure they are feeling. One girl sighs, "This is more stressful than exams." Elizabeth agrees despairingly, "I don't even want to go anymore." The girl with the raccoon eyes talks about putting on makeup: "I'm so scared. I've never done this in my life. I told Ted that I just wanted to go in sweat pants."

Starting to stress out, the girls discuss how much harder it is to be a girl than to be a boy, and exclaim nervously:

-I love the way guys say it's easier to be a girl!

-That's crap!

-Bullshit!

-No way!

-They yell at us when we just eat salads and then they yell at us when we are too fat.

One girl who has been working on her makeup in front of a full-length mirror for a long time pauses, smiles at herself in the mirror, and says in a breathy voice, "Hi, Ken." The raccoon eyes girl, whose makeup is almost complete, asks, "How do you take this crap off?" Elizabeth moans, "I feel sick. I don't want to do this."

Further down the hall, two blond girls wearing sleek black dresses and with their hair up are putting the finishing touches on their makeup. One of their mothers stands outside their door. She murmurs, "They look like movie stars." Another mother is taking pictures, saying hi to all the girls, talking to them, making a fuss over them in a high shrill voice. The daughter looks embarrassed that her mother is there.

An African American girl, Sunny, who has been helping everyone do their hair in the bathroom, comes into Kristin's room. Leaning on a bookshelf and relaxing, she suddenly sees a small black dot about the size of a ladybug on her dress and screams in a shrill voice, "Oh my God! I got black on my dress!" Horrified, several girls bend to look as she asks no one in particular in a wobbly voice, "How'd that happen?" Everyone stares at the little black spot in disbelief, not knowing what to do. In an even shakier voice Sunny asks, "Who has something to take it out?" A girl runs and gets a wet towel and dabs at the spot. It doesn't work, and now the dress is wet. Someone calls for a blow-dryer, and I run to the bathroom and grab one. They hand it person to person until it gets to Sunny and the girls trying to help her.

Sunny is helpless with shock, and Elizabeth takes charge, trying to help her. They decide to go into the bathroom to work on the dress. As they pass by me, I see a large tear roll down Sunny's cheek. In the bathroom Elizabeth kneels down and uses the blow-dryer on the dress, which now has a larger black spot and a large water stain and is puckered. Tears stream down Sunny's cheeks as she shouts, "I'm not going!" Elizabeth guides the distraught Sunny to her room by the arm. As she enters her room, she cries out in despair, "How the *hell* did I get *fucking* black on me?" A little while later the girls sprint several dresses (spares that they happen to have in their rooms) down the hall to Sunny's room. A friend of hers tells me that Sunny is going with a group and does not even have a date. Later I see her leave for the prom in her original dress, tears dried.

After almost everyone is ready, a girl comes in wanting Kristin to do her makeup. Concerned that she will not be ready in time herself, Kristin says, "I need to get my dress on and stuff." The girl replies, "You go ahead and take care of what you need to do first, but I do want you to do my makeup." When she returns a short while later, after almost everyone has left, Kristin, Elizabeth, and another friend are heading out the door. She again asks Kristin to do her makeup, and Kristin replies quietly, "But we don't have time." A look of terror and panic crosses the girl's face, and she says through clenched teeth, "Don't fuck with me at a time like this!" Kristin sighs softly, says, "Okay," and quickly applies the girl's makeup.

Boys

As I walk to the boys' dorm, I see a boy dressed in his tux walking from one faculty apartment to another looking for someone to tie his bow tie. Another boy sees him and yells, "You look pimp!" In the boys' dorms, all doors are closed without any sign of group activity. No one is in the common room. One or two boys stride purposefully down the hall. One stops and asks if I know how to tie a bow tie. Others quietly emerge from their rooms and swagger out of the dorm. One boy is wearing sunglasses. Outside, a group of boys asks me to take a picture as they pose, arms over each other's shoulders. I ask them if getting ready for prom is a group activity and they reply, "No!" One boy adds, "Except that we had Mr. White tie our bow ties." I don't see any evidence of drama or catastrophes. All is amazingly quiet and calm.

The Dance

We drive for about an hour to a boat for a harbor cruise. The students gossip that a boy is getting a hand job from his date. "He just put his jacket over his lap. You could see the jacket going up and down," a student reports.

Dinner is served fairly soon after we board the boat. Sam, a friendly day student, calls me over to sit with his friends and him during dinner. Part of the discussion during dinner centers on Sam's girlfriend (not a Bolton student), who has "forgotten" both her underwear and to take her birth control pill that day. Tyler wonders, "She forgot. How do you forget your underwear?" She giggles and replies, "I was in such a hurry and then I was like, I didn't care." Later that evening Sam reaches over the white tablecloth and passes condoms to his two friends. As day students with girls who did not attend Bolton, they would have ample opportunities for sex after the prom, unlike the more closely chaperoned Bolton students.

Twice during the prom I see girls in tears rush to the bathroom followed by several of their friends. One of the girls is upset, her friends tell a concerned faculty member, because her freshman date is sitting at a table full of seniors and is not saying anything. Later that evening, I see the same girl laughing with and touching a different boy as they make their way to the stairs that lead to the upper deck, where other students are making out. He tries to carry her up the stairs over his shoulder like a sack of potatoes but can't quite manage it. She laughs, and they hurry up the stairs giggling. I do not see her freshman date rush to the bathroom in tears.

Lots of girls dance together. No boys do, but they stand on chairs or tables around the dance floor and are dancing by themselves. Somehow it seems that if they are elevated, it is okay to dance alone. The students later claim that alcohol was brought in and that sex took place on the boat.

As the students board the bus for the ride home, the chaperones mark their names off on a list. On the way home the students joke about what people are going to do and keep asking for the lights to be put out. There are reports of students having sex on the bus. Once back at Bolton, the students are required to check in at their dorms immediately, except for the seniors, who have a closely chaperoned senior sleepover in the field house.

Dancing Between Two Worlds

For the girls, prom is a collaborative activity. They get dressed together and do each other's makeup, hair, and nails. They lend each other jewelry and shoes, dance together, and come to each other's aid when crises occur. Their focus on what others think adds to their need to conform to an ideal of beauty. If they feel they do not meet this standard, they experience considerable stress and pressure.

For the boys, on the other hand, prom is largely an individual activity. Although many do not choose their tuxes alone, they do get dressed alone. They do not worry as much about conforming to a particular ideal in appearance or at least take great pains not to show that they care. They do not have public crises over their appearance or their failure to gain the approval of others.

:: SPORTS TEAMS

Although the students describe the boys' sports teams as less relationship-centered and more task-oriented than the girls' teams, the intensity of the team bond, their desire to be part of a particular team, and specific team rituals reveal the importance of the group connection and belongingness for the boys. Throughout my research, the boys manifest their great desire to be members of sport teams and part of the "brotherhood" bond of some of the male teams, especially hockey. Despite the intense bond between teammates, the boys engage in few organized bonding activities for sports, and those they do engage in are different from the secret "getting psyched up" gifts of candy, balloons, and cards for the girls. The boys' bonding appears anti-relational:

-We have helmet boxing. You put on your helmet and gloves and fight each other.

-We had fighting on the van yesterday.

-Mostly we just beat the hell out of each other and become friends for it. We respect each other.

The boys claim that the girls' sports teams are more relationship-oriented and social than the boys'. One explains, "I think it's more of a social event for them. [In a high voice mimicking that of a girl] 'Oh, we'll go play. It will be fun.' [In his regular voice] And most of the guys are going just to play."

The few boys' rituals also appear more intense than those of the girls. One year most of the boys on the varsity soccer team, except an African American with dreadlocks, shaved their heads as an act of unity. Another year the football players buried their jock straps in the end zone after a successful season. The girls made fun of them by then burning their bras on the field hockey field. Recently the boys' varsity soccer team started a new pre-game ritual that exceeds anything other teams do by holding a team dinner the night before games and then all standing by the chapel and saying the Lord's Prayer followed by a cheer.

It seems, however, that boys do this to enhance group solidarity in order to achieve a result—victory on the field by working as a team—but not to deepen the interpersonal relationships with one another.

Although the girls' relationships with each other are more intense and caring, the flip side of these relationships is that the boys are able to leave personal differences aside, whereas girls cannot. For girls, bad relationships off the field affect how they treat each other on the field. One girl explains, " 'Cause if girls don't get along with each other, they never will." Another adds, "Yeah, you'll see people giving you a bad pass to the ankles or . . ." Boys, on the other hand, are able to work together during games for the sake of the team.

The students also contend that if boys are fighting for the same position on a team, "the competition is only on the field." For girls, the competition is "everywhere." A group of girls explains that girls "fight forever" over it, while "guys can just be like, 'You know what? This is just a sport. He's better than me.' They can accept it easier than girls can." The girls add that they always "take it personally" and "won't, like, talk to that person."

While traveling to and from (as well as during) sporting events, the girls engage in gender behavior that is much more other-directed and social than the boys. Despite all the show of emotions and connections, the girls have needs for autonomy and demonstrate their anti-relational side by hostilities and factions on and off the field. Moreover, the boys' self-focused behavior allows them to fit in and become part of the team, a relational aspect that is very important to many of them.

The boys' varsity tennis coach mentioned to me once that when his team had to share a bus with the girls' lacrosse team, the girls' "rowdy" behavior "amused and astonished" the boys. He explains, "The boys sat as far from me as possible" and listened to their Walkmans and slept, while the girls "chatted the whole time," listened to music on a boom box, and danced in the aisles. He was surprised at how "one girl talked with the coach the whole time," as if they were best friends.

:: COMMUNITY SERVICE

The Bolton students' attitudes toward community service again demonstrate how a focus on other is the essence of the performance of femininity while a focus on self is the essence of the performance of masculinity. Volunteerism has long been an important aspect of upper-class culture due to the belief that if one is privileged, one has a responsibility to give back (Domhoff, 2002). This tradition is particularly strong among upper-class women, whose clubs and organizations are often based on volunteerism. Often an upper-class woman's social value rests not on her career, as a man's does, but rather on her position in volunteer organizations.

This gender imbalance is visible at Bolton. Although Bolton Academy has a community service program, it is not a thriving one. The number of students who participate is low, with girls constituting almost 80% of the volunteers in the program. According to the previous director of the program, the girls seemed to have a "genuine interest" in helping others, while the few boys who volunteered were transparent about their motives of wanting to avoid the time commitment of playing a sport or having it look good on their resume. Although some boys are interested in participating in some community service activities, they often "never make it" because the events start early in the morning or take place on Sunday. He cites a Big Brother–Big Sister program at the school or Sunday morning maintenance work at a nearby camp for children with terminal blood diseases to illustrate how many girls enthusiastically embrace helping others but few boys do.

At 8:00 A.M. one Sunday in the spring, nine bleary-eyed girls, ranging from sophomores to seniors, and one junior boy pile into vans for a community service project at a nearby summer camp for children with cancer. They will rake leaves, carry firewood, paint fences, or stain cabinets for the next three to four hours. The one Asian boy seems out of place, and when someone jokingly asks him why he is there, he replies that it will look good on his college application. Later that night I visit a boys' dorm and ask them why girls participate in community service more than boys. The boys respond: "They seem to be more caring," "Guys are more lazy," and "Waking up at eight o'clock for a guy is a lot rougher than for a girl because girls are usually up and they're used to doing their hair and all of that stuff and guys can just wake up and go to class." The boys make no apology nor display any hint of guilt in relating how girls are "more caring." It appears entirely acceptable, even desirable, for boys to be uncaring.

In a survey of 178 students conducted by the school in 2002, the students consistently ranked community service dead last among the aspects of their education they deemed as important. The lack of real interest in community service by both genders, but especially the boys, reflects the reality of the relatively low value placed on other by the entire school community as well as how being concerned with other is viewed as a female trait and interest. The reasons the boys cite for the girls' greater participation, such as that they are more caring, demonstrate that a concern for other is viewed as feminine. That the boys attribute their lack of involvement to being "lazy" indicates that a focus on self is expected and associated with masculinity.

:: MAGAZINES

As with most American teenagers, the Bolton students gravitate toward magazines that help them to be better at the game of gender. In effect, the magazines are scripts on how to perform masculinity and femininity. The importance of examining magazines lies in how they reflect and reinforce larger cultural inequalities and ideals. These provide keys to understanding the pressures the Bolton students face and the "rules" that guide their relationships with both same-sex and opposite-sex peers. Currie (1999) describes how teen magazines perpetuate the "beauty myth," that the "the quality called 'beauty' objectively and universally exists. Women must want to embody it and men must want to possess it" (p. 34). Teen magazines embody the relationship between the sexes: "Men look at women. Women look at themselves being looked at. This determines not only most relations between men and women but also the relations of women" (p. 32). These cultural patterns are visible at Bolton, as the content (both the articles and the advertisements) of the magazines the girls read and how they read and utilize them are other-oriented, while the boys' magazines and how they read them are self-oriented.

This work corroborates previous research describing the differences in how magazines and other media depict men and women. The media requires women to maintain higher standards of physical appearance, especially with regard to thinness and beauty, targeting them with these messages (Silverstein, Perdue, Peterson, & Kelly, 1986; Andersen & DiDomenico, 1992; Nemeroff, Stein, Diehl, & Smilack, 1994; Silverstein, Perdue, et al., 1986). Others have documented an increasing thinness in the cultural ideal for females (but not for males) in American culture and media (Garner et al., 1980; Silverstein, Peterson, & Perdue, 1986; Petrie et al., 1996). Some have correlated exposure to media portrayals of beauty and attractiveness with low self-esteem and eating disorders in women (Stice, Schupak-Neuberg, Shaw, & Stein, 1994; Stice & Shaw, 1994; Striegel-More, Silberstein, & Rodin, 1986).

The Bolton teenagers say they learn about becoming men and women and about sex from a variety of sources including magazines. Many of the girls turn to friends and then "definitely" the media: "I know I read a lot of trashy magazines." The boys turn for sexual advice to doctors, the Internet, porn, peers, and magazines. Typically the boys exclaim enthusiastically that they turn to *Maxim* magazine for sex tips.

The students would much sooner turn to magazines than to their parents for answers about sex. One girl exclaims, "Oh, I would never turn to my mom!" "Oh God, no!" is how the boys react. One boy exclaims, "I don't talk to *anyone* related to me." The students explain, however, that they do learn a great deal about sex from their friends. One girl describes how she "had to show" one of the other girls "how to give a blow job."

The girls read many magazines of the same genre, which portray an ideal of physical appearance and interpersonal relationships. While the older Bolton girls read *Glamour, Vogue, Cosmo, Elle,* and *Mademoiselle,* the freshmen and sophomores are more apt to read *YM* and *Seventeen.* Many also treat catalogues such as those from J. Crew, Abercrombie and Fitch, and Victoria's Secret as magazines.

A typical edition of *Glamour* (July 2002) guides girls on how to achieve physical "perfection" and relationships and thus femininity.[8] The cover of the magazine portrays a slender female model in a strapless dress with her long blond hair billowing back. The headlines, which appear in bold type on the cover, are almost exclusively beauty- or relationship-oriented: "Guys Talk, Talk, Talk"; "Men's #1 Piece of Advice for You & 1000 Guys Tell What Makes Them Stay Loyal"; "Lazy Woman's Guide to Spectacular Summer Hair"; "Healthy Breasts at 20, 30, 40"; "The Top Sexual Health Questions You Wouldn't Dare Ask Out Loud"; "Got a Tissue? Friendship Stories You Will Never Forget."

The articles and even ads feature women and focus on achieving a physical ideal and on relationships. The articles deal with fashion, offer beauty tips, and provide advice about how to get or maintain relationships; 65% of the ads in this particular issue are for beauty products, and most of the rest draw on physical appearance for their appeal, such as in ads for gum ("Gets teeth whiter. Keeps teeth whiter") or razors ("In just one stroke, your skin stays smoother longer"). In only five instances do men appear on the pages of this magazine. The males almost always appear as backdrops for women and generally do not appear in "beefcake" poses.

These magazines form an important part of the girl culture at Bolton. When one girl proclaims, "I don't read magazines. I think they're stupid," the other girls look at her in disbelief. Most girls love reading them because "they're just so much fun" and they are "oriented to our interests. Like they always have that section on fashion," "and guys," "and the love and the quiz zone." When I ask if they read other types of magazines, one girl looks at me as if I am crazy and replies, "I just don't like newsmagazines."

The magazines read by the African American girls at Bolton differ greatly, which corresponds with their different focus. Most report reading *Essence*, *Black Enterprise*, or *Ebony*, which are geared toward women of color, are more career-oriented, and focus less on looks. Although one African American will "glance through mainstream mags such as *Mademoiselle*, *Seventeen*, and *Glamour*," she and the other black girls prefer *Ebony* and *Essence*, which contain articles on "more weighty issues, not what color of fingernail polish is best or what kind of jeans to wear." They are "less about beauty," and "you have to get to a certain point before you can appreciate them." She relates to them because "they provide women role models and inspiration."

When the girls read these magazines, they share, discuss, and read them together in other-oriented ways. One girl says about a friend, "She comes knocking on my door, 'Did you see this?'" and mimics the screeching noises her friend made. Another girl adds, "Amanda and I sit in my room and just make fun of the *Cosmo* articles." Reading the magazines frequently becomes a group activity because "it's just fun" to read them together. One girl explains, "I'm always reading the horoscopes, and I'll be, 'Hey what's your sign?'"

In something akin to femininity by association, the girls use the pictures (most often the ads) from the magazines to extend the performance of femininity to their walls. Almost every girl plasters on her walls numerous cutouts of women (and much less often of men) from their fashion magazines or catalogues. This public display is the ultimate in shared reading. One girl explains that she reads the quizzes and horoscopes in the magazines "with people," and "the rest I read by myself or we tear them up and put them on our walls." Some of the girls place cutouts on the walls to provide inspiration to meet an ideal in physical appearance, while others find them beautiful or meaningful to their lives in some way. One girl explains, "I think that women in general are more beautiful than men and I think to have men on your walls is tacky." She has put up so many pictures of women "to make it a more feminine room and to make it more me."

For many of the girls, the pictures symbolize the performance not only of femininity but also of upper-class wealth. The ads on their walls are often for upscale products, designer perfumes, clothes, or jewelry. One girl who has a collage of magazine ads featuring both men and women and expensive designer labels states that the theme for her collage is "just companies that I like, Tiffany, Gucci, Burberry."

Sometimes the girls make collages out of single body parts cut from these magazines. One girl has a collage "dedicated to female breasts" as well as to a female model's butt "because she's known for her butt." Another girl has a collage of male and female abs on the back of her door that is "just to remind me to do sit-ups."

Although the majority of the pictures on their walls are of females, many of the girls also have pictures of males. Often the male models appear along with women. The only "beefcake" pictures are the male models in the Abercrombie and Fitch catalogue, whom the girls refer to as the "Abercrombie guys." The girls put the Abercrombie guys on their walls "because guys are cute" or because "I think a lot of them are gorgeous."

The dorm room of two girls stands out because it is decorated exclusively with pictures of males. One of the girls (who has complained about being overweight) explains that she decorated her walls with male models from the magazines "because the girls in magazines are always so perfect and skinny, it just makes me feel worse about myself." Her roommate has done the same with her half of the room because she "just likes guys better."

In contrast to the girls, the boys at Bolton mostly read one magazine, *Maxim*, which focuses on fun and self-indulgence and is a guide on how to perform masculinity.[9] In one typical edition (August 2000), the cover features scantily clad women in black leather. At the top of the cover, the words "sex, sports, beer, gadgets, clothes, fitness, greed, lust, sharks, eye-gouging, hiroki" promote what the magazine is about. Splashed across the cover in bold type are the lead articles: "Master Sex Moves—The Complete Guide," "Eat My Cleats! The World's Bloodiest Sports Rivalries," and "The Be-aooooo-tiful Girls of *Coyote Ugly* World Exclusive Photo Shoot!"

Besides pictures of beautiful, scantily clad girls, *Maxim* contains often humorous stories about ways to have fun and be "manly" through sex, alcohol, music, movies, and gadgets. The central themes are fun, self-indulgence, self-reliance, being cool, and getting girls. It doesn't address how they should look or be. One section on penises tells men not to worry if you don't measure up because "what women want is a self-confident man." Another article entitled "The Move" describes unusual sex moves and promises its readers, "Read on and prepare to become a man—or at least act like one in bed." The "How To" feature teaches the reader how to survive in shark-infested waters (while a similar feature in *Glamour* teaches the reader how to decorate a room).

The focus of the articles and advertisements is on women, but with the aim of sex, not relationships. Most of the articles and advertisements feature beautiful female models, many of whom are wearing scanty clothing in suggestive poses. Many of the articles and advertisements could be considered anti-relational, such as one article that reveals how to get lesbians to have sex with you, and another that advises how to get lipstick stains out of your collar if you are two-timing. Similarly, many ads feature one man with many women.

The advertisements in *Maxim* differ greatly from those in *Glamour* not just in how they appeal to their audience but also in the products that are advertised in the magazines. Of the ads that appear in this particular issue of *Maxim*, 72% are for products that can be considered fun or self-indulgent, such as CDs, TV shows, movies, alcohol, and cigarettes. Less than 1% are for appearance-related products (one for hair gel, one for a hair growth product, one for a muscle-building product, two for fragrances for men and women, and one for deodorant).

Although a few of the boys read other magazines such as *Men's Health, Playboy, Hustler,* and *Sports Illustrated,* the vast majority enthusiastically endorse *Maxim* as their magazine of choice. One boy who says he is "different than most people" and whom the others agree is "weird" reads *Newsweek, Time,* and *Washington Report on Middle Eastern Affairs.*

Because *Maxim* is geared to their interests, they enjoy it. "It has women," one boy explains. Another adds, "It's got neat articles. Like, it has an article on how to make booby traps. It's amusing. It's fun to read." Another laughs, "*Maxim* you don't have to, like, hide whenever the dorm parents come around." Others say they use *Maxim* for quick reading or masturbation.

Although reading *Maxim* is primarily a solo activity, some say that they discuss the articles. One boy explains that you read it "by yourself because it's serious reading and you have to . . . concentrate on them [the girls]," a comment that receives snickers and jokes about mastur-bation. One boy notes, "No one really discusses *Maxim*. Everyone just picks it up and reads it, but nobody discusses it." One boy mentions sharing it "when you find fine girls in *Maxim*; you're like, 'Dude, look at this!'" Another adds, "If you're reading it, you might be like, 'Hey, page 52, check that out.' But that's about it."

Sometimes the boys tear out pictures of girls from *Maxim* and put them on their walls, but not with the frequency that the girls do with their magazines. Generally, the pictures contain only one or two girls in revealing poses, and never advertisements.

When I ask the boys to compare their readership to that of the girls, they say that *Maxim* is not quite as much a part of their lives as the girls' magazines are for the girls. One group of boys first comments on how much they also like the girls' magazines. A big tough hockey player states, "I actually read all those girl magazines too, like the quizzes and stuff." Another boy adds, "Yeah, I love the quizzes." The boys note that the girls have more magazines and read them more because "they always worry about the latest beauty tips and fashion tips."

The boys say that the girls like to read *Maxim* as well. One boy notes, "You'd be surprised at how many girls read it and say they like it." There is further evidence that the girls often read male magazines, as one year a dorm parent found *Playboy* while doing a room inspection in the sophomore girls' dorm.

That both *Maxim* and *Glamour* always have girls on the covers not only is symbolic of the entire focus of the magazines but also demon-strates the differences in the students' masculine and feminine ideals. While *Maxim* promotes fun, "manly pursuits," sex, alcohol, and being part of the "in" group, *Glamour* promotes perfection and relationships. The girls choose to read magazines that will help them to become more "feminine" by reaching a physical ideal (to be like the girl on the cover) and to foster relationships. The boys choose to read magazines that help them to become more "masculine," learn how to have fun, and be cool (in order to get the girl on the cover).

:: DORM ROOMS

The way the Bolton students decorate their dorm rooms provides visual evidence of the essence of gender performances. The rooms are their only private—or, if they have a roommate, not so private—areas to which they can escape. Some rooms are singles (private rooms), but most are doubles and a few are even triples because of overenrollment. As the boys will readily tell you, the girls' rooms are bigger and nicer than their own. Every year the students draw lottery numbers for their room pick. At an auction to raise money for faculty enrichment and scholarships, parents bid for their child's first choice of rooms. Parents paid $2,400 for the first pick of dorm rooms for seniors, $1,200 for juniors, and $800 for sophomores.

Most of the rooms are similar: small with white walls and industrial carpeting. The simple furnishings include a bed, desk, chair, dresser, and closet. When the students first move in, the rooms are bare and stark, but they quickly decorate them to make themselves more comfortable and at home. The students bring keepsakes from home, buy or collect things once they are at Bolton, or create decorations from available materials such as magazines to adorn their walls.

Many students bring their own small couches, chairs, or tables, the most prized of which are couches that are passed down from student to student. One girl's couch is "very meaningful" to her because it "belonged to a girl a few years ago, and then she passed it down to Hillary, who passed it down to me. I'll pass it down to somebody when I leave." Prefects (student leaders who help in the dorms) are allowed to have small refrigerators in their rooms.

Csikszentmihalyi and Rochberg-Halton (1981) explain that the objects people display in their homes have meaning and "constitute an ecology of signs that reflects as well as *shapes* the pattern of the owner's self" (p. 17). Cross-culturally, they found that the displayed objects often symbolize "the power of the bearer" in order to affect others and that for males the objects revolve around "virile virtues such as strength, bravery, prowess, endurance," but for females the objects represent "seductiveness, fertility, and nurturance" (p. 26).[10]

At Bolton, the students also display objects that represent their ideal self, what they want others to think about them or what they would like to be. At the same time, these items serve to shape and help them perform gender. Because of the importance of their rooms as "their space" and as a way to present themselves to the other students from scratch, looking at the different ways boys and girls decorate their rooms reveals the essence of the gender performance (see Steele & Brown, 1995). Also important are the items the students describe as most meaningful to them, often objects used to perform masculinity and femininity.

Girls: People Count

The rooms of the girls are filled with people: pictures of family and friends, random pictures cut out from magazines or catalogues, and things associated with people that are "just important little sentimental pieces of my life." Their most meaningful object usually is other-related, such as pictures of family and friends or an item that they associate with others. Almost all of the girls have either collections of magazine cutouts or pictures of family and friends covering their walls. One girl has a collage of pictures from eighth grade, and another has pictures of all her "friends that have gotten kicked out of this school." Others have posters with encouraging sayings such as "Challenge" and "Courage." One girl has a collection of what she calls "little psych notes to myself," such as "You can do it!"

A wide variety of other-oriented objects include the phone ("I can escape from this bubble. If I just need to call my mother, I can call my mother. If I need to call a friend, I can call a friend. It keeps me sane"), a necklace ("My sister gave it to me. . . . I'm close to her so when I'm here I wear it and it reminds me of her"), and a grandmother's tablecloth hanging on a wall ("We have a cottage at Cape Cod, my mom's mom, and this was on the table when I was little. Some of my best childhood memories are there, and she's dead, so it reminds me of her").

The items the girls have in their rooms are also often relationship-oriented or sentimental. Many of the girls explain, "Oh, I have so many stuffed animals!" One girl has a letter from her brother posted on the wall. The red tapestry on another girl's wall is her "favorite color, and it's from the same place where my friend got her eyebrow pierced." One student covers every inch of her walls with memories and pictures, including "a deflated heart balloon my ex-boyfriend gave me for Valentine's Day." She also has a canopy over her bed that was made by her sisters "so I would miss them." One girl explains that a surfing poster "was, like, my dad's when he was in college or the Navy." Another has a Camel poster her brother gave her. One hangs her brother's football jersey on the wall.

Some of the things the girls have on their walls do not appear to be directly connected with others. Many have tapestries that they say are not meaningful but which they just like. Several girls have mementos of travel or places they have lived. One girl has license plates from all the states that she has lived in, another a map of her town, and another a map of world with pins stuck into it to mark the places she has been.

Many of the girls have posters: a selection of subjects includes the band 'NSync, the photographer Ansel Adams, animals, sports (both male and female stars), the children's book character Pooh Bear, the actress Marilyn Monroe, and the cartoon character Scooby Doo.

Few of the girls have anything typically achievement- or team-oriented on their walls. A couple have their sports letters pinned up or pictures of their sports teams, but I only saw one sports trophy, a jersey, on the wall. The girl who displayed this was an excellent field hockey goalie, and the jersey had been awarded to her at camp that summer by an Olympic field hockey goalie.

Female beauty and expensive designer labels are the main themes in most rooms, representing the girls' ideal selves, the ideal of femininity, and the status markers by which their femininity is judged.

Boys: Things Matter

The boys' self-oriented room decorations and most meaningful objects differ greatly from those of the girls, revealing a much different ideal self and vision of masculinity. Rarely do the boys tear out pictures of people from magazines, with the exception of a few of sexy *Maxim* women. Although many of the boys have a picture or two of family or friends hanging on their walls, it is not nearly the number that the girls display. Instead, the boys' rooms are filled with posters showing images of sports, beer, music, movies, cars, and scantily clad women. Many of the boys have the same beer poster: a picture of a large number of bottles of different types of beer and the caption, "Life is full of difficult decisions." Many have music posters, the most popular being of Bob Marley, Eric Clapton, Phish, Led Zeppelin, rap artists, and the Grateful Dead. Lamps with black-light bulbs as well as posters that glow when the black light shines on them give the room a cool look.

Only a few of the boys have collages, and these are sports- or interest-related, not people-related. One boy's collage contains mostly sailing scenes, an ad for some medicine featuring a "cute" girl, and pictures of a cat and a dog. Another boy's collage features pictures of mountain biking, sailing, and a girl.

The markers of wealth and status on the boys' walls differ from those of the girls. The boys are more apt to have achievement markers displayed on their walls, including sports team pictures, trophies, and pennants as well as signed or famous players' jerseys. One boy has on his wall his space blanket from when he ran the Boston Marathon.

Another has a poster of the French Alps "because I went skiing there over winter break." Many of the students have their yacht club burgee or the emblems of their favorite sports teams hanging on their walls.

Many of the boys' rooms focus on a variety of sports, while others are dedicated to one sport, mainly hockey, and their participation and achievement in that sport. Many of the boys explain, "Most of the stuff in my room has to do with hockey." One boy's "hockey room" has hockey posters, a team jersey, hockey pictures, pictures of his father and brother, female supermodels cut out from a magazine, a movie poster, a hockey banner, a picture of a bloody hockey skate and an arm, the student's statistics for the hockey season, a Vince Lombardi speech, "the goals we used for the hockey team this year," pictures of different hockey teams he has played on, a beer poster, a Canadian flag (he is from Canada), a poster of the famous hockey player Wayne Gretzky's wife in a bathing suit and hockey gear, and a black light.

Pictures of scantily clad women and alcohol are part of making a room look cool. Many boys have black lights and beer posters. The performative aspect of these decorations becomes clear when I ask one boy if the reason he has so many beer posters up is that he likes beer. He responds, "No, not really, I just put them up." Many of the boys tell me they would put up more sex and alcohol pictures if they were allowed.

Some of the boys' rooms are bare. One boy who has absolutely nothing on his walls explains, "I don't really care that much. I'm just waiting to get out of here." Two sophomores with almost bare walls say, "We just haven't decided what we want to put up yet," even though it is April and the school year is almost over. Many of the Asian students from Korea and Thailand also have bare walls. The only wall decoration of a Korean boy is a two-by-three-inch Korean flag.

A few of the boys have posters of famous men, often sports stars, on their walls for inspiration. One athlete places a basketball poster of Michael Jordan on his wall "because he's the best basketball player ever. I look up to him and wish I could be like him." A serious student has several "motivational" posters of famous men, explaining, "That's what my room is to me. Just different things that cheer me up. If I'm having a bad day, I can just walk in and say, 'Hey, there's Muhammad Ali,'" someone who represents strength and perseverance.

The boys' most meaningful objects in their rooms are self-focused objects that demonstrate or are tools to achieve masculinity. Even the idea of having something meaningful runs against the code of masculinity. Whereas the girls often think of so many meaningful items in their rooms that they have difficulty deciding which one to pick, the boys have difficulty coming up with any meaningful object. Picking items that are less emotional or "deep" than those of the girls, the boys focus on an item's utility.

Almost all of the boys list a self-oriented item as their most meaningful object, but one student could not name anything: "I have nothing. I have nothing meaningful in my room." A few male students list other-oriented objects such as pictures of family, friends, or a girlfriend. The most frequently cited self-oriented items are furniture and appliances, especially the bed, because the boys "love to sleep." One boy answers, "My garbage can because I use that the most (it is overflowing). My fan. It keeps me cool. Air freshener spray because sometimes it stinks in here."

Sports-related items such as hockey sticks, lacrosse sticks, and snowboards, computers, and music-related items are the next most frequently listed items because of their utility and not because they are associated with others. One boy's most meaningful object is "my crew jacket. I worked all season for it. It's a varsity jacket." Another boy lists his guitars or his computer, saying "They are my life." Another boy picks his "computer or bed, because I use them a lot."

Rooms of Self and Other

The students decorate their dorm rooms and present objects as meaningful in a way that invokes masculinity and femininity by association. Their decorations are divided along the lines of a focus on self and other, revealing how they wish to present themselves to others. By decorating their rooms with pictures of family and friends and citing as meaningful objects that have some connection to others, the girls demonstrate their ideal selves as revolving around other. By putting up ads of expensive brand names as well as pictures of beautiful women, they promote an image of femininity based on the status markers of beauty and prestige. The boys, on the other hand, cite trivial objects or objects useful to themselves (self) as the most meaningful, distancing themselves from emotions. By surrounding themselves with black lights and posters of sports heroes, famous musicians, sexy women, and alcohol, as well as other status and achievement markers, the boys promote a masculinity based on coolness and present their ideal, high-status selves through traditional status markers of wealth and achievement. These symbols of strength, power, fame, proficiency, and status contribute to their ranking in the social hierarchy and the ultimate goal of belongingness.

:: WHAT DOES IT MEAN TO BE MALE AND FEMALE?

The divergent ways in which the male and female students at Bolton manipulate and negotiate the opposition between self and other as they perform masculinity and femininity are evident in such areas of everyday life as their relationships, casual discourse, sports, community service, magazines, and dorm rooms.

The performances of self and other become so gendered that they literally define what it means to be masculine or feminine, or male or female. Rather than being natural tendencies, numerous cultural punishments and rewards serve to enforce these prescribed gender ideals despite evidence that the needs and desires of many of the students do not naturally fit within the confines of these ideals. Often the pressure from one's own sex to conform to gender-"appropriate" behavior is stronger than pressures from the opposite sex. That the gender ideals and expectations of self or other do not always coincide with an individual's personality or traits is evident for both sexes.

Paradoxically, due to the students' ideals of masculinity centering on a focus on self, male students appear best able to secure relationships and connections with others if they do not overtly demonstrate sensitivity, selflessness, caring what others think, and caring for others. The opposite appears true for female students, who appear to be most successful in relationships and in making connections with others if they do not overtly demonstrate independence, sexuality, power, competence, or any lack of caring about what others think or about others (and one could argue career success, autonomy or power) in order to fit the ideal of femininity. Because this disparity between self and other is central to the gender ideals of these students and because mate value and conformity are primary concerns of adolescents, the cultural rewards and punishments that encourage this divergence are particularly effective; this results in a high degree of sexual dimorphism.

Because the values of self and other form the basis of the students' gender ideals, this gender dichotomy also permeates the oppositions the students face between equality and inequality, individuality and conformity, freedom and constraint, and excellence and fun. The boys and girls' covert needs and desires as well as the social pressures and consequences they face to conform to the accepted gender ideals are evident in their everyday struggles.

4 ::

Cute Girls, Cool Guys

Researchers have described sets of polar oppositions as the primary conflicts within cultures (Lévi-Strauss, 1969a, 1969b). The oppositions of "devotion to the pure, intimate inside and the corrupt public outside" found in Iranian society and "feelings and desires (*ninjo*) against social duty (*giri*)" found in Japanese society can be compared to the importance of the opposition between individualism and conformity found in the United States (Beeman, 1986a).

The desire to be an individual and stand out yet simultaneously conform and fit in lies at the root of these teenagers' self-esteem and identity, yet the contradictory qualities of individuality and conformity pose a dilemma for these adolescents, who are expected to achieve both at the same time (Tocqueville, 1945; Spindler & Spindler, 1982; Varenne, 1977; G. L. Hicks, 1976; Beeman, 1986b; Mascolo & Li, 2004). The value of individuality stems not only from the notion of the "rugged individual" (Tocqueville, 1945) as the cornerstone of American culture but also from the competition to attract mates and establish status during adolescence. The value of conformity arises from the way similarity enhances the solidarity that fulfills the human drive to establish and sustain "belongingness" (Baumeister & Leary, 1995; Gabriel & Gardner, 1999). Only through successfully achieving both conformity and individuality can students achieve high romantic and social status and corresponding high self-esteem.

The Bolton students approach these values differently, as they openly value individuality but covertly cherish conformity. Publicly, both genders postulate individuality but feel intense pressure to fit in and to perform the ideal in masculinity and femininity. They also seek solidarity, striving to bond with peers and establish friendships as well as to separate themselves from parents, school personnel, and other adults.

Boys and girls at Bolton manipulate the opposition between individuality and conformity differently due to the different ideals for masculinity and femininity. Compliance with what is considered appropriate behavior paves the way to relationships and connections with others.

Research demonstrates that the correlates for popularity and peer acceptance among adolescents vary greatly because it is simply complying with accepted behavioral norms that appears to make individuals popular (Rubin, Bukowski, & Parker, 1998). As a result of the interconnection between divergent gender, class, race/ethnic, and sexual norms, the Bolton students perform divergent masculinities and femininities. As West and Fenstermaker (1995) argue, "No person can experience gender without simultaneously experiencing race and class" (p. 13). In her study of differences between how middle-class and working-class girls constructed and expressed opposing femininities through clothes, cosmetics, and attitudes toward sexuality, Bettie (2003) illustrates how social class structures not only one's opportunities but also one's gender and sexuality, and social class is itself constructed in relation to gender and race. Bettie asserts that women perform "different versions of femininity that are internally linked and inseparable from their class and race performances" (p. 15). Other researchers add behaviors involving smoking and compliance with school rules (Eckert, 2004; Ortner, 2003; Trautner, 2005) to class and ethnic performances of gender. Organizations themselves articulate ideas and presentations of gender that are mediated by class (Trautner, 2005).

The degree to which individuals abide by gender stereotypes is closely connected to both class and race/ethnicity. Researchers have described African American women as less likely than other ethnicities to accept culturally dominant, gender-stereotyped beliefs and behaviors (Binion, 1990; Dugger, 1986; Henley, 1995). Some studies have not found discernible differences between African American males and males of other ethnicities in the degree to which they adopt traditional gender attitudes and behavior (Smith & Midlarsky, 1985; Stanback, 1985). Others, however, have noted an identity described as "bravado" or "macho" among African American males living in high-risk neighborhoods (Cunningham, 2001; Spencer, Cunningham, & Swanson, 1995; Cunningham & Meunier, 2004). Black teachers are less stereotyped in their beliefs and behaviors (for a review, see Meece, 1987).

Research in America has correlated popularity for boys with athletic ability, gender-appropriate athletic participation, toughness, and social skills and popularity for girls with physical appearance, gender-appropriate athletic participation, social skills, and parents' socioeconomic class (Adler, Kless, & Adler, 1992; Holland & Andre, 1994). One aspect of popularity on which all studies seem to agree is that it is more acceptable for girls to act in gender-inconsistent ways than for boys to do so, and that boys who display female-stereotypical behavior are ridiculed and disliked more often by both boys and girls than are girls who display male-stereotypical behavior (Fagot, 1985; Moller, Hymel, & Rubin, 1992).

These interconnections between class, race, and gender are readily apparent among the Bolton students. The girls' popularity at Bolton is often based on their socioeconomic status, which directly relates to their ability to wear the right brands and the amount of focus they place on their appearance, including the pressure they put on themselves to be thin. At Bolton, the role of socioeconomic status is also salient for boys, but it appears to play a more complicated role than it does for the girls. For boys, two conflicting axes of power, athletic power and wealth, are important for popularity. As these two traits rarely seem to occur in the same individual, the boys and groups of boys who possess these opposing traits often vie against each other for status. Which characteristic wins out appears to be a matter of class. For the less wealthy students, athletic power appears to dominate, while for the wealthiest students, it is money and the accompanying attention to appearance that win popularity with other boys and with girls.

Central to the students' ideals of masculinity are individuality and the expectation that boys need not and should not care what others think of them, either in appearance or in behavior. A boy performs masculinity by displaying a disregard for others, focusing on individuality, self, and self-gratification, and engaging in cool or "bad-ass" behaviors that demonstrate power. A girl performs femininity, on the other hand, by displaying conformity and caring what others think of her appearance and behavior. Femininity rests on being cute, maintaining control over herself, and denying her sexuality in order to maintain a good reputation.

At Bolton, the girls are judged and pressured to conform to an ideal of appearances so as to be deemed "cute." A girl's femininity and status are determined almost entirely by her ability to conform to a narrow physical ideal few attain. Even the behaviors associated with the process of trying to achieve this ideal—such as being self-conscious, being unhappy with her looks, and spending time on her looks—are viewed as feminine traits. Also central to the performance of femininity is the expectation of control, as girls face pressure to conform to a contradictory and convoluted standard of sexual behavior that requires them to control and deny their sexuality.

For Bolton boys, on the other hand, although appearance is undeniably important, status is achieved by being a "bad-ass" or cool and demonstrating power. The performance of masculinity requires them to be self-reliant and not to care what others think of them as well as to be self-focused and self-indulgent. Unlike the ideal of femininity, which is limited to a few key characteristics, the ideal of masculinity involves the boys meeting the masculine ideal of being strong mentally and physically, self-reliant, self-driven, self-confident (not caring about their looks), athletic, not caring about others or what others think (having a "bad-ass" attitude), not working too hard (which would result in being deemed a nerd), being good-looking, being able to provide, and partaking in drugs, alcohol, and sex. Although attractiveness is valued in males, it is just part of being considered cool, and a boy's excessive attention to his looks is viewed as feminine, negating his masculinity.

The differences in how the Bolton students negotiate individuality and conformity can be expressed as the pressure to be "perfect" for girls versus the pressure to be "the best at everything" for boys. Because a focus on other is symbolic of femininity, the overt quality of conformity is valued in females. Because a focus on self is symbolic of masculinity, the overt quality of individuality is valued in males. Consequently, the girls desire to be perfect—in other words, to conform to an ideal based primarily on appearance. The boys, on the other hand, desire to be the best and to be popular, with their pressures involving status and ranking.

Both genders demonstrate covert needs and desires that do not fit into the prescribed gender performances. The girls display covert individuality through their intense rivalry, competition, and dissatisfaction with the pressure to look good and to constrain their behavior, both sexually and otherwise. The boys, on the other hand, covertly demonstrate conformity as they strive to fit the wide variety of behaviors, appearances, and abilities necessary to be considered cool. Time and time again the students feel the most pressure to conform to stereotypical behavior and ideals of appearance from same-sex peers because of competition. Researchers (Maccoby, 1998) have described similar behavioral differences, establishing that gender, class, and ethnicity, rather than being a set of characteristics determined by biology or culture, are performances that can be strategically changed depending on the context.

:: THE OVERT VALUE OF INDIVIDUALITY

Although the Bolton students value both conformity and individuality, they uphold the value of individuality both in their public chapel speeches and newspaper articles and in their private conversations. In their chapel speeches, many students preach the ideal of "not following the crowd" and "being your own person." The basis of one boy's senior chapel speech is "be yourself and don't conceal the real you." Another boy recommends people find their own "individual road to happiness," referencing other speeches in which the students recount their own individual pleasures. Many girls also urge individuality. One girl describes how she escapes from the conformity surrounding her:

> I was able to see by refusing to be blinded by the superficiality of society. I have removed the mask I once wore so proudly day after day. I removed layer after layer of plastic coating from my body, which was said to protect me from the outside world. I was not informed it would retard my growth and very existence; it would restrict my education, and inhibit my talent. Oh no, I was not told it would bury my individuality deep within my flesh. It was the comfort zone of conformity, which allowed me to blend in with all the other plastic beings. . . . I constantly push others to travel the path less traveled, the path of individuality.

:: THE COVERT VALUE OF CONFORMITY

Performing Class

Similar to gender, class is both an economic reality and a performance. Bettie (2003) describes how the adolescents she studied performed class to both distinguish and distance themselves from other socioeconomic groups. The girls often performed a different socioeconomic standing than they actually occupied by adopting particular behaviors or modifying their appearance in order to fit in with the group they identified with. Similarly, Trautner (2005) describes how strippers at nightclubs catering to clientele of different socioeconomic classes use "their appearances to simultaneously do gender, heterosexuality, and class" (p. 778). She describes long red nails, tight clothes, dark or bright red lipstick, bleached blond hair, and more acceptance of a variety of body types as being symbolic of working-class sexuality, while long hair, thin bodies, coiffed hair styles, glittery eye makeup, long lightly colored nails, being tan, and wearing perfume were symbolic of middle- and upper-class sexuality. In these classed versions of femininity, the more upper-class clubs put a greater emphasis on the dancers fitting more rigidly defined (thin) body types, hair styles (long), and clothing (covering more, and more elaborate), as well as an overall greater attention to appearance.[1]

The students at Bolton also "do" class in correlation with gender. Despite the overt value the students place on individuality, they conform to their new environment by changing the way they dress, the way they talk, the music they listen to, and the way they act in order to fit into the wealthy, conservative, preppy culture of Bolton Academy. They often cast off their class of origin, depending on whether they are at Bolton or at home.

Students who are neither wealthy, conservative, nor preppy face pressure to change in order to fit in. In one dorm, the boys who are not from New England or who are not wealthy feel pressure to conform to "New England society" and "to be a certain way." One boy from Washington, D.C., complains:

> If you listen to rap or whatever [at home], you're part of the in crowd, . . . and here I told one kid that I like rap music and he was like, "You like rap music? Do you consider yourself African American? *We* [said in a snobby tone] listen to the Dead."

Because of the isolated nature of Bolton, the students have unusual influence over each other and have created their "own popular culture." They note the similarity of music tastes: "Everybody begins to listen to the same music" and "You walk through the quad and everyone's playing the same song."

The Preppy Style

The preppy style associated with wealth and privilege is not just a style of clothing; it symbolizes a different way of life and mentality. In every culture, clothing not only is utilitarian but also symbolizes a person's or group's identity. Sahlins (1976) describes how clothing incorporates a symbolic system that produces social distinctions and creates meaningful differences between categories and subcategories. According to Eckert (2004), an individual's clothes serve "as a direct and intentional expression of group values, a marker of boundaries" (p. 216). Preps distinguish themselves by their choice of footwear, the colors they wear, and how they wear their collars, and these differences take on great meaning (see Birnbach, 1980).

The prep performance of masculinity and femininity relies on exclusiveness and wealth. The most popular brands are the most expensive and those that indicate a privileged lifestyle, especially anything nautical. Whether the designer's label is clearly visible or discreetly hidden, the students are attuned to the subtle differences that allow them to judge the cost or authenticity of the clothing (such as Sperry Top-Sider shoes that were actually worn sailing). Eckert (2004) describes how "economic means are reflected both in rapid turnover of clothing—exhibited through wardrobe size and swift style changes—and in the quality and expense of individual items" (p. 216). The items that carry the most meaning at Bolton and elsewhere, however, are often the subtle markers of category membership such as popped collars (ones that are standing straight up), a gold nautical rope bracelet, a family crest ring, or pink boxers with flowers on them because "these subtler differences, which can be achieved only through private information, are the ultimate indication of group membership" (Eckert, 2004, p. 216).

For girls, the preppy look centers around pastels, especially pinks and greens (often in a patchwork pattern), pearls or jewelry from Tiffany's, and belts and tote bags from Vineyard Vines. In warmer weather, sheath sundresses from Lilly in pink, yellow, white, green, and periwinkle are popular, while girls wear cashmere sweaters, short skirts with bare legs, and Ugg boots in winter. The parts of the body covered or revealed and the looseness or tightness of clothing indicate social status and are central to the prep performance of femininity. Because the preppy style is modest, tight clothes or clothes revealing cleavage are considered low-class, but bare stomachs and short skirts are acceptable.

For boys, the most popular clothes are polo shirts with the "right" logo (Ralph Lauren is the highest-status), brightly colored pants (Nantucket red is popular), Brooks Brothers jackets (a loud madras jacket inscribed with previous owners' names is the highest-ranking, as one senior passes it down to another every year), cashmere sweaters, and ties, belts, flip-flops, and boxers featuring nautical themes (sailboats, starfish, whales, sharks, or fish) or critters (ducks, turtles, squirrels, crickets, or frogs). Wearing the color pink evokes the divergent performances of masculinity among the boys at Bolton. The members of the "high-class club" wear pink clothes (including boxers) but would not be caught dead carrying a pink backpack or having pink in their rooms because "pink is for girls." They also care about their looks and the quality of each other's clothing. This stands in direct opposition to the hockey players, for whom wearing pink and caring about how you look (or about whether or not your sweater is cashmere) are unheard of and considered effeminate. The athletic boys mock the preppy boys as the "pink team," questioning their masculinity for their color choice and lack of athleticism. Although the African American boys do not wear pink, they care how they look and smell. They describe taking care matching their clothes (even matching their sneakers with their shirts), showering often, and using scented products such as aftershave. Because the preppy boys wear clothes that other boys avoid at all costs and regard as "feminine," they set themselves apart and project the ultimate power and superiority of wealth by performing what is usually considered the antithesis of masculine behavior.

A popped collar appears to signal the essence of prepdom, and so how the students—both boys and girls—wear their collars designates them as preps or non-preps. A few of the students tout their non-prep status through the clothes they wear, claiming, "I don't even *own* a polo shirt." Others conform partially to the prep look and frequently wear polo shirts but wear the collar down. "Prepped-out" students always pop their polo shirt collars. The significance of these different collar positions is dramatic. On one occasion I asked a group of students to change how they were wearing their collars. Those with their collars down were to put them up and those with them up were to put them down. The students felt so uncomfortable with their collars the "wrong" way that they complained: "Oooh, I can't do it!" "Yuck!" and "Oh, it feels so weird!"

The girls describe how students "deck out" at Bolton and how they dress similarly. Certain brands such as J. Crew, Lilly, Vineyard Vines, North Face, Ralph Lauren, and Abercrombie and Fitch serve as the model for the students. One girl explains, "Individuals tend to dress just like other individuals, so everyone is almost dressed alike." Tellingly, one girl asks, "How many times have you seen the same outfit on, like, five different people?" Her friend agrees that many of the students are "like J. Crew mannequin models."

Noting the conformity to the prep style traditionally worn by the "haves" in New England, one boy asserts:

I hate to say this, but if you had someone who dressed, like, punk style, with the high boots and the colored hair and all sorts of piercings all over the place, I don't think anyone at this school would talk to them. Even though people say they aren't, everyone pretty much conforms to the whole prep aspect of the school.

A boy says one girl is "a perfect example": "When she came into this school, she didn't dress like anyone else. She had all the piercings and the punk clothes. And by the middle of the term she had completely changed entire clothes." Another boy notes the transformation of another girl:

She came in with the whole hippie look, and now she's starting to get into the whole prep expensive clothes aspect of things. Like everybody just falls into the same trap or mold or whatever you want to call it.

Some students purposely perform class by conforming to the look when they come to Bolton, only to revert back to their own styles when at home. One girl explains, "Here I'm *really* preppy. And at home I'm more laid back." Another girl reveals:

I used to wear more punk clothes and stuff. I came here and I bought clothes to fit the dress code. Like, I shopped at Abercrombie, which is like a big thing for me. But I don't go as far as everyone else is, which is to be identical to everyone else.

At this, Kara, a black girl who excels academically and athletically but also places great importance on appearance, agrees, "Yeah, I think there's a little too much J. Crew shopping going on at Bolton, to where you see the same outfit a little too much." A wealthy girl, Sarah, explains, "Yeah, but that's what I buy anyway. That's the hard thing, there are people who change to be that."

Not only do the students change their style of clothes in order to fit in, but they also change their behavior. A girl from the South tones down her southern drawl at Bolton and picks it back up at home. A black girl from California notes, "There are certain people who I look at and I know good and well when they go home they don't look like that, they don't act like that." She cites the example of Melody, a girl in the room from a poor area in California, and adds "I know where she comes from. . . . I know where she hangs around."

The boys also face pressures to conform to the preppy style of clothes and behavior at Bolton. One boy, Bryan, admits that at home he usually wears his pants low in a hip-hop style, but when he is at Bolton he does not. He adds, "If I get a strange haircut at home, it's not strange. Here it is." I frequently observe the other boys making fun of Bryan for his clothing or jewelry. In one instance, the boys pick on him for wearing a baseball hat the wrong way:

-Why do you wear a Fremont hat?

-I don't know.

-Why do you wear it sideways?

-Do you think we're in the hood?

-You're a white kid at boarding school, you're not in the ghetto.

Although the international students do not adapt to the preppy style as readily as the American students, they still abandon the styles from home to create an Americanized look. When one boy from Hong Kong left Bolton at the end of the year, he discarded in the Dumpster outside the dorms a suitcase full of unworn handmade suits from Hong Kong that he had brought with him when he had arrived. (Some of the items thrown into the Dumpsters by students at the end of the year are salvaged by faculty members for their or their families' own use.)

Some students from wealthy areas drop status clothing in order to fit in at Bolton. Elizabeth, who is from Greenwich, Connecticut, explains:

The thing is, I know that here I do get dressed up and I do care what I look like, but at home it's *much* more, like, status. Like, I wouldn't wear all the status stuff that I wear at home, like jewelry and handbags and all of that other stuff. I just leave that behind when I come here because it doesn't matter.

Groups and individuals who do not change to conform to the preppy style highlight the interconnection between the performance of gender, class, and ethnicity, basing their self-identity on not being preppy and not selling out to the prep crowd and upper-class values. Sara, who is proud of her Colorado heritage, hinges her nonconformity on her Western (versus Eastern and prep) pride by wearing boots and a large cowboy-style belt buckle. One boy who does not conform is an intelligent day student who wears punk-style clothes and a Mohawk. Considering the traditional prep/town rivalry and how the day students say their local friends think they are snobs, his nonconformity sends a message that he is not selling out.

Two distinct groups on campus eschew the preppy style, their identity revolving around their opposition to being preppy (in both looks and behavior) and not selling out. One group is the hockey players, many of whom are from working-class Catholic families in Boston or Canada and who are often in social conflict with the preppy boys. Their nonconformity stems from their middle-class pride and resistance to the upper class. Ranking high socially, these boys are such a large, strongly bonded group that they withstand the pressures to conform and even distance themselves from the preppy boys.

The second group is the African American students, whose nonconformity stems from ethnic pride. Because adopting the preppy style would be tantamount to "selling out" to the rich establishment, they maintain a different look from the majority of the students. Only two wealthy African Americans girls at Bolton conform to the preppy style, standing out from the rest.

While discussing how the students at Bolton conform to the preppy style, a white girl mentions that she wore Reefs (the quintessential preppy flip-flops worn in all weather) in the middle of a snowstorm, saying "I wore Reefs tonight. What was I thinking? It's freezing." At this Kara, an African American girl on scholarship, exclaims:

> Yeah . . . it's not just dress code, your whole mentality, your way of life, wearing Reefs in the snow! I've never seen such stupidness in all my life! I didn't want to bring it to a race thing but I was like, I know no black person would come out with Reefs in the snow. It's blistering cold. They have a coat on, hood, hat, scarf, and Reefs.

The girls laugh and respond, "Mercedes and Chanel [the only two wealthy African American girls on campus] would have!" Kara retorts, "They are the only idiots that would do that!" For a few wealthy African Americans, their assimilation of the preppy style indicates that socioeconomic bonds predominate over ethnic ones.

Another African American girl, Nicole, who has a beautiful dancer's body that she shows off to full advantage by wearing very tight clothes, "gets away with" wearing clothing that is different from the other girls' at Bolton. She muses, "It's funny. I see people wearing stuff I wear and the teachers are like, 'What are you doing?' and I'd wear it and get away with it. I don't know because—" At this one of the other girls interjects, "Like that damn fur coat." Nicole laughs, "Yeah, like that fur coat. I can get away with a fur coat, but everyone else can't get away with a fur coat. I don't know why." One of the white girls who is from a poor area reasons that, unlike herself, Nicole has never changed her style in order to mold herself to "that J. Crew image."

Performing Gender

The students at Bolton face pressure to perform divergent and often opposing masculinities and femininities. For the very preppy boys, the wealth and status signaled by their pink polo shirts and cashmere sweaters symbolize their masculinity. The mostly middle-class hockey players' muscularity and athleticism are central to their gender identity. The African American boys combine athleticism and appearance (looking and smelling good) into their performance of masculinity.

For the girls, good looks are central to the performance of femininity, yet differences exist. The wealthy girls strive to act "classy" and to be "perfect" and "thin," focusing on their and others' appearances. The less wealthy girls are less concerned with appearances and thinness, being more comfortable to "burp and fart and get up and pee with or outdrink the boys." The African American girls combine both the focus on clothes and looking good (but not being thin) with the freedom to "hang with the guys" and often act less stereotypically than the other girls.

In trying to distance themselves from behavior associated with the opposite gender, these students engage in extreme gendered performances. Some aspects of the boys and girls' performances are similar. Neither sex views being really smart as part of their gender ideal. Boys are allowed more leeway to be smart as long as they don't look as if they are trying too hard. As one boy writes, "My peers would hesitate in allowing others to see the amount of work they have to do each day." The girls view the feminine ideal at Bolton as being "really, really, really dumb," saying, "Boys don't like girls who are too outgoing or talk too much" and that they want "silent dolls an their arms, beautiful silent dolls," especially when boys are with their friends. Feeling this pressure, the younger girls describe how they "dummy down" and don't say much in the presence of boys. Some girls "never say anything" in classes where there are boys they like because they fear they might "say something stupid" or appear too "nerdy."

Although conformity is important for both genders, their gender ideals force them to approach it differently. The boys conform by not seeming to conform or care what others think, while girls conform openly because a focus on other is symbolic of femininity.

Private Writings

In their private writings, both sexes disclose their covert ideas or desires that they hesitate to share with others, revealing how important it is to fit in as well as to stand out and be popular. The covert nature of male conformity manifests itself when one boy contends that although "many deny it," he believes the biggest issue he and his peers are facing "is the position that I hold at Bolton. That is my image, what others think of me. Whether I have a girlfriend, am on a varsity sport." The girls, on the other hand, wanting to fit in, do not openly express individualistic desires of status or popularity, but their desire to be perfect reveals their covert desire to stand out.

The pressures facing the boys and girls are different. The girls feel pressure to conform to a cultural ideal of beauty ("I am dealing with anorexia, depression, so much is based on physical beauty") and a model of culturally sanctioned sexual behavior ("[I'm dealing with issues of] sex and feeling pressured if you haven't had it, or juvenile, or then some feel slutty or like a skank if they have. It's hard, either way you feel bad") in order to be perfect and fit in. Although many girls mention drugs and alcohol, their concerns in regard to these suggest not pressure but rather "making choices."

The boys, on the other hand, feel "unbelievable" pressure "to act cool and be liked and to be popular," because "you don't want to go through four or three years at school in hell with no friends." Their pressures to conform to a standard of behavior includes ranking high, taking drugs and drinking, having a girlfriend and sex, being on a varsity sport, looking strong or "ripped," and acting cool. One boy explains, "People with alcohol and drugs are considered the in-crowd, whereas people who do not participate in these activities on campus are isolated by the users because of the lack of socializing."

The boys' writings reveal the pressure to perform masculinity rather than act on their true desires. Because many of the boys neither naturally fit the code of masculinity nor desire to fit it, they strategically alter their actions in order to fit in. One boy writes "how hard it is to be popular and stay popular," especially "when you want to do something but can't because you won't be cool anymore." Another complains that the

Bolton students highly value and consider cool "disgusting" behaviors such as "drinking too much or chewing tobacco or men shaving their testicles." Because "drugs and drinking are a persistent issue" at Bolton, a freshman notes he must "be strong and not give in—*just say no!*" Another writes, "Drugs, sex, etc. . . . is expected and sensitivity is blocked."

A few of the boys feel pressure to be "strong and buff" and good athletes. One boy writes:

> One issue is being strong or more "ripped." I feel pressure to be in the weight room and to be strong physically. Also, I feel pressured to be great at sports. I do enjoy playing sports, but I feel that I have to do too much at times.

Rather than describing his own need to conform, one student reveals how he forces his roommate to conform to accepted ideals: "I have issues with my roommate about him taking a shower. I solve this by punching him till he goes into the shower."

Looking Good

Appearance, an important element of human existence (Etcoff, 1999; Jackson, 1992), is primary during adolescence as boys and girls become interested in promoting their value as mates (Schlegel & Barry, 1991; Dittmar et al., 2000; Simmons & Florence, 1975; Cawley, Joyner, & Sobal, 2006; Freedman, 1986). Appearance plays a vital role in the gendered performances of the students as they hold an ideal physical stereotype (both physical appearance and clothing style) against which they measure each student.

At Bolton, the dual pressures of individuality and conformity are central to the paradox of appearance. The students strive to stand out and be noticed, yet at the same time they undergo immense pressure to fit the beauty mold valued by their peers. For girls the pressure is to be thin and pretty, for boys to be "buff" and handsome.

The girls are allowed and even expected to attempt to conform openly to these rigid and demanding ideals for physical appearance. Although the boys are given more latitude in upholding physical standards, their quest is made more complicated because they must hide their conformity and not appear to care about their appearance or spend much time on it, or else they will be labeled effeminate.

Although appearance is important to the self-esteem of both boys and girls, a focus on looks and concern about what others think is strictly part of the feminine and not the masculine ideal. The girls also demonstrate their need to stand out by their descriptions of the intense competition between girls over appearance. The males, on the other hand, contrast the girls' focus on appearance with their own disinterest, trying to outdo each other in how little they care and making fun of boys who care too much about their appearance. Their hidden desires to conform, however, are demonstrated by their longing to be more muscular and taller, their enthusiasm over the thought of gaining 15 pounds of muscle, and their written accounts of caring about their appearance but trying not to show it.

Girls: Looks Are Everything

For girls, "looks are everything" at Bolton. During the middle of study hall, a girl comes in with her hair partially up, partially down, saying, "We're half done in the process of doing my hair. That's why I look like this." I ask if they are cutting her hair, and she replies, "No. We're just blow-drying it. We were having a hair day." The girls continue to discuss their hair and whether it is straight or naturally curly. When I ask how important looks are, the girl doing her hair responds, "Everything is, like, looks here."

The clique of wealthy senior girls, also known as the "senior princesses," "bitch squad," or "rich bitches," earns these labels because they are very concerned with their own appearances and critical of others. "I'm sorry. I will *not* date anyone who is not cute . . . or not athletic," says Mercedes.

The girls' competition over appearances reveals the hidden realities of individuality and the desire to rise above others and stand out. One girl explains:

> What I think stresses me out most about looks is to compete with other girls. I really wouldn't worry about a guy seeing me with unshaven legs or something, but the fact that all the girls have silky smooth legs, I'm like, "Oh, should I have silky smooth legs too?" It's the pressure with the girls.

The girls frequently say that they have low self-esteem, which they attribute to this competition. One freshman girl, Jen, who considers her brown hair and curves as not fitting the ideal in appearance, blames her "total" lack of confidence to her being "afraid of what other people think. I care too much, I really do." She admits, "Some days I'm afraid of myself. I'm afraid of what I think of myself."

Many girls feel dissatisfied and self-conscious about their bodies. The ritual in one dorm called "Topless Tuesday" is heralded by some girls as allowing them to overcome this self-consciousness. This ritual is called "Topless Tuesday" because it takes place late on Tuesday nights after the dorm parents are in bed and the girls gather in different states of undress, often in just underwear and boots, and watch TV. They also knock on others' doors and try to get reactions. Girls from that dorm state:

-I think it's kind of cool that we're comfortable enough with our bodies to be walking around.

-And we trust each other not to criticize, you know . . .

-'Cause there are so many girls who are so uncomfortable with their bodies and how they look naked.

-Because a lot of us in [the dorm] weren't comfortable with our bodies until Penelope showed us the light and her headlights on top.

Although some boys obsess over their looks, the girls do so more because they are judged solely on looks, while boys are judged as a whole package. The girls claim, "Girls settle more for personality than for looks." Another girl agrees, "Like, you see a lot more pretty girls with not good-looking guys, I think, than good-looking guys with not as pretty girls. Definitely."

The juxtaposition between the feminine ideal, which includes being self-conscious and self-critical about one's appearance, and the masculine ideal, which does not, is demonstrated by the bitch squad members, who describe how self-critical and unhappy they are with their own looks but condemn boys who show any insecurities. Chanel, a thin and attractive black girl, comments, "I always find something wrong with me." The other girls agree, "I think girls just want everything to be perfect." The girls say that for the boys "their only thing" is being "jacked" and mock the non-muscular boys as "pathetic, especially if they're seniors." One girl comments, "Some guys care how they look. I think Kevin [her ex-boyfriend] cared more how he looked than I did. That was wrong!"

Since caring about looks and spending time on appearances are part of the feminine but not the masculine ideal, the boys who do are criticized as "pretty boys" or effeminate. Although the boys often care how they look, the girls contend that showing it reduces their masculinity:

-If they care as much as we care, that's sad!

-It's such a turn-off.

The ivy-covered walls and manicured playing fields of prep schools
give the aura of excellence and exclusivity.

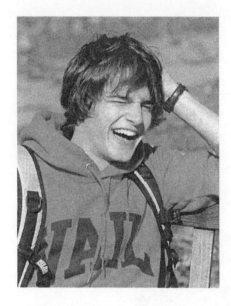

Girls often envy the boys' fun and relaxed demeanor, but the boys feel pressure to be successful, wealthy, and the best of everything.

Despite rigorous academics, girls feel social pressure not to be "too smart" and to silence themselves in class, while boys try not to appear as if they are working too hard or are overly concerned about their academics.

The girls feel pressure to look and act perfect. Short skirts, popped collars, and pastel colors, especially pink, dominate prep attire.

Small classes, large round tables, individualized attention, and extra help typify prep school academics. Some schools require formal dress, while others allow more informal attire.

A jacket passed down from one senior boy athlete to another and inscribed with each recipient's name underscores the importance of athletic status.

The state-of-the-art athletic facilities of prep schools rival those of colleges and have become more elaborate as schools strive to attract top students and athletes.

Prep schools offer a wide range of sports, including crew, horseback riding, and squash. They also offer extensive programs in art, theater, dance, and music.

Sports, the most common road to popularity, fill a large part of boys' lives, whose desire to make the team often overshadows all else.

The forced proximity of boarding school often serves to reduce racial barriers and to bring together students from different backgrounds.

Where students sit in the dining hall reveals the different cliques on campus. Cliques based on wealth often supplant other differences.

Students socialize out of their windows with members of the opposite sex because intervisitation is strictly regulated.

A rare moment of girls and boys relaxing together in a boy's dorm room.

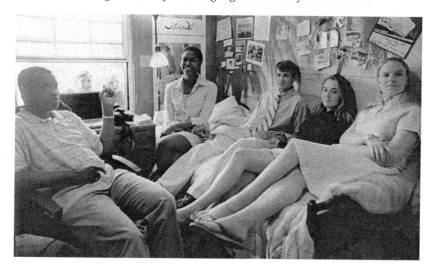

Graduating from prep school means that students become "part of a club."

Graduation mirrors the prep school focus on success and excellence.

-I would so much rather date a guy that didn't care about the way he looked at all.

A girl giggles, "A certain friend of mine's boyfriend plucks his eyebrows." At this, the girls hoot and laugh.

The boys who do not care about their looks are more attractive, more interesting, and more sexually appealing to the girls. One girl comments, "Guys who don't care are more cute." Another contends, "Boys that are self-conscious are just so *boring*!" The girls expect the boys to act masculine, not vain, self-conscious, or otherwise "feminine":

-And I hate it when guys don't have any respect for themselves. If they can't be like, "Yes, I'm okay with me as I am," then it's such a bother.

-Ugh! You just want to be like, "Shut up."

-You're not a girl!

-Exactly.

-A guy who spends more time getting ready than I do, I would lose interest.

-I hate vain guys.

A "bad-ass" attitude also increases a boy's masculinity and sexual appeal. The girls in one dorm say that what makes one boy "so hot" is his attitude. Adoring chinstraps (a thin strip of facial hair on the chin), a girl gushes, "Oh my God, they are *so* sexy!" As she hyperventilates and fans herself, the girls laugh and debate whether or not a hockey player who has a chinstrap is good-looking. When Katherine, a wealthy girl who prefers clean-cut, preppy guys, says, "He looks like a 40-year-old man. He's got a beer belly and a receding hairline," the other girls reply, "But he has sex appeal." All agree when the girl who likes chinstraps contends, "You know what makes him so hot is that his attitude is like, 'I don't give a fuck.' That's what makes him so . . ." At this, she sighs and fans herself again.

Boys: It's All About Confidence

Although the boys care about their appearance and say males are becoming more concerned with looks "than in the past," they agree that looks are more important with girls and "less with guys" due to the lack of competition with each other over looks because of the girls' interest in other traits. The boys in one dorm assert, "Guys are much more pleased with their looks than girls," noting, "Girls are never pleased" and "Girls have to worry about 'Why aren't I the super-attractive blond one that all the guys fantasize about?'" Debating whether boys work out to "feel good" and be better at sports or to look good, the boys agree, "It's a self-satisfaction thing" but "not pressure." The boys, however, feel pressure from other males to date a good-looking girl. One boy says that if you date an unattractive girl, "the other fellas, you know, they're like, 'Man, she's kind of ugly.'"

The boys seem bewildered why those girls who seemingly fit the ideal are not satisfied with their looks. When one boy reveals how several girls who are quite thin did not eat for two weeks before a play they were in because they had to wear revealing clothing, the other boys exclaim:

-Damn, she's hot!

-What's she not eating for? She barely weighs a hundred pounds.

-Oh! She's *so* hot!

Although the boys admit they are attracted to girls by appearances, a boy's looks are "not that big an issue" because girls like boys for other reasons. One boy, Bobby, who is a good athlete, funny, and well-liked but called "an ugly motherfucker" by his dorm mates, dates Brook, one of the most attractive girls in the school. He tells the other boys, "The secret for getting girls is confidence." They laugh, "Yeah, but where do you get it?" Another group of boys contends that girls, unlike boys, "go out with ugly guys. They go for that inner beauty."

Like the girls, most boys are critical of other males who care about their looks. "Guys don't give a shit" and those that do "are labeled with . . . feminine qualities." Because self-consciousness and dissatisfaction with one's looks are strictly part of the feminine but not the masculine ideal, "guys don't talk about it."

The attention given to appearance varies among the boys. One boy says that some males "are really obsessed with their looks and they'll, like, spend hours on their hair and put gel in their hair and look all nice and other people don't care." When boys spend time on their appearance or admit to being self-conscious and caring about their looks, other boys tease them. After one of the boys says, "Everybody's self-conscious, everybody—males and females. Not as many guys say it publicly, but everybody is," the others counter that boys "don't care as much as girls."

When he insists that "some guys care about their looks as much as girls do," the others pressure and haggle him until he admits that he does. He adds, "But I'm not the only one. What about Mike? He does his hair *every* night."

The boys also criticize girls caught trying to be attractive, but mostly only if they fail. One notes, "You can tell when a girl is really trying, and it is sad." Another adds, "It's pathetic." In contrast, although the girls in the bitch squad obsess about looks, the boys do not condemn them for it because they are able to achieve "good looks." One boy says these girls are "going for looks all the way, but then again they sort of have it, so . . ."

Often the boys try to outdo each other in showing how little they care about their appearance, illuminating how caring about looks cuts against the masculine ideal. In one dorm, when a boy says that his friends "wake up five minutes before class and they'll be set," another quips, "I usually wake up five minutes *after* class." In another dorm, after a boy says, "I would prefer to not have holes in revealing places, but other than that I don't give a shit," a friend jokingly boasts, "I do 1,000 sit-ups a night to make sure. *No!* Pfffff. I've never done a sit-up in my life!" A third says, "I think I've brushed my hair once in the last year." Despite this bravado, many boys do want to be muscular. One boy explains:

> I don't obsess about being this huge guy, but, like, everyone wants to be comfortable taking their shirt off and not be self-conscious about it.

Class and Ethnic Differences

Social class factors into how much emphasis the students place on appearance.[2] Students from poorer areas typically say, "Looks are more important here than anyplace I've ever been!" The wealthy students, on the other hand, say that their hometowns are similar to Bolton in terms of concern for appearance and wealth. In one dorm, when some of the girls say that "no one cares" about looks at home, adding that, "the majority of people here are more shallow and materialistic than most of the people I know outside of Bolton," Elizabeth exclaims, "Not in my town, it's not. Oh my God!" She and the other wealthy girls describe the pressure in their towns to look good always.

The wealthier students, concerned with brand names and the quality and expense of materials, are viewed as judging others on looks and thinking of themselves as superior. One boy says students judge others on the labels of the clothes they wear, explaining, "If they have a Brooks Brothers shirt on and you don't, they'll think that they're obviously a better person because of it." Another notes the socioeconomic roots of caring about looks: "If they have money to spend, then they spend it and show it."

The girls in one dorm mock some wealthy boys who the girls think are overly concerned with their looks, calling them "obsessive-compulsive." The girls label as a "sick, sick person" a member of the "high-class club" whom they caught looking at his reflection in a window and fixing his collar.

Reveling in the nicknames "bitch squad" and "rich bitches," these wealthy senior girls admit that they pay the most attention to appearance:

-Our dorm puts more effort into getting up in the morning. Like we blow a fuse every week because everybody's blow-drying their hair at the same time.

-People go from room to room searching for an outfit. You're like, "Oh! I need to wear pink!" So you, like, go through everyone's room looking for a V-neck pink ¾-length sweater because that's what you want to wear. It's not like roll out of bed and throw on a collar and blazer. It's, like, get dolled up.

They attribute their interest in appearance to their personalities and upbringing. Mercedes, a wealthy African American who is a prominent member of the bitch squad, comments:

But I think it's just our personalities, I'm sorry. A lot of other halls, I'm sorry, but they just don't care about how they look. Because of just the way, I guess, that we've been brought up.

The others agree:

-But I think that's why we're all friends I think. I mean that's why we're friends.

-Yeah, that's the way I was brought up.

The wealthiest boys occasionally go against the ideal and admit to caring about how they look. Saying that "the ugly kids don't pay that much attention" to their looks, the boys in the "rich dorm" explain that their focus on appearance is due to how their parents raised them. In one dorm, a wealthy boy admits to the others, "I can actually say I care about my looks because my mom cared a lot about her looks." Another agrees, "My mom wouldn't dare . . . let me out of the house without wearing expensive clothes." In another dorm, Tad, whose father is governor of a southern state, says his friends at home take steroids "just for looks" and teenagers "dress much dressier" than the kids at Bolton, adding:

> Where I'm from, it's a real, you know, like, I guess a real wealthy area and everybody there wants to drive a nice car and wear nice clothes, I mean, everybody there has fake tans, even the guys. I mean, I go into the tanning bed when I go back home.

At this, several of the other students ask incredulously, "Really?" laughing and snickering. Tad shrugs and says, "I don't care. That's what everybody does there."

The boys often criticize the wealthiest girls, especially the bitch squad, for their focus on looks, explaining how one girl gave her senior chapel speech on how she had to look "cute" and how she and her friend "played tennis so that they could wear little skirts and look cute. That was her chapel speech." The way the bitch squad passes judgment on others also draws the boys' criticism:

> But they judge . . . they judge everybody by what they look like . . . a lot of the girls, not so much on the guys. They're worried about name brands and things like that.

Ethnicity also influences how much emphasis individuals place on looks. The only group at Bolton viewed as placing as much importance on looks as the wealthy are the African American students, especially those from New York City. Although the members of these two groups are, with a few exceptions, at opposite ends of the socioeconomic spectrum, only the wealthy students are viewed negatively because they are deemed to judge others. Never did I hear other students criticize the African Americans' attention to appearance or label them with effeminate qualities. Coincidentally, the African Americans at Bolton are often star athletes, while few of the very wealthy students are.

A few African American girls contend that the reason they pay more attention to appearances is because it's a "city versus country" thing. Kara, who is part of the New York City group, explains that "it's a city thing": "Because me and my friends from New York City, we're so used to getting up every day and putting ourselves together every day. That's just what you do." Others, however, say it is due to ethnic differences.

Despite their attention to appearance, the other students do not view the African Americans negatively because the black students do not judge others. They often contrast Kara and her group of African American girls from New York who attend to their looks with the wealthy white girls of the bitch squad, stating, "But she [Kara] doesn't care. She doesn't judge."

The black boys say their ethnicity affects their attention to appearances and hygiene. Comparing his own attention to appearance with that of his white roommate, a black student, Jared, says, "For me they're important, but this guy, sometimes he doesn't shower for days." He then says that the ethnic differences result from the standards of the black women they want to date:

> White girls and black girls are different. They're two different types of people, right. Black girls are more critical of how guys look than white girls are. So black guys, you have to smell good and brush your hair and stuff like that, whereas white guys don't have to do all that. Like they [white girls] appreciate it no matter what you look like.

When a white boy responds "Some white girls are pretty critical too," at first all the boys agree: "It's not really color of the skin. It's more personality." But when a white boy ventures, "But you can go out on a limb and stereotype, but blacks tend to care more about what they wear than whites do in some ways," Jared agrees enthusiastically: "They *do*. They have to match." The white boy, pointing at Jared, who is wearing blue shoes and shirt, continues, "They have to match baby blue Jordans with the shirt or whatever." Jared agrees wholeheartedly: "You have to match. That's what I'm saying. You can't go out looking like Joe and Chris [two white boys present who are known for not caring about their looks] and not matching." Later when I am conducting room tours, Jared says, unlike the other boys, that the most important things in his room are "my shoes and my clothes. If anybody touches my shoes or my clothes, I'll beat their ass. I mean it. I really do. That's the only thing that would make me angry, because I have so many shoes and so many clothes and they cost a lot of money."

Even though Jared and other African American boys admit to caring about their looks, they are not attributed with female qualities. Because they are often large and athletic, they have demonstrated their masculinity to such an extent it cannot be harmed. In this case, Jared has also given an "acceptable" reason for caring about his looks: in order to get girls.

Exactly why the wealthiest and the African American students focus more than the others on appearance warrants further investigation. For both groups, economics plays a central role. The wealthiest individuals use appearance to secure their social dominance. By placing importance on expensive labels or materials, they exclude the less wealthy and reconfirm their superiority. The time, attention, and money often required to fit the ideals of appearance also set them apart. African Americans, on the other hand, have been discriminated against for centuries, so perhaps for some, "keeping up appearances" has become a matter of pride, a way to illuminate their worthiness and equality.

The Pressure: Girls

Parents and other girls (and to a lesser degree boys) exert pressure on the girls to look good, each for different reasons. The parental pressure centers largely on one issue, weight. As one girl explains,

> I don't actually put pressure on myself until my parents say something to me. And they're like, "Anne, you look kind of like you need to lose some weight." And I'm like, "Shit! I need to lose some weight."

Most of the other girls agree, telling their own tales of parental pressure.

Although this parental pressure to be thin is commonplace, it is the most intense and harsh among the wealthiest students, illustrating the dramatic difference of socioeconomic class. One wealthy girl has "a whole family just absolutely beating down on her. She is a dancer, and they're saying how fat she looks." Wealthy Katherine says, "If I go out of the house without makeup on, my dad's like, 'Gee, what happened to you?'" At this, a girl on scholarship replies, "My parents are the exact opposite. If I'm doing it up, they're like, 'Ashley, geez, who are you impressing?'"

The members of the bitch squad feel "a *lot* of pressure" from their upper-class parents. As one of the few wealthy African Americans, Chanel explains how her parental pressure differs from that of most of the other African American girls:

> I guess it's where you grew up in society, like what happens around you. My mom's like, "Oh look, I fit into size two. [Evil cackle] What are you fitting into right now?" My dad's like . . . "How about that nose job? Coming up soon, no?" Thanks!

The scholarship African American girls see Chanel's plight as different from their own because they receive little pressure to be thin from their own parents:

-She's taking Metabolife pills because her mother tells her she's fat. And Chanel has never been fat, ever, *ever* been fat. And now she's lost like 30 pounds, passed out this last year because she took eight pills at one time. And it's just like so sad and sick that your own mother tells you, "You look fat and have to change."

-You ate yesterday, quit complaining.

-And beat down her self-esteem.

The main pressure the girls feel from other girls centers around style and clothes, while the pressure from boys is to look good overall. Many of the girls regard the pressure from other girls as being more pervasive than that from boys: "I think girls are a whole lot more critical of girls than guys are" and "Girls criticize each other on looks more than guys ever would." One girl confesses, "I've never really cared what I look like in front of boys. What really gets me is sly comments from girls . . . like 'Isn't she grody.' It's stuff like that." The bitch squad's emphasis on appearance coupled with the competition between girls gives rise to "ridiculous amounts of pressure."

This pressure surfaces when a group discusses how girls with large or small breasts feel uncomfortable changing in front of the other girls. A girl with large breasts admits, "I know Jeanna and I were very uncomfortable changing in the hockey locker room." A teammate responds:

I know. I felt sorry for Hooty. First of all, we called her Hooty McBoob, Chesty LeRew, Busty Saint Clair, and we would just joke. But you could tell she wasn't comfortable. We would joke because we wanted her to be more comfortable . . . People would be like, "Damn, her tits are huge!" That's what makes people uncomfortable.

The pressure from boys to look good comes not so much in the form of comments but rather in the fact that boys do not date heavy girls. A freshman girl complains that since she doesn't fit the model of beauty, blond, blue-eyed, and slender, the Bolton boys will never be interested in her:

Here, I just feel that no matter what I do, no one's really going to give a shit about you. And it's really hard to be wanting to love yourself when you realize that when you try and make yourself look pretty, you're not getting anything back. And I feel it a lot here. . . . I miss feeling appreciated.

Many of the other girls agree when her friend Jen adds:

I've never felt appreciated by a guy ever in my entire life. Honestly, never ever. I have been used by every single guy I have ever been with. I'm talking not one single exception. Not one.

The girls believe the boys feel more pressure to have good-looking girlfriends than the girls do to have good-looking boyfriends. Because girls care about "who your boyfriend is" and not just whether he is good-looking, they take personality into account. Although "there is definitely a looks component," the only real pressure they have is not to date a "loser."

The Pressure: Boys

Although the boys do cite some pressures to look good, the standards they are expected to live up to are much lower than are the girls'. While the girls repeatedly use the word "perfect" to describe how they want to look, boys use phrases such as "not like a scumbag" or "not like a slothful pig." The main pressures come from girls and parents, not from other boys. The parental pressure concerns haircuts or style of clothes ("classic") but not necessarily to be handsome. They also face pressure to be strong or "buff" from fathers, brothers, or other males.

The pressure on the boys to have a good-looking girlfriend is great because a good-looking girlfriend directly affects a male's status. Whether or not his girlfriend is good-looking can "bump him up" or "bring him down" in status. When I ask if boys face pressure to have a good-looking girlfriend, one boy replies, "Yes, but I don't give a shit." The others then proceed to make fun of his girlfriend, saying, "His girlfriend is good and ugly" and "She is thoroughly butt," while making it known that their own girlfriends are "hot."

Some individuals are able to resist these pressures. When the boys give one student a hard time for liking a girl they find unattractive, telling him, "You're never going to live that down," a friend comes to his defense and says, "She is a really nice person. Do you know her?" Brushing his remarks aside quickly, someone shouts, "We're not talking about personality here, we're talking about raw physical appearance." Everyone laughs, and the boy is uncomfortable. Despite this pressure, the boy and girl in question have a serious relationship all the next year.

"Get the Face Book!"

The rating systems the students use to rank each other, most of which revolve around the face book, exemplify the pressure to conform to a valued standard of appearance. The face book is an annual booklet put out by the school that contains a head shot of every member of the Bolton community, including students, faculty, administrators, and maintenance, business, and kitchen staff. The school intends it to be used for identifying and contacting members of the school community, but the students use it as a vehicle to rate the opposite sex. The students in every dorm use rating systems as well as know about ones that the other gender uses. The rankings are sometimes made public and posted on dormitory walls, are shown to members of the opposite sex, and at least one time during my research were briefly posted in the school building for all to see before being taken down.

The girls use the face book to create a wide variety of ranking systems, including a "top ten list." Comments about various photos include "Wow, he's really hot," "Wow! That'd be nice," "He's good-looking," "Hottie," "Cutie," and "Nice guy." Sometimes they rate the boys with whom they would date and have sex. In one dorm, the girls explain:

-The night after the face book comes out, it's like our tradition. We whip it open and do the top ten guys.

-It's like it's all based on people's pictures. It's ugly.

-Yeah, it's not nice.

The girls claim that their rating systems differ from those of the boys because they include personality and are less harsh, less sex-oriented, less public, and less organized. Although looks are important, the girls also value personality, intelligence, and athleticism. One group of girls explains that an unattractive male can rank high ("Oh, he's ugly, but he's really nice, so that makes up for it") and an attractive male can rank low ("Oh, that kid's a jerk. He was so mean to his last girlfriend"). Another girl claims, "If he's nice, his rating will go up." Another adds, "'Cause the best-looking guy here gets a 6 if he's an asshole." The girls contend that the boys are "much meaner" and more "shallow" because they rank only on looks.

In stark contrast to the boys' rating systems, one girl's system is based "all on cheekbones! Oh my God, they are so sexy!" She explains, "Like last year, I had hearts and stars and smiley faces and stuff," adding, "Heart is, like, cute. Smiley face is, like, okay. There's a star for sexy, and 69 . . . I want to stop on that! Oh yes!" At this, everyone laughs, and she turns bright red, admitting that 69, or wanting to exchange oral sex, is her top rating.

The bitch squad says their face book is "the most wanted face book on campus" because they "ranked every single person." Distinguishing themselves by rating not only boys but also the girls, they declare, "I think girls do it naturally, I'm sorry. I think girls, like, rate everybody who walks by, whether you're a guy or a girl."

Aware of the boys' ranking systems, the girls often feel uncomfortable and pressured by them. The girls identify the boys' rating system as based on three categories: "fuckable, datable, and not at all . . . wouldn't touch with a ten-foot pole." Others describe it differently: "You wouldn't let them do anything (that means they're ugly as sin) . . . Then, like, you'd let them . . . suck your dick . . . and then you'd fuck them."

Sometimes the boys' ranking systems are public in nature, involving "top ten lists" and "pictures cut out from the face book and they had them in order." One group of girls complains, "It's ridiculous—they have, like, bulletin boards and hang up charts." During the research, a girl tears down a list the boys attached to the announcement board in the main school building of "the ten prettiest girls and what they would do with them." The girl, who is on the list, complains, "I think it is so degrading." She notes the irony of the situation: "All the girls who were on the list were mad that they were on it, but all the girls who were not on it were mad that they weren't."

The boys describe rating the girls on the amount of sexual contact they would "allow" the girl to have with them, but they do not feel much pressure from the girls' rating systems. Tyler, a handsome "bad boy" who this week is on the verge of being expelled for "being with" his girlfriend, screams with excitement when asked if they have rating systems for the girls, "*Yes!* The face book. Boom! It's done." Another boy adds, "If there's a guy's face book on campus that doesn't have a rating, that means he was doing a rating with someone else in their face book."

Although "every guy has their own personal rating system," which ranges from "doable" and "not doable" to "top ten" and "one through ten," only a few boys take personality into account. Basing their ranking system solely on looks, the boys in one dorm admit, "We were pretty harsh. I mean, there might be three or four girls that actually got a decent rating." Their system was based on different colors of circles: blue if they'd have sex with the girl, black if they would let her perform oral sex on them, and no circle if it "was a girl that you wouldn't touch."

Most ranking systems are sexual in nature. The boys explain, "In some cases, it's not just hot and not hot, but person I'd want to fuck or person I do not." Professing that I am the "only female" [he] ever told this to, one boy explains the rules of "the game":

> If you see a cute girl, you point her out on the clock and say, "Game." And the game is, you go to a party at 8:00 and start drink- ing, what time would you have sex with the girl? So if the girl is really cute you can do it as soon as you get there at eight, you don't need any beer, that's how good-looking she is. If she's kind of ugly, it's 9:30.

Another boy adds, "If she's a 1:30, ouch!" The boys laugh about how late it could be for "really ugly" girls.

The disparity between the rating systems of the two freshman boys' dorms reveals the degree of individual differences in the performance of masculinity. In the freshman dorm that is regarded as less "cool" and of a lower social standing than the other, many of the boys take personality and intelligence into account when ranking the girls. One boy says:

> For me, I mean I want looks and all, but I also look just to see, like you know, that they're not some ditzy airhead, like money-driven. I just want them to be funny or, like, athletic or just fun to hang out with, someone you can make conversation easily with and not just sit around.

The other boys agree. Zander, who takes pride in not conform- ing to the "cool" ideal, says, "I'm notorious for finding something in everybody, you know." Finding girls attractive whom others do not, he explains, "I'll be like, 'Wow, she's kind of hot.' And they're like, 'No, dude.'" His individuality is rare among the students at Bolton.

In contrast, the rating system in the "cooler" freshman dorm, "where all the girls go," is sexual in nature. The boys explain:

> There are three categories. The highest is girls you'd actually kiss, like make out with and actually date. The girls you'd have sex with. And then the girls you'd just let suck your dick.

The boys claim to take the girls' lists, which they label as "stupid," less seriously and feel less pressured by them than the girls feel by the boys' lists because the girls' lists are based on factors other than looks. This lack of concern may also be partly due to the pressure for males not to appear to care about looks or be self-conscious about appearances. When one boy, Ben, gloats that he made a girls' list rated by "the whole dorm," saying, "I was on that list. I was on that list. Yeah!" the other boys exclaim, "You're a bitch, man. You self-conscious bitch." Ben explains, "It just boosts my ego. I was number three." At this, one of the other boys mimics shrilly, "Look how it boosts his ego. 'I was number three. I was number three.'"

Changing Oneself

Feeling pressure to conform to an ideal as well as valuing a focus on self more than a focus on other, both the girls and the boys would reduce their other-oriented traits and gain more self-oriented traits. Most girls at Bolton would choose to be "skinnier," "much skinnier," "like ten times [thinner], like size zero," or prettier if they could change one thing about themselves. One girl asserts, "Ninety percent of girls would want to be prettier or thinner." The girls in the freshman dorm focus on appearance, saying they would change their body or face or lose weight.

Other than appearance, the girls would change in ways regarded as more self-focused and less other-focused. Some wish to be "smart," while others would change their other-focused priorities (as in "I'd do stuff for my friends before I'd do my homework, and that's pretty bad") or be "more carefree," "have confidence in my body," not be "so oversensitive," not be "such a worrywart. I worry so much," and relax ("I think I get too stressed over things that I don't need to get too stressed over").

Although almost all of the girls eagerly relate what they would want to change, the boys have more difficulty answering, demonstrating either relative contentment or the social restraints on male self-consciousness. The boys typically respond, "I wouldn't change" or "That's a hard one." It frequently takes a while for anyone to answer.

Eventually, the boys admit that they would change their appearance to be taller or more muscular: being "bigger and stronger is the number one quality." Although the connection between appearances and athletic ability is not clear-cut, by being bigger or taller the boys could achieve both.

Like the freshman girls, the freshman boys demonstrate the most dissatisfaction with their appearance. Considering they are the smallest at the school, if they could change anything about themselves, it would be their height, to be taller.

Other than changing their appearance, the boys would become more self-focused and less other-focused, saying "I'd be a lot less self-conscious," "I wouldn't want to be as worried about what other people thought about me," and "I'd be more outgoing."

Gender Ideals in Action

Katherine, a popular, attractive girl, calls me in the middle of the final exam period to ask if I can drive her and some friends to Wal-Mart. "I really need to go," she pleads, so I agree to pick them up. On the ride into town I ask if they are stressing over their exams. "Not as much as we should be," they respond. I ask them what they want to buy, thinking that it must be important. Katherine responds, "I want to color my hair." Another girl answers, "I want to get munchies." Once there, Katherine heads straight for the hair color department and finds a color she likes. She keeps asking her friends and me, "Should I do it? What do you think? Would it be an improvement?" One of her friends answers, "I honestly love your hair the way it is now." Katherine discounts her praise and asks if we can try Kmart instead. Once there, she finally settles on something.

Then they look for snacks. Katherine, who many students think has the perfect body, selects seltzer water, and her slender friend picks up some ice pops, adding, "They're only 30 calories each." The heavier girl in the group grabs a bag of chocolate chip cookies and a bag of Doritos. At the purchase counter, she acts guilty, saying as an excuse: "My mom never buys this stuff, so I have to eat it now. I should be able to eat anything I want during finals anyway, right?" When the cashier gives her change, she grimaces and hands back a penny. "Could you take this? I have way too many pennies." The cashier looks at her as if she were crazy and stammers, "Y-yeah, sure." One of the girls confides, "I feel so bad for these people. I'd never been in a Kmart in my life until I came here."

On the way home one of the girls says how upset she is at her roommate, explaining that even though it is finals, she "has, like, five friends in our room all day and they're making so much noise." Then she whispers, "They're trying on all my makeup."

Katherine asks her, "Did they ask you?" She answers softly, "No." Katherine declares, "I'd be mad." Her friend answers softly again, "I am!" but goes on to say that she is not going to complain because she is not "very good at confrontation."

The Mr. Bolton contest raises money for the freshman class and the charity of the winner's choice. Each form selects three boys to represent their class and to compete for the crown of Mr. Bolton. The areas judged are beach wear, evening wear, and talent. Seven girls are the judges.

Backstage before the event, John, a large football player who is popular despite not fitting a physical ideal, practices carrying his pretty blond escort over his shoulder. A small freshman watches, saying to no one in particular, "I can't do that!" He quickly turns to his escort, an attractive blond girl who is about six feet tall, and says, "No offense! I'm just 110 pounds of pure muscle." He flexes in a self-deprecating and joking manner for all to see.

The show begins with the swimsuit competition. Few of the boys fit what would be considered the ideal in terms of body shape and size. Aware of their physical limitations, the small and thin boys make fun of their physique by donning floaties on their arms and showing their muscles as if they were ripped. Others are self-conscious about being too heavy or not cut, keeping their shirts on even when the crowd hoots for them to strip them off. Only one boy, Mike, seems comfortable with his body and proudly shows it off onstage. As a senior tri-captain (captain of three varsity sports) whose body is well developed, ripped, and lean, he is the only one comfortable being dressed in just a swimsuit in front of the whole school. They all stand onstage showing off their muscles (either mockingly or in seriousness) as the crowd hoots. At one point, Mike tweaks the nipple of a skinny junior, who jumps and yells, "Ow!" The crowd roars.

For the talent portion of the competition, the boys lip-sync to music, sing, play the guitar, or recite poetry. The one talent that stands out from the rest is John, who takes off his shirt to reveal his ample girth and does belly tricks. After he shoots a quarter out of his belly button, he squeezes the fat around his belly button with both hands and says it is a doughnut. The crowd roars.

The final event is a question-and-answer period, where the contestants are asked what being Mr. Bolton means to them and to what charity they would donate the prize money. John first answers flippantly about finally getting dates, but then responds from his heart that the charity he has chosen helps disabled people find jobs. This charity means a lot to him because "my father was one, he was blind." The other contestants do not have heartfelt answers about helping others.

In the end, John, the boy with the largest belly of any of the contestants and who did belly tricks for the talent part of the competition, wins the title of Mr. Bolton because he demonstrates humor, personality, and heart.

What Girls Want

In describing the ideal man, the girls at Bolton focus on "personality," "self-confidence," "intelligence," "humor," "wealth," and "athletic ability." Several groups of girls are "picky" compared to boys because they want personality and other characteristics, and not just looks. While many of the girls describe the ideal male as "just really nice and funny," many others state that teenage girls (including those at Bolton) are often attracted to "egotistical, athletic, rude jerks."

The girls list numerous self-focused characteristics other than appearance when describing the ideal man and often do not even mention looks. Some of the girls list more other-focused attributes:

-I'd rather have, like my best friend, like, a guy to watch a game with or something like that.

-He'd have to be a good listener.

-Someone I can hang out with.

Another girl notices the incongruity, saying, "That's not a man . . . that sounds more like a woman."

The girls' standard of good looks is often forgiving, a far cry from the perfection they demand in themselves. The girls in one dorm contend that although looks are important for initial attraction, they think ultimately personality and other characteristics are more important in the long run. They add, however, that looks do matter in the extreme:

-I'm going to sound really shallow, but you can't be with someone you find incredibly disgusting.

-Unattractive.

-There has to be some sort of small amount, like he doesn't have to be good-looking, it's just, like, he can't be heinous.

Perhaps it is considered unacceptable for girls to be so self-focused as to care about looks in males, and the girls who do are referred to by themselves or others as being "shallow." One girl notes, "We want good-looking guys, but we don't want to say it." Also, because girls are looking for "attention," personality becomes more important to them than looks. One girl observes, "Girls want attention, so they're looking for a personality, but boys just want sex, so they're looking for a hot girl."

The freshman girls who have felt used and unappreciated by males talk about the characteristics that they are looking in a boy:

-Loving.

-Caring.

-Sweet.

-Just to hold me. Is that asking for too much?

-Someone you can trust.

The most important characteristics for a male to be considered good-looking are "eyes," "smile," "good cheekbones," "hair" "taller than me," and "teeth." Only afterward, if at all, the girls mention body or muscularity. If they do mention muscularity, it is addressed in extremes: "some sort of definition," "look stronger than you," "can't have chicken legs," "good butt is crucial," and "I hate *really* muscular guys."

When describing the most important criteria for a male to be good-looking, the girls often include "personality." For girls, personality seems to be inseparable from looks. The girls typically respond, "When it comes right down to it, personality is the most important criteria for a guy to be good-looking."

During a group interview, while the other girls mention things like hair and teeth, one girl blurts out, "He has to be muscular!" This happens only once in my interviews, and the girl later confides in me that she is gay.

Some of the girls contend that there are some criteria they would look for in a husband but not necessarily in a boyfriend: "intelligence," "motivation," and "money." Despite an American ideal of marrying strictly for love, many of the girls unabashedly would consider other factors, especially wealth, when marrying. Announcing that they will "definitely" consider factors other than love when marrying, the girls, both wealthy and poor, white and African American, describe the importance of "financial security."

Although almost all of the girls focus on wealth, most of the less wealthy girls are not looking for a "guy who's loaded" but rather "secure enough so I can, like, stay alive but not so I can go to these ritzy places," "send my kids to college with no problem," and "be able to travel." One of the girls envisions marrying for "100% love and 120% everything else. [Money's] just that extra that needs to be there."

There are some class and ethnic differences that show up in what girls say they want. Both the wealthy girls and the African American girls place special importance on style in males. For a man to be good-looking, the girls in the bitch squad mention style and shoes as the most important criteria:

-First comes style. If you can't dress, no, I'm sorry. Then comes
body, then face. If I'm looking at a guy, I'll look at his shoes first,
then I look at clothes. I have a fetish for shoes.

-Oh! I look at shoes too.

-And if they fill up the clothes properly, then you look at the face. And if they have a cute face, then . . .

Believing that males focus on style too, Mercedes notes:

And I'm sure guys look at that too, like, "Does she dress cute? Will she always dress cute?" You know. 'Cause guys want that perfect woman on their arm when they get married.

At this, some of the girls not in the bitch squad snicker. Mercedes retorts, "I'm sorry, but it's true!" She adds, "No matter what they say, especially athletic people, they always want that trophy wife on their arm. My dad told me so."

The girls in one dorm debate the importance of clothes in a man's looks, the difference in opinion falling along lines of wealth and ethnicity. Although most of the girls state that style is not an important factor in a man's looks, Elizabeth responds that it is "very important." An African American girl on scholarship agrees, "It's what attracts me." At this, a girl from a poor area on the West Coast says that a boy wearing "the dirtiest T-shirt and the dirtiest jeans" actually makes "him look hotter." When the other girls protest about males being "hygienically clean," she adds, "I like clean guys but not, like . . . I go for the punks and bad-asses. I don't like guys that are preppier than me." Elizabeth counters, "See, I like really preppy guys, *really* preppy."

What the Girls Think the Boys Want

The girls think that what makes a female good-looking to the boys is to be "skinny." One girl contends, "If guys see you as heavy, they'll just rule you out. Even if you're really attractive." When some girls say the boys consider size four ideal, a girl adds that only the "coolest" guys focus entirely on a girl's weight and looks: "If she has a good personality . . . certain guys will be attracted to her."

The freshman girls identify the boys' ideal as "blond," "blue eyes," "really skinny," and "big boobs." The girls comment:

-Here at Bolton [the boys] like their blondes and they're, like, size fours. You know, they all have a uniform. They're all size four, they all wear black pants, they all wear platform Steve Madden shoes—

-They all have their straight blond hair.

-I don't think guys are interested in, like, different types.

The other characteristics the girls believe the boys value are largely other-oriented. Although occasionally the girls mention self-oriented characteristics such as being smart, having a sense of humor, and being athletic as things the males find attractive, they claim that the boys consider the ideal woman to be limited or other-focused: "Big-breasted girls who don't have an opinion on anything," "Someone who doesn't talk very much, listens," "They like goofball girls. Someone who won't threaten their masculinity," "Someone who wears no clothes," "No personality whatsoever!" "Very social," "Rich, spoiled, and materialistic," "Is a bitch to everyone but them," "Will put out," and "Really, really, really dumb."

What the Boys Want

When describing their ideal woman, the boys focus on looks. Although some boys describe the ideal woman as having a "good personality" and being "fun," "intelligent" and "respectable," the others say that she has to be "good-looking," "attractive," or "definitely hot." Their ideal is specific as to hair color (blond), eye color (blue), and cup size (C).

Although the boys focus on a girl's weight and body, a "good" body is a top priority more often than being "skinny." Using the terms "not fat" or "morbidly obese," they desire shapeliness in girls. One boy who has a substantial potbelly says, "She can't pack a lot of pounds, especially in the stomach region." Others wholeheartedly agree, "Oh, she *has* to be skinny! She cannot be a fat girl! Fat girls are not allowed. Definitely not being fat is number one," and "You *can't* be fat and attractive!" When one of the boys comments, "You can be attractive and kind of chubby," the others agree, "We're talking full-on, beast-like, 'Grrrrr! I'm going to eat you, give me a doughnut' type of thing.'" Usually weight matters only in extremes: "If they really are too overweight, I can't consider them. It's not a good thing, I don't feel good about it, but it's the truth."

Many of the boys claim that for them the ideal in appearance is someone whose weight is at neither extreme. Although one boy doesn't want "a big ball person," he doesn't want someone "who has, like, broken ribs to get a waist two inches wide. I want in between." Others say that boys at Bolton are "down with skinny-like twig girls" but prefer a nice butt, breasts, and body.

Many boys say that the relative importance of face and body depends on the nature of the relationship: "If it's just for a hookup or something more. If a girl has a really good body, but her face, you know, makes you want to lose your lunch, then it's okay for a hookup."

The majority's desire for the "model mold" contrasts with the opinions of a few boys, such as a freshman, Jeff, who insists, "I don't have a perfect woman. I'm ready for anything." Occasionally the boys add self-focused characteristics to their lists: "She can't be crappy to talk to . . . like, has to have some kind of personality," "sense of humor," "fun to be around," "athletic," "smart," "rich," "classy and intelligent," and "honesty is key." When a boy who is considered a nerd says he desires an independent-minded woman, however, the rest of the boys snicker and roll their eyes.

The boys mostly focus on other-oriented characteristics of the ideal woman. One boy's ideal is "someone who will baby me, rub my feet, give me back rubs, and cook for me." Another's ideal is someone who "likes everything you like. You don't want somebody who's going to argue with you the whole time or drive you crazy." One boy desires "someone who's willing to cook and clean." Another says his ideal woman is "someone who doesn't complain, basically, someone who doesn't let everything in life bother them." In one dorm, when a boy jokes that the ideal woman is "a strong, independent woman," the others jab him, shouting, "Shut up!" like that is the last thing they want.

Linked to the boys' definition of the ideal woman is her reputation. The issue is difficult for the girls to negotiate because, on one hand, the boys argue that she must be "fast," "easy," and "horny." "She's gotta like to get together with you in a back room somewhere and have sexual encounters," one says, and another puts in, "You *cannot* go out with a prude girl." On the other hand, she cannot be "slutty," "she can't be a whore," "she can't be like some hussy. Just absolute skank. She just can't keep the change with everybody."

Although all the boys agree that a girl cannot be a "whore," they debate the importance of sexual availability:

-She has to be willing.

-No, she doesn't.

-Shut up. *No,* she doesn't.

-It is very *nice* if she is.

-Yeah, it's nice but not essential.

Unlike the girls, the vast majority of the boys "definitely" plan to marry 100% for love. Although other factors might affect their choice, the boys tend to be more apologetic than the girls. One boy admits:

I want to say that [he would marry 100% for love], but I don't know what other factors might influence me a little bit. Money. Connections. It might be some things that might sneak in there. It might unconsciously influence me or something. But I want it to be by far mostly for love, but you never know if that might influence it or something.

Among the boys, too, there are some class and ethnic differences in terms of what they look for in girls. The wealthy white boys often use the word "perfect" to describe the ideal woman. The ideal of perfection represents the exclusivity of wealth. One wealthy white boy, Andrew, details the ideal woman's perfect looks:

Blond hair . . . a perfect body, you gotta have like 34 to 36C, perfect everything, perfect curves . . . blue eyes . . . just like a perfect face, perfect feet, feet are important, just the full package, everything's got to be exactly perfect, hands, feet, all the little stuff too.

After others mention personality, he remembers that as well, but quickly reiterates that an ideal woman is

someone who you can definitely show off, though, to your friends. That's a big thing. Someone you could walk into a party with and "Oh, my God, who are you with!" kind of thing. That is so important, I think. Really.

Ethnicity as well as class correlate in the type of behavior the males desire in a woman. The wealthier boys generally want someone perfectly feminine who is "classy" and not "dirty," "sloppy," a "hippie," or a "slob." The less wealthy white students, such as the hockey players, and the African Americans, on the other hand, desire someone more laid-back and casual who can "outdrink me" and "hang with the guys . . . and can burp and fart in front of 'em."

What the Boys Think the Girls Want

The boys believe that the girls focus less on looks and more on personality and other characteristics such as "appeal," having the right "lingo," "attitude," "personality," "humor," "social standing," "wealth," "athleticism," and being "clean" and "hygienic."

Feeling less pressure to conform in appearance than the girls, the boys contend that "looks don't matter" to the girls because "ugly guys" with positive qualities can still "get hot girls." While the girls have a "more varied range" of what they look for in a male's appearance, the boys have "a more standard way of describing an attractive girl."

Several of the boys' dorms, however, believe that big muscles and a good body are the number one criteria for a male to be considered good-looking. In the "jock" dorm, the boys claim that a good-looking male has "to be pretty large," "jacked up," and "buff." Not surprisingly, since the freshmen are the youngest and smallest boys on campus and often have a hard time getting girls, they also focus on being large and having big muscles. The lower-ranking "non-athletic" dorm focuses entirely on what they do not have: "They have to be jacked" and "athletic."

When discussing what the opposite sex considers the ideal, the boys frequently answer, "Me," demonstrating or at least postulating self-confidence and self-assurance. In almost every dorm, one or several of the boys say, "Me!" except the freshmen in the lower-ranking dorm. There, the boys say, "Anybody but us," demonstrating low self-esteem due to the disparity between themselves and the ideal standard. Not one single girl answered "Me" during the entire course of the research. This display of self-confidence or bragging is acceptable and encouraged behavior strictly for males.

Although the boys are not as pressured appearance-wise as the girls, they feel pressure to excel in many other areas because the ideal male is the "most popular, most athletic, best whatever. He's just got to be the best." He is "someone who does everything well and doesn't have any flaws" and "somebody who's intelligent, somebody who has money, somebody who is good-looking, who has a good physical stature and is manly and who can protect and support." Another contends, "He's someone everybody likes. He's the captain of all the sports teams. He's the president of all the clubs. He's everyone's friend."

Being "too smart" is not part of the ideal of masculinity. The boys report, "Smart people don't get the girls as much." One studious boy, Pete, vents that girls are not looking for boys on the honor roll because they are "too focused on their work" and "spend too much time out of socializing, out of play."

The boys also feel pressure to be wealthy because the ideal man is supposed to be a good provider, to be "rich," and have "a lot of money," "an income of at least $150,000." Others say that the ideal man must have a high-status career: "He has to be, like, a doctor or a lawyer or something, or something well-established" or "a banker." The boys note how some girls will only date boys who are wealthy and in the "top social clique," claiming, "Some of the girls on this campus are out for the money."

Although the boys say that the girls focus on "personality" instead of looks, a boy's self-focused behavior or attitude appeals most to the girls. At Bolton the guys who "have an edge" get all the girls, while "nice guys and dorks" get left in the cold. One boy contends, "Girls like guys who have edge, like, who are bad, like, kind of have badness, you know, they aren't all nice and stuff." The others agree: "They go out with the mean guys and then they get mistreated and then they want to talk to the nice guys, the dorks," adding, "Yeah, they comfort them, and then they diss the dorks and go back to the mean guys again. Girls are weird. I don't get it."

Overwhelmed at the prospect of living up to these ideals, the boys say that although the pressure is great for women to look good, "the overall ideal is higher for men to try and live up to" and "Guys don't have as high standards as women." While boys only take into account looks and personality in girls, girls take into account those plus a whole host of other attributes.

The cultural ideals described by the students demonstrate not only what they themselves value but also their pressures because of what they believe the opposite sex values. Both the girls and boys feel overwhelmed by the ideals they think they need to live up to in order to attract same sex friends and romantic partners. In order to live up to the ideals that they themselves have set, these teenagers pursue the extremes of self-focused and other-focused behavior.

From "Mad Fine" to "FUBAR"

The terminology the students use to describe others' looks highlights the different ideals they hold for males and females.

Girls

The girls use a large vocabulary of words to describe a good-looking woman: "pretty," "beautiful," "gorgeous," "elegant," "attractive," "stunning," "cute," "oh, I would love to be her," "bitch," and "why?" (as in "Why her and not me?"). The girls have no trouble listing these words, ten in all, using them often. The last three terms, which are more comparative in nature, are used only by the clique of wealthy senior girls, whose members are known to judge people on their looks.

The girls also use many words, 26 in all, to describe a good-looking man. While "sexy," "gorgeous," and "hot" indicate the top of the scale in terms of attractiveness, other words include "cute," "fine," "fit," "damn fine," "doll," "cutie," "sexy mama," "handsome," "sweet," "good-looking," "beautiful," "mmm, break me off a piece of that," "fox," "hotty," "nice," "whooo," "damn," "oh my God," "whoa," "good dresser," "fuckable," "rapeable," and "babealicious." Sometimes the girls don't use words at all, but as one girl explains, "I grunt, definitely."

The terms differ in connotation. One girl states, "Sometimes if a guy is really hot, I'll say that he is beautiful too, just to get that extra good-looking." Another adds that good looks and sex appeal do not always go hand in hand: "Some guys are good-looking but not sexy, and some guys are sexy but not necessarily good-looking." Two other girls explain the difference between "hot" and "sexy":

-When someone's hot and someone's sexy there's a huge difference. If he's hot, he's hot. But if he has sex appeal, it's like you want to jump on him and rape him.

-Sexy is like, "Damn, I want some of that!"

The term "good-looking," many of the girls explain, is used for older men such as faculty members at Bolton.

The girls also have many terms for an unattractive female: "heinous," "ugly," "she looks bad," "hideous," "ewww," "ohhhh," "poor thing," "that sucks," "who does she think she is?" "I sympathize with you," "I'm sorry, come over and we'll do a makeover weekend," "there's always plastic surgery," "foul-looking," "raunchy," "skanky," "ho," "trashy," "ho bag," "disgusting," "painful to look at," "nasty," "gross," and "horrible." The girls list 24 terms, some of which connote sexual promiscuity.

Some of the girls who don't use negative terms say that they usually comment only if someone looks good, not bad. However, these girls would call a girl unattractive if she were with an attractive male. At this, a girl responds, "You guys are so cruel. I would never say that about somebody." The girls retort, "You'd think it." She agrees, "Darn right! But I wouldn't say it."

Judging girls' appearances more than boys', some girls frequently use negative terms for females. One girl exclaims, "Oh my God. I use 'heinous' all the time." Others agree, "Girls are more critical of girls," and "We judge girls a lot."

The girls' terms used to describe a bad-looking male include "disgusting," "heinous," "nasty," "ewww," "gross," "ugly," "hideous," "bad hygiene," "raunchy," "skank," "crusty," "dirty," "ohhhh," "he looks wack," "he looks like the shit at the bottom of my shoe," "not attractive," "an ugly motherfucker," "yucky," "smelly," "disgusting," "putrid," "greasy," "slimy," "repulsive," and "grody." The girls list 25 terms, and a main theme involves dirt or filth.

The girls say that the boys are "definitely" much harsher on the unattractive and that girls "have more compassion for, like, boys who are overweight or something." While the girls feel "bad" for unattractive boys if they are "sitting at a table alone by themselves," the "guys'll make fun" of unattractive boys and girls.

The wealthy senior girls' clique gives perhaps the ultimate insult, saying they would not even notice an ugly male or think enough of him to use a term to describe him, except:

-Only if they come and talk to you. That is the only time you notice ugly guys.

-Like, if you even put enough effort into recognizing them. Like if a bad-looking guy comes up to especially one of *us*—

-We're like, "Ewww, what are you doing?"

-We're, like, nice to them. We're not disrespectful, but we don't even think about it. Like we don't think enough [of him] to be like, "Oh, he was ugly." I think we would just overlook it.

Boys: Judging Girls

The males list many terms, 54 in all, to describe a good-looking female: "titties and ass," "phat" (which they define as an acronym for "pretty hot and tempting"), "trick," "monstrous jugs," "hot," "mad fine," "slammin'," "bangin'," "delicious," "smokin'," "tight ass," "fabulous," "pretty," "succulent," "fine," "hottie," "fly girl," "sexy," "fox," "damn" (accompanied by a catcall), "beautiful," "gorgeous," "glamorous," "sparkly," "picturesque," "perfect," "boomin'," "tight bangin'," "blazin'," "babe," "piece of ass," "kinky," "grade A top choice meat," "attractive," "enjoyable," "doable," "quite fine," "foxy," "damn sexy," "bitchin'," "cute," "wicked fine," "bonerific," "drop-dead gorgeous," "sick," "holy shit," "she's got a rack," "bomb," "guns," "cannons," "breathtaking," and "heart-stopping." "Hot" and "gorgeous" are often ranked as the top of the scale. Using twice as many terms as the girls list for a good-looking male, the boys often refer to erogenous body parts.

The connotations of the boys' terms appear more complex than the girls' since the importance and complexity of girls conforming to sexual standards of appropriateness plays a more integral role in the meaning of the terms.

The boys explain that the connotation of "hot" and "good-looking" differ because "you can be 'hot' and not that good-looking. Hot's sex appeal." Another boy notes:

> Good-looking and hot are two way different things. A good-looking girl is pretty and a hot girl is beyond pretty. Like, a hot girl makes herself hot, and a pretty girl . . . it's just the way she is.

Another adds, "Actually, all hot girls put tons of makeup on and wear materialistic clothes." Some of the boys say that the term "hot" conveys a negative connotation because it has a tint of sexual promiscuity attached, explaining, "Hot's kind of, like, leaning toward skanky." Words such as "gorgeous" and "beautiful" mean she is "a lot" more attractive.

Many of the boys agree with one who says, " 'Gorgeous' is by far the top":

> -It's like drop dead.

> -Yeah, "gorgeous" is, like, beautiful, glamorous, perfect, everything.

> -Picturesque.

> -"Gorgeous" is like, nice, you know, the curves all around.

> -It's, like, sparkly.

They contrast "gorgeous" with "hot" and "sexy," which rank lower.

The boys use these same terms to describe older women such as female faculty members or other boys' mothers. One boy comments to another, "Have you seen William's mother? She is *hot!*" In one dorm, the boys discuss the teachers they find hot:

> Miss Adams. My God! I dropped her class partially because I could not pay attention in her class because all I could think about was throwing her on her desk and doing crazy-ass shit there. Oh my God, is she hot!

In contrast to the large number of terms for good-looking women, the boys have few terms for good-looking males. To comment on another male's looks is considered "against the guy code." When I ask for terminology for a good-looking male, the boys first are silent and then laugh. Although they notice if another male is good-looking, they say that "guys don't acknowledge other guys' looks." One boy explains, "You never say anything . . . you notice, but you never say anything." Another adds, "I do it inside. Inside I'm like, 'Whoa! I know what's going on there.'" The boys report, "I might say, 'He's not ugly,' but that's it."

Homosexuality is associated with noticing another male's looks. When asked to provide terms for a good-looking male, many boys say, "No, I don't swing that way" and "I'm staying away from that one!" The boys explain that although they might notice anther male's looks, if they comment on it, they would be considered "gay." Boys don't talk about another male's looks except to comment on his muscles, mainly using the term "jacked."

The only other terms they admit using are "he's not ugly," "good-looking," "attractive," "he's a dude," "tool," "player," and "pretty boy." Although the terms total eight compared to the girls' ten, the number of times and the readiness with which the terms are given underscore the striking difference between the boys and girls. Many of the boys can't give any terms at all, or they just list words they would say in front of a girl but not other guys. The girls, on the other hand, readily recall their terms and say how often they use them.

The boys use almost twice the number of terms than the girls do to describe an unattractive female. These include "brutal," "nasty," "ugly," "hideous," "FUBAR" (acronym for "fucked up beyond all recognition"), "coyote," "chicken head," "goat," "doughnuts" ("on the scale from one to ten they get a doughnut, a big zero"), "pass," "oily," "sniggle tooth," "draggle tooth," "hurt," "busted," "couch ass," "trunk butt," "tank ass," "she took a dive out of the ugly tray," "beast," "cow," "dog," "slutface," "horse," "skank," "cross-eyed," "not pretty," "ouch," "she fell out of the ugly tree," "she was run over by a Mack truck repeatedly," "gross," "trash," "bagger," "nasty," "ho," "ho bag," "slut," "whore," "whore bag," "butt ugly," "disgusting," "nasty," "pig," and "ohhhh." The boys also use certain unspoken signs to indicate to each other that a girl is unattractive:

-I think when guys see a bad-looking woman they just look at each other and you know.

-You just look away.

-You're like, "Ohhhh."

Whereas the girls use many terms referring to dirt or filth to describe the unattractive males, the boys use many terms referring to animals and sexual promiscuity to describe unattractive females.

The boys also have a limited number of terms for an unattractive male, which include "I want to kick his ass," "he's just ugly," "fag," "goofy-looking," "he's an ugly dude," "poor soul," "why," "tool," "winner" (said sarcastically), "not a dude," "freak," and "waste of space." One boy says that he would just laugh. Unlike the bitch squad, which doesn't "associate with ugly people," one boy claims, "You'd want to hang out with that dude 'cause then it makes you look better." In one dorm after a boy first says that males would say "nothing" about an unattractive male, he adds seriously, "Actually, Matt is butt ugly." Matt, who is in the room, turns bright red but does not respond. The boys' 15 different terms for an unattractive male contrast to their 24 terms for an unattractive female.

This terminology study reveals how much more important appearance is for females than for males. The boys use far more terms for females' appearance, both attractive and unattractive, than the girls do for males' appearance (99 versus 52), indicating the importance of a girl's looks. The girls use more terms for members of the same sex (34 versus 23), which indicates their concern with the appearance of other females. The number of sexually descriptive terms used by both genders to describe unattractive females together with the sexually loaded terms used by the boys for attractive women highlight the importance both genders place on appropriate female sexuality.

The Cost of Looking Good

Feeling immense pressure to conform to a cultural ideal of masculinity and femininity, many take extreme measures to conform. Because thinness is the main element of attractiveness in girls and the essence of their femininity, they take extreme measures to lose weight. On the other hand, because "being jacked" and achieving athletically are core elements of masculinity, the boys sometimes take health risks to gain weight.

Girls: Never Too Thin

Restrictive diets, excessive exercise, appetite suppressants, obsession over food, and severe eating disorders are all evident among the girls at Bolton. According to the school counselor, although the peak occurrence of eating disorders occurred a few years before this research, food issues still remain among the girls. During the height of the eating disorder boom on campus, I witnessed firsthand the atmosphere in the girls' dorms through Lauren, a girl who confided in me.

Lauren, a junior, tells me one day that she is concerned about eating disorders among her friends. She reports that her "whole dorm is obsessed, obsessed with food," eats "nonfat everything," and constantly does sit-ups. This obsession started with one girl, Amy, and then it just "snowballed."

Lauren explains that the girls go to one extreme or the other. One of her friends, Caroline, says, "Well, I might as well eat this cake. I'll never have a boyfriend anyway." Lauren adds, "All she does is eat because she's depressed." Most everybody else, she explains, only eats "bagels, cereal, apples, and water." The girls never take trays at the dining hall but just small amounts of food on plates: "If you get a plateful, people look at you." Weight and exercise are competitive between the girls: "They'll say, 'How far are you running?' or 'Oh, you're running? I should run too.'"

Lauren is concerned because a close friend of hers, Britney, who has a solid athletic build and excels at sports, has lost 40 pounds in one month. Pretty with long dirty-blond hair, a winning smile, and a wonderful sense of humor, Britney is wealthy and seems permanently tanned from all her family vacations. Now that Britney has lost weight, Lauren reports, "everyone is telling her how great she looks. Her periods have stopped, and they won't let her do crew because they don't think she has the strength. Crew used to be her life." She then adds, "And now she has a boyfriend, so that's going to make her want to do it [not eating] even more."

Lauren blames Amy for the current wave of eating disorders because she needed a dieting pal and recruited Britney. "It's like, 'I'll teach you how to lose weight,'" Lauren claims. Lauren's friends now smoke or do drugs instead of drink because those are not fattening, and they make up excuses for not going to dinner or eating, such as, "I just went to the Grill [a local restaurant]."

Lauren says the school should kick out "girls who are really bad" to keep others from following their example. She and several of her friends went to the administration at the beginning of the year and told them that Amy had a severe eating disorder and needed to leave. "She was expelled for two days and then came back unchanged," Lauren explains.

Lauren blames mothers and their attitudes for many of the problems girls have with food. For Amy's problems, she blames Amy's mother as well as boys, her peers, and the media. When Amy's mother came to pick Amy up, she entered Lauren's room, sat on her bed, and asked, "Do you think Amy is skinny? What size do you wear?" Amy's mother "is super skinny. She drinks, like, one milk shake thing a day and that is all." When the school called about Amy being anorexic, her mother didn't see a problem: "She's like, 'I work out every day and eat only nonfat foods. What's the problem?'"

The girls who have eating disorders must sign a contract that requires them to be weighed once a week at the health center, to maintain their weight above 100 pounds, and to attend group meetings with a counselor. Lauren says, "Some girls just won't sign." If they fail to meet the guidelines of the contract or if they refuse to sign, they are expelled. Sometimes they are allowed another chance after they attend a meeting with their parents, their advisor, and a health center representative. If they don't keep their weight up, they are not allowed to return the next year.

Lauren is worried about Britney because she once weighed 160 pounds and lost over 40 pounds in one month. Britney constantly asks her how many calories different foods have and has not eaten a thing since returning from Christmas break: "I mean nothing. Oh, she might have a Jolly Rancher once in a while." She told Lauren that "if I have one spoonful of cereal, I feel like I'm going to throw up," and that she is scared that that one spoonful will make her fat.

Lauren reports that "the boys are telling Britney how good she looks and not to gain any weight, not to lose any, but to stay the same." "It's really scary," Lauren adds, "All of my friends have a little of it [anorexia], but she is bad. Some of the things she said were so awful. I know she was asking for help." About one month after returning from Christmas vacation, Lauren comes to me upset because Britney has just been sent home for losing too much weight. A doctor examined Britney, finding her condition serious, so she was given a medical leave and sent home to be treated for anorexia. If Britney returns to Bolton Academy, she must eat three meals a day at her advisor's house. Lauren says that Britney asked her, "How do I fool them, how do I get around the rules?" Britney never comes back to Bolton.

I always suspected that Lauren herself was struggling with issues of anorexia. A perfectionist in grades as well as everything else, she held leadership positions at the school and was a favorite of students and faculty alike. Soon after Britney left, Lauren began to say she had "just eaten" when she came over for advisee dinners. She took to wearing baggy clothes. She was playing varsity hockey but would work out on the treadmill after team practice, saying, "We really didn't work out that hard today." Because of the reputation of the coach, that was hard to believe. She became even thinner.

I attempted to talk to her about it, as did others, and our advice must have finally sunk in. She went to therapy while at Bolton and gave her senior speech on anorexia and how she had been able to overcome it. When she came to visit me *a year after graduating from Bolton, she was a vibrant, healthy young woman who showed no signs of her old disease.*

The students report that although there is more awareness and peer resistance to eating disorders than there used to be, eating issues of all types, including severe eating disorders and use of drugs, remain prevalent among the girls at Bolton. The girls maintain that "loads" of girls, up to 80%, have unusual diets in order to lose weight. They talk about several girls who "just absolutely, you know, shrank, and they sent them home . . . and they went to the hospital and all that stuff." They think "a couple of people" should go home "right now" because of their eating disorders.

Many girls become anorexic not in order to attract boys but rather to compete with and get attention from other females. One girl says that anorexia is "weird" because "the guys don't like skinny people. They're kind of, like, 'She needs to get meat on her bones.'" Instead, girls want to get attention from their peers, "'cause it's, like, 'Wow, you're so skinny. What size are you . . . three, four, zero?'" One of the girls muses, "It's so funny—guys want to look swollen and girls want to look emaciated."

At Bolton, an emphasis on thinness is often a class and ethnic issue. Connected to their greater emphasis on appearance in general, the wealthiest girls describe the most parental pressure to be thin, desire most to be thin, and focus the most on weight. These findings coincide with other research reporting that higher-class girls reported greater levels of restrained eating, greater body dissatisfaction and distortion, and placing greater importance on physical appearance and less importance on achievement and family life (Ogden & Thomas, 1999).

A girl who transferred from a public high school in a wealthy area contends that there are fewer eating disorders at Bolton than at her old school, where "like 82% percent of the girls had eating disorders." Agreeing with her, others speculate about why. One girl thinks that it is because "food is our main event. Like, when you want to do something with your friends, it's, like, 'Do you want to go to dinner now?'" Another decides that it is due to "all the sports and stuff" and that when you participate in sports, "you need food." Another student cites the lack of privacy, "People don't have the privacy to go throw up in their own bathroom." One attributes it to Bolton's busy schedule, saying that girls don't have "time to be anorexic" and "there's so much else to do to concern yourself with."

Many girls point out, and it appears to be true, that often female athletes don't have as many issues with their bodies and food. One girl explains, "I think that some of the girls who are into hard-core sports don't change their diets at all, just because they need the energy. Hockey players, basketball players, softball players." In one dorm, as the girls debate the percentage of the girls at Bolton who are on special diets, one large hockey player who is on scholarship from Canada cannot believe the numbers that the other girls are proposing. She suggests a much lower figure and keeps saying, "Really?" This girl seems far removed from the food issues that the other girls describe.

Other research confirms this link between athletic involvement and eating issues. Athletic participation has been correlated with significantly higher self-esteem and body esteem among girls (Novick, 1999; Morgan, 2004). The number of unhealthy weight control behaviors has been found to be lower among female athletes, although it remains a significant issue (Croll, 2003). Athletes of both genders also rate higher on indexes of both general and mental health (Steiner, McQuivey, Pavelski, Pitts, & Kraemer, 2000).

That there are fewer eating disorders among females of color appears also to have a cultural basis, as research describes ethnic differences in body image. Some research finds adolescents of color to be more satisfied with their bodies and have fewer concerns about dieting and weight loss than whites (L. K. G. Hsu, 1987; Schwartz, Thompson, & Johnson, 1982). Other research, however, indicates that although black females are as dissatisfied with their bodies (especially their weight) as whites, they see fewer negative implications in being overweight because, unlike the white females, they do not view thinness as essential for being attractive (Thomas & James, 1988). Although perhaps not to the same degree, females of color still demonstrate great concern with their weight and unhealthy eating habits (Rosen et al., 1988). At Bolton, the students of color did appear to have fewer eating and food issues, except the few wealthy students of color, who appeared to be just as concerned with being thin as the wealthy white girls. A former young African American faculty member who headed a group concerned with diversity and tolerance on campus explains that eating disorders are usually never an issue in the lives of the African American female students because their families are "worried about getting food on the table" and their mothers "would kill them if they threw it back up."

The girls report that there is "a *lot*" of diet pill use and abuse of performance drugs in order to lose weight, estimating that between 30 and 50% of the girls at Bolton take supplements or diet pills. One group of girls adds, "The whole school is on antidepressants," so "probably half the school is on some kind of medication that affects their diet, not necessarily because it's supposed to, but it's like a side effect."

In order to perform better academically as well as to lose weight, some girls abuse performance drugs such as Ritalin. At the beginning of the year Bolton expelled several high-achieving girls for abusing Ritalin and cough syrup. Although abuse of performance drugs has dropped due to lack of availability, the girls quickly add, "There is still a lot" and "They are still very, very much around."

Because of the academic intensity of boarding schools, the girls note there is "definitely" more abuse of performance drugs, caffeine, and amphetamines than at public school. The girls take these substances to help them perform during exams as well as "even on regular nights when you have a lot of work. Like, I know people who are popping the caffeine pills regularly." One girl believes that the abuse of these drugs is so high at prep schools because "even if you're not competing academically, you're competing for sports or beauty or something else. Like you're always competing with somebody."

Boys: Pumped!

The boys face fewer negative consequences in their quest for the ideal in appearance, claiming that there is little steroid use and only "very few use creatine [a protein supplement] here or whey protein." One student explains, "Legally, it's about as minimal as you'll find anywhere."

Agreeing that steroid use at Bolton is "definitely less than at home," many credit the characteristics of a boarding preparatory school for minimizing the use of illegal muscle boosters because steroids are "easier to get a hold of at home," students are "isolated to campus," there are different types of kids who attend Bolton, there is a lack of privacy, and there is less athletic pressure. Others add, "This isn't also, like the bigtime sports school either," so "there's not that much pressure on being as strong as you possibly can" and that "here it's just the type of kids are different and they're . . . like, a stereotype would be that they're more intelligent about it." Another contends, "Kids that are going to go pro, like football or NHL, don't usually come to a place like this, and maybe they do steroids."

Other boys disagree both about the lack of steroid use at Bolton and that the characteristics of prep schools discourage the use of steroids. One group of boys contends that some of the recent students at Bolton did use steroids because of athletic pressure:

-The desire to be so good at hockey because you're expected to be and maybe you have a little disadvantage because you're a little skinnier or smaller than the average player. They'll take steroids to overcome that disadvantage. There were some here last year.

-Here, all over.

Although steroids might not be used much at Bolton, protein boosters are prevalent. The difference between boys taking protein supplements and girls with eating disorders or taking appetite suppressants is that boys want to perform better athletically and not just improve their looks. The boys at Bolton typically take them "for performance and athletics, like, most the guys wouldn't work out and go through all that just for a *girl*," but they admit that "it's definitely true" that looks also play a role in why males lift weights and want big muscles.

Although the girls are often more intense in their efforts to achieve the ideal, both boys and girls demonstrate the extreme lengths to which they will go, even at the risk of seriously damaging to their health, in order to secure relationships and connections with others.

Sexuality

Perhaps in no other area of their lives is the pressure to conform to gender ideals as dramatic as in their sexuality. Despite their true inclinations not to behave in accordance with prevailing gender ideals, most students conform or at least openly play the role of the appropriate gender due to strong cultural pressures, which include the girls' fear of being labeled a "slut" and the boys' fear of being labeled "gay."

Sexuality has been described as providing the key to the innermost and truest part of the self (Foucault, 1978). It is not surprising, therefore, that Ortner (1991) asserts, "Class differences are largely represented as sexual differences" (p. 178). In her analysis of performances of sexuality in exotic dance clubs, Trautner (2005) describes the performances of middle-class sexuality as being more voyeuristic in that the women were unapproachable, and through slow music, far-off gazes, and fluttering caresses that did not directly touch their breasts, they created an image of dream-like, unattainable perfection. The working-class performances, on the other hand, were more interactive, animated, and varied, and the women were more explicitly sexual. Similarly, Bettie (2003) describes how although there were no class differences among the girls in the amount of sexual activity they engaged in, the *appearance* of sexual promiscuity, as symbolized by tight clothes and heavy makeup, was central to working-class girls' performances of gender and in opposition to middle-class respectability.

These class differences in the ideals of female sexuality correspond with what I found among the Bolton students. The extreme differences in male and female sexuality typified by the opposing ideals of power and control, the strong sexual double standard, and the failure to acknowledge female sexuality appear to correspond with the upper-class ideals of the dream-like perfection and purity of females. The students' views concerning ideal sexual behavior are extremely gender-specific. It is important for the students' self-esteem to stand out as being "hot" and sexually attractive, yet they face intense pressure to fit a gender-specific standard of sexual behavior and activity that rests firmly on the divisions between self-gratification and power, on one hand, and self-denial and control, on the other.

For girls, the pressure is immense to be other-focused—to look for love, not sex. They are expected to control themselves and their sexuality and thus care what others think so as to maintain a good reputation and not to be viewed as a "slut." For boys, they feel pressure to be self-focused—to want sex, not love. They are expected to demonstrate power, to have sexual relations (or at least to have had one encounter and not be a "cherry"), to gratify themselves, and to be proficient and well equipped.

To be heterosexual is probably the most intense pressure for conformity of any kind at Bolton, especially for the boys. For a boy, to be homosexual calls into question his entire manhood, but for a girl, homosexual behavior does not negate her womanhood to the same extent or with the same consequences as for males.

Sexual Ideals and Pressures: Girls

The students unanimously decry a strong sexual double standard at Bolton that allows boys but not girls to be sexually active. Speaking indignantly of the "unfairness" of the double standard, the girls face the social calamity of being labeled a "slut" if they transgress the appropriate gendered sexual behavior. As a result, the girls feel inhibited expressing and even acknowledging their sexuality as well as giving in to sexual desires.

For the girls, the importance of maintaining a "good" reputation among students and faculty, on one hand, and of not appearing immature or being a "prude," on the other, creates contrary pressures and dilemmas. Each type of sexual pressure has its own label and negative connotation. The girls feel pressure not to be a virgin, but they feel "juvenile" if they have not had sex and "slutty" if they have.

Not all the girls subscribe to the double standard. African American girls often criticize male promiscuity, their criticism standing out from the resigned acceptance shown by the other girls. One African American girl insists, "For myself personally, if a guy is a ho, he's a ho . . . no names mentioned!" At this the other girls laugh and identify those boys by name. She continues, "I think they *were* just praised for it, but now I think they're starting to get a little of the heat for it too."

The sexual double standard endures largely because girls are judgmental of other girls. "Definitely we judge each other more," they explain, adding, "Girls will down each other and call each other ho's." If a girl "sleeps around," other girls will say, "Ooh, she's dirty," but if a boy does the same thing, other boys will praise him: "Yeah, man, you got more play. Good for you."

Many of the girls show confusion, resentment, and despair over the differences in sexual expectations:

-I've begun to lose a lot of faith in guys lately. It's just, I don't know, I've been screwed over by every guy ever and I just don't have faith in the male race any longer. I've had enough.

-I don't think you can win. Girls are either a prude or a slut. If you're a prude, you're called a bitch. If you're a slut, you're a slut.

-Like there really is no middle ground, there really isn't.

Self-esteem is closely linked with conforming to these cultural ideals. One girl claims, "If you don't have a good reputation, you lose a lot of self-respect." Another feels "scrutinized" everywhere she goes, and so "when I'm not in the dorm, I put on a mask, let's go to class, be intellectual, and then come back here, it's like, I fall apart at the seams." Other girls joke that their best friends "know way too much" and if they ever got into a fight they would have to "kill" them.

The girls constantly worry about their reputation with the faculty and administration. The girls care so much because they think the faculty plays favorites with the students who do not have "a reputation." The girls also say that they "have to care" because the faculty "can screw with your life here" and "they have so much input in your future."

The pressure for girls to have good reputations revolves around not being viewed as a "slut" by other girls, boys, and the faculty. The definition of a slut varies greatly among the girls and is often integrally connected to the amount of sexual experience a girl has had. The primary characteristics of a slut are the number of people a girl has sex with, the time frame in which it happens, and if she is "in love."

The girls generally define a "slut" as a girl who "fucks" "a lot of people in a small period of time." They often add a relationship component, claiming if you "sleep with him and you're not going out with him, you're labeled." A girl who likes sex differs from a slut as long as she has sex under the right circumstances. The girls make the distinction: "Just because you like sex a lot doesn't mean you're a slut, especially if it's with the same person; then you're just having sex a lot." However, even a virgin can be deemed a slut depending on the clothes she wears, how she acts, or if she kisses or has oral sex with lots of different guys.

Perhaps not surprisingly, the girls who have the most sexual experience give the most lenient definitions. One girl who is extremely sexually active defines a slut as "like if you have sex with four people in one night, that's slutty." A semi-experienced girl contends, "Or four people in one week, even, that's slutty." An inexperienced girl claims, "Or in a month." The experienced girl disagrees, but the inexperienced girl insists and a few other inexperienced girls agree with her: "I think four different people in a month is a lot." At this, the experienced girl looks uncomfortable, saying with a rather insulted air that she thinks "four different people in *a night* is a lot." Everyone seems uncomfortable because they know this girl easily fits their definition of a slut.

There is no term for males' sexual behavior that has the same negative connotation as "slut." The girls mention "player" as a term to describe a promiscuous male but add, "'Player' is used for somebody who has, like, charm, who girls still would go with." They conclude that "dirty" is the only word that strictly carries a negative connotation.

Engaging in mildly "kinky" sex (such as the use of foods as sex aids) does not make a girl a slut, nor does there appear to be a large double standard for engaging in kinky sex.[3] The girls are more concerned about whether it happens in a monogamous and loving relationship than whether it is "non-standard" sex. Most of the girls describe kinky sex as "very acceptable," so acceptable that how to perform it is part of their popular culture. One girl explains:

If you look in a magazine and you see . . . there's, like, what, 30 new ways to please your boyfriend and it's, like, 30 new things you should do . . . it's kind of just common things now.

Just as boys pressure each other to lose their virginity, the girls pressure each other not to be virgins as well as not to be "sluts." Although some girls want to lose their virginity, they also feel pressure from other girls:

-With girls there's the competition like, "You're a virgin?"

-It's like, "You're a virgin? Oh, good for you." [Said negatively]

-Yeah, it's seen as bad.

Debating the pros and cons of losing their virginity, the girls display their wide range of beliefs concerning sexual activity. In one dorm, when one girl announces, "I almost wish I was still a virgin," the others disagree, saying that girls who do not have sex are "missing out" and that "I just think there's nothing to save." One girl comments, "It seems like losing your virginity has gotten to be such a big deal and, like, people just want to get rid of it." A Muslim girl voices her opinion on abstinence, stating, "Personally, I think sex is meant for reproduction, and if you're not ready to have children, then I don't think you're ready to take the chance to have sex." The other girls look at her like she is from Mars.

Feeling dissatisfaction and regret about losing their virginity, the girls in one dorm say:

-You want it to be so great and then it happens and you're like, "What the *hell* did I just do?"

-It's like you want it [your virginity] to be over and then people always regret it after it happens too.

Several girls hate the boys with whom they lost their virginity, and others "basically regret everyone" with whom they had sex. One girl comments, "No one likes the first person they have sex with." Another emotes, "Oh, I hate him so badly!" Another muses, "I don't know him," and on realizing her admission, she turns red, sputtering, "Oh my God! I have to leave."

Sometimes losing one's virginity is viewed as a state of heart and mind rather than a physical change, especially if the girl involved was raped or very young. After taking a poll, the girls in one dorm discover that 5 of the 12 girls in the room are virgins. A non-virgin tells the virgins, "Be proud of it," saying she lost her virginity when she was raped at 15 but adding, "I don't count it as losing my virginity, though, because it was rape and he didn't cum." Commonly girls who were "too young to say no" or raped say, "Well, I guess I technically lost my virginity when I was 13, but I didn't have sex again until I was 16."

The severity of the repercussions for a girl's reputation and self-esteem if she fails to meet the sexual ideals and the rewards if she succeeds become evident in how the boys regard two similar girls. Both Lilly and Rebecca, who are best friends and pretty and "feminine," don't do sports and are very interested in clothes and makeup. While Lilly is sexually experienced and rumored to have herpes, Rebecca has "done a good job maintaining her celibacy." As a result, many boys write off Lilly as a "bus-station skank," while they "all obsess" about Rebecca.

Sexual Ideals and Pressures: Boys

While the males face intense pressure to conform to the standard of being sexually active, proficient, well equipped, and heterosexual, they also face pressure to conform to self-focused behavior of using girls for sex, being cruel, and not wanting relationships in order to prove their masculinity.

The boys readily describe a sexual double standard at Bolton: "If a girl goes out with six different guys in a year and fucks them all on the first day, then she's a slut," but if a guy does the same thing, "he's not a slut, he's just a man. A guy's not a slut, he's a fuckin' 'way to go, atta-boy!'" Some girls, however, will look unfavorably on a male who has "too much" sex. An African American boy explains:

> -'Cause, see, girls get considered sluts if they have sex with guys by both guys and girls, but if a guy has sex with a lot of girls, guys are like, "Yeah, I guess that's cool" and girls are like, "That's terrible."

> -You're a player.

> -Yeah, girls don't see it as good, either way.

Unlike the girls, many of the boys view the double standard as right "because girls are seen as pure" and "good and holy" and "it's just the way things are, the way it should be."

A boy's reputation for being sexually proficient and experienced is important. In one dorm, a boy notes, "Yeah, like if you're still a virgin by the time you're 18. Yeah, that's no good. Sorry." The only exceptions are for concrete reasons, such as a Muslim who says, "It's against my religion," and another boy who warns, "Or if you have herpes like me." The only other acceptable reasons are if "you have no penis. Or like some horrible debilitating war injury. Or you're a quadriplegic."

Although a boy's reputation is important at Bolton, the boys discuss it with a different degree of intensity and fear than the girls. A boy says, "What people here think of you *really* matters because you can't get away from them." Another boy claims, "At public school, teachers didn't care. Here they care." Another asserts, "Here, you're with people 24/7 and you gotta impress people." At this point, a friend lets out a huge belch. The first boy pauses and then says, "You really do."

Perhaps in response to the lower tolerance for a sexual double standard among the African American girls, Adam talks differently about reputation than the white boys in his dorm. He tries to convince the others that reputation is "everything in the world" at Bolton because of the way girls talk, but the others do not agree. One boy comments, "It's not everything, that's money." Adam insists, "Reputation matters a lot," explaining:

> Say I have a bad reputation with one girl, right. Now I break up with that girl, or whatever, now I try to talk to another girl. That girl that I broke up with told her my reputation, so now I have a bad reputation and it keeps going with me in life. Because girls talk. All they do is talk, talk, talk! And my reputation keeps traveling and traveling and I am all by myself on my deathbed.

The boys' definition of a "slut" as someone who has sexual intercourse with multiple partners in a short period of time with no emotional attachment revolves almost exclusively around the number of sexual encounters. In contrast to the girls, the boys do not mention other factors such as the way a girl dresses, agreeing that, except for extreme cases, a girl has to have sexual intercourse to be deemed a slut. This lends credibility to the contention that the girls judge other girls more harshly than the boys do.

Like the girls, the boys contend that it is the number of different people and not the amount of sex that makes a girl a slut. One boy explains, "When you're a slut, you want it all the time, you do it all the time, and that's just nasty. If it's with the same person, see, that's monogamy. That's beautiful." The boys consider how many sexual partners a girl could have before being deemed a slut and agree that the girl who "blew 24 guys in one year" would be a slut.

Because male promiscuity is not looked down upon, the boys note that there is not a term similar to "slut" for males. Sexually active boys are envied by the others and attract some girls who like experienced partners. The boys explain, "Yeah, the guy is like a pimp!" This term carries a positive connotation because "its meaning now in slang is kind of good." One boy adds, "All the guys are envious of him." Others claim, "From like a girl's perspective, he can be, like, a scumbag. But from a guy's perspective, he's not. Even girls who call you an asshole, they hook up with you."

A boy can be seen as having too much sex, but the sexual activity must be extreme and even then other males still often look up to him. The amount of sex must be "a lot higher than a girl," with some suggesting, "I think you'd have to get over 20" in a school year. A boy who dates and is having sex with three different girls (three-timing) would have too much sex, but if he has sex with three girls all at the same time, he would be "the man!"

Engaging in mildly kinky sex is acceptable for a girl as long as it occurs with one partner and includes emotional attachment. The boys usually desire such encounters, saying that a girl can do "anything" if it is just with one partner and "all guys fantasize about that shit." The use of food as sex aids would "definitely" not get a girl labeled a "slut." One boy explains, "That's not kinky. That is so ordinary."

Only one boy describes a double standard for kinky sex but adds that it is subjective:

> Like the guy's the man and the girl's kind of . . . You like it if
> you're having kinky sex with a girl, but if she's having it with
> someone else you call her a fuckin' whore.

Although I took this to be a humorous response, it reveals much truth about the competition and jealousy behind how others judge.

The only type of kinky sex the boys frequently mention as unacceptable is for a girl to have sex with more than one person at a time:

> -That's a slut. That's basically a whore.

> -Even if she only does it once. If she does it once with more than
> one guy, you can definitely classify her as a whore.

The boys note the double standard, recognizing that if a male has sex with two girls at a time, "you're above everybody else." The only other type of kinky sex that will get a girl labeled a "slut" is if she engages in "tossing salad."[4]

The different types and intensity of pressures the Bolton boys face to achieve the masculine ideal of being sexually experienced, proficient, and well equipped become most apparent during their casual discourse and self-interviews, when I am not present. In one dorm, Adam, an extremely athletic and popular black boy, leads a discussion during a self-interview, asking the others if they are still virgins and, if so, why. While a few admit to being virgins, it is browbeaten out of others. Adam takes a poll, and five of the nine boys are virgins. The virgins unanimously say that they are not happy about being virgins and desperately want to have sex: "Every decent girl I see I think about fucking" and "I look at girls and am like, 'What would it be like to fuck that girl?'"

Tim, one of the four boys who said that he was not a virgin, had lied, and the others find him out, an incident demonstrating not only the complicated nature of girls' sexual reputations but also the pressures on boys to have sex and not to focus on relationships. Adam asks Tim, who has complained about not having enough sex, "Does your girlfriend give you head? I wouldn't stick with a girl if she doesn't even give you head." Tim responds, "No, no, no, it's, like, lots of head," but then he sheepishly admits that he has not had vaginal sex. On finding him out, the other boys exclaim, "If you've only had a blow job, then you are a virgin because you haven't fucked a girl!" One boy adds, "None of this oral-sex-is-sex bullshit. A mouth is not a pussy!" Adam asks, "Okay, you sleep around on this girl?" When Tim answers no, Adam replies, "Well, then your ass is stuck." Tim sheepishly admits, "I'm aware of that now. That's why I'm looking around." It is obvious that it is not "acceptable" for Tim to focus on his commitment to the relationship and that he feels pressure to assert his focus on "self."

During a self-interview on sexuality, a group led by Paul, a popular hockey player, uses my questions on terminology to make fun of a boy for being sexually inexperienced. The other boys, many of whom bragged about their sexual experience and proficiency, make fun of Doug, a boy described by a teacher as "quiet, smart, and hard-working." During the interview when Paul reads the question, "What terms do you use to refer to a male that has too little sex?" many of the boys laugh and say, "Doug!" When Doug says that he does not think girls enjoy sex the same amount as boys, they accuse him of having a "little dick," masturbating excessively, and being a "fag." Someone asks Doug why he is putting up with the abuse, and he replies, "I don't care," but it doesn't sound like he means it.

Whenever another boy passes by the common room, the other boys ask, "What do you call a man who has too little sex?" and whisper for him to reply, "Doug." When he does, they all laugh uproariously. Finally Doug leaves. The boys joke that he is in his room crying, hanging himself, or "he's sittin' there with the tweezers pulling his penis saying, 'I know you can make it another centimeter, baby.'" Finally one boy says, "I'm going to go check on him. I've been his roommate for three years, so . . ." He returns and reports that Doug has left the dorm.

That the boys face pressure to measure up to each other sexually is clear when they try to outdo each other with tales of sexual endurance and performance. In one dorm a boy attended a party the night before at a day student's house and claims, "I had sex five times." A little while later, Paul, the boy who is leading the discussion, asks each boy when he last had sex. The pressure is obvious. The boys give answers like "last Wednesday," "last Monday," "winter break," and "too long ago." One boy, who answers meekly, "Thanksgiving," is suspected of lying and being less experienced than he claims. Paul states, "He's blushing. I think he's full of shit!" and the others laugh. Paul then asks the boys, "How many times?" The others answer "twice" or "once." One of the boys answers, "At least five, maybe six." Paul then laughs, "I had it twice that day and 24 times over a four-day period. That's kind of sick." This receives much laughter.

The boys then compare their records for masturbation:

-What's your record? How many times a day?

-Quattro.

-Are you serious? Holy shit!

-Jesus Christ, man, you're going to hurt yourself!

-We single guys have to take advantage of it.

The boys also face pressure to be well equipped sexually, that is, to have a large penis. On a six-hour bus ride to go whitewater rafting for the senior trip, Tyler, who is rebellious, outrageous, and candid, asks if he can take my mike and go to the back of the bus to ask questions. Since I was conducting interviews in the front on the seniors' thoughts before graduation and the seniors had stopped coming up, I agree. He starts out asking the same "boring" questions that I had been asking but soon switches to topics on his mind: oral sex, masturbation, and penis size.

The intense pressure boys face to have a large penis is demonstrated when Tyler interviews Tina, an attractive and popular black girl. Tina is sitting next to a male student, Eddie (also black), who reportedly has liked her since freshman year, but they have never gone out. Tyler asks Tina, "Does size matter? Do you personally prefer a big cock to a little cock?" When she responds, "Yes," he asks, "What's more important, length or girth?" Tina responds, "Thickness." Tyler then asks Tina to show him how big is big enough for her. She shows them a bottle, from what I can tell a Snapple bottle. The boys erupt, "That's fuckin' enormous!" and "Holy . . . ! I think I'm done." One of the boys then asks Eddie, "So, Eddie?" Sounding dejected, Eddie responds, "I can't measure up to that."

The boys then discuss the size of the average penis. They decide that it is the size of the rather large microphone they are using. Tina exclaims, "So the average size is like this microphone? Are you kidding me? That is like a toothpick!" The boys shriek, "Oh shit! We're going down!" Tina asks again, as if she can't believe it, "This is average?" When all the boys respond that it is, Tina and her friends laugh and continue making fun of the size, insisting, "That is really small!"

The boys seem deflated by the girls' responses, and Tyler resignedly continues the interview, this time focusing on racial differences and penis size. Tyler says to Tina, "So you must be into black guys, from what I can tell. You can't just say every single black guy is hung like a fuckin' horse because it's just not true." Tina agrees but adds, "Black guys tend to be larger." Tyler then states to no one in particular, "Doesn't that suck if you're a black guy and you have a tiny dick?" Tina replies, "But it happens." Eddie interjects, "Like Frank." Tyler exclaims, "Is he? I didn't know that! Did you know that Frank was small?" he asks everyone in a loud voice. He adds, "Asian people, let's not even talk about how tiny their dicks are!"

Although boys at Bolton do not admit to or discuss many of these types of sexual pressures during the interviews, these incidents demonstrate the types of everyday pressures they face. Sexual experience, capacity, and equipment are all important aspects in the students' ideals of masculinity, and not measuring up to these ideals affects their self-esteem.

Despite the pressure to have a reputation for being sexually experienced, the boys rarely have "scoring" contests or keep a scorecard of conquests. Instead, they compare tallies verbally. As a boy in one dorm explains, "Guys are a lot more apt to brag about girls they've hooked up with than girls are. I mean, guys are always talking about it." He has not written it down, but "I've got mental notes." Although most of the boys in the dorm have never heard of males keeping a scorecard, one boy states, "Actually, I've seen that" at Bolton. He adds, "Not notches on a bedpost, but they actually marked it on a piece of paper, freaking tallies." Others exclaim, "Holy cow! I've never seen that."

How Much Sex?

The Bolton boys and girls face additional sexual pressures from the cultural ideals setting forth how sexually experienced a future spouse should be. For the girls the ideal is that they should have little, if any, sexual experience. Although some of the boys want experienced partners, many more want to marry women with minimal experience and would prefer to marry a virgin. Sexual inexperience and experience are associated with positive and negative attributes. The boys associate sexual inexperience in females with ineptitude and being a "complete idiot" sexually and too tight ("I can *not* have sex with virgins . . . my dick will *not* fit," states a popular hockey player), but also with future fidelity and cleanliness. Experience, on the other hand, is associated with high sexual appetite, being open to "freaky stuff," being "fun," and being competent at sex, but also with being "damaged goods," having STDs, being dirty, and future infidelity.

Most of the boys prefer that their wives have limited sexual experience. The sentiment "I wouldn't want her to be loose" or a "slut" is common. The main reason given is cleanliness. One boy wanting a more experienced wife argues, "Yeah, but she might know some new tricks that your little virgin wife won't." One of the other boys responds, "Yeah, but you don't want herpes when you're 40." At this, one of the other boys quips, "I'm 17 and I already have herpes."

While about half of the boys desire virgin wives, most of the others want their future spouse to have "minimal, definitely minimal" sexual experience or at least a limited number of partners. The boys commonly say: "A virgin is the ideal," "A virgin, and then I'd like her to get very experienced," and a virgin would be "ideal. I mean I would like her to be."

This male preference for marrying a virgin or someone with limited experience underscores the pressure girls face to remain within the bounds of appropriate sexual behavior. The contradiction between the boys' current sexual desires, played out in the pressure they place on the girls for sex, and the value they place on relative inexperience of girls belies one of the major contradictions of femininity the girls at Bolton must negotiate.

Although the boys face many pressures to conform sexually, the male sexual ideal to be experienced is straightforward. Almost all of the girls would prefer their husband to be at least as sexually experienced as, or more experienced than, they are. Many girls consider it "very important" for a male to be sexually experienced: "I get frustrated giving commands," "I don't want a guy fumbling on me," "It's really nice to have a guy who's *really* experienced" and "I want my guy to know more than me." Although a few of the girls like the idea of "breaking a guy in and teaching him," asserting, "I would rather have no experience at all than too much," none says she would prefer to marry someone who has less experience than she does, and none says she would like to marry a virgin (except one girl who is Muslim).

The girls at Bolton "definitely" do not want to marry a virgin. One girl states, "I wouldn't want to marry someone who's never experienced it." Others announce, "I definitely want him to be experienced," and "I don't want a virgin. I want a guy who knows what he's doing."

The two reasons given for wanting experienced husbands are so that they will be faithful and proficient. Several girls argue that if males have sexual encounters before marriage, they will get it out of their system:

> I wouldn't want a husband who after five years of marriage . . . wants to find out what others and stuff is all about. You know, I want them to experience it all before they marry me, so . . . you know.

The main reason for wanting a sexually experienced husband is that the girls equate experience with the ability to please women sexually. One girl exclaims, "Teach me something. Throw me against the wall." Another says, "He has to know what he's doing or it would suck." Others agree that with someone experienced, "sex would just be better."

Acknowledging Sexuality

The freedom to acknowledge one's sexuality and expect sexual fulfillment is an integral part of the sexual ideals. The male sexual ideal stresses a focus on self and self-pleasure, while the female one revolves around pleasing others rather than being pleased. Whereas the male ideal not only allows for but encourages a focus on sexual needs and enjoyment as well as sexual self-fulfillment and lack of restraint, the female ideal denies female sexuality and focuses on restraint and giving rather than receiving pleasure.

The boys' openness about their sexual needs contrasts sharply with the girls' reserve. Although the girls have sexual desires and enjoy sex, they do not discuss their own sexual urges, desires, or needs. The boys, on the other hand, are very open and almost try to outdo each other in discussing their sexual needs.

Many girls contend that females enjoy and want sex as much as boys. One girl unabashedly asserts, "I enjoy sex as much as *any* guy would." Others claim that boys enjoy sex more because they "always nut" (have an orgasm), while girls are not always sexually satisfied. One girl explains, "I don't think a guy cannot enjoy sex. I think a girl cannot enjoy sex." Others agree:

-It depends who you're with, if he sucks—

-Yeah, but even if a girl sucks, a guy will still enjoy it.

-How can a girl suck?

-It's better than their hand, okay, that's the bottom line.

The girls generally agree that the boys face more pressures to demonstrate their needs and that it is more accepted for boys to be open about their sexual desires. Although boys seem to want sex more, they "publicize the fact that they want it, and if a girl wants it, she may not say anything." The girls also contend that boys feel much more pressure from peers to want and to have sex than girls do. When some girls say, "Guys like it more at this age or they feel like they want it more," others comment, "But a lot of it's pressure from their friends to want it" and "Yeah, boys pressure each other to have it."

Although the boys cannot agree on whether or not females and males want or enjoy sex the same amount, they do agree that "guys talk about it more" and "are more open about it." Some of the boys contend that the girls do not want sex as much because they lack testosterone. Others exclaim, "Hell yeah—girls like sex as much as guys," but "they are just worried about what people will say" and so "girls try to hide it." One boy asserts:

Girls are hornier than guys! They just don't talk about it. Are you kidding me? Girls are *really* horny. They just don't talk about it because it shows weakness. That's why guys are so weak, 'cause [girls] know that you're horny and they aren't going to give you sex 'cause they know you're horny so they tease you.

When the other boy questions, "Why don't they give it to you, then?" He replies, "'Cause they're smarter than you. You're a guy. They can hold out longer."

Oral Sex

The expectations and the importance placed on giving and receiving sexual pleasure are part of the students' performances of masculinity and femininity. The performance of femininity centers around a girl giving more pleasure than she receives. The performance of masculinity, on the other hand, centers around getting as much pleasure as possible, and maybe, or maybe not, giving pleasure in return.

The amount of oral sex the girls perform, even though they generally do not enjoy it, reveals that gendered behavior is often not the result of real needs or desires. Because girls are supposed to care more about giving rather than receiving and because oral sex is less damaging to their reputations than vaginal sex and is "expected," most willingly do it even though they find it distasteful and "get nothing out of it."

The students recognize that a great deal of female-on-male oral sex takes place on Bolton's campus. Its frequency is due to its quickness, how much the males like it, and freedom from worries about pregnancy and (they mistakenly think) STDs. The girls do not regard it as "really" sex, so it is not as "big a deal." Remaining a virgin, girls can please their partners without the labels and ramifications of vaginal sex.

Many of the girls explain that oral sex happens more because it is "easier and guys always want it" or because "people are pressed for time and stuff." Others claim that oral sex occurs more often because "sex is too complicated." A downside to oral sex is that it carries somewhat the same stigma that vaginal sex has for a girl's reputation. In one dorm, a girl notes, "Once people find out that you're giving head, you get harassed by the guys." Another adds, "Yeah, like who gives the best head."

Although some boys contend that vaginal sex occurs more on Bolton's campus, most say that oral sex is more common:

-'Cause it's easier if someone comes into the room to cover it up.

-Just put a towel over her head.

-It's easy and quick.

When one of the students who said that he has more sex states, "All I'm saying is, fuck oral sex! It isn't real," they all agree but add that oral sex has its advantages:

-I think that's clear but, you know, in a pinch it's better than nothing, and it's a lot better than a hand job, 'cause let me tell you this, I can do it a lot better than she can.

-Definitely! Right on with that.

The boys also say oral sex is more frequent because it is a precursor to sex as well as safer in regard to pregnancy and STDs. In one dorm, the boys are unanimous that oral sex occurs before vaginal sex:

-'Cause it's part of fooling around.

-Yeah, yeah, it's not quite sex yet.

-It's getting the mood set.

-She's not going to have a baby from oral sex, and herpes is less likely.

Despite the large amount of female-on-male oral sex, not one girl says she likes to perform oral sex, and the girls would unanimously prefer to have vaginal sex rather than give oral sex. In one dorm, all but a few of the girls agree that oral sex comes before vaginal sex and is usually viewed as the step before vaginal sex. When one of the girls comments that she would have vaginal sex first, several of the girls are amazed and question, "Are you kidding? You have sex before giving a blow job?" To which the girl softly replies with a giggle, "Yeah, I don't want to go down there." The girls then agree that they would "rather have sex than give oral sex." At this, an African American girl who had said that sex comes first asks incredulously, "But you'd have oral sex before sex even though you'd rather the other?" When most of the girls reply affirmatively, she states, "I'd rather just jump in the sack."

Although the girls in one dorm acknowledge the large amount of oral sex that takes place at Bolton and that it occurs first in a relationship because "you have to go in order," they unanimously and enthusiastically agree that they "would rather have sex than give a blow job." One girl sighs, "It's so much easier."

One girl prefers vaginal sex to oral sex because she gets something out of it too:

> At least sex, I can tell myself in my mind, "Well, I got something out of it too" . . . but if I'm giving a blow job I can't justify it in my mind. The fact that you can't justify it screws with your mind and just makes you feel dirty. . . . So I feel like [with] sex I can be like, "Yeah, I wanted it. To get laid, it was my doing." But when I say, "I gave a blow job," I don't get anything out of it. It's more degrading.

Even though most girls would rather have vaginal sex because that is seen socially as "a bigger step," most girls, especially virgins, give oral sex.

Male-on-female oral sex is rarely mentioned. The few times it is discussed, some of the girls regard it negatively. In one dorm, several of the girls "don't like guys going down on them." One of the girls comments, "It's nasty." Another adds, "I feel bad for him."

Most of the boys also do not like to give oral sex. Although a few of the boys enjoy giving it, most make comments such as, "Who the hell wants to give that?" "It's disgusting!" and "I ain't doing that shit!" One boys admits the unfairness of girls having to perform oral sex but adds, "I mean, I feel bad for the girl, but they have tits and all those other good things we can play with, but we have that, so I'm sorry, but that's the way they have to go."

Again the responses Tyler receives on the senior trip to his provocative questions reveals much about the pressures males and females feel to conform sexually and to perform oral sex. Tyler asks the girls about oral sex, and one of them says that boys receive more oral sex because "I think it's a tendency for guys to be more assertive about what they want, as far as like sexual favors and stuff." Tyler ventures, "So the girls want it, but they're not going to ask for it." The girl replies, "Exactly." Tyler asks, "They're not going to demand it. Are they expecting it?" The girl responds, "I'm sure they wouldn't mind it. I'm sure they would enjoy it, but like I think they're just hoping that if they make the guy feel good enough and make him feel good, then he'll return the favor."

Tyler then asks her about males' attitudes toward receiving oral sex. He states knowingly, "A guy is expecting it, and if it doesn't happen, they get pretty pissed." The girl agrees, "They do. They get pissed. And, like, the guy will demand it, basically. Like, maybe not with words but, like, you know." Tyler adds, "With his fingers. 'Get down here.' They'll just whip it out and be like, 'Okay, now it's your turn.' But a girl won't get pissed if it doesn't happen?" The girls agree.

Tyler proceeds to yell to other students near him to elicit their views on oral sex. When he asks the boys if they are "willing to do it to a girl," they respond dividedly. Many say they will not perform oral sex. One says, "Lay it on the table, not below the navel." Another associates giving oral sex as negating one's masculinity, stating, "If you give oral sex, you're fuckin' queer."

Others are more open to it, especially if the girl is very attractive. One boy equivocates, "I don't know. Depends what the girl looks like." Another comments, "I'm not against it at all." One boy adds, "If I like the girl or she's extremely hot, I'm willing to do the deed." One boy even claims, "I actually like it quite a bit. As long as she's clean, yes." This is too much for Tyler, who has made it clear that he is "completely against it," and he exclaims, "You are? Dirty motherfuckers!"

Now the boys turn the tables on Tyler, asking him his own questions: "Are you willing? Have you ever given oral sex?" He replies, "Yes, and I hate it. I don't like that shit." At his response, two of the boys state that they "love it." One says, "I think it's great." The other adds, "I think it's amazing. A good time. A good time. Having a girl squirm all over the place because of you. Oh yeah!" In general, the boys who like giving oral sex give it freely, while those who do not feel no pressure to do so.

Tyler then asks the girls again, and three more girls say they'll perform oral sex. He then asks if they enjoy it. Their responses are lukewarm, to say the least. One answers, "I don't mind doing it. It doesn't bother me. It doesn't faze me one way or another." When Tyler asks her, "Do you expect oral sex in return?" she states flatly, "No."

Tina, the pretty and popular African American girl, stands out because she demonstrates a degree of self-orientation not evident among the white girls who discuss the issue. She shocks the interviewer by stating matter-of-factly, "I don't give head." Tyler exclaims in horror, "You don't give head! Oh, what a waste!" She adds coolly, "Not all guys like getting blow jobs." Tyler repeats unbelievingly, "Not all guys like blow jobs?" He then shouts to all the students on the bus, "Is there any guy on this bus that doesn't like getting blow jobs?" He receives a loud chorus of nos.

Later, however, Tina is very other-focused concerning sexual intercourse, as she would rather give than receive pleasure. Tina states that she has never really had an orgasm during sex and says, "I would rather give an orgasm than get one." "You don't want to have an orgasm?" Tyler asks incredulously. She replies, "Because it's something I don't usually get. I'm more into pleasing than being pleased."

Boys seem to perform oral sex if they enjoy it, but do not if they don't. Girls, on the other hand, feel obligated or expected to perform oral sex whether they enjoy it or not, and most do not. Males expect or demand oral sex, while the females do not. Although both genders state that they do not like giving oral sex, the boys seem to be much less pressured to do it anyway.

Ethnic and Cultural Differences

Due to ethnic and cultural differences, African American girls and girls from other countries differ from the other girls in their willingness to perform oral sex. In one dorm all the girls describe oral sex as happening first in relationships at Bolton except for one African American girl and a German girl who explains, "Back home, it's the other way around."

Ethnic differences in sexual preferences and expectations also surface when a group of boys describes the sexual "progression" among adolescents. Bobby, the only African American in the group, has different expectations than the other boys do. When one boy, Tim, says that his girlfriend gives him lots of head but that they have not had sex, Bobby replies, "That's messed up, man. How can you get head before you get ass?" The other boys explode, "What are you talking about?" and Tim bursts out, "Of course you get head before you get ass. I got a hand job before I got head or pussy, that's the progression." The others agree, "That's the progression. When you're, like, 14 you get a hand job, when you're 15 you have sex, and you get head somewhere in between."

Bobby explains the differences that exist between the sexual activity of black and white girls: "Black girls don't like giving head. See, that's why I didn't understand." One of the other boys agrees: "I've fucked black girls before. They don't like giving head, but white girls . . .," Bobby responds, "See, that's why I didn't expect that, because black girls don't give head, you know."

Thus, even though boys and girls share similar sexual needs and desires, the freedom to acknowledge one's sexuality and expect sexual fulfillment appears to be part of the masculine ideal but not the feminine one. The African American girls stand out, at least in regard to oral sex, for not succumbing to pressure to do something they do not enjoy.

From Virgin Queen to Hoochy Mama

Both the number of terms and the negativity of the terms for students who have too much or too little sex reveal the sexual ideals for each gender. Similar to studies examining slang terms for "male" or "female" used by university students (Sutton, 1995; Munro, 1990), the number and types of words used reveal considerable differences in what are acceptable and unacceptable characteristics for men and women.

The girls have a relatively large number of words for both males and females who have what is considered too much sex. The girls list 16 terms for a female who has too much indiscriminate sex, which include "slut," "whore," "self-conscious," "insecure," "ho," "stupid whore," "cum rag," "skank," "prostitute," "tramp," "hooker," "promiscuous," "nympho," "hooch," "hoochy mama," and "cum-guzzling gutter slut."

The girls list 13 terms for a male who has too much indiscriminate sex, which include "dirty," "slut," "schmuck," "player," "ho," "man whore," "man ho," "gigolo," "pimp," "asshole," "jerk," "hockey player," and "libertine." The girls explain that most of these terms do not have the same negative connotation as the words for female sexuality. Also, many of the girls claim, "There aren't any" or "They aren't really used."

The girls have the same number of terms for males and females who have what is seen as too little sex, but the tone or degree of negativity varies greatly. The 11 terms for a female who has too little sex include "prude," "virgin queen," "tight," "unhappy," "missing out," "innocent," "poor girl," "deprived," "just not wanting to have sex," "frustrated," and "suffering from LOP—lack of play." These terms are not very negative and are not said with a negative tone. Many have the connotation of control, and they do not strike at the essence of femininity.

The 11 terms the girls use for males who have too little sex include "gay," "loser," "impotent," "lame," "ugly," "sad," "gay ball," "small dinky," "homosexual," "gay ass," and "erectile dysfunction." Unlike the terms for females, these terms are negative and are said with a more negative tone. Because the terms often focus on homosexuality and connote a lack of power, they question the essence of a male's masculinity.

Thus, the large number of negative terms for females who have too much sex and for males who have too little and the focus on homosexuality for males but not for females indicate how essential sexual activity is for a boy's masculinity but not for a girl's femininity. Heterosexuality, sexual experience, and competence are vital for a male to be seen as masculine, while a female's sexual history defines what kind of female she is but does not question the essence of her femininity.

The disparity between the number and negativity of the boys' terms for males and females who have too much sex is even greater than those of the girls'. The 15 terms the boys use for a woman who has too much indiscriminate sex are "slut," "ho," "skank," "butt whore," "chicken head," "ho bag," "whore," "bus station skank," "prostitute," "dirty putang," "penis popper," "pussy giver," "nympho," "my fantasy," and "sperm bank."

The boys' 9 terms for a male who has too much indiscriminate sex include "player," "yeah!" "the man," "wife beater," "shaft," "bad motherfucker," "the king," "gigolo," and "pimp." Four of the nine terms are extremely positive, and the others do not have a negative connotation. Several dorms cannot list any and only say, "There is no such thing" or "That question is irrelevant!" Others list one or two and then add, "But it's not derogatory" or "But it's not a bad term." Some of the terms, such as "the king" and "the man," connote power.

The boys' 16 terms for a woman who has too little sex include "prude," "bitch," "ugly," "cold," "worthless," "my girlfriend," "deprived," "not fun," "tease," "frigid," "cocktease," "tight," "dumb little bitch," "stupid," "a waste of pussy," and "new."

The boys' terms for a man who has too little sex include "fucking dick," "ass," "gay," "pussy," "priest," "someone who hasn't had the opportunity," "loser," "faggot," "insecure," "fag," "bitch," "wimp," and "pussy." Although the boys list only 13 terms compared to 16 for the girls, they are much harsher in their focus on homosexuality, a lack of power, and a negation of masculinity.

Thus, the boys and girls use the most terms for females who both have too much sex and too little sex, illustrating how a woman's sexuality is of public concern. Each gender's terms for males who have too little sex call into question a male's power and thus his total masculinity. The boys' terminology demonstrates that the option of a male choosing not to have sex if presented with the opportunity would be considered unacceptable male behavior. This terminology confirms the sexual double standard that exists among the students at Bolton and reveals the conflicting nature of female sexual ideals.

Homosexuality

Girls

Because of the conservative nature of both the students and faculty, the girls generally agree that boarding schools are the most "homophobic place in the world." One girl asserts, "I have never been in an area, in a school, in a place, *anywhere* that is as homophobic as this."

The girls also agree, "The faculty are a big reason it's like that here. There are a lot of old-fashioned people." One girl recalls an incident where one young male faculty member was "openly really dick" to another faculty member who had come out of the closet and admitted his homosexuality. This homosexual faculty member, although much loved by the students, addressed the school in chapel one morning after some of his artwork had been vandalized with anti-homosexual slurs. He explained to the school, "Being homosexual is only part of who I am." Soon after, this teacher left the school.

The girls believe that the students are more tolerant of homosexual faculty than they are of homosexual students. One student explains, "I think it's different with teachers. I think people are okay with teachers being it but *definitely* not students."

The girls contend that for the most part at Bolton "females are more tolerant" and that "guys aren't tolerant at all." The only negative remarks the girls make publicly are that they feel "uncomfortable" with homosexuality or that it's "hard" to see. Some girls wish the students would be more open at Bolton and challenge those who disapprove of homosexuality. Some of the girls condemn others' use of the word "gay" and take delight in the thought of homosexual students "coming out" to challenge rigid constraints of heterosexuality among the students at Bolton. One girl comments, "People should just stand up and say, 'I'm bisexual, so you all know, and you don't have to ask me again . . . and life goes on.' Just to break Bolton's window."

Because of the lack of openly homosexual boys on campus and intolerance, the girls say, "I'd fear for a guy if he became open here." Hearing of openly "gay girls but not guys" at Bolton, the girls believe that girls are more "accepting" of homosexuality. A few girls argue, however, that "girls are more scared of having a lesbian on their hall." The girls agree that they are more willing to befriend a homosexual, while boys are scared they themselves will be tainted by any sort of acceptance.

One girl who confided in me that she is a lesbian reveals the hidden nature of intolerance among the girls and how she (and presumably other homosexual students on campus) must hide her sexual orientation. During a group interview she asserts, "There are so many homophobic people at this school it's not even funny. I mean, this school stresses diversity but . . . never mind . . ." She trails off and does not finish. The other girls in her hall do not know she is homosexual. Later she writes me:

> I have often assumed [Bolton] to be a much more open and understanding campus than many, however, the constant use of the words "fag" or "gay" have and still continue to make me uncomfortable. They have shamed me, and made me much more protective of what I share with other people about myself. I've had many late-night conversations in the dorm where the degradation of gays has occurred though I have yet to stand up and say something. Many of my friends are homophobic. At this school I will never be confident enough or comfortable enough to speak my mind on my own sexuality.

Boys

In their everyday lives, the boys face immense pressure to prove and confirm their heterosexuality. The fear of being labeled "gay" and the huge stigma attached to it intensify their other-focused behavior. Unlike the girls, the boys are openly negative about homosexuality. The males find it necessary, perhaps, to act in this manner in order to distance themselves as far as possible from the dreaded homosexual and his lack of masculinity.

The vast majority of the boys exhibit disgust, hatred, and contempt toward homosexuals. The contempt with which the boys in one dorm talk about homosexuality illustrates the grave intolerance on campus and perhaps explains why not one boy is open about his homosexuality:

-If a male student came out of the closet—

-We wouldn't talk to him.

-Yeah, we wouldn't talk to him after we all beat him senseless. [Laughter]

Many of the boys do not even want to discuss homosexuality. In one dorm, when I ask about homosexuality, one boy states, "Let's skip that one!" and the other boys utter words of disgust and reluctance to "talk about fucking homos."

Many of the boys claim that female homosexuality and bisexuality are more tolerated and even viewed as a male fantasy. One boy comments, "Women bi's are okay, but guys aren't." Another boy adds, however, "No. Girl bi's are only all right if they are willing to do a threesome."

The special circumstances of boarding school are seen as contributing to the intolerance for homosexuality. The boys in one dorm explain, "There is no tolerance" for homosexuality, "not when you're living with the fucking people." Others contend that homophobia is more pronounced at Bolton "because of living together and showering together." One boy adds, "It *really* matters, even if it's a really cool person." Another describes "gay bashing" as "so social. If lots of people are together and they see something on TV, they are like, 'Turn off the TV!' and 'Break the TV.'"

Homosexuality is yet another way in which the Bolton students view prep school students as differing from other adolescents. One group of boys is adamant that "there are no gay kids here." They admit, "Yeah, there's lesbians, but there ain't no gay guys." The boys then question how many homosexual males there really are at prep school and, after citing the reported national average, comment, "I don't think one out of ten prep school students is gay."

Both the difference in the overt intolerance of the male and female students at Bolton for homosexuality in their own gender and the threat homosexuality poses to males' entire manhood are connected to extremes in gender ideals. Males are allowed and even encouraged to be openly abusive to others, especially other males with whom they might be in competition, and thus homosexuality violates the very definition of manhood. This intolerance transforms into immense pressure, almost entirely among the boys, to prove that they are not gay, and the fear of being labeled as gay accentuates the gendered behavior among the boys. Despite the intensity of the negative attitudes toward homosexuality, just a few years after my research at Bolton the climate was slowly beginning to change, and a few faculty members and students openly supported gay rights and were open about their own homosexuality.

:: FITTING IN WITH FRIENDS

The many direct and indirect ways adolescents feel pressure to conform to group standards are evident among these students. At Bolton, because of the unique situation of boarding school with its constant exposure to peers as students sleep, eat, study, and play together, the wide variety of individuals in such close contact, and the particular institutional values, peers groups are of primary importance. As Cookson and Persell (1985) contend, "One of the consequences of the intensity of the prep crucible is that the usual adolescent behavior of seeking peer group support and approval is heightened" (p. 21). Both the large degree to which peer groups influence individuals' behavior and the variety of ways and intensity with which this influence takes place are evident in the daily lives of these adolescents.

The effects of the peer groups are strong because they influence the students' behavior in two ways. First, the students respond to the pressures they feel to conform to group standards in order to maintain membership in that group. Second, the divisions the students create among themselves based on group membership exacerbate differences and often cause groups to pressure their members to exhibit extreme behaviors in order to fit in. The symbolic oppositions central to these students' lives center around their need both to belong yet to distinguish themselves from others. Thus, individuality and conformity are negotiated differently in the gendered performances of these boys and girls. Both genders face intense pressure to stand out and rise above others as well as to conform in order to be popular. Masculinity is performed by acting cool and having power, and femininity is performed by being cute and having control. Yet, despite these gender ideals, both genders covertly desire or display the unapproved qualities and often must hide them because they are not part of the accepted performances.

The masculine ideals of individuality mirror the overt values of all the students as well as larger cultural and institutional values, while feminine ideals of conformity are diametrically opposed to what is publicly valued. This difference results in the devaluation of both women and femininity by both boys and girls. The girls face the near impossibility of being perfect. Males, on the other hand, while they do not face as much hypocrisy, must still meet high expectations of being the best at everything as well as survive the expectation of a lack of intimacy, caring, and dependency.

The sexual attitudes of these adolescents are a mixture of sexual conservatism and liberalness, differing substantially from what others describe as a sexual liberalness among American teenagers.[5] The students at Bolton are sexually conservative in that they describe intolerance for homosexuality and social persecution for females who do not conform to the amount of sexual control expected. On the other hand, they describe a sexual liberalness not noted by other researchers in that social punishments, such as being deemed a "slut," are reserved for girls who have "too many" partners and not what type of sex they practice with their partner. The students also describe sex as being more casual and "not such a big deal" as it used to be, with such casual sex being accepted as part of "the teenage scene."

This sexual conservatism and liberalness are incongruous and undoubtedly cause much sexual confusion and frustration among the girls. Despite the students' own descriptions of American adolescents becoming more sexually liberal, these students either have maintained or reverted back to a sexual conservatism. This conservatism can be explained by New England's traditional conservatism as well the scare of AIDS and other STDs (although the students at Bolton do not appear to be particularly worried about these diseases).

5 ::

Differences at Bolton: Race, Class, and More

How the students manipulate and negotiate the opposition between equality and inequality reveals their intense need to separate from others in order to belong. By endorsing inequality and separating themselves from others, they secure connections and belonging, preferably among a high-status group. Whether it is in regard to gender, socioeconomic class, race, sexual orientation, day students versus boarders, form standing, or peer groups, these students create divisions among themselves in order to belong and gain status in the social hierarchy. The students then perform gender, class, and ethnicity in an effort to maintain relationships and status.

Researchers have paid little attention to social class, especially the upper class, in current research on peer groups (see Rubin, Bukowski, & Parker, 1998). The *crowd*, a large peer group based on reputation, and the *clique*, usually smaller groups of same-sex and same-race friends (Kinderman, McCollom, & Gibson, 1996), are the primary social groups of adolescence. Researchers report that not only do teenagers in America typically spend with their peers more than double the amount of time they spend with adults (Csikszentmihalyi & Larson, 1984) but also that this time spent with peers is largely unsupervised by adults (B. B. Brown, 1990). Adolescents report that their friends are of more or equal importance to them in terms of support and advice than their parents (Buhrmester, 1990, 1996; Furman & Buhrmester, 1992). Further, developmental changes occurring in adolescence have been found to increase the influence of peer groups in regard to appearance, values, attitudes, and participation in illicit behaviors. Despite their importance to teenagers, membership in these groups tends to wane in late adolescence (Gavin & Furman, 1989), and usually by senior year in high school both the importance placed on belonging to a clique and interclique conflicts have declined (Larkin, 1979) and students tend less to clump peers into a narrow range of types (Brown & Clasen, 1986).

Researchers recognize not only that individuals "do difference" as "an ongoing interactional accomplishment" (West & Fenstermaker, 1995) but also that peer groups are important in the formation of gender, class, and ethnic/racial dichotomies. Members of groups create differences between themselves and other groups where none previously existed (Harris, 1995). The cohesion within a group is heightened when group members compare themselves to another group (Turner, Hogg, Oaks, Reicher, & Wetherell, 1987) and perceive themselves as more alike or different from the other group than they really are (Wilder, 1986; Williams & Best, 1982; Turner et al., 1987). This human tendency to create differences between ourselves and others and then to "do difference" is evident as the Bolton students negotiate a variety of roles and hierarchies in their daily lives.

The peer groupings found among the Bolton students are different in some respects than those described for other adolescents because of their immersion in boarding school life and their mostly upper-class social status. Perhaps because of the intensity of contact and the institutional emphasis on competition and success at prep school, divisions based on cliques, race, socioeconomic classes, class standing, and being a day student or a boarder are especially prominent. Among the Bolton students there is a correlation between a student's high socioeconomic status and the relative importance the student places on class and difference. At the same time, however, the smallness of the population and the many (often forced) commonalities among the students result in some unusual connections and a special closeness amongst the students.

Although the cultural and institutional emphasis on independence, hierarchy, and excellence appear to give extra impetus to the need to separate in order to belong, most students generally reveal an unfailing overt belief in equality and often insist on relative equality in their lives vis-à-vis the outside world due to the special characteristics of boarding school. The students explain away much of the inequality at Bolton as due to the need for connections with others, rationalizing the disparity between their values and their realities by focusing on comfort levels, similarities, and upbringing rather than on discrimination or inequality. Certain inequalities such as race and class are cloaked within a "discourse of invisibility" (Ortner, 2003), but the students admit to inequalities between genders, peer groups, and boarder versus day students and unabashedly argue for more inequality between forms. Although the boys and girls publicly endorse equality, they privately find security and acceptance by enforcing the inequality that affirms their membership within select groups.

The interplay between social categories is multifaceted, and individuals must come to terms with or prioritize conflicting identities. The Bolton students are continually "doing difference" (West & Fenstermaker, 1995) in their social interactions, harboring many different identities, which they stress or mute according to the context. The clash between race, ethnicity, and class is strong for some of these students, and their performances of these opposing identities define the dimensions of each category and its relative importance in their concept of self.

Students from the lower classes and students of color are expected to acquire the "habits of the heart" (Kuriloff & Reichert, 2003) of the upper class from their education at Bolton, but many resist in an effort not to sell out, and some experience academic and social difficulty as a result. The African American students are exceptionally successful at Bolton, giving credence to the suggestion that African Americans at elite private schools are able to negotiate the academic and social geography of the school more successfully than other marginalized groups because of their collective power to address class and race issues, which allows them to accept and embrace the benefits of their elite education without selling out (Kuriloff & Reichert, 2003).

:: OVERT VALUE OF EQUALITY

In public both the boys and girls demonstrate an unfailing belief in equality, concerned that everyone be treated "fairly" at Bolton, especially in terms of disciplinary situations and privileges. Often the inequalities concerning disciplinary cases, race, socioeconomic class, day student versus boarder, form standing, and gender are paramount in the students' minds and on their list of grievances against the school administration or society in general.

The majority of the platforms presented by the students seeking election either as school president or as a member of the Disciplinary Committee focus around treating everyone at the school equally. One male running for president appeals to the students' concerns for equality, assuring them that if he is elected he will provide "more freedom and comfort. . . . All we students want is consistency in decisions made by the Disciplinary Committee."

Almost all of the Disciplinary Committee platforms revolve around the need for equality. One girl writes, "We are all kids and we all make mistakes. I do not think it is right that some kids get let off the hook and others are harshly treated." Another boy echoes this belief in equality, writing, "Every student sent before the Committee should receive the same attention and be given the rightful punishment for his or her actions; no special treatment should be given to anyone."

Many newspaper articles in the school paper report how frustrated the students are with the "inconsistency" of the disciplinary system. In an article entitled "Disciplinary Consistency Questioned," the students write, "Many of those [students] polled believed that there was favoritism in the rulings of the headmaster. These respondents felt that girls, varsity athletes, faculty favorites and students with money received an easier time."

Endorsing equality, some students talk about the pain of bigotry and exclusion in their chapel speeches. One Jewish girl talks about how she was shunned as a playmate by other families when she was growing up and how she came to deny her heritage. Announcing that hiding her background is over, she lets everyone know that she is Jewish and proud of it. Another girl places large graphic paintings at the entrance of the chapel depicting her grandfather in a Nazi concentration camp. In her speech, she describes his ordeal and then explains that her paintings help her to celebrate his courage and to understand and come to terms with the horror her grandfather experienced. A Chinese American girl speaks about the pain of lining up after a hockey game to shake hands and having opposing players call her a "chink." All of these students advocate equality, calling for tolerance and an end to discrimination.

:: COVERT VALUE OF INEQUALITY

Despite this overwhelming public emphasis on equality and fairness, the students at the top of the social, class, form, gender, or racial hierarchy show and sometimes endorse inequality and favoritism as natural and "only right." Such inequalities are undeniable among the students at Bolton and are often paramount among the students' concerns.

On Martin Luther King Jr.'s birthday, Nicole, an African American student on scholarship, delivers an eloquent speech to the school community outlining the amount and types of inequality and "ignorance" occurring on campus. Nicole first contends, "Ignorance is running rampant on this campus." She then asks a series of questions, each referring to recent incidents at Bolton that all ran counter to the ideal of equality:

> Why has music, the international language, the medium that breaks cultural barriers, divided us as a community?
> Why has sitting at a table with people you culturally identify with, those that look like you, talk like you, and understand you, become a reason for alarm?
> Why has befriending people outside your race created an uncomfortable situation inside your race? Race is a color line, a possibility, not a basis for friendship.
> Why does being here and not being able to pay for it make you less of a commodity to your peers?
> Why is being a teenager an automatic signal of immaturity and rebellion? Wisdom is a state of mind, not an age. Maturity is not directly proportional to age.
> Why is sensitivity gender-specific? Gender is your biological makeup, not your psychological makeup.
> Why can't a student at a place where they should feel the safest be able to walk through the locker room without being confronted by unnecessary hate?

One of the issues she touches upon is how tastes in music divide the campus. Often the proponents of traditional rock, the preppies' music, devalue and do not accept rap, country, punk, emo, metal, and hardcore. This intolerance of alternative genres of music is indicative and perhaps symbolic of the intolerance among people as well. The music war on campus is a fitting metaphor for the intolerance and closed-mindedness often evident among the student body.

Music tastes have changed drastically in the few years since I conducted my research, and now almost everyone at Bolton listens to rap, evidence of the strong influence of mainstream youth culture. This trend is similar to what is happening nationwide, as rap's influence has been far-reaching and in line with the rapidly growing, covert prestige of black English vernacular among white teenagers, who incorporate words from hip-hop music into their slang in order to appear cool (Chapman, 1986; Sutton, 1995; Munro, 1990). A current Bolton student tells me that the white students now often attempt to act "ghetto" to look cool, adding "I constantly hear rap music blaring, and I hear the preppy white girls say things like 'word' or 'peace' or 'fo' sho'.'"

The music incident Nicole refers to in her speech occurred before prom, when some students were reported to have said that they didn't want "black music"—their term for rap—at the prom, as there had been the previous year. This provocation upset many of the African American students.

A music war also rages in the music folder of the campus web page. Often students will bash one of the alternative music genres, and others then react, not only promoting the merits of the genre but also telling everyone to have an open mind. The exchanges are heated. The types of bashing include such postings as "I hate rap, that's all I wanted to say," "Rap is worthless and pointless," "You know what music is really horrible? Punk and emo, that stuff is pathetic," "If you listen to frickin' metal, that is not music . . . metal and hardcore are both just a bunch of yelling and random stuff mixed together to make a sound. *Not music*," and "Country sucks so much it is unbelievable. Country should be banned from this world."

The tendency for mostly boys to do the bashing might be explained both by the acceptability of open conflict for boys as well as the idea that such bashing is, as one girl postulates, an effort to be "cool."

∷ GOING TO DC

Believing that everyone should be treated equally, students view the school's disciplinary system negatively because of perceived inequalities when students get in trouble and have to go in front of the disciplinary committee (DC). Every dorm describes the disciplinary system as "inconsistent," explaining that the administration "can tell who they want to get and who they don't want to get" and "It all depends on whether they like you or not."

Despite their unwavering belief in equality, both sexes sometimes rationalize the inequalities and say that they can "understand" it. One girl states about favoritism, "That's just how it works out anywhere." Others add that some favoritism does "make sense." Some boys complain that athletes are "absolutely" favored. Another boy understands why the administration might keep exceptional students and not others in order to maintain the institution's strength:

> I know they want the best for our school and that's great and everything, but sometimes I wonder if that's right. And not just athletes, anything that would make Bolton better and that a student can give them, they'll keep them.

Others agree: "You can't really blame the school" because "if something's going to benefit the school they're going to have to go against the system a little bit." The boys identify the favored groups as the "athletes" and the "rich."

Although the students *understand* this inequality, rarely do they *endorse* it. If they do endorse it, they do so usually because they are part of a group receiving the preferential treatment. The wealthiest students sometimes openly assert that because they contribute more financially to the school, they should get preferential treatment.

The students' belief in equality is so strong that it often overrides the usual positive attitudes toward beating the system or breaking the rules and not getting caught. In one case, the students are up in arms because the headmaster used a "silver bullet" and allowed an African American boy, Ben, to stay at Bolton after his third offense. The students contend, "He got more chances because he was black or because he was a hockey player and singer." When a black girl argues that the headmaster was right in letting Ben stay because of the dire situation at his home, arguing, "Everywhere you go in life there are loopholes," the other girls vehemently disagree. Labeling his treatment as preferential, the boys condemn Ben for not changing: "He was ripped every night, walking around Halsey and Penderson at three in the morning like a retard. . . . He probably got too many chances. . . . 'Cause he didn't change."

:: RACE

In most schools and institutions in this country, whiteness is viewed not as an ethnicity but rather as the norm, with nonwhite individuals seen as "ethnic" and "other." This separation of whiteness as "non-ethnic" serves to hide its privileged status (see McIntosh, 1988). Fine (2004) argues that we must focus not only on the disadvantaged but also on the "micromoves by which Whiteness accrues privilege and status in schools," how "Whiteness grows surrounded by protective pillows of resources and second chances," and how especially upper-class whiteness "provokes assumptions of and then insurances for being seen as 'smart'" (p. 245).

At prep schools, whites have numerous advantages, not only the obvious advantages that wealth, high social status, being the majority, and lack of prejudices bring, but also much more subtle ones (see McIntosh, 1988). White students do not have to worry that others assume they are lazy or violent or will steal their things. If white students get in trouble or don't do well, they do not have to worry that their actions will be viewed as indicative of the failings of their race. White students do not need to fear being outspoken lest they be labeled as "uppity" and their futures compromised. Similarly, they do not have to feel that others believe they are less deserving of being at the school and are there simply to fill a quota or serve as a token for diversity.

Race relations at Bolton are a complex mix of acknowledged racial tensions and self-segregation and an unfailing belief in equality and insistence by the students that race is "not an issue" at Bolton. The students often explain away racial issues as due to the simple need for connections with "similar" individuals.

Several major race-related incidents occur during the year that upset the students. First, a swastika is found carved in the girls' locker room in the gym. One of the most beloved teachers at Bolton, who is Jewish, stands up at a school meeting and, crying, says this incident has shaken her and her family.

Several racial slurs occur among the students, upsetting many of the African American students. At chapel on Martin Luther King Jr. Day, several African American girls give what some consider inflammatory and accusatory speeches lambasting the entire school community for standing by and not actively doing something about the racism occurring at Bolton every day.

Despite what many refer to as a "difficult year" with more tensions than usual, most of the students say race relations at Bolton are better than in the "outside world." Citing their exposure at Bolton to other races as well as the low level of racism tolerated by the school officials and students themselves, the students say repeatedly (especially the white students, but even the most critical minority students tend to agree) that due to the forced proximity and interactions, the students at Bolton Academy are better educated about different races and are more tolerant. (This coincides with the conclusion of Festinger, Schachter, and

Black [1950] that mere proximity is an important factor in relationship formation. Nahemow and Lawton [1975] found that pairs of best friends who differed by race or age were particularly apt to live close to each other. Wilder and Thompson [1980] demonstrated that individuals form positive views toward others they spend time with, even if they are from a group previously disliked.) The students believe that a type of education takes place when different groups are forced to eat, sleep, have classes, and participate in sports together, and that this lessens racial disharmony. They point out that several of the students recently elected to the post of class president and other important leadership positions have been African American.

Most of the students believe that although the minority students are not very well integrated with the rest of the students, race is "really not an issue" at Bolton. One boy comments, "There really aren't any barriers to begin with. It's ten times better [than society at large]." The white students typically state: "I think it's cool here," "There's no problem with race here. I haven't seen any," and "I think it's really good here, to tell you the truth."

Although race relations on campus are "relaxed in general" and many students of different racial/ethnic groups are "close friends," there is still self-segregation. The students note: "All the Asians live together," "The whole Asian thing," and "All the black people sit together" at lunch.

The students explain this self-segregation as "natural" and claim that it results from a deep need for connections with others. Some white boys say of the black students, "Well, they kind of segregate themselves," but add that "it's not necessarily in a bad way" and "no one has a problem with that." One boy comments, "You find some sort of connection, you know. I mean, it's just more natural." Another adds, "It happens everywhere" and segregation "lets them find a better social connection somehow."

Some students point to language to explain why Asian students self-segregate, lumping all the Asian students together even though they speak many different languages. This becomes apparent in one dorm when one boy says, "It's not ethnicity. The Asian kids separate themselves and hang out together so they can speak Thai." At this, others exclaim, "Are you kidding me? They don't all speak Thai. Half of them speak Korean...." The first boy insists, "Yeah, some, but they hang out together so they can speak their language." Others again refute his claims and point out, "But they don't speak the same languages." The first boy then states that their self-segregation is because "they have a connection. . . . It's just one of those things. They separate themselves."

Racial segregation differs among the ethnic groups at Bolton. Although both Asians and blacks tend to hang out by themselves, the Asians are more segregated while the blacks are "more social with everyone else." The students attribute this difference to a "pretty substantial" language barrier the Asian students face.

The students tend to explain away the segregation between the different races as being due to similarities, not because of discrimination. They assert that the different races stick to their own because "they enjoy each other's company," "they share things," "birds of a feather flock together," and "that's what they choose to do." One girl faults parental teaching for any racism: "If there are any issues, it's few. And it's just that their parents are racist, and that's what they were taught." Another girl says, "At our age, being teenagers, we're all really insecure, so we need a place of comfort where we can be, like, really comfortable with our friends. And, like, find that secure place."

The numerous incidents and amount of tension, the accounts of the African American students, and the insights of several students (both white and black) that racist ideas are prevalent but hidden at Bolton betray a complex reality full of inequalities. Some white students are uncomfortable that the African American and Asian students separate themselves in the dining hall, citing it as evidence of racial discord at Bolton. The whites view the minority students as self-segregating, rather than being segregated. One African American points out that because the African American and Asian students are the minority, they are more noticeable. Both black and white students explain away the racial separation that occurs between the black and white students, who are otherwise socially integrated, as a "comfort" issue and not one of discrimination or exclusion. Often the black students want to sit together, and because their being together is obvious, they are forced to defend their sitting together as not excluding others. The segregation of the Asians, on the other hand, who are rather separate from the rest of the Bolton community, is explained as due to comfort issues as well as linguistic, cultural, and musical differences.

The exceptions to this racial division among the students reveal the interconnection between gender, class, and ethnic performances. Repeatedly it is pointed out that "there are exceptions," and three girls stand out by crossing the color line. Two are Mercedes and Chanel, the wealthy black girls who are members of the "bitch squad" and whose friends are almost all white (although their boyfriends are black). These girls have issues with the other black girls. The other is a middle-class white girl who has mainly black friends and dates blacks. Although all are seemingly well accepted by the ethnic/racial group they join, they have issues with the ethnic/racial group they have left. Similarly, the black students who date whites (in all cases these are males) are often viewed as traitors by other black students.

Most of the students agree that the special circumstances of boarding school result in fewer racial issues, attributing this to how quickly others would find out about any racism due to the speed of the rumor mill at Bolton, the low tolerance of both the administration and other students for racist behavior, and the education that exposure to other races/ethnicities brings with it. A boy notes, "You kind of find it hard to be racist when you get to know someone of a certain race. When you really get to know them, it's like, 'Oh, I like them.'" A girl agrees, explaining that at her old public school "in honors classes you would never see a black person or a Hispanic or anything. You were totally separated from them."

Others observe that at boarding school people blend more not because the students are the same but because "there are less of a lot of the same kind of person . . . so you tend to be more open with who you hang out with."

Race relations at Bolton are either better or worse than at home depending on where the students come from. One boy from a wealthy area says, "There aren't any people, like, other than white people" where he lives, so to him there is more obvious racism at Bolton. Students from more ethnically mixed neighborhoods mostly view racism to be less of a problem at Bolton. One states, "It's definitely a lot less, especially coming from my school, which had the neo-Nazis. It's a lot less strained here. Like, there's a lot less bigotry and ignorance in terms of racist stuff."

Some boys discuss the covert nature of racism at Bolton:

-There's racist stuff but not, like, open.

-There are the people, but it's not generally accepted and you can't get away with it.

-A lot more people look down on it here, so kids that are racist have to hide it more.

Other boys notice that racism is kept hidden at Bolton: "There are definitely some racists here. They are definitely closet racists, though." They explain that at Bolton students are not "open about" it because:

-There are more authorities watching over us.

-If you said something that was racist to somebody that took it seriously, you'd be out in a second.

-They just don't say it. There's not less racism.

The only black boy present, who has been sitting quietly and listening, finally adds, "I think it's underground. There definitely isn't more or less here. It just isn't as open."

In one boys' dorm where no minorities are present, the boys' dialogue is very racist. After they compare the large boats that their families own, they criticize diversity day, a day the school uses to celebrate diversity on the campus. During the conversation, they call the black group of kids on campus "soul train" and then continue:

-Somebody always lets something slip, whether it's nigger, coon, or whatever . . .

-So what? Fuckin' spic, chink, gook, fuckin' . . .

-WASP.

-Dude, WASP is a good thing. I'm a WASP.

-Wop. Yea, Wops suck.

-Fuckin' greaseball.

After several boys mention how the Korean and Thai kids never sit together, but say they cannot understand it because "they're all the same," another boy responds, "To us, but to them it's like the whites and the blacks."

Although the black boys are generally quiet about race issues at Bolton, many of the black girls are vocal about them. Daudi and Kesi dominate a discussion about race in one dorm, not hesitating to share their views. Because of the music issue at prom and other incidents, the race issues at Bolton are tense. Earlier, a black teacher called the girls out to talk about these racial tensions. I did not know what was being said, but I could tell that there had been some confrontations between students. When Daudi and Kesi return and I ask about race relations, they laugh and one says, "It depends if we're talking right now or when I first came here," adding that current racial tensions are "a little heated!" and "right now it's like a powder keg going off."

The race issues at Bolton have taken a toll on Daudi and Kesi, as they make clear:

-As much as we say that we live in this bubble, I have to deal with so much more here than I would at home. It's different.

-It's so intense.

-Yeah, it's a different intensity level. If I was at home I would just turn off, walk out, go home to my house. But this is my house.

-Exactly. This is your house, your town, your state.

-Your school. This is your everything right now.

The students' views of interracial dating mirror this ideal of equality and the hidden reality of inequality. Describing interracial dating positively, some students claim "nobody cares" and "it's not a big deal" and that quite a few black boys date or "hook up" with white girls. However, the contradictory views, although infrequently aired, demonstrate the complexity of the issue. One boy comments, "I think what happens is that some of the students who come here, white or black, some of them grow up in communities that are all white, all black, all Chinese, so that when they come here, it just seems wrong." One girls views some people's acceptance as a facade:

I think there are a lot of people who pretend to accept it but in their minds are like, "Whoa, what's going on?" And they put up a front at this school because they feel like they need to be obligated to be like, "Yeah, we're cool with it."

The people who openly disapprove of interracial dating are black girls and parents of white girls dating black boys. I first become aware of this parental disapproval when the girls are talking about their parents' attitude as well as how a white girl's mother did not want her to go to prom because her date was black. The black girls disapprove of interracial dating not because they are against it but because they get left out of the mix. Not once during my ten years at the school did I see a black girl dating a white boy, although the opposite happened quite frequently. In one girls' dorm, the black girls' frustration is obvious. When a white girl comments, "Honestly, I think it's a lot more lax here" than in society at large, a black girl, Kara, points out the selective nature of this acceptance: "Black guys and white girls is relaxed, it's free. But I have yet to see a black girl with a white guy." Neema, another African American girl, who is large, adds, "I tried. I tried a few times," proceeding to describe how she had approached a few white males but they had not been interested. The black girls admit that this trend is similar to what one would find in society at large.

When several white girls say that they are now are open to dating black boys, this does not seem to make the black girls happy. One of the white girls states, "To be honest, before I came here I never would have thought about it, like, dating someone who's black, but now my opinion has definitely changed. Because some people I've just gotten to know and . . ." At this several other white girls chime in, "Yeah, I'd go out with a black guy" and "Yeah, definitely." Neema agrees but adds that the lack of options also makes a difference: "I never would have thought as much about going out with a white guy, but here your options are severely limited. If I say I'm only going out with black guys, well, four are taken, and one I don't like." Kara interjects, "And one doesn't shower!" The black girls then describe the gender differences in acceptability in inter-racial dating:

-It seems like black guys are a very hot commodity right now . . . anyone will go out with them . . . whereas [laughs] black women have a stereotype of being aggressive and domineering.

-Too much to handle.

-That it's harder to date outside of your race as a black woman.

The African American students face the challenge of being ethnic/racial and class minorities at Bolton as well as the pressures of not selling out to the white establishment. The conflicts of African American students have been described by both researchers and by former prep school students themselves (Anson, 1987; Lorene, 1991; Zweigenhaft & Domhoff, 2003; Kuriloff & Reichert, 2003). In order to succeed in the white establishment, African American students at prep schools feel that they have to learn how to "act in a certain way" and that they are at prep school (or the perception is that they are there) to learn how to act white. Their experience at prep school increases their "elite cultural and social capital" and allows them to accumulate economic capital (Zweigenhaft &Domhoff, 2003). (Zweigenhaft and Domhoff describe the graduates of a scholarship program as being aware of their having acquired this "elite cultural capital" and being aware of its value. The students describe the knowledge to include both academic mastery and the confidence to fit in socially with the upper class.). Many students try to achieve these advantages without "selling out" to the values of the white elite, learning how to shuttle between black and white cultures by changing their dress, speech, music preferences, and behavior when among whites in order to become part of elite society. The amount of resistance the African Americans at Bolton demonstrate to assimilating into white society appears greater than that described by Zweigenhaft and Domhoff (2003) for earlier generations of scholarship students.

Often the African American students at Bolton describe "toning down" their ethnicity when at school and not "making waves" but at the same time maintaining class and ethnic divisions in order not to sell out. Non-preppy clothing and footwear choices help them to maintain their ethnic identities. Although many of the African American boys date white girls, they don't view it as selling out; however, the black girls do, judging by the resentment they express. The black girls regard a tall, handsome, muscular football star who is black and a senior as a "male ho" because he had sex with a large number of white girls, many of whom are sophomores.

Sheena attends Bolton through the program A Better Chance, which prepares and places poor but academically motivated African Americans from New York City at prep schools. Sheena is candid to the school community and me about her belief that racism abounds on campus. Although the high number of racial issues at the school this year is unusual, she believes "the problem has always been here, people are just being more bold about it." With recommendations for colleges on their minds, Sheena contends, "Many blacks will just 'shhh' in front of large groups and not say how they really feel" or talk about the severity of the racial issues because "you don't want to stir up trouble."

Bolton Academy is not alone in instances of bigotry, according to Sheena, because she and others have experienced blatant racism on the sports field when playing other preparatory schools. She mentions that players from opposing schools "say some foul things, very, very foul" to Grace, who is the only black on the field hockey team. Sheena plays junior varsity basketball, and often at the end of the game when the opposing teams shake hands, the girls on the other team do not want to touch her.

Sheena then talks about more personal incidents such as when "somebody was like, 'Do you wash your hair?'" Noting how their style is "so different" from that of the white girls, she adds that "khakis versus black pants" is another thing that bothers her: "It seems completely innocent but . . . we black girls like to wear black. It goes with everything, black pants, black blazer, black shirt, black shoes. You can look sharp any time. Certain colors don't go with khaki, that's the problem. Okay, so people are like, 'You're always wearing black, blah, blah, blah.'"

Although Sheena sees a lot of racism at Bolton, she believes, as do many other students, that in some ways it is better than the "real world" because of the exposure or education that takes place at boarding schools. She describes her own "horrible" experiences with her white freshman roommate: "I knew it when I walked in the door. . . . the look on her mom's face and on her face. It was like, 'Could you hide your emotions just a little bit?' Oh man, that was hard! Of course we ignored it, me and my mom, you can't just be like 'Why are you looking at me like that?' So my roommate was spasmodic and scared of me. . . . She actually had a lot of fear, and that didn't make me feel good, you know. It didn't feel good at all. And then the dorm parents get mad at me because she's running down to them every night because she thinks I'm going to kill her. . . . But now it's been two years and we live on the same hall together and everything's fine."

When her roommate found out Sheena was in honors courses and earned good grades, she was "shocked": "I got the high honor roll first term and she didn't, and stuff like that, it killed her. It absolutely killed her. And the next year I was in honors math and she was not in honors, and it ripped her apart. But now it's absolutely fine. Now if she has a problem in math, she'll come to me and be like, 'Can you help me with this?' And I'm like, 'Yeah, sure.'"

To attend Bolton, Sheena underwent an intense process to make it into A Better Chance. She and her family made many sacrifices and continue to make them so that she can have this opportunity. Her father, who has a heart condition, works two jobs to pay the small tuition required and to send Sheena the money she needs for all the little extras that come up. Sheena talks about how guilty this makes her feel and the pressure she feels to succeed and not to let everyone down.

The story of Davis, a funny, warm, and charismatic African American, also reveals many of the special issues the students of color face at Bolton. During one interview Davis explains the types of issues and additional strains he is facing at Bolton. Downplaying stresses and pressures, Davis reveals, "I kind of feel like I have to escape my father and my uncle and my grandfather and my stepfather." He proceeds to explain, "My grandfather, he used to be kind of, like, an alcoholic, kind of, but not really an alcoholic, like a borderline alcoholic. And my uncle, he went to jail, he spent most of his life in jail. And my father spent a lot of his life on drugs, right, and my cousin, he drives a nice car and I don't know what the hell he do, right. So sometimes I kind of feel like I'm next in line. You know what I'm sayin'? Like if I don't do certain things it's all going to fall through. It's like a pattern. You know, so I feel like I have to escape that pattern, and I guess maybe that's why I'm here. I just needed to get out of the environment that they were in because when you live in New York there's a lot of temptation. There's more temptation in New York than here, because here it's, like, secluded. So I guess maybe that's why I'm here, because if it came down to it, I would have more reasons not to be here than to be here, which is kind of unfortunate but that's the truth. . . . So I'm trying to escape the male line of the people in my family."

Davis's dorm bonds during my interviews, and at the end of the year during my last session they open up to each other and become sentimental, almost mushy. One of the topics of their last, long interview includes how their ideas of each other have changed over the course of the year. A white boy admits to Davis, "I don't really mean to sound racist or anything, but I didn't really know too many black people before I came here and I was kind of, like, scared of you." At this, the boy's roommate interjects, "Yeah, he had a knife under his bed for, like, two weeks!" The first boy continues, "I was like, 'Who is this kid looking at me all the time? Is he going to rob me?' The first couple days you were here you didn't say anything. I was like, 'Jesus Christ, he must not like white people or something.' Because you were obviously in a dorm with all white people except for Ben."

At this Davis states, "Well, um, I really don't like all white people, just some." To which a different white boy responds, "We don't like all black people either." The first white boy continues, "And then you, like, came out, and you started, like, talking and whatever. And you're probably one of my favorite people here, so . . ."

Davis's white roommate, Jay, tells his own story of how his prejudices were removed when he got to know Davis: "Yeah, when I first met Davis, like, the day we moved in, I came in and his mom had tattoos and Davis was chilling with his do-rag and I was like, 'Oh shit, I'm a white kid.' And then Davis was like, 'Hey, man!' [he says this in a high squeaky, voice] and I was like, 'All right, we straight, I can kick this kid's ass!' And the intimidation factor was out the window."

The boys all laugh, and Davis retorts, "I personally know that Jay can't kick my ass, but I think I intimidate a lot of white people. I think a lot of people think I'm racist in this school because—" Jay interjects, "You look like a thug." Davis agrees: "Yeah, I walk around in my do-rag and sometimes I just look at your ass and I don't say nothing. You know, I think I lot of people think I'm *racist and stuff, but I'm really not. But I'll be honest with you. I don't like all white people, but I don't like all black people either. I don't like half the black people here, so—"*

One of the white boys interrupts, "I don't like half the people here." Davis concludes, "So it's not even a black and white thing. It's a people thing."

∷ THE INTERNATIONAL STUDENTS

The international students at Bolton provide a glimpse of how the values and conflicts found among the American students at Bolton may differ from those of teenagers in other cultures. The primary difference is that the value of self appears stronger among the American students at Bolton than among many of the international students, especially those from India, Asian countries, and Latin America. Many of the international students have a much greater cultural value of other in the sense of more focus on family, respect, duty, hard work, academics, success, and sexual and moral conservatism.

A group of girls from Mexico and South America note, "We have much more respect for our parents than the teenagers here" and "The kids here have too much freedom. Their parents let them do anything." They believe that the boys and girls at Bolton "lack manners," adding that the students have more sex than adolescents in their own cultures and are sexually more "loose" and "easy" here. The students at Bolton are also more concerned with "looks and money" than their friends back home, and class and race are bigger issues at Bolton. They find it more difficult to be an adolescent at Bolton than in their countries because "parents don't give kids here enough structure and because there are more pressures because of all the choices."

Many male international students also describe less individualism in their own cultures. A boy from Hong Kong states, "Here people always talk about getting away from their parents. In Hong Kong people don't just want to get away from their parents like most people say they do here." Duty rather than autonomy or independence guides a boy from Thailand, who explains, "In Thailand, we basically obey our parents. We just do whatever they say. For example, I came here. I really don't want to come here. But my parents forced me to." Some of the Thai students are also sponsored by their government, and their endless drive to succeed reflects their stress and their feeling of duty to achieve.

A focus on fun and the different measures and expectations of success also differentiate American prep schools such as Bolton from schools in other countries. Many international students say that their concentration on academics distinguishes them from the other students at Bolton. One girl from Germany says that her focus on academic excellence separates her from her peers:

> I hate parties. I don't like talking about how cute this boy is.
> And I don't care if I am wearing makeup or not. I am interested
> in the arts, literature, music, and a lot of other things. I like school.
> I like learning, but some people can't understand this and don't
> accept me.

The international students often comment that "fun" in the form of sports and freedoms is not as highly valued in their country's schools, but excellence in academics is stressed. A boy from Thailand explains, "Sports are not as important where I live." A student from Hong Kong agrees, "It's not as competitive as here. Academically, it's more competitive, but not sports." A French boy comments on the academic rigor, lack of fun, and the lack of freedoms in the French academic setting: "In France, you can't choose your class. We only have sports three hours a week. So you work from eight until five or six with no free [periods]. You take two foreign languages. You work a lot." Two Korean boys note, "There is more pressure in other cultures for grades, success" and "Success is taken for granted here."

Like other New England boarding schools, Bolton Academy enrolls many Korean students. These students often band together, speak Korean among themselves, and remain on the fringe of the school community. Although they are generally excellent students and good citizens, and are only infrequently brought before the disciplinary committee (except for plagiarism issues), their separation and cultural differences make both the students and faculty feel "uncomfortable." Pursuing an accelerated agenda, they focus mainly on excelling academically and attending a good American college. The most obvious cultural difference and the one that causes their American counterparts and the faculty the most concern is their tradition of an established power structure and hierarchy. As is the custom in Korea, the oldest Korean boy at Bolton has power over and responsibility for the other Korean students. Because of the boarding school environment, there are many avenues for this hierarchy to come into play and to be abused. It is common to see the girls and younger boys serving as "little slaves" to the older boys in a manner that borders on and in some cases surpasses the school's definition of hazing. The older boys expect favors from the others and have immense power over them, even to the point of physical abuse. The girls will clear their dishes at the dining hall and vacuum their rooms. The oldest boy makes the travel arrangements for the other Korean students.

Because they did not come out of their rooms for the group interviews nor did they actively participate in the activities that I followed, my study does not represent the Korean and other Asian students adequately.

I first met Han, a boy from Thailand who attends Bolton on a one-year scholarship through his government, at a homesickness support group the school counselor holds at the beginning of the year. Very homesick, he shows all of us pictures of his family and home. He feels considerable pressure from his government and his family to achieve at Bolton.

He is quiet and shy and rarely speaks. Despite his intelligence, he has difficulty speaking English and being understood by the American students, which makes it hard for him to make American friends. Students often make fun of him and his incomprehensible English, laughing outright when he speaks up in class. Han finds sports, New England weather, and American teenage morality a trial. His only friends are a few other Asians. Because he seems lonesome and isolated, my children and I make a point of talking to him whenever we see him, but we never can understand a word he says. We just smile a lot. Thanks to his advisor, who suspects a problem, Han is discovered to have hearing issues, and his government, after much coaxing, agrees to pay for a hearing aid.

Despite our friendly connection, whenever I visit his dorm he is the only boy who does not come out to the interview to enjoy the brownies and camaraderie. Instead, he stays and studies in his room, which has no decorations other than a flag of his country and a few pictures of his family and his JV squash team.

In his senior chapel speech at the end of the year, Han speaks about the honor, prestige, and pressure of receiving his government's scholarship. He tells how he had passed many tests and beat out many other students to earn the prestigious award of his government's scholarship to study in the United States. He speaks of making his parents and country proud. He tells how hard he has worked in order to succeed and to pay back his country. He speaks of how much the Bolton experience and friendships mean to him. Although he had few friends, he asks to stay in touch with everyone and thanks the student body for their friendship. As he talks and talks and talks, students snicker and roll their eyes. Still he talks. Finally, the headmaster gently tells him it is time to stop.

People suggest he was making up for not talking for the whole year he was at Bolton.

∷ THE HIGH-CLASS CLUB AND THE BITCH SQUAD

Similar to the performance of gender and ethnicity, the performance of class depends on the individual and can change depending on context such as who one is with or where one is. As mentioned earlier, most students strategically perform class to conform to the wealthy preppy style, at least while they are at Bolton. Two groups, the "high-class club" (boys) and the "bitch squad" (girls), stand out, not necessarily for their wealth, because there are other students who are equally or more wealthy who are not part of these cliques, but for their extreme and exclusive performances of wealth.

Class is another area in which the Bolton students openly espouse equality, while at the same time describing much inequality as well as a covert belief in inequality. Like racial issues, class issues are often explained away (especially by the wealthier students) as simply the need to establish connections with "similar" individuals who have a similar "upbringing" or "the same hygiene," and not discrimination or elitism.

As they do for race, many of the students state that class issues are not a problem at Bolton or are at least less than society at large, but at the same time they notice self-segregation at both ends of the economic spectrum, classism, and reverse classism. Furthermore, many of the students have negative attitudes toward day students or hockey players, many of whom attend Bolton on scholarship. Although I never hear socioeconomic class mentioned overtly as a reason for their disdain, many of the day students and hockey players feel looked down upon by their more wealthy peers.

In many ways boarding school has unique class issues. First, although the cost of attending Bolton is very high, the students who attend Bolton cover the entire range of socioeconomic classes because of many scholarship awards.

Second, being total institutions, boarding schools are a moneyless society. The students need little money except for ordering out for food or when they go shopping. If they need things at the bookstore or school snack bar, they can charge it to their parents' account. Because of this, students rarely carry money, and therefore in many ways money becomes a non-issue.

A third reason is due to a tradition of "inverse snobbery," where the wealthiest and those with the oldest money often look like they have the least. "Part of the socialization of power is learning how to conceal wealth, or at least minimize its importance by never openly referring to it" (Cookson & Persell, 1985, p. 28). Because of this, knowledge of others' social class is a complex issue, although it soon becomes known nonetheless.

The students at Bolton regularly express their belief in equality of the social classes and the relative lack of social class problems or divisions at Bolton Academy. They claim, "I think it's not really known. It's not really talked about" or "It's just the person, not a financial status" or "not an issue at all."

Many students believe that the nature of boarding school minimizes class issues:

> You're sort of evened out. You're in the same classes. You're on the same sports teams. So also dorm makes a difference, because you really get to know the people in your dorm. So you're sort of evened out by doing the same thing every day.

One boy observes that there are many fewer class issues at Bolton because "you're around them so much, you take them for who they are, not how much money they have really." Nicole notes how the special circumstances of boarding school "even out" the large disparities in wealth among the students:

> The school kind of evens out money though because at one time or another everybody's going to run out in their account and there are people here with millions and millions of dollars who are like, "Man, can I borrow $2," asking people who don't have any money to borrow $2 for pizza. It kind of evens out at school . . . until you go shopping with credit cards.

At times the students cite the economic diversity in the school as the reason for the lack of social class issues at Bolton, yet at other times they credit it precisely for class issues. When they came to Bolton, many students expected to find a lot of "rich snobs" but found "people that were nothing like that" because many students were not rich, and those who were rich often were not arrogant. A group of boys claims that Bolton is not "like a public school" because at the public schools in their towns "it is all rich" and there isn't "one poor kid," so the students "compete for money. It's all about competition."

Other students blame the "glaring differences between the haves and the have-nots" at Bolton for the social class issues that exist. One boy comments, "Well, there is a difference between the trust fund kids . . . who are never ever going to have to work a day in their lives, and then there are the rest of us that will." At this, one of the other boys interjects, "Who will have to work for a brief five-day period." Another boy contends that there are class issues at Bolton, "but in the outside world there are different social differences." He explains that the public high school he went to "had all sorts of weird people, like the goth kids, and then there were, like, the neo-Nazi fascist kids, who kind of freaked me out . . . They scared me quite a bit."

Still others assert that the economic similarity of the students results in better class relations because "when you're in, like, a society where almost three-quarters of the school is the same as you, there's nothing to flaunt." The boys claim that "because everyone's the same, really," no one is "really left out unless you're a loser."

That some wealthy students "just don't show" their wealth indicates how class is a performance and explains why class issues at Bolton are less significant than people might imagine. The students often talk about how some people show their money, while others don't. Nicole observes:

> That's the difference between old money and new money. New money be running around with all their jewels, "Look at me!" And then you have these other people, laid-back, looking like scrubs, they got money for days, money like "Whoa." . . . I've seen some really rich kids do some really ghetto things like look in the cushions for coins to buy a soda. It's experiences like that that make us all the same, you know.

A group of boys ridicule some students with "new money" who live "lavishly" and are "out on the green in their little polo shirts and they're like, 'Hi, Buffy' [said in an affected tone], and they want to live that way." They criticize this group: "They think that they're cooler, but I think most people wouldn't really think that they're that much cooler."

As they do for race, students attribute the "close relationships" between the students in the boarding school environment for making class issues less noticeable and less important. One girl explains, "You don't judge them because you know them." Kara admits that she had "a lot of stereotypes" about "rich white people" before she came to boarding school, but her attitude has changed:

> It's different than the real world, I think, because you're thrown in, you have to, you can't just have your own little issues about certain groups of people. Like, how can I come here and be like, "Oh, I hate white people?" Oh well, if I don't like white people, I'm screwed because right now I'm in a roomful and when I go to class I'm in a roomful and you just have to drop those things. . . . Now everybody's a human being and has their own qualities.

When a diversity group from Brown University comes to Bolton and tries to address class along with race issues by having different groups, such as those students on financial aid, step forward, the students are outraged. The girls of the bitch squad assert that the diversity day event was "awful" and that "it was so offending to our community because they were saying, they were trying to tell us this [class] was an issue for us. And it wasn't an issue." One girl concludes, "I think that day brought more, more tension between people than there even was." Another group of girls criticizes the diversity day event as "so bad" and "the worst day ever" and that something like that is not "right" at Bolton. One boy calls the Brown group's pinpointing the students on financial aid as "unheard of" and "absurd" because "they were seen as, of course, the same as everybody else, you know. And that was like the first time anybody in the community had ever thought of it."

Despite these claims of equality and relative ignorance and unimportance of wealth, the students concurrently describe much interest in the wealthy and many class inequalities and tensions. For the vast majority of the students, the focus on wealth or social class is reserved for the wealthy, not the poor. The contention of one group of boys that social class becomes an issue only when people "act like they have a lot of money" is typical. The students target the rich as the "issue" in class divisions. It is undeniable that there is a great deal of interest in the amount of money others have and the power that goes with it.

"Basically everyone knows" each other's social class, especially if they are wealthy. The girls wonder about who has money and look for telltale signs of wealth: clothes, "where people are from," "the way they act," and parents who "act a certain way" at parents' weekend. The boys identify certain signs of wealth: cars, clothes, and an "attitude toward life [that] is much more light." One boy claims, "You can tell within ten minutes of meeting a person if they're like Carter, whose father is, like, the richest man ever, whose father is a congressman and is worth what, 800 mil?" The boys, intrigued by Carter's wealth, separate him from the high-class club because "he's not like them" and isn't a "snob."

The boys often say that the girls are more aware and concerned with social class, noting that while social class issues are "not as much with the guys," "girls, like, show it off." "Guys actually try to hide it" and "the guys don't really care, but the girls, yeah." Girls display their wealth through their clothes. And if a girl is very wealthy, "you'll find out. Girls will talk about it, even." Many boys contend that girls care more about who has money because they are always trying to impress. One boy asserts that this is because "guys aren't as hard on each other" and girls are "more into each other's personal lives," and "that's when it gets into the social classes." He adds:

> They're always more interested in what they wear. Because they're all interested in impressing the guys. And some have the funds to overly impress and never wear the same thing twice and others have to wear the same thing twice, you know.

The economic status of students is a worthy topic of conversation only if they have a lot of money, not if they don't. A boy explains that "it's on a one-sided scale" and that "if you don't have money, people don't know about it. They just think you're an average person. There isn't prejudice if you don't have money, but there's definitely sucking up if you do." The boys proceed to discuss Will's room:

> It has a $1,500 entertainment system, and then he has a computer solely for the purpose of DVDs. He has never had a keyboard hooked up to his computer. And then he has a dartboard that he's probably going to have to pay close to $1,000 in wall damage because of all the holes. And then he has 100 DVDs. He has a $300 leather office chair, a $2,000 La-Z-Boy. And this is all in a tight little single.

The students focus not on the poor but rather on the wealthy students who sometimes feel awkward or uncomfortable around the others. One boy explains:

> I think a lot of kids, they try to lower themselves to the standards of everyone else, you know, because they don't like being set off as, "Oh I'm the rich kid." They don't like being called that. You know,

they just try and lower themselves. And everyone just tries to stay the same because no one likes to be the oddball out, you know.

Some of the students view having wealth as "a big issue" at the school because it influences people's friendships. In one dorm, some kids convince a wealthy boy to buy them all "a pair of sneakers and sunglasses and they all charged it to this one kid's credit card and the kid didn't care because it was his parents' credit card number." This wealthy boy readily makes friends because he

> buys food for the whole dorm every Sunday night. He'll just say, "Where are we ordering from?" and then everyone gets food. And you'll, like, see kids who have never talked to this person before in their life all of a sudden come up to him and start talking to him because they know he has money and they know that they'll get benefits from being his friend.

Some wealthy students appear "snobby" by segregating themselves. The boys identify the cliques based on social class: "All the rich snobs hang out and live in Wentworth dorm" and "The rich kids stick to them-selves." The girls often assert that Bolton "definitely" has more cliques based on social class than at public school. One girl exclaims, "Oh my God! I didn't even think that much money existed." The students rou-tinely pinpoint the "really wealthy people cliques," the high-class club and the bitch squad, as being exclusive. They describe the girls' clique as wearing only expensive preppy J. Crew and North Face clothes, living in Greenwich, Connecticut, and being rich. But those in this clique claim that the poor students "tend to seclude themselves too, though," saying, "Maybe they don't belong or something."

One group of boys passionately describes the classist behavior of one girl and the preferential treatment given her family because of their wealth. When the boys bring up the subject of snobs, one boys screams, "Alexandra!" Other boys chime in, "I was just going to say that!" "Oh my God, I hate Alexandra!" and "Alexandra sucks!" When one boy reveals, "Her dad was put on the board of trustees because he's expected to give, like, some unreal number, like $10 million, to the school," the others insist:

-Who cares? She still sucks. She's still worthless.

-She's a girl who's bad at life.

-She's gross.

The boys then debate whether one of the boys in their dorm who is "really, really, rich" shows it. Some state, "He shows it in his room" with his "$200 clock" and his "$1,100 chair" and his attitude, "He's like, 'Oh, that's not cashmere!'"

Only the bitch squad and the high-class club endorse inequality or openly talk unfavorably about students without money. The girls in the bitch squad relate how clothes reveal the wealth of a student and how students who do not have money to buy expensive brand-name clothes stick out.

The poor students are not looked down upon but in most cases are admired. Even the bitch squad girls, after saying that the poor students do not fit in, later talk highly about them because they realize the poor students are often the best academically and give the most back to the school. They admire how the poor students "take more advantage of this school," are "more involved," and "appreciate it more." One student notices that some of the rich kids for whom the tuition is "a pinch full of money," "petty cash," and "nothing big at all" are more apt to get bad grades and get into trouble because "to them it's, like, 'I'm not wasting money.'" She contrasts this with what happens if you are not "financially secure":

> You realize what a great opportunity this education is and you're like, "Why would I pay, like, $30,000 here to fail," and . . . you get more involved 'cause you're like, "I'm never gonna have this opportunity back . . . there's all these people at home who don't have it."

Although many students say the wealthy self-segregate due to their arrogance or elitist attitudes, some say that they bond because of "similarities," "common interests," "experiences," or how they "grew up." Some wealthy boys contend that even though the different classes stick together and form cliques, it is not negative. Believing that they simply share things in common and like the same things, many explain away social class segregation in the same manner as race segregation. One boy explains, "The upper-class people kind of stick together, then the middle-class [students] kind of stick together, and some of the lower-class [students] stick together," but he doesn't "blame it, though, because . . . that's how they grew up . . . like, they know what you're talking about and stuff." The other boys seem to agree: "They're just different. They're just different."

One boy then equates different classes sticking together to different races sticking together because of shared interests:

You know, you have common interests and experiences with people that are similar to you. I mean, probably, and this may be a generalization I would think, but I think the Asian people have more in common with themselves and their likes and dislikes, and type of music and stuff, than with someone, say, me. I don't know anything about Korean or Japanese music. I've never even listened to it.

At this, an Asian student quietly protests, "That's not, like . . . that's not what they talk about." The first boy responds, "No, I know, I know. But it's just . . . it's one . . . it's a 'like.'"

Throughout the interviews, the girls in the "rich bitch" dorm claim to be friends not because of their wealth or arrogance, as other dorms contend, but because of the similarities in the way they were "brought up." These girls demonstrate the complex interconnection between gender, class, and race/ethnicity as they manipulate the relative importance of each of these characteristics in their concept of self. In this instance, class seems to be a stronger force than race or ethnicity, as the primary voices among the "rich bitch" clique asserting their similarities are the African Americans Mercedes and Chanel. Mercedes attributes the cliques' friendship to their similar looks, style, and hygiene:

> If you look at your group of friends, you kind of are friends with people who are like you. Like, you're not really friends with people that are totally opposite from you, you know, looks-wise. You kind of match up with people with the same style, or, like, the same hygiene, or whatever.

She continues to explain how looks are important to her family and how they segregate themselves from fat, ugly people or people from the wrong area:

> 'Cause I know especially at home, like maybe it's just because it's in the South, but, like, no one who we're supposed to associate with can be . . . No, I can't say that, that's mean. But it's, like, no one in my group of friends and my mother's group of friends is, like, ugly and over a size eight.

"It's the same at my house," interjects one of her white friends. Mercedes continues, "And I'm sorry, and you can't be from—" She stops, knowing what she is about to say is not acceptable to voice out loud.

Concern with brand names is widespread at Bolton. When a girl says that people care only about the prep style and not expensive brand names, her friends correct her immediately: "Brand names are big with *everyone*." She insists, "You can look just as preppy and cute in clothes without brand names. No one is checking to see where you buy your clothes." The others shriek in disbelief and horror, "Stacey! People are *so* concerned here with where you buy your clothes."

The poor students sometimes find the wearing of brand names of utmost importance. In one interview, two black scholarship girls from New York City talk about how the people at Bolton Academy who have money do not know how to spend it. Tamara declares, "Let me be a gajillion-padillionaire and I will show you how to spend it. First of all, he [one rich boy] don't even be dressing right!" She adds, "The only person who's got money who knows what to do with it that I'm looking at is Steve, because he's stylin'!"

The attitude that often comes with money rankles the students. One girl explains that it is not how much money you have that makes you a "snob," but "it's more what you say." The students often describe the behavior of the bitch squad as elitist and cliquish. Most of these girls come from Greenwich, a wealthy town in Connecticut, and exhibit behavior "typical" of people in that town. The girls explain: " They come here and act like kings of the world" and "like you're better than everybody." One girl notes how they also judge others: "You'll walk in wearing something, and they don't like it, and they'll sit there and, 'Uhhh [rolls her eyes], they have no taste at all. I can't *believe* they're wearing that!'"

Outraged that one of the Greenwich girls criticized the pronunciation of her name, a black girl adopts a snotty tone to mimic what the Greenwich girl said: "'Ewww, why does she say it like that?'" The girl adds:

> I'm like, "It's *my* name. *You* may say it wrong. *You* don't know how to say it. You can kiss my butt because I really don't care." Any person who would take the time to think that *they're* saying my name right. The girl has no sense. She's stupid, and she's dumb.

Overtly hostile behavior, which generally is not part of female interaction, is unique to the bitch squad:

> The difference is that they're backstabbing. Where we'll talk shit about them and won't bother associating with them, and they'll talk shit about us openly and we'll hear it. Like I'll walk by and they'll be like, "Ewww, what is *she* wearing today? [said in a snotty

tone]. She's such a bitch, she's such a slut." Like they do it within ear range so you can hear it.

Judged by the "rich bitches" for her clothing, Kara says:

I've never seen people wear the *exact* same clothes. It's not even the same style. It's the same clothes from the same store, the same rack, or whatever, and I'm not used to that. And then you wear something that's just a little bit different and it's a big deal here.

She then says how the bitch squad made snide comments when she wore a bright orange pantsuit: "it was a big deal" to them.

The students also frequently say that the high-class club, made up of about ten of the wealthiest boys, is arrogant:

Some of the guys have this thing called the high-class club and they'll be like walking around, and they'll like see one of their friends who's in it too, or whatever, and they'll be like, "Hi, where's your tie from? Brooks Brothers? All right, just making sure." It's kidding, but at the same time it's not.

Another girl states, "The way they talk to people, it's like everyone around them is to serve them." Another girl interjects, "That's because they have maids and servants." Another adds, "I asked Chris if he does anything at his house and he's like, 'Sometimes I bring my dishes to the sink.'"

The dorm where most of the wealthy boys live is "all about the money." For one Halloween these boys dressed up as millionaire snobs in khakis and oxfords and made a show of having pizzas delivered to the dining hall instead of eating the school's food. "They were holding $100 bills and, like, wiping their foreheads with them," one girl exclaims.

In one instance, Tamara, who is African American, tells a group of white girls about the offensive and classist behavior of Chad, a member of the high-class club:

Last year Chad said to me—it was like the first time he had ever spoken to me—I was like, "Gosh, it's so quiet here." And he was like, "Yeah, you must miss that random sound of gunshots." I was like, "Oh, not in my neighborhood, sweetheart, maybe in yours." I mean, where do you come off thinking that? And to say it so boldly and that be like the first statement you ever say to somebody.

One of the white girls from a poor area interrupts, "There *are* random gunshots in my neighborhood. It's fishermen." Tamara continues, "You *know* he thinks people who don't have money are beneath him." The others agree, and one adds:

> He was asking me where I was going to college, and I said,
> "I don't know. I haven't heard on financial aid." And he was like,
> "You mean it really matters on money?" and I was like, "Yeah,
> actually it really does."

At this, Tamara explodes, "Not brains for him!" One of the other girls exclaims, "He's lucky he has money, though, because he's dumb as shit." Tamara concludes, "He'd be dead if he didn't have money!"

Reverse discrimination also occurs. One girl, Courtney, who lives in a wealthy town, describes the reverse discrimination that she faces at Bolton:

> I come here and everyone's like, "Oh, you're from New Canaan,
> la di da," and they just, vroom, immediately threw this whole
> stereotype on me. So I think it's a lot more apparent here.

Later during a discussion on wealth, Tamara asserts that there is "a certain arrogance that is seen with money" and starts to pick on Courtney. She asks, "Courtney, do you have money? I'm checking out that Tiffany's [heart bracelet] up there, or is that not real?" Courtney sighs in exasperation and exclaims, "Sorry, God!" Tamara continues to pick on her, using a condescending tone: "Did you get it for your birthday? Are you going to get a car next year?"

The girls often remark that "those Tiffany bracelets and necklaces" like the one Courtney was wearing are indicators of class and wealth at Bolton. The bracelets' appeal is widespread. Even though Tamara is on scholarship and has difficulty paying her tuition, she says, "I really want one" of those "really, really expensive" bracelets. Other girls comment:

> -I think it's stupid everyone here has one.

> -Honestly, I don't like it because it's become like a cult thing. "You
> don't have a bracelet? Come on, get one. Get one."

At this, Kara comments about the bracelet, which has a chain-link pattern, "You know, I'm black. I try not to have anything that resembles chains on my hands." Others add, "I don't think people get those Tiffany bracelets to look good. I think they get them to fit in." They conclude, "They're a mark of who has money."

Some boys also experience this type of reverse discrimination. One wealthy boy resents that some students target him as rich and ask him to buy them things, complaining: "People are like, 'You're rich. You can order me a pizza.'"

The boys sometimes claim that rich girls at Bolton, concerned about their reputations and image, seek to maintain their "elite" status and will only "get with rich guys." One boy says that this happens at all schools, both public and prep, but a friend quickly disagrees and argues that he sees a "huge" difference:

> Girls here won't get with a guy because of their reputation [i.e., what others would think of them for doing so], while at public school and any other school that's not a boarding school, if they wanted to, they would. If they liked a guy, they would.

The white students at Bolton attribute this concern with image and reputation to affluent culture. One boy, a self-proclaimed authority on the wealthy ("I live in Greenwich, okay?"), argues that although other students often say, "Oh, the girls are different in my hometown," for him "the girls you see here *are* the kind of girls that are in my hometown." He adds that in Greenwich the focus is on "all reputation and talking, just like here," and says it is "a product of, like, the culture, the affluent society." The others agree, and one boy proceeds to explain why not only the rich girls but also the rich boys care about their reputations so much:

> 'Cause they care. That's what snobs do. They care what people think. They feel good because people put them where they want to be [better than others]. And they need to feel better than others and that's why a lot of girls, and guys too, do that.

Despite little open negativity toward the poor at Bolton, the scholarship students often feel added pressure, pain, disappointment, anger, and envy due to their lack of funds. The scholarship students, both black and white, often talk about how hard it is to have to worry about financial issues as well as all the other things everyone else has to worry about. One girl feels bad that she can't do all the stuff the others are doing for prom, like getting her hair done. Another comments:

> I think the people who don't have as much money feel like more pressured to get better grades so they can be on the honor roll

every single time so they're going to get their financial aid and stuff like that, whereas the richer kids, if they don't do as well, their parents don't. . . . We feel more pressure to get the better grades. You have to get good grades. You have to go to college. You have to do this. You have to do that.

One girl explains, "When everyone else is walking, you have to run."

Stealing is an issue both on and off campus. Frequently the students report on a Web page that someone stole money from their rooms. An incident of mass shoplifting also occurred during a school outing to the local mall. Often the students believe that it is the wealthy who steal, which evokes frustration and anger from the poor students. In one e-mail with the subject line "Thank you for stealing money from me," an African American scholarship student writes to the school community:

> To the students and faculty of this lovely institution of knowl-edge . . . I would just like to thank that person who came into my room while I wasn't there and kindly stole 30 dollars out of my wallet. . . . I hope that the Good Samaritan realizes that he/she took all the money I have left (except the 38 cents in my debit account). I furthermore appreciate the gesture especially since the person who stole it probably really needed the money to go out on luxurious excursions or add 30 dollars to their massive trust funds.

Examining how the issues of class play out in the Bolton students' lives adds to current research on adolescent peer groups by revealing how social class affects peer groupings and the relative salience of "dif-ference" and class segregation among the most wealthy. Class often is more important than race, but not gender, in their peer groupings. The tendency of both the upper-class boys and girls to base their group associations on attention to appearance, wearing the right brand names and expensive jewelry, sporting tans from their vacations to exotic des-tinations, thinness for girls, and wearing preppy pink for boys reveals how they distinguish themselves from and maintain a distance from those of lower social status. Even in a context where most students would be considered upper-class, and one where there are no cars or houses to indicate social status, the wealthiest students tend to self-segregate into cliques and maintain boundaries of "difference" based on their wealth.

∷ PREPPIES AND TOWNIES

Viewed as separate from the rest of the Bolton community, the day students believe they are valued less by the school administration and the boarding students. Traditionally day students are a fringe element at boarding schools, and the day students at Bolton believe that they are no exception. Because prep schools are traditionally located in the country, rivalries arise between the rich "preppies" and the poor "townies" from the surrounding areas. The Bolton day students feel affected by this antagonism. Not only do they not fit in at Bolton, but they also view themselves as different from their old friends at local public high schools because they attend Bolton. However, the day students regard themselves as smarter and as getting better grades than the boarders. The high percentage of day students who win academic and top scholar awards and join the honor society every year corroborate this.

The life of the day students is in some ways similar to that of the boarders but in other ways quite different. The day students arrive early in the morning and sometimes eat breakfast at the school. They often spend their breaks between classes in the day rooms, separated from the boarding students, who usually head back to their dorms. After classes, the day students attend sports. After sports, the day students either go home or stay for dinner and work in the library. Many of the day students report they stay for dinner for the social aspect, not the food. One day boy likes to eat at school because it is more social and because he does not have to "set and clear the table the way I do at home." Many of the day students do not leave campus until late at night.

The subject of day students rarely comes up among the boarders; when it does, it's often in the context of discussing the day students' intelligence, talking about a party they went to at a day student's house, or complaining about having to attend the academic awards ceremonies, which they derogatorily refer to as "the day student awards." For the majority of the boarders, the day students are a non-issue.

Despite "missing out on some stuff," the day students like being day students and feel they have "the benefit of both worlds." The day girls feel that they get all the advantages of prep school and "take advantage of all the facilities," "but then at night you can go home to your own bed, my own room, like my family and I have the home-cooked meals there." Although "it's easier for the day students to work . . . it's a lot easier to focus," they mention that they feel "a lot more pressure" from their parents.

The boys prefer to be day students because of the freedoms and fun available to them that are not available to the boarders. One boy explains:

> During the week it's more fun to be a boarder. But during the weekend it's more fun being a day student, because I can go to New York or I can go to a friend's house without calling up the headmaster and four other people to see if that's okay.

Others assert, "You don't have half the rules, like study hall and stuff" and "There are more freedoms."

A boy who was a boarder the year before and is now a day student believes that "day student life is definitely better. You have more freedom. The faculty isn't breathing down your throat all the time." He contends, "The boarders party more . . . but we party better." He explains that day students party better because as a boarder, "it wasn't really partying. If you ever did anything, it was just sitting in your room stoned or whatever." He concludes, "There is definitely more moderation and more fun as a day student."

Caught in the middle of the traditional preppy-versus-townie rivalry, the day girls feel they do not fit in and are not accepted fully by either group. One girl explains, "People who are living in trailers drive by here every day and are like, 'Oh my gosh, this is a school?'" She adds that even day students are viewed as snobs, and therefore "it is very hard for day students in town to come here because we lose a lot of friends over it." She explains that "once you become a preppy," people don't want to be associated with you because "all of a sudden I am prissy, I am elitist."

Repeatedly the day students say that attending Bolton Academy has broadened their horizons. One girl describes how she and her fellow day students "went into culture shock" when they first came to Bolton: "As a day student we were like, 'I know where the [convenience store] is' to 'Where's Beijing?'" Rachel, an excellent student who is involved in many extracurricular activities, discusses how attending Bolton has opened her eyes to the world:

> One of the greatest changes for me has probably been my global perspective and just the idea of getting out of here. I have friends who have already been pregnant, had abortions, have a job, have their own place now. And I never thought about it growing up, but now that I'm here I say, "They are never going to leave. They

are never going to leave." And some of them don't want to leave; it's not a bad thing. But for me, it kind of scares me. I couldn't imagine being happy knowing that I never stepped anywhere else, knowing that I had never just dipped my toe in the water to see how it was. I mean, maybe I'll travel all over the world and decide that this is the best place, but some people never get that chance.

Rachel adds that for boarders the experience can be a "bubble" because they "don't see the surrounding community, and when they do go out they're still separated. It's almost like they don't see them [the local people]."

The day students describe a large division between themselves and the boarders. Some day boys say, "I don't really talk much with the boarders so I don't really know what their life is like," and "I'm just not really close friends with a lot of them." Other day boys mention how sports have helped them bridge the day/boarder gap. One athletic boy views the "sports tie" as stronger than whether one is a day student or boarder. He adds, "I actually don't think there's much difference between day students and boarders. . . . I'm friends with both."

Often the day students feel mistreated and devalued by both the boarders and the school itself. A day girl mentions how a boarder had "spent the entire class bad-mouthing day students. He was like, 'You live in *Milltown*?' He was like, 'This school should be all boarders. I hate day students.'" Many of the day students feel devalued by the school itself. One girl contends, "The school doesn't like day students. They're trying to get rid of us. I swear to God they are." Some of the boys contend teachers and administrators favor and are easier on the boarders but "ride day students harder" to get their work done.

Socioeconomic differences are one of the main reasons day students feel like outsiders from the rest of the Bolton community. One girl explains that at spring break day students usually do not travel, but adds, "It's not like a conflict. Day students are just like, 'Wow, they are so lucky to be able to do that.'" Other girls add that the socioeconomic differences affect their social life in subtle ways such as clothing:

I think it plays in socially like the way you dress. Like the difference between day students and boarder. Like for some boarders J. Crew is like their life. And I think that's different.

Other girls add, "There's probably more emphasis on clothing [brand names] if you're a boarder probably because you have enough money to get it." One boy often feels uncomfortable "when my jacket's from Filene's and everybody else's are from Brooks Brothers" and "when somebody has on Gucci shoes and I have on Birkenstocks or sandals."

One way the day students see themselves as different from the boarders is that their relative poverty makes them appreciate attending Bolton and want to give back to the school more. Typically the day students comment, "A lot of boarders are here not so much because they want to be here. I think that, like, more day students are here because they want to be here" and "Day students appreciate what they get more. Like we appreciate the opportunity to be here because, like, we know it's a lot of money for our parents to spend on our education."

The academic success of the day students also creates a rift and sometimes even antagonism between the day and boarding students. Rachel, who receives many academic awards, explains that this antagonism flares during the academic convocation awards ceremony:

> There's a huge running joke about convocation in the fall where people actually keep tallies [of] how many day students and how many boarders win. And someone kept a tally one year and it was, I don't know, three to one, or two to one, day students, and the [enrollment] numbers are reversed, two to one boarders, so that is always a very tense time. "Oh, there's another day student" is whispered . . . That's why I think that day students have developed the habit to just not talk about it [good grades, awards or high SAT scores]. You just work your hardest, do your thing, but don't talk about it and when you do get that award, don't look too proud, don't smile too big . . . . I think I have great relationships with the boarders, until it comes to that time of separation.

A day girl runs for school president this year, and despite unequaled academic and leadership experience and being a clear favorite of the faculty for the post, the other students quickly vote her out of the competition.

Less concerned with clothes and image, the day girls note that boarders are more concerned with being "sexy." One girl says, "Day students are more laid back." This relative lack of attention to clothing appears to be both a matter of logistics and focus. Rachel, who has short bright red hair and does not dress in the latest fashions, explains, "Sometimes

I see boarders with, like, three outfits on each day. They go back to their rooms and change all the time. I'm like, 'What are you doing?'"

Many of the day girls talk of being pressured by the boarders for rides, to supply alcohol, and to provide a place to go and party off campus. One girl conjectures, "I think boarders kind of use day students. I'd use them if I was a boarder." Another adds, "There's a lot of pressure and there's even more risk because as soon as there's alcohol found in the dorms, day students are immediately pointed out as suppliers even if we don't." Despite the perception, some of the girls argue that it is easier for the boarders to misbehave than for them. One girl offers, "They can get away with a lot more here than we can at home, even though it seems like everyone really cracks down on them. Like, there's stuff kids do here that I could never do at home."

Because this is their "chance of a lifetime," the day students are more "cautious" about getting in trouble than the boarders. They say that "more boarders than day students . . . don't really think about the consequences" of getting kicked out because "they're like, 'I can just get a second chance and then go to another private school.'" The girls claim, "For most of us, this is it. Like, if we get kicked out of here, it's, like, public high school and community college."

The day girls claim that the boarders "don't have a lot of respect" for them. One girl comments, "I've driven boarders and I'll be like, 'You've checked out?' Like, I make sure they do everything. And they're like, 'I haven't checked out.' And I'm like, 'How could you forget? You could get me kicked out!'"

One area in which the day students view themselves as similar to the boarders is in coping with Bolton's intense schedule and workload. A driven day student, Amanda, explains, "I think a lot of the things we complain about are the same: 'We just want to have fun,' 'Why is this place so stressful?' 'Why is all our time mapped out?'" She adds, "We're just kids. We want to have fun."

Although the day girls say that they are so different than the boarders, they too display the same need to be "perfect." Many claim that the pressure to be perfect comes from comparing themselves to others: "I think it could be considered a type of competition with each other" and "We want to prove to the world that we can do everything and do it well."

The day boys stand out from the other students at Bolton due to their drive to succeed and their belief that attending Bolton is a path to success. One boy correlates attending Bolton with having a more "successful life." He states, "[Bolton] just basically has stronger academics, which will help me get into a better college, which will help me get a better job and just basically help me have a more successful life." According to many of the day boys, the best thing about being at a prep school is "the prestige it carries with it" and "meeting the kids here because all the kids here are going to go to college, and they have successful parents."

Unlike the boarders, the day boys feel considerable pressure from others, especially their parents, to succeed. Many explain that they have much more pressure put on them by their parents than their friends at the local high school because of the money their parents are spending.

Also unlike the boarders, almost all of the day boys state that they feel greater pressure to excel academically than athletically. One boy, however, feels more pressure for sports because his parents know he is a good student and will work hard at academics:

> I think I have more sports pressure than academics because my parents know I do my work. They don't have to worry about that. So they just want me to excel in athletics too. My dad just wants me to train whenever I have free time. Like if I'm watching TV, he's like, "Why aren't you running? Why aren't you lifting?"

There is no love lost between the day boys and the day girls. Both view the other as the lowest on the totem pole at Bolton. The boys describe the day girls as "fake," "territorial," and "evil": "They all complain to each other and stab each other in the back every chance they get." All the day boys believe that the boarder girls are "*much* better-looking" than the day girls. The girls describe the day boys as "so scary" because the day boys have traditionally been known to haze. The girls explain: "They beat the hell out of each other. You can hear them downstairs, like screaming and stuff, it's so horrible." The girls add that the day boys are also more ostracized than the day girls: "Boarder boys don't talk to half the day boys at all. . . . Like you don't see a lot of day boys going into the dorms, but we'll go into the dorms, and it will be okay."

:: FORM HIERARCHY

The equality and inequality between the different forms (grades) at Bolton Academy is one area where the students generally claim that there is too much equality and openly argue for inequality. Many students, especially the boys, vehemently argue for more inequality between the forms, believing that students at the same grade level as well as the school as a whole are able to bond better when inequality and a definite hierarchy exist.

Since connections are the ultimate goal, this inequality helps promote belonging by separating. Their views on class hierarchy stand in sharp contrast to their views on equality.

The seniors enjoy certain privileges the other students do not. These include senior breakfast, where seniors can eat an hour later than the underformers (and thereby have more time to sleep in the morning), doughnuts after Monday senior chapel, a senior couch in the main school building, and a senior lounge in which to watch TV or relax between classes. The seniors also are allowed other traditional privileges during the last few months before they graduate. Posted on the school Web page are the spring senior privileges for one year:

Senior Privileges for Last 2 Months

No blazers (except for revisit day)
No study hall (except for students with a D or lower)
10:30 check-in on weeknights
Seniors may order food up until 10:30
No waiting for sit-down and informal meals
Doughnuts after Monday and Wednesday chapel
The school will provide a DVD player for the senior lounge

Because thirteen seniors had a D or lower that spring, they did not receive senior privileges.

Viewing school rituals and traditions as largely responsible for establishing and maintaining a hierarchy based on seniority, the students bemoan Bolton's lack of such traditions. Although Bolton has some traditions and rituals, they contend that those at other schools are "on a much larger scale" and are "a much bigger deal." The Bolton traditions range from an "ugly" plaid jacket passed down from star athlete to star athlete and seniors singing the Weenie Song to the freshmen at 10:00 on the first night of school ("We love you weenies, oh yes we do, we love you, we love you") to naked runs where large groups of boys (and sometimes girls) streak naked from their dorms late at night and ring the victory bell.

By far the students' favorite tradition is Grunt Day, which takes place in the spring and is a fund-raiser for the sophomore class. The sophomores sell themselves as grunts to the other students, who bid on them. The buyer then writes up a contract of what the grunt is expected to do and the grunt can decide whether to sign or not. The students often reminisce about great moments in grunt history. In one dorm the boys recall how Tyler "had to wear spandex shorts to chapel and whenever anyone yelled, 'Charge!' he had to run into a tree." Tyler adds, "Or a wall, like full speed. I was, like, cut and bruised by the end of the day. It was great." One of the boys comments, "And it was funny as hell!" Tyler agrees, "It was great. I had fun."

At many prep schools hazing of the underclassmen is part of the prep school rite of passage. Many of the Bolton students who have attended other boarding schools describe such hazing. One boy says, "The hazing was crazy at Winston. I saw kids duct-taped to trees naked. I've seen kids pissed on, dragged up and down fire escapes, thrown into lakes in the middle of winter." Another adds, "At my brother's school they duct-taped a kid to a luggage cart in his underwear and sent him up and down an elevator for an hour and a half and then threw him into a lake."

There are also newspaper accounts such as the suit by a former student at an exclusive prep school much like Bolton but more competitive. Alleging that assaults are routine on younger students, the student described to the press the type of hazing that was common: "Three or four boys will often pin a single boy down, grab his testicles, shove fingers up his rectum, then lick his face." Because of a "code of silence among the students," he claims hazing was "widespread and appeared to be intertwined in the fabric of the school's environment" (Schemo, 2001, p. A16).

The students insist that there is no hazing at Bolton, especially "nothing of that sort" and "really not much at all." One boy elaborates on why hazing is not a real issue at Bolton: "We're not that competitive. Like at Cole [his old school, a prestigious pre-preparatory school] that kind of thing was much more apt to happen because it was much more competitive." He adds, "This is more of a family school." Others also attribute the difference to the intolerance of the administration.

To overcome "boredom," the upperclassmen sometimes play pranks or mildly haze the underformers at Bolton. One boy explains that when his dorm is bored, they wake up the sophomores in the next dorm, turn on the lights, plug in the vacuum, close the door, then run away.

The vast majority of upperclassmen and many underclassmen wish there were more rituals and traditions at Bolton, ones to celebrate and create more inequality between the forms. They reason that inequality is needed to teach the underclassmen "respect for seniority," to submit to their place at the bottom of the school hierarchy, and to "prepare them for the hierarchical nature of society." Many also believe that organized initiation rites are "fun" and meaningful and bolster the morale and the unity of the student body by "making character at a school."

The students bemoan that over the years the administration banned many rituals because it found them to be offensive or to amount to hazing. Once the lacrosse team used to strip one of the freshman players at the end of the last practice and make him run back to the dorm naked. The coaches and administration put an end to this tradition. A few years after this research took place, the headmaster ended the Grunt Day fund-raiser for the sophomore class.

Although most of the girls desire more traditions and rituals at Bolton, they rarely call for inequality between the forms but rather say that the traditions would add to the unity of the school and be more fun. Even the girls in a sophomore dorm want more traditions and rituals and good-natured hazing because it would be "a lot more fun." In a senior dorm the girls describe how unifying their one hazing incident as a class was when they sang the Weenie song to the freshmen in their dorms on the first night of school:

> That was, like, the *best* moment for our class. I mean honestly,
> until graduation that was one of the few moments that we were
> like totally a class. And it didn't matter who you are, or how long
> you'd been here or whether you know the words to the song or
> not, it was just the fact that we were out there screaming and
> like . . . harassing the freshmen.

Unlike the girls, the boys want traditions and rituals and even hazing in order to promote inequality between the forms and to teach the freshmen respect, submission, and their place in the hierarchies of the school. Typical are the opinions of the boys in one dorm who contend that the freshmen are "little pricks" and "run around like they are kings of the world":

-They need to be beaten. They need to be hazed.

-They need the paddles.

-I'm not saying it has to be physical, but they need initiation so
that they can learn to fit into our social project, which has a defined
hierarchy.

Many of the boys view organized initiations positively because "what doesn't kill you makes you stronger" and that "if you can't deal with them, then there's a lot in the real world you won't be able to deal with."

Not all students think that the student body at Bolton should be more hierarchical. Many freshmen claim that they already face a great deal of inequality and do not like "the clear hierarchy between forms." Typical is one boy's complaints: "Living a life where upperclassmen are better or are perceived to be better should be addressed. Many upperclassmen think they are superior to a person only a few months younger than them, and that is wrong."

∷ CLIQUES

The cliques in the student body demonstrate how the profound desire to fit in and belong coincides with the need to exclude. Despite disliking the cliques for their exclusiveness and inequality, the students perceive a hierarchy of social acceptance with inequality implicit in the exclusiveness of the highest-ranking groups.

"Dealing with the different cliques on campus" is one of the students' biggest issues. The subject of cliques is always a topic of enthusiastic conversation, with students all talking at once and wanting to describe the number of cliques and the exclusiveness of some of the groups. The students consistently identify the various cliques on campus and the differences between male and female ones. As they do with race and class, some of the students believe the nature of boarding school minimizes the number of cliques. A boy explains: "Here you have to live in a dorm. So no matter what, you are going to have to associate with people you wouldn't be hanging out with otherwise."

In addition to cliques based on class, ethnicity, and day students or boarders, the girls list cliques based on form, sports, popularity, personality, and special interests. The boys add intelligence, hair color, and style of clothes. The girls divide the groups as "freshman girls," "hockey boys," "the 'we're fabulous and have a lot of money' clique," "dumb jocks," "dorks," "computer nerds," "music people," "rich bitches," "day students," and "NYC plus NJ group (the African Americans)." The boys identify groups as "rich," "freshmen," "Korea," "Asian," "Hong Kong," "chorus," "Abercrombie," "blond," "Caucasian," and a variety of sports-based groups. Certain sports are more cliquish than others: "Hockey sticks together, and then lacrosse sticks together." The boys explain that they include intelligence because "the smart kids don't usually hang out with, like, the jocks."

While the girls view the boys' cliques as based on sports and on "how they act," the boys describe their cliques as based on race, class, and sports. Both genders have a hard time deciding what the girls' cliques are based on, but ultimately the girls say their cliques are based on "grade level," "looks," or "popularity." The boys contend that for girls "it's more physical," "more popularity," whether or not they are "slutty," as well as "a certain intelligence level that goes along with it too. You can't be too smart." Others also say that the girls' cliques are based on how girls "act":

> For girls it's more than looks, though it's also a certain personality. Because if you're a girl and you look great, you know, whatever they want, but you still don't act the way the little clique wants you to act, you're still not going to be accepted by it.

Both genders view the girls' cliques as more stable and absolute and the boys' as more flexible and rotating according to seasonal sports. As one boy observes, "Girls have their cliques and they stay." The boys explain that their cliques are flexible because "you can, like, hang out with the kids in your dorm one night and then if you have a game you hang with your team." One boy says, "With the guys . . . it goes a lot by sports, like who's on your team at that time becomes kind of your friend." They assert that cliques are based on sports teams more than dorms or other interests because that is whom they interact with most outside of class. One boy jokes, "Being naked in the locker room together really brings us closer together." These descriptions confirm theories that males focus on larger group relationships, while females focus on closer personal relationships (Baumeister & Sommer, 1997; Gabriel & Gardner, 1999).

The students attribute the girls' social stress to the exclusivity of the girls' cliques combined with their need to be part of the "right" group. A group of freshman boys claims, "Socially, it's a lot more stressful for females than for males 'cause for females it's all about *who* you hang out with, *who* your male friends are, *who* your female friends are." One boy adds, "I don't think [for males] it's as important who your friends are as long as you're happy with your friends. For a girl, it's like 'I have to be with the popular girls or I'm worthless.'"

The students claim that some male cliques are stable and are based on "people's ethnic background or social class." Four groups are relatively fixed: the rich boys, the hockey players, the black kids, and the Asian kids. Many boys describe the wealthiest students as "the only real set clique" and as "alienating themselves from everybody else" the way girls do, and they say that these boys are "idiots." This group consists of "the typical preppy boarding school kids" who "think they're better than everyone else." Because of the rich boys' exclusiveness, the other boys often describe them negatively and question their masculinity. One boy observes, "I think of them as, like, girlie because of it. Like, they don't have any other friends."

The hockey team also appears to be more fixed and is an exception to the rule of rotating sports teams. A hockey player explains, "Certain teams, like I know the hockey team seems to stay friends through the whole thing," and all but one of the others agree. Although it is not apparent at first, one reason that hockey players are a more fixed group is due to class. Many of the hockey players are at Bolton on scholarships, and membership in this clique seems to fall along class lines. Not coincidentally, there is often animosity between the hockey clique and the rest of the boys.

Although a few say that the minority students "always separate themselves," most agree that these boys are not a true clique because they intermingle and do not view themselves as superior. While the African American and Asian students self-segregate, the students from other countries and backgrounds assimilate into the general population. One boy says, "The blacks and the Asians have their own separate areas, but the other nationalities kind of blend in." Not all foreign students blend in easily. Some boys harass a French student in the group for not fitting the American standards of cleanliness, appearance, and sociability. Because he has longish hair pulled back in a headband (a very European, but not American, thing to do), the boys scoff, "What are you wearing!" They say that he is not part of any clique and "sits by himself," adding:

-He's French and nobody likes French people . . .

-He smells.

-Jean-Paul, go into your room. It's too late for you to be out here.

Even the most enduring cliques, those based on race, can change. One Korean boy says his clique "is changing because a couple of years ago the Thai people only hung out with Thai, and Korean people only hung out with Korean, and now everybody hangs out together."

Both genders view the girls as more competitive and hostile to each other both within and outside their cliques. Many students describe the competition and the covert animosity between the girls' cliques, especially the bitch squad and a group of pretty juniors. The girls assert, "Guys will beat each other up and then be best friends the next day," but "girls hold grudges." The freshman girls express frustration because girls and their cliques are more contentious than those of boys. One says, "I think boys are more loyal than girls. They're not the backstabbing bitches girls can be." Another adds, "I think there's a lot of competition between girls. Even your best friend can become your worst enemy in just one day. With guys that would never happen."

The girls' cliques are different from the boys' because the girls segregate themselves more from each other. One boy points out, "The difference between girl cliques and guy cliques is that guy cliques are cliques, but there's, like, intercliqueing. There's no intercliqueing of girl cliques. They're all just vicious." Another boy explains, "Girls have that thing where all girls just pretend to be friends with other girls. There's a lot of that going on." A third contends, "All girls do is walk around together and give the nasty bitchy look." The boys cite numerous covert but dramatic fights within the girls' cliques, contrasting them with the boys' disagreements, which are overt but less of "a big issue":

-[Boys] just call each other an asshole.

-Yeah, and, like, an hour later you go back and hang out in the room with him.

-Or five minutes later.

-Guys don't let little, minor, tedious things get to them.

Some cliques rank socially higher than others. The cliques at the top of the hierarchy are the most exclusive and based on status or popularity. Male popularity depends on rank in the social hierarchy and being cool. A freshman writes, "Who is socially higher is a big issue. Many of the people who are looked up to have girlfriends, do drugs, and are 'cool.'"

At the top of the social scale are the most exclusive and self-segregating groups: the rich students, hockey players, and popular kids. Most of the other students view these groups negatively because the groups think they are better than everyone else. The "guys that have a lot of money" are often viewed as the most exclusive group and the only "real clique."

The "popular guys" (mostly good athletes) are another exclusive clique described by the students. They hang out with "only pretty girls," especially the "senior princesses." Some boys call them the "2 cool" clique because "they act too cool." Most agree, "The 2 cool crew sucks!"

Unlike most of the other students, the girls at the top of the social hierarchy, the self-proclaimed "bitch squad" or "senior princesses," do not describe cliques negatively, saying that they exist "but not in a bad way." An African American member of the clique frankly proclaims, "We don't really associate with ugly people." Other girls in the group claim cliques are based on "similarities" and that "you hang out with people that look like you." Instead of saying that cliques are based on class, beauty, and popularity, as the other students do, these girls never mention class or popularity and claim that cliques are based on "age, personality, and sometimes sports."

The "dorks" or "nerds" and other low-status groups are at the bottom of the popularity ladder. In one dorm, when the girls contemplate what kind of label to give their own group, they are careful to differentiate their group from the "dorks":

-What are we?

-The smarties. We're not dorks, though.

-We're clean kids.

-We are the good kids.

The boys in another dorm describe the "nerdery" as low end of the scale in the hierarchy of cliques:

-You don't have to be smart to be in the nerdery, you just have to be weird.

-It is sort of like the outcasts of every other clique in the school have come together to form their own group.

-But there are a few groups that are even below the nerdery.

The boys often maintain a pecking order during their discussions by picking on individuals of lower social ranking. In one dorm, a popular boy says to an unpopular boy, "You don't count. You don't have a life. You don't go out of the dorm. . . . You have nothing. You are nothing. You are out of the social realm."

The "unpopular" students view the consistency of their groups not as due to exclusivity but rather as a result of their being ostracized by the rest of the school community. One boy in the "nerdery" admits, "I personally sit with the same four or five people at lunch, but I don't go out of my way to exclude people. It's just that nobody wants to sit with me."

:: THE DINING HALL

When I ask about the different cliques on campus, the students tell me over and over again that all I have to do is look at the seating in the dining hall and I will see all of the cliques. So I do.

Because the same groups always sit together, the seating in the dining hall reflects the different cliques at Bolton. One girl exclaims, "I've been sitting at the same table for the last four years. How strange is that!" A boy points out that where different groups sit is so stable "you might as well designate" certain tables to different cliques. Another agrees, "I can count on two hands the number of times I've sat somewhere else." One boy explains:

> If you see someone, you can probably pick out what table they sit at. Like, "Oh, he's an athlete; he sits at, you know, in this section over there," or "He's this type of kid; he sits back there," or "That girl's like this. She's such a geek; she sits in that corner."

The wide variety of terms the students use to label the different groups in the dining hall (and in other areas of campus life) highlights the numerous divisions within the student body as well as the social hierarchy that exists among the student body. Because of the importance of the dining hall in the students' discussions on cliques, I ask the students to draw a picture of the dining hall and then label the tables with the terms they would use to designate the group that sits there.

In general, the students agree upon the composition of the different cliques and where they sit. Most of the students identify similar groups mostly based on race, social class, sports, special interests, day students, academics, or popularity. Almost every student places particular tables, especially the more prominent ones such as the "hockey table," the "black table," the "senior girls' table," and the "nerdery," in exactly the same spot. Although certain groups are fixtures in the dining hall, the less prominent or easily identifiable or labeled groups vary more.

The students' terminology reflects the hierarchy between the groups. Some groups are consistently labeled "nerds," "losers," "sucky people," "rejects and outcasts," and "worthless." Others are consistently labeled "snobs," "senior bitches," or "social climbers." Even though the latter terms are largely negative, they indicate a high social status.

Individuals do not label their own group or table negatively. The senior girls, whom the other students consistently label as "snobs" or "bitches," describe themselves as the "senior girls." Similarly, the boys referred to as the "nerds" or "losers" call themselves "music people," the "creative table," or "non-athletic." The students at some tables use the same neutral terms that others use: the "hockey table," the "black table," or the "freshmen."

The terminology used by the boys and girls differ in several ways. The girls use fewer negative terms in their terminology. Although the girls call some groups "bitches," "unpopular," "nerds," "obnoxious jerks," "annoying hockey guys," "druggies," "music people geeks," "snotty people," and "potheads," the boys use harsher and more negative terms: "tool," "bitch," "sucky people," "Lambert [the name of a dorm] retards," "sketchy people," "dumb girls," "rejects and out-casts," "lazy people," "thing one and thing two," "dorks and misfits," "soul train," "nerdery," "stoners and weirdos," "worthless," "ugly," "losers," "outcasts," "Nathan and his peckerheads," as well as many derogatory terms referring to male homosexuality (discussed below). One boy went so far as to label *every* table where girls sit as simply "bitches."

The boys also classify groups of girls (not boys) by looks, while girls do not. Girls use the terms "cool" or "popular." While some boys use these terms as well, they also use "cute girls," "good-looking girls," "not good-looking girls," and "blond Greenwich girls."

The boys also use terms that refer to sexual preference in a derogatory manner for other males, while girls do not. Whereas the girls use terminology such as "upper-class social climbers," "prep Greenwich," or "snooty people" to label the tables where the wealthier boys sit, the boys use similar terms as well as "fruitcakes and pink team," "fruity group," "pink team and Colin and his bitches (a.k.a. fags)," and "boys pink team." Other groups are sometimes also targeted. One boy designates a group as "crew [the sport] fags and day student queers."

:: DORMS

Not only are individual cliques labeled and put into a hierarchy, but also entire dorms have certain personalities or reputations. Those that rank low are denied connections because of their low status. There is much agreement between all the students, both boys and girls, on how the different dorms are regarded. Although the girls' dorms appear somewhat equal, each having its own label and personality, the students place the boys' dorms in more of a hierarchy, with some of the dorms clearly at the bottom and others at the top of the social ladder.

Some sophomore girls describe the different personalities and reputations of the girls' dorms in this manner:

> This is the sophomore hall. Over there are the seniors, down there is the insane hall, the crazy ones, over there are the sleepers, and [in] Bailey are the ones that don't want to be bothered with anyone. And freshmen are across the street.

They describe the boys' dorms in this manner:

> [In] Halsey are the popular jerky people. Wentworth is the money dorm. Pratt is sort of just random people . . . Penderson is really sketchy. Bright is music. Lambert is just the dorm they got stuck in, the reject dorm basically.

A "rich" dorm that is "all about money" is also viewed as the "the racist dorm."

The students in the dorms know what their own labels are, especially when they are derogatory or flattering. In Carter, the dorm others describe as the "rich bitch" dorm, the girls laugh and agree loudly when I ask about dorms having reputations:

> -Ours has a reputation that is totally false.
>
> -No, it's not!
>
> -We're the bitch rich girls.
>
> -Yeah, but a lot of people think that we party a lot, but we definitely don't.

The girls do not argue with the titles of "rich" or "bitches" but do claim, "We definitely don't party." When I clarify, "Are you the bitch rich girls? Is that part true?" many respond, "Yeah."

The girls in Carter have an ongoing feud with a group of pretty juniors in Colt. The Carter girls describe Colt dorm like this:

-Colt is the bad-ass dorm. They get away with everything.

-They do get away with everything.

-They're so, like, uppity two-shoes.

In describing the boys' dorms, the girls describe two dorms as "bad," one "a partying dorm" and another as "quiet. Pratt, you don't ever hear anything about."

The girls in Colt also revel in their reputation as the "crazy dorm." After describing an adjacent hall as "the calm ones who just go to sleep," they proclaim, "We're crazy!" The girls explain that they have this reputation because of their unusual rituals, which include "booty patrol," in which they pull down their pants and moon each other, and "topless Tuesday." Taking pride in their reputation, they delight in shocking the rest of the students. One difference many of the boys see between themselves and the girls is that they believe that the girls more often actively decide to live together than the guys do and therefore "the girls' dorms are a lot more cliquey."

The boys are well aware of their dorm's reputation and place in the dorm hierarchy. The boys in one dorm, Lambert, which is separated from the others by some distance, feel left out of the social scene and stigmatized as "losers" by the rest of the students. The boys in this dorm even say that "Lambert sucks." One boy exclaims, "Lambert is the gay dorm." Another adds, "This could have been a hospital. It's all white and sterile. I feel like I'm dying here. I feel like I have an infectious disease and have been quarantined." They explain, "They always show our dorm to all the parents. Yeah, it's classy and professional." The boys in Lambert conclude, "It's a nice dorm, but it's not fun."

The boys in other dorms are also aware of their negative reputations. In one dorm the boys describe their dorm as "the social outcasts," saying, "If you live in Bright, you either are really, really smart or you play music." The boys in another dorm describe their dorm as "the projects" and "the ghetto." They describe other dorms in the following ways:

-Wentworth is the rich dorm.

-Bright has intelligence going for them.

-Lambert are just the kids nobody wants.

-The outcasts.

A few dorms hold themselves in high regard. The boys in one dorm full of hockey players and partiers talk about another dorm as the "social retards" and call themselves "bad-ass mofos."

The two freshman boys' dorms, although none of the upperclassmen differentiate them, openly describe a hierarchy. Both the higher-ranking dorm, Weld, and the lower-ranking dorm, Lowell, know their place. One boy in Weld declares, "Compared to Lowell dorm, I think we're sort of superior. I mean, how else do you want to put it? I mean, you look at them and they just live so dull." As a means of explanation, the boy adds, "This dorm is way more involved in sports." The boys in Lowell agree that their status is lower. "We're the lower-class dorm. All the pretty girls go over there, and we get the rejects," says one boy. Another adds, "But now Kyle has scared even them away, and nobody comes here now."

:: CULTURE OF INEQUALITY

Both the boys and girls publicly value equality over inequality while they demonstrate and describe much inequality. The ways the students negotiate this dichotomy between equality and inequality are part of their gender, class, and ethnic performances.

Individual and group differences in the emphasis of equality or inequality are also readily apparent. Those at the top of certain social hierarchies, such as the wealthy students of the "bitch squad" or the "high-class club" or the popular hockey players, display the strongest beliefs in inequality. Those at the bottom, such as the girls and the African American scholarship students, often display and vocalize most clearly the value of equality. Despite the overall emphasis placed on equality, the reality is that both male and female students perceive inequality in their lives.

The relative emphasis the wealthier students place on inequality and difference is also apparent in the importance of their class-based cliques. The relative importance of class over ethnicity is made clear as the wealthy African American students tend to belong to the wealthy cliques and often distance themselves from the much poorer African American scholarship students. Despite some degree of reverse classism and their disparaging remarks concerning the self-segregation and attitudes of superiority of the wealthiest cliques, the less wealthy students often reveal their desire or longing to be part of that group.

As society's values are "manifest in the settings and circumstances of its institutions and organizations" and elite private schools are "effective agents of hierarchical distinctions," the "acceptance" of educational inequality (Peshkin, 2001) and the existence of private schools such as Bolton Academy reveal the cultural acceptance and even encouragement of the inequality that results from the American values of individualism, excellence, and competition. As the Bolton students negotiate equality and inequality in their daily rituals, they mirror these larger cultural values.

6 ::

Perfect Girls, Best-at-Everything Guys: Managing Pressure, Having Fun

The incompatibility of the opposing values of excellence and fun and the related tension between freedom and constraint, along with the students' dual desires and pressures, mark two of the most volatile struggles the students engage in at Bolton. The institution of preparatory school is based on the value of excellence: excellence in academics, excellence in sports, excellence in the arts, and excellence in citizenship and leadership. It is a value that the students hear repeatedly from the administration and faculty and often parents, a value that many seem to have internalized. As the different influences push students to achieve excellence, many strive to attain it, often in all areas at the same time. Girls report intense pressure to be "perfect," while the boys feel they must be the "best" at everything.

Many students feel pressure to achieve and go to the "right" college, pressure coming from themselves, their families, their peers, and Bolton Academy. Hinging its reputation on where its graduates matriculate, the school prominently displays the senior college list in the school catalogue and in the program at graduation. The names of students on the honor roll and high honor roll are displayed outside the academic dean's office for the whole school to see. The pressure for excellence and its external signs is great.

Even though the academic challenges and requirements are intense, most of the students believe that it is important to have fun and that they deserve it. This "hidden curriculum" (Crosier, 1991) is a perfect example of how the students actively create their own culture in an environment strictly regulated and orchestrated by adults. Not only do the students break the rules to have fun, but a culture supporting and glorifying rule breaking has become an important part of student life.

The students talk about the amount of sex and partying that take place on campus. Many students are called before the disciplinary committee each year for school violations, and an average of 10–15 students are expelled. Academically, a number of students strive to do as little work as possible, and a few do so poorly in their classes that they are subject to restrictions or are not asked back (the equivalent of being expelled) for having unsatisfactory grades.

How the students at Bolton negotiate and manipulate excellence and fun is in many ways peculiar to attending a preparatory boarding school and also varies from individual to individual. Although some individuals focus more on having fun while others focus more on excellence, still others try to combine the two, with most students struggling to reconcile these opposing values.

Pursuing excellence and fun are gendered activities. Caring about grades, working hard academically, and feeling stress and pressure are part of the performance of femininity but not of masculinity both at Bolton and among American students in general. Academic effort has become feminized because although achieving academically is viewed as masculine, studying and trying hard academically are conceived by American youth as feminine and socially unattractive for males (Lasane, Sweigard, Czopp, Howard, & Burns, 1999; Grabill et al., 2005; Adler, Kless, & Adler, 1992). Although academic success, like success in general, is viewed as masculine, it is more highly regarded if it comes naturally, without vulnerability to academic planning and preparation (Ablard & Lipschultz, 1998). Male students who plan and organize assignments are regarded as neurotic or easily stressed (Grabill et al., 2005).

Similarly, having fun (especially illicit fun) is masculinized, as it is part of the performance of masculinity but not femininity. American youth view consumerism and leisure instead of hard work to be the masculine ideal (Osgerby, 2001). Gendered performances are largely responsible for the differences in the degree to which girls and boys at Bolton focus on fun, how fun is defined, the pressures they face to engage in illicit fun, and how they approach various aspects of sex and partying.

:: OVERT VALUES OF EXCELLENCE AND FUN

Publicly the students praise both excellence and fun, and these values are evident in their senior speeches and newspaper articles. In their chapel speeches, many of the students celebrate the ideals of excellence. Frequently, the students urge the audience to work their hardest in order to have "no regrets," a phrase often used by a popular coach. One girl's advice to the other students is to "give it your all, and take everything you can out of it . . . no regrets." Another girl urges, "Don't have any regrets about what you could've or should've done." Some of the boys also encourage excellence. One boy urges the other students to "play to win and have no regrets . . . live every day to its fullest potential . . . adversity only makes you stronger . . . and train for excellence, not mediocrity."

Other boys, however, celebrate the value of fun in their chapel speeches. One boy urges, "Have some fun. Eventually this world we live in will end and we will have to grow up sooner or later." One boy tells his audience, "Life is too important to take seriously."

In some of the senior chapel speeches, boys talk about their regret in not achieving excellence while at Bolton. Several boys wish they had studied harder while at Bolton. One boy tells the students that he did not work hard enough and now is not able to go to college because none of the colleges to which he applied accepted him. He urges the other students to take their work seriously.

Conversely, others regret how hard they have worked and the lack of fun they have had since coming to prep school. Several stellar students, both male and female, who focused almost solely on excellence while at Bolton tell the student body that they regret studying so hard and not having more fun. One of these boys urges his audience to "live life to the fullest, try to enjoy every day."

Several students implicitly demonstrate the value of fun by contrasting their lives at Bolton with those of their friends in public school or college and speak wistfully about how much more fun they would be having if they were not at Bolton. One male postgraduate student (a postgraduate year at a prep school allows recent high school graduates, usually athletes, the opportunity to mature, develop their academic skills, and have more options for college) tells his audience:

> I could be in college right now, doing who knows what, or I could be studying. I could have girls in my room without having to ask

permission, or I could be studying. I could call people between the hours of 8 and 10 at night, or I could be studying.

One girl tells the audience that she regrets coming to Bolton Academy because she "lost all the little things about high school that seem to have the most meaning":

I went to public school my whole life. When it came time for high school I had never even thought about going anywhere else besides public high. None of my friends went to private schools or anyone in my family. Every morning my brother would drive me to Dunkin Donuts and then school. School was easy. If I didn't want to go to class I didn't have to. All I had to do was write a little note and sign my mom's name. I was pretty good at that. After school I could do what I wanted, go out with friends without having to sign out in a book and call three different people. I had real weekends, not just one night. Friday nights we'd go to football games, not study hall at eight o'clock. I could actually go out on Saturday nights and not have to be in at 11. Everything was just fine, but come hockey season my freshman year I was playing first line JV, fourth line varsity, on the guys' team. I was playing on three teams and none of them were that good. I knew if I wanted to play hockey in college I would have to go elsewhere. So I did. When it came down to it I did not want to leave. I had to leave everything and I was not ready for that, but unwillingly I did. Now, I feel like I've lost almost all of the high school experience. These were supposed to be the best years of my life but I don't think they were. I didn't get to go to the football games, homecoming dances, or state championships. I couldn't take a limo to my prom then go to after-prom parties. I didn't get to play in the powder puff football game or decorate my car for the pep rally. I lost all the little things about high school that seem to have the most meaning. I should not have any regrets, but now I do. I guess I gained a couple of things from Bolton—I received a good education and am playing hockey next year at [college]—but those things do not make up for the things that I have lost.

:: REALITY—INDIVIDUALISTIC AND GENDERED

The reality of how much excellence or fun the students have in their lives at Bolton varies, following both individualistic tendencies and gender patterns. At Bolton the girls slightly but consistently outperform the boys in academic performance. For example, for the four academic years from 2001–2002 through 2004–2005, senior girls' GPA led that of the boys by an average of 0.14 (based on a 4.0 scale), junior girls outperformed the boys by an average of 0.16, sophomore girls outperformed the boys by an average of 0.21, and freshman girls' GPA led the boys' by an average of 0.02. In total, the girls' GPA was 0.13 higher than the boys'.

The pattern in the differences in academic performance, with the freshmen having the least difference, the sophomores having the most, and the seniors and juniors in the middle, corresponds with the amounts of pressure the students often describe to fit the gender ideals. The freshmen are new and have not been exposed long, the sophomores feel the most pressure, and the seniors have matured a bit and describe themselves as not worrying as much about fitting in.

The gender ideals for both sexes encompass conflicting aspects that both encourage academic success (being perfect for girls and being the best for boys) and discourage or hinder academic performance (such as placing importance on looks for girls and acting cool for boys, which includes not studying or trying hard academically). Because of their opposing ideals, the way the boys and girls perceive, respond to, and handle academic pressure differs.

The agenda of a typical Friday school meeting reveals the realities about how both the ideal of excellence and the ideal of fun play out in the lives of Bolton's student body and how they vary for different students. As the meeting commences, the head of the math department reads the results and awards of a recent math team competition. The Bolton students won the championship, and he calls out the students' names and congratulates them. He then calls the headmaster forward and presents him with the trophy. After the students and faculty make sports and music announcements, the dean of students informs the school that a student committed a second tobacco offense and reads the restrictions for that student. He then announces that Sunday detention will have to be moved to a new room because there are too many people to fit in the normal location.

:: EXCELLENCE

Believing in the value of excellence, most students undergo considerable stress and pressure to achieve it in their daily lives. An article in the school newspaper explaining why the school placed new restrictions on phone and Internet use reported that, according to the academic dean, "about 90% of the symptoms of the students who reported to the health center last year originated from lack of sleep." The school counselor also told me that in her opinion the majority of issues the student body faces, especially among the girls, are the exhaustion and stress of trying to reach perfection in all areas.

Stress and Pressure

The amount of stress and pressure the students manifest correlates directly with their gender performances.[1] Since feeling stress and pressure is part of the performance of femininity, girls say that stress and pressure pervade their daily lives at Bolton. When asked if they are under pressure, the girls commonly respond, "Oh my God!" and then in a torrent list their many pressures. Typically the girls say, "You get pressure from everywhere!" and complain about the "impossible," "hectic," and "constant" schedule at Bolton and how they have no free time. One girl gushes, "I have tension headaches here. I go to bed with tension headaches." Another asserts, "I think there's a lot of pressure to be the best." Others claim that they have "tons" of pressure "from everyone, all angles," citing pressures for "work," "to get good grades," "to be popular," and for "sports."

One girl writes:

> It's hard to keep an equilibrium of everything right now and it isn't unusual to have mini-breakdown episodes every other night. The stress is definitely there in every aspect of our lives and the hard part is deciding which ones have priority: the college application, the boyfriend, the troubled friend, or the championship game.

Having "too much work, not enough sleep," the girls report "staying up till one or two in the morning and working on Sunday, our *one* free day."

Frequently in conversation the girls use the word "perfect" to describe the ideal of excellence they feel pressure to achieve. One girl's quest for perfection stems from the pressure she feels "to go to the best college, to be the best person, the best everything." Another comments, "I feel pressure to be perfect. You have to be like the smartest, and the best at sports and the prettiest and like the best in like everything."

Many girls describe the need to be the "perfect student" for colleges. One girl comments:

> I think there's more ways to feel the pressure to be perfect than physical appearance, especially when it comes down to looking at colleges and they all just want this *perfect* student. You know, you try to see which ways you can help this and help that and be well rounded, but it's really hard to be perfect at *everything*.

Another adds, "I feel like I have to have perfect grades or my parents won't let me come here anymore."

Because feeling stress and pressure is not part of the performance of masculinity, the boys downplay their pressure and stress and often deny that they feel any at all, especially in the group interview setting. Typically, when asked if they are under a lot of pressure, the boys respond, "Not really," "No, not at all," or "I'm not under any pressure at all." One hockey player says, "I never have stress. When I do, I'm usually like, 'Aaaghh,' and then I beat something up." Another hockey player says, "If I have enough work to be stressed, I just don't do it." Pointing fingers, the boys say, "He is," indicating another boy, who in turn denies it and responds, "Who? Are you?" It appears that some really do not feel pressure, while those who are under pressure do not want to admit it.

Some boys reluctantly admit that they experience "a little" pressure from "parents, grade-wise." One boy explains, "My parents expect me to get good grades, but I have to get good grades to go to college, so I don't really think they're putting pressure on me." Another student admits, "My dad knows I'll be disappointed in myself if I don't get good grades, so he doesn't put much pressure on me." When the boys claim that one boy has pressure, he retorts, "I don't." A Japanese boy pinpointed as having lots of pressure admits softly, "Kind of, yeah." After discussing how Asian parents pressure their children to excel, one of the boys jokes, "Or you get whipped!"

The boys repeatedly downplay their pressures as "all about how much you put on yourself." When one boy explains that "some kids bug out. They're just like, 'I can't take it anymore!' and they just like freak out and they have to go home for weeks at a time," the others quickly assert, "If you do a lot of activities, like football, dean's assistant, and Key [the group that gives tours to prospective students] then you can become stressed out. But if you're not involved in a lot, then you don't become that stressed," and "The only way you can get stressed out is if you procrastinate." Others agree, and one adds, "Yeah, no matter what anyone says, there is plenty of time to do your work."

The boys report spending a great deal of time watching DVDs or playing computer games, Xbox, or PlayStation, even during study hall. One senior reveals, "It is really difficult for me to get my work done. I guess it is kind of my fault for providing the dorm with an entertainment system and always wanting to challenge the other guys in FIFA games." Others explain:

-I know very well that in exactly half an hour I will be very stressed out because I have a paper due tomorrow, but I'm sitting here eating doughnuts. This paper has been assigned for a week but I'll be stressed because of Kirby's Adventures [a computer game] and doughnuts.

-I've seen more DVDs since I've been here. . . .

A few boys admit feeling a great deal of pressure. One boy comments, "Personally, I think I'm under as much pressure as I will be in my entire life." He explains that he is under pressure from both his parents and himself "because I can't afford, like, out of pocket money to go to college so I have to do well in everything so I can somehow go to college." A junior reports feeling pressure from himself and his parents because "they say this is the year that really counts, so they want me to buckle down and keep my grades up."

In their private writings, the boys admit to much more stress and pressure in their pursuit of excellence than when in group settings. This divergence suggests that behaviors such as working too hard, caring about grades, and feeling pressure are hidden because they run counter to the accepted performance of masculinity.

Most of the boys write that their stress and pressure are either general or connected with the pursuit of academic excellence. One boy writes his stress is "college, getting accepted. At this rate I hope to have gray hair when I'm twenty." Another boy writes, "There is too much pressure to do well. Competition is great but can become too much at times." Several students identify the need to be the best as a source of their stress. One boy explains, "I am dealing with the pressures of trying to be good at a lot of things (academics, athletics, student council). It's a lot of pressure, but I like it. It pushes me to do better."

The boys often write about their desire or pressure to "succeed," and unlike females this often includes their future careers. One boy writes, "Success is all that matters." Another writes, "There is a ton of pressure right now on who's going to succeed in life and who's not. Each decision we make, it seems is huge." One says that boys feel "the pressure to surpass [their] parents financially and in stature in the future."

Many of the students view future success as dependent on attending a good college and thus cite getting accepted at one as a main source of stress. One boy writes:

> The main thing is grades because what college you go to basically maps out your life. People say it doesn't and try to persuade us that it doesn't mean anything, but of course it does and there is nothing we can do about it.

Another writes, "The quest for college weighs down heavily upon seniors, for now we think it means everything in the world to go to the best college."

The boys also report striving for excellence and feeling intense stress and pressure to excel in athletics. Many write that their major issues are "trying to be a good athlete," "trying to make sports teams," or "worrying about making the hockey team and having a good season." Many emphasize the relative importance of athletics in their lives. One boy reveals that his major issue is "athletics—that is a huge part of life for me. It almost comes ahead of academics." A freshman describes how important it is to be a part of the varsity hockey team: "There is no other real desire of mine but to play on that team. I'm on the JV team now but would give up virtually anything to play on that team."

Unlike the girls, the vast majority of the boys scoff at the thought of feeling pressure to be perfect, and when a few do admit to it, they almost always describe it as "self-pressure." When asked if they feel they have to be perfect, the boys typically laugh and respond with a chorus of nos. Often someone shouts "What?" as if he's never heard anything so strange. Although they sometimes admit to wanting to be perfect in certain areas or in certain endeavors, the boys passionately deny feeling like they have to be perfect in any general way. One boy stands out who admits feeling the pressure to be perfect, but "only from myself." At which one of the others explains, "He's a perfectionist." In his private writing, another boy admits to pressure to be perfect: "Everyone wants us to do good and possibly be perfect. I think it is good but sometimes they are too hard on us."

Pressure Points

Girls

Saying that girls experience more pressure and stress from striving for excellence than boys, the students explain that girls are more competitive with their peers, that they care more about pleasing others and what others think, that they are more insecure, that they feel more guilt about disappointing others, and that they internalize their failures more than the boys.

Most of the girls claim that their pressures for excellence come from other people: advisors, parents, coaches, colleges, and Bolton. One girl explains, "It's craziness. You got it from your parents. You got it from your teachers." The girls often feel a "ridiculous" amount of pressure from other girls, claiming that girls compete "in everything, looks, sports, academics," something they don't view as being so intense for the boys. The competition between girls at Bolton is so great that they are "embarrassed to go to class" or "talk in class 'cause you feel stupid." The girls conclude, "Girls are really self-conscious. . . . there's a lot of pressure."

Attempting to please others, the girls feel that their stress is magnified because they get "caught up in the stupid little nothing" of insecurities of what others think and competition. Unlike the boys, the girls "care a lot more" what others "think about them" and feel guilty about disappointing others. One girl writes that it is hard to believe "how much pressure is on you to get good grades and do well so your parents will be proud." Another girl reveals:

> I am a perfectionist. I want perfect grades. I want perfect hair, perfect body. I want everything perfect about me. I want a perfect personality. My perfection is more a need to be loved. I don't think I do it for myself but for my parents and the people around me.

Yet another says:

> Like I couldn't really care less which college I went to, but my parents really cared, and so by making them happy, I was happy. And by making my teachers happy, I was happy.

The girls also "feel really bad skipping a class, not even because like if you don't go to class then you don't know what's going on, but like to have to talk to the teacher afterward and be like, 'I'm really sorry.'"

The girls contrast this with the boys' attitude: "Guys don't really feel like they have to, like, live up to what the teachers think because they don't get that guilty about it."

The ultimate source of the girls' pressure to be perfect and please others is the desire to secure relationships with parents, teachers, boys, and friends. One girl describes how the pressure she feels to be "perfect" comes from wanting friendships:

> That's why I was afraid to come back this year, because I was like, "There are going to be all these new girls who are going to be better at everything." Ask anybody—I was *so* scared. I was like, "Everybody's going to like them better than me because I'm not good at anything other than, like, being your friend."

Although the girls on scholarship feel added stress and pressure due to the economic drain of private school for their families, the African American girls feel more pressure because of the added strains of representing their race and not letting down their families and friends. Typically, one African American girl feels pressure from her "whole family," who "pitch in" to help her afford prep school. Because she is the first person her family has been able to send away to boarding school and her whole family thinks "it is such a big deal," she feels that she is "holding up all these people." This student adds:

> And then all these teachers that you become really close to and then all of a sudden they have all of this faith in you and the entire time you just keep going and you're never forgiven for your mistakes here because people expect so much of you. And no matter what there is so much pressure for college and all that.

One of the scholarship girls describes how her mother's ill health and effort to afford prep school make her feel "selfish," which increases her stress:

> I felt so bad. Like, it was sophomore year and I'm trying to do my thing or whatever and my mom gets sick. And I'm like, "I should be at the hospital with her. No, I'm here trying to get a higher education." And I feel guilty because I'm like, "Am I being selfish?" I even called her up yesterday and I was like, "Mom, I'll come home if you want me to," praying that she'd say, "No, stay, stay, stay." But it's such a strain on her. I don't know if I'm being selfish or not. I want to stay here. I want to graduate from here but . . . And that's hard to deal with.

Boys

Only a few boys admit feeling pressure, and almost all of them claim that it is self-induced pressure. One boy "sometimes" feels pressure but adds, "It's from myself." Other boys declare that their pressure is from "self," "all self," and "basically, completely self." When one boy mentions, "I put myself under pressure," the other boys laugh, "We know Mike! This kid shoots himself if he's like five minutes late." One student reflects, "You kind of create your own pressure, I think." Others agree, "You got to get good grades for college" and "You have to get good grades to stay here." Although some of the boys first cite "some" pressure from parents, teachers, or advisors, most agree that it really comes from themselves. Often the students say that attending prep school increases the pressure they put on themselves. One says, "It seems like I have to be the best. This is how I grew up and I love competition, so it's all good."

Occasionally the boys say that their pressure comes from other people, usually their parents:

> I'm under a lot of pressure to achieve from my parents. My parents are real sticklers for grades and stuff and if I get a C, it's like an F. And if I pull off a D, it's like hell on earth. It's not good.

The boys contend that parental pressure is often augmented by the large sum of money parents spend to send them to Bolton. One boy explains:

> I think parents put a lot of pressure on students because they're like, "We're paying $30,000 for you to go to school. You better do a damn good job and not disappoint us." And then it's like, "Oh my God! I can't screw up."

Another boy admits, "They don't *say* that to me, but I feel it." Another adds, "Yeah, I don't want to do bad. I don't want them to be mad at me." Several of the boys feel a "ton of pressure" from the hockey coach "primarily." One boy explains, "I'm terrified of Mr. Green [the hockey coach]." Another student writes, "Worrying about what team I'm on for hockey is important. I want to make my family proud, especially my grandfather, but it's a lot of pressure."

The Ivies

The Bolton students often focus on their or others' desires for them to attend a top college, Ivy League if possible. Despite parental and student expectations, very few of Bolton's students matriculate at an Ivy League school. For schools such as Bolton, an average of only 3 to 4% go to Ivy League schools, although a larger percentage, 8 to 10%, go to top-tier schools. This failure to meet the expectations of the Ivy League adversely affects the self-esteem of many students.

Girls

Most of the girls want to attend a prestigious college, preferably an Ivy, but they think that this is important mainly to please others. Typical is one girl's assertion that from a parent's and teacher's point of view, "The reason you came here is to get into the Ivy League colleges." The girls describe "a lot" of pressure on them for college, "starting in, like, your junior year." "They put the pressure on pretty heavy," says a girl about college counselors and parents. The competition among students is another source of pressure. One of the girls explains, "It's what you talk about for, like, six months." Another adds, "Yeah, it's all really pressure about what other people are doing."

This pressure appears as strong among the African American students. Kara leads a discussion in her dorm on how important it is for their parents that they go to an Ivy League college. Kara asserts, "My mom calls, 'You're going to Yale, right?' 'Yeah, right, Mom.'" Another girl laughs, "My parents gave that one up a long time ago." Kara continues, "My mom's like, 'Why aren't you applying to Ivy League colleges?' 'Because I won't get in!' 'Don't sell yourself short!'"

The girls typically claim that to go to a prestigious college is "not that important really" for them but that it is "definitely" important for their parents, and "it's more important for your parents to know you're going to the right college, which makes it more important for you." Attending a prep school has made the pressures for college greater. The reasons for this have to do with the money their parents are spending for them to attend Bolton, that parents and college counselors view getting into an Ivy or other prestigious college as "why we're here," and the importance Bolton places on where its students go to school by publishing lists at graduation.

Heather, a wealthy girl, describes a much different scenario:

> In my situation the most frustrating thing is I'm like, "Mom, I'm having such a hard time, I want to drop out of school." Just joking. And she'll be like, "Whatever makes you happy." It's like, "No! You're not supposed to say that."

At this, she gets lots of offers to trade moms. Heather continues:

I was like, "Mom, I don't know what I'm going to do. I'm not going to get into college." And she's like, "Well, you can always drop out and work at Bloomingdale's. You like shopping there, don't you?" I'm like, "Are you kidding me?"

Again she gets more offers to trade, and the other girls do not give her much sympathy. One of the other girls interjects, "Trust me, you all, there is not one side that is better. Both of it is stress and pressure. Whether it's you putting the pressure on yourself or other people putting the pressure on you, it's just the way it is."

Differing markedly from the others, some very motivated and stellar students describe how much they want to attend prestigious colleges. The vast differences in how individual students negotiate the values of excellence and fun are evident among these girls. As the girls discuss how going to a prestigious college is "very important" and "huge" to them, one girl, Samantha, comments:

I just want to go to a college where I can party. I just want to go to a party school. . . . Well, I figure if you're only going to go to college once, you might as well make it a fun one. You only live once.

The rest of the girls continue to discuss how they would love to be one of those students who can brag, "Oh my God, early acceptance to Harvard!" Unimpressed, Samantha states, "I'll just be a stripper." The others do not miss a beat and continue to discuss how their quest to attend a prestigious college started out in preschool, when they were four years old, and how going to a top college will result in their lives "working out really well."

Unlike the girls in the other dorms, these girls do not feel pressure from their parents because they are so self-motivated, but they still want to make their parents "happy" and do not want to "disappoint" them. The girls explain that they do not get "that much" pressure from their parents because "I already exert enough on myself, so whatever I do, they know I'm doing my best, so they don't put any pressure on me," and "my parents know that I'm so demanding of myself." Samantha mentions nonchalantly, "My parents don't give a shit as long as I'm not living at home."

Boys

Feeling similar pressure to attend a prestigious college, the boys seem markedly less affected by the pressure from others. Although some students cite intense pressures to get into an Ivy League college or to continue family legacies at prestigious colleges, most downplay this pressure from others. Focusing on their own wants and desires, many boys claim that the only pressure they feel is to go the college that is "right for me"; others say that their parents have "given up" on them.

Going to a prestigious college is "so important" and "very important" for the boys. Some of the boys claim, "It's expected" and "That's why we're here." Some feel pressure to continue a family legacy. One boy says, "I've got to go. My whole family has gone to the same college, so if I don't get in. . . . I pretty much have to go there." So intense is the desire to attend a prestigious college that a student's self-esteem plummets if he gets rejected. One boy explains:

> College is really important for some, and some, like, overrate it.
> I'm not saying college is not important, but they base their life on it and when they get rejected, sometimes . . . lowers their self-esteem.

Although the boys feel parental and social pressures to attend an Ivy League school, they downplay these pressures. Facing pressure "from kindergarten on" to go to a prestigious college or "you're going to have a terrible life," one boy says, "And then I realized it's all B.S., so what I'm worrying about is going to a college where I'll be happy and succeed." Many assert, "There are different types of colleges—the ones your parents want you to go to, and the ones that suit you best" and "make you happy."

The boys often tell how their parents have "slowly" come to accept that they won't be attending prestigious Ivy League schools. One boy typically explains, "I've taught them to lower their expectations."

Some of the male students question whether a prestigious college will help them be successful in life. In one dorm, a boy comments, "As long as I get a job and make my 35 mil by the time I'm 25, then I'm good to go. I don't really care what I do." Another asserts that although "a lot of people, especially at this school, are enamored with going to an Ivy League," he believes "an education is what you make out of where you go." At this, a wealthy boy blurts out, "Yeah, my dad had the shittiest education and he's a trillionaire." He explains how his father went to a state university but still "makes tons" of money. He claims that "some of my parents' best friends" went to prestigious schools and haven't been nearly as successful, adding:

> The people who tend to put pressures on themselves that go to all these prestigious schools tend to be the ones that fail life because they break down right after it all.

Coping with Pressure

The differences in how the boys and girls cope with stresses and pressures are directly connected to the differences in their focus on self and other in the performance of gender.

Girls

Although disagreeing about which sex pushes itself harder academically, the students agree that the girls internalize and react more to the academic stresses. One girl explains:

> I think [the boys] put it off better. They'd be like, "Well, you know, I have four tests tomorrow." Where I'd be, "Oh my God! I've got four tests! Oh my God!"

The girls believe they feel more stress than the boys because they "take themselves more seriously," "care more what other people think," and internalize their failures. A girl explains, "If something bad happens to a girl, she's like, 'Oh my God! My life is over.' Whereas a guy just brushes things off and they're like, 'Oh well.'" Several girls add:

> -Like I've never seen a guy getting upset for getting, like, a C and I'm almost in tears.

> -I'll, like, sit down and not talk the whole class if I get a bad grade.

> -I'll be in a bad mood the whole week if I do that.

Many girls argue that the boys are also stressed, but they don't show it "half as much as girls do," "just don't talk about it," and "just don't let it come to the surface." The girls explain:

> -Girls seem to talk through it. Guys bury it.

> -Guys never talk about their problems.

During times of intense stress, the girls act in volatile ways. One girl comments, "Oh my God! Don't even talk to her because she's just going to bite your head off today." Others describe how girls respond to stress:

-Freaking out! No one is friends.

-Crying, like, there are tears like during exam week.

-Like, you'll walk into someone's room during exam week and you'll see someone just freaking out or just crying.

-A *lot* of breakdowns.

-A *lot* of emotional—

-Catastrophes.

One of the girls adds, "Like, during exam week, three people started crying the same day. I was like, 'Oh my God! It's because it's exam week.'"

To manage this stress, the girls engage in mostly other- or group-oriented stress releasers. They explain, "We listen to loud, out-of-control music and sing it at the top of our lungs. It's, like, the entire dorm." Although one girl says, "I do things more by myself," most describe themselves as participating in "totally" and "definitely" group activities. The girls explain:

-We put on Christmas carols and sang to the Christmas carols.

-To, like, really cheesy, cheesy Christmas carols.

-And, like, danced around and sang.

-And we put up a tree and did secret Santa.

The main ways others deal with stress are by eating and "goofing off" together. One girl explains, "Food is my escape. When I get stressed out, I just eat. It doesn't matter if there are people there or not. It's more fun that way, though." They describe other stress releasers:

-Sometimes we just sit around and talk about the things that are making us stressed, but it doesn't really help anything.

-We get really *dumb*. Especially exam week, we get really dumb. We're so educationally drained that we're like, "Duh!" and run around like idiots with our pants hiked up.

-Or we'll watch a movie or something.

The girls explain that their stress releasers are generally group activities because:

-You can't goof off by yourself.

-Unless you're sulking in your room.

-That's really no fun.

Boys

The boys believe that they handle their pressures differently than girls because "guys just suck it up, guys just deal," whereas girls are "uptight," are "so stupid," and have "little stupid crises." One boy exclaims, with a sigh of exasperation, "I think girls at this age are just dumb because they can't rationalize things." The boys make fun of the girls' "crises" such as their concerns with matching clothes, being thin, and "their reputation with guys." A boy concludes, "It's amazing that some girls just live their lives . . . worrying about what I think of them."

The boys handle stress in more solitary and physical ways. One boy comments, "I think if a guy has stress, he takes it out on himself. He deals with it himself. But a girl will take it out on everyone around her." Another adds, "Girls can work themselves up into riots and go berserk." They view girls as dealing with stress "emotionally" and "taking it out on each other," while boys "deal with it physically." One boy explains, "Instead of, like, crying, we'll, like, break something or get into a fight."

The sexes also handle their academic stress differently. One boy notes:

I know that, like, if girls have a lot of work to do, they begin staying up really late to do it, and guys will be like, "You know what? This is too much" and go to bed. And I know that, like, a lot of girls can't finish what they're doing until they're done with it. There's the sense that it has to be perfect.

The others agree, and one says, "Yeah, girls tend to pull a lot more all-nighters than guys." Another adds, "Girls will stay up until like three o'clock, and guys, it's twelve and they're done. They brush it off."

The boys and girls deal with failure differently. The boys contend that girls "go into deep depression and think their life is over," whereas boys "just deal with it: 'Okay, another day.'" One boy confides, "We're just as affected by it. We just don't show it."

That the boys do not admit to having stress may be due to the "bad-ass" image that is consistent with the ideal of masculinity. One serious student contends that the nonchalant attitude of his peers concerning exam stress is a facade and that "a lot of people don't want to take it seriously because they think they look cool by not caring." At this, one of the boys says, "I care about my grades. I'm lazy, but . . . all I'm saying is that during exam week I don't feel any, any extra pressure. I just feel like there's more free time that I *should* be studying."

Unlike the girls, the boys relieve their stress generally alone rather than in groups. Many boys mention "working out" or "going running," which they usually do by themselves, whereas the girls do the same activities but usually do them with a friend. Some of the boys sleep. One boy explains, "I'm definitely more the physical type. So far I've broken two lamps." Another adds, "I'll throw notebooks or something." A third adds, "How I deal with stress is I'll go into the weight room and nearly kill myself." The one group activity the boys mention is playing "helmets and gloves," a type of boxing match with hockey helmets and gloves.

Masturbation is also a common stress releaser. After a group has declared that they engage in stress-relieving activities "very independently," a boy notes that "they may take it out, like, in sports or alone in their beds." When some boys declare that masturbation increases during exam week and other times of great stress, one boy observes it is already so prevalent that "I don't think it *can* go up." When a Muslim boy announces that he doesn't think there is more masturbation during exam week, the other boys protest loudly, "It's against his religion. He doesn't count!" and then all say that they think it does.

Finals

Girls

A visit to the girls' dorms during exam period confirms how feeling stress and pressure is part of the performance of femininity. In the "crazy" dorm, the girls gather when I arrive with an evening snack, looking exhausted and dressed mostly in tank tops and pajama bottoms or sweatpants. As they munch on brownies, grapes, and sorbet, they freely talk about their stress. Exhausted and run down, they bemoan how little they have slept because they have stayed up for nights studying. One girl complains that she has worn pajama bottoms and sweatpants for a week and a half, and another exclaims that she only wants to look pretty again. A girl, who is lying on the floor while her friend gives her a back massage, claims that during exams, "girls crave massages. My back and neck are killing me, killing me. I have knots everywhere."

Contributing to their stress is their need to be perfect. One girl feels "guilty" when she sleeps:

> It can be, like, four in the morning and I don't know my stuff and I'm like, I can't function right now, but I can't go to bed right now and wake up in the morning and be like, "I tried my hardest."

Elizabeth mentions her parents' "complete" lack of understanding:

> I talked to my dad, like, five minutes before study hall and I was like, "I am so tired," and he was like, "Well, why don't you go to bed, sweetie? Make it an early night." I was like, *Are you kidding me?* I have so much work to do."

One girl notes that the work, stress, and pressure seem endless:

> You go through four years of kind of doing this, of sleep, work, trying to manage it and everything, and then if you think about it, when you go to college, it's four more years of that.

Some girls attribute their heightened academic stress to women having to "prove themselves," while men do not:

> -I think guys are just so used to having like opportunities for, like, education or whatever and not that like in our generation women didn't, but I just think it's like ingrained in us that we have to prove ourselves and that we're worthy.

> -Girls are always trying to prove something, prove to your teachers, prove to your parents.

One girl cites "guilt" and internalizing failure as causing girls to be more stressed than the boys:

> I think girls guilt-trip themselves, almost. Like if you do bad, you get so emotional . . . guys are like, "Oh I did bad on a test. It's not me. . . . It's the teacher that made the test." They blame other things, whereas a girl's like, "Oh, I'm so stupid. I should have studied more." They start attacking themselves, where the guys put the blame somewhere else.

Another claims that girls feel more stress because they connect everyday failures to the rest of their lives, while boys do not:

Everything's connected to your future and what's going to happen to you and what's happening to you now. And guys don't make connections. They're just like, "Oh, I failed that test." They don't think about how it's going to affect their GPA and getting into colleges. It's just they failed a test.

The girls in other dorms feel the same during exam period. In a "studious" dorm, one girl cries out, "I'm *mad* stressed!" Another exclaims, "'Stressed' doesn't even begin to define my demeanor. I'm not even in my body. I'm just here." All then moan about how stressed and tired they are.

Although a few of the girls "refuse to" pull all-nighters or "just don't do it," many more do. One student says, "What I do is pull an all-nighter and then in the morning eat peanuts . . . protein." After the last time one girl pulled an all-nighter, she "downed about six cans of Surge." One girl describes her common experience of going "to sleep at two and then you have your alarm set for four, and it just jolts you awake and you try to sit down and your hand is just shaking when you try to write." The girls say how "fun" it is to see the sun come up when they pull all-nighters. They compare when they last went to sleep and when they woke up and how little sleep they have gotten in the last few weeks. One girl then asks the others, "Have you ever fallen asleep on a keyboard and had the keys imprinted on your head? I typed one paragraph and then I was just going to like sleep for fifteen minutes and then type another one." The girls are obviously exhausted. When the food is gone and I pack to leave, they giggle and talk almost deliriously about lines from silly TV shows and movies. As I leave and thank them for their time, one girl shouts, "*Thank you!* It feels so good to laugh again. I haven't laughed in weeks!"

Boys

I also visit some of the boys' dorms during exams, and the difference is striking. Toting huge quantities of brownies and jugs of milk, I offer food in exchange for them letting me see what their lives are like during a time of high stress. The boys who live in the "random" dorm run from the halls into the common room and attack the brownies and milk. They plop down on the couches and chairs to eat and talk. They are rowdy, and I don't notice the same glassy-eyed tiredness as among the girls. Although some boys say they are "very stressed," others say they are not.

Unlike the girls, the boys often talk about masturbation and how effectively it reduces stress. In one dorm a senior attributes the boys' more relaxed state to the amount of masturbating they have been doing. Others admit that masturbation is one of their primary means of stress release.

The boys also observe that the use of alcohol and drugs increases during exams. Because this line of conversation does not provide nearly as much humor for them, they quickly return to the topic of masturbation. "Girls are more stressed because guys masturbate," one boy claims. He then adds, "Three or four times a day we're in there whacking off. It is a great stress reliever. Girls don't do that. Could you just see a girl, 'Oh, I'm so stressed I'm going to play with myself'?" This causes much raucous laughter and a tirade of comments about the differences between male and female masturbation.

One boy says that the girls' lives seem to be overtaken by their studies, while the boys carry on as usual. He also mentions how the girls study together, while the boys do so much less frequently:

> You see girls all sitting around a table at the dining hall and they have note cards and are all quizzing each other. The guys are talking sports. No one is cracking a book. I haven't made one note card in my four years at Bolton.

Despite their cavalier attitude, some of the boys reveal that they are quite stressed. Pete asserts, "I stayed up until four studying, and then when I got up this morning, I had a panic attack and spent all day at the infirmary." He adds that there are many students, both male and female, "wigging out" and that the nurse is "swamped with people having panic attacks." Another boy, Tyler, who is in trouble academically due to his focus on fun, adds, "I'm stressed because if you don't do any work all year and then it's like, 'Oh shit, I should have done that.'"

This relaxed atmosphere does not appear to be related to how studious the boys are. In the "intellectual and music dorm," the boys describe an equally low level of stress. One of the boys says that his stress is "low because I just don't care." The boys laugh at the thought of pulling all-nighters and are unanimous that they don't. One boy observes, "I'm actually not stressed at all. Squash is great." Another says, "I just don't have much stress because I don't let it get to me." Another boy asserts, "At this point if I know it, I know it. If I don't, I don't. It's no use to cram." One stellar student disagrees: "I cram and I do a lot better." He adds, however, that he does not pull all-nighters. Another boy concludes, "I just refuse to pull an all-nighter *ever*. I did a few of them my junior year, and I'll never do it again."

Even the boys who feel stress often describe it positively, something the girls never do. One of the boys notes, "The last four years I've been really stressed, but I think it just pushes you to work harder."

The Toll Stress and Pressure Take

The consequences of all this stress and pressure play out in accordance with gender ideals, resulting in different responses for the boys and the girls.

Stimulants

The students' stress and pressure can be measured by the amount of legal or illegal stimulants they use in order to help them stay awake or perform better. Although both genders use caffeine, the abuse of performance drugs is largely a female phenomenon. In almost all cases, these drugs also have the effect of suppressing appetite, and this only increases their use by girls eager to lose weight.

The girls report that legal drugs, especially caffeine, in the form of coffee, diet pills, soft drinks, and No-Doz, are used more than illegal drugs to help people stay awake and perform better. The girls use caffeine to stay awake "six or seven days a week." One girl reports that "drinking Coke is my job," while another says she takes No-Doz. According to the girls, use of No-Doz is "*very* common"; the product is used "all the time." Some estimate the use of No-Doz is a "good 99%," while others put it more at 70%. A girl comments, "I OD'd on caffeine [No-Doz] in ninth grade and ended up in the hospital. It sucked." Another concludes, "The amount of No-Doz consumed is *ridiculous*."

The prescription drugs the students report using illegally in order to stay awake or to perform better are Ritalin and Adderall. Almost all the girls' dorms list Ritalin as the number one drug used among girls at Bolton. Frequently the girls explain that the high level of Ritalin and Adderall use is due to their intense schedule and workload. Although "some people are weird and just do it for fun," most take Ritalin "when they have work to do. What you got to do to survive." This is corroborated by the school counselor, who contends that the abuse of performance drugs such as Ritalin is "rampant" because students "see no other way to achieve."

The boys also cite the frequent use of drugs to help students stay awake and perform better, but often say that the girls use them most. In one dorm, when I ask how frequently students use legal stimulants, the boys explode, "All the time," "It's ridiculous," "Ha!" and "Every day, all day." Some students "use No-Doz six times a day" to help them stay awake or perform better, and others use prescription drugs obtained illegally for the same purpose. A boy comments, "Yeah, a lot of people do Rit[alin] for that." Some contend that "75% [of the students] take some kind of drug" to help them stay awake or perform better. They also claim that 25% of the students take illegal drugs for the same purposes.

Although the boys mention Ritalin as one of the drugs used by the students at Bolton, it is not listed as frequently as it is among the girls. In one boys' dorm, for example, it is listed as the eighth most frequently used drug, and in others it was listed as the sixth, fourth, or second. Adderall is never mentioned.

Eating Disorders and Binge Drinking

The consequences that befall some of the Bolton students due to their pressures follow the gender performances of self and other—eating disorders among the girls and binge drinking among the boys.

The eating disorders and binge drinking at Bolton Academy can in many ways be tied to the performance of class, ethnicity, and gender. Eating disorders and abuse of performance drugs among adolescent girls have been related both to the upper-class focus on appearance and the female focus on relationships. The majority of girls at Bolton are upper-class whites who feel pressure to be perfect in all areas, and their dissatisfaction and obsession with their appearance, especially their weight, are among the major issues they face. Eating disorders are most prevalent in white upper-middle-class and upper-class adolescent girls due to the child's attempt to be perfect and to live up to her privileges (Bruch, 1973, 1978) and the pressure they face to "have it all" and fit the multifaceted ideal of being successful career women and at the same time being thin and beautiful (Gordon, 1990). Anorexics typically grow up in families in which there is an extraordinary emphasis on achievement and external appearance (Gordon, 1990).

As eating disorders are an other-oriented type of response, they fit into the performance of femininity. Eating disorders are based on a focus on the other (caring what others think), constraint (controlling one's body and therefore one's life by not eating), excellence (to achieve perfection and be the skinniest), conformity (achieving the thinness needed to conform, and then some, to the ideals of thinness) and close personal relationships (getting a boyfriend and being in the "in" clique).

Although researchers have linked the loss or lack of relationships and eating disorders (Maine, 1991), I contend that they also contain a covert competitive aspect and are about independence, autonomy, and rising above others. There is often a competitive aspect involved in eating issues as to who can be the skinniest and the prettiest. Vanity also plays a role. The competitive aspects of appearance are revealed on a sign in the room of one of the "rich bitches" that reads: "Dear God, if you can't make me thin please make my friends fat."

Male binge drinking can also be linked to upper-class performances and the culture of affluence. Luthar (2003) makes the association between unhappiness and wealth as being due to the pressures to work and acquire material goods, competition, hierarchy, the lack of time for internal rewards and relationships, high levels of stress, and the potential for much self-doubt and insecurity. The unique association between substance abuse, depression, anxiety, and popularity among peers found among affluent youth along with the stresses associated with the rigors of prep school, pressures to excel and succeed, and the need to be the best can account for much of the binge drinking that occurs among the boys. When these children of privilege, whether at preparatory schools or elite colleges, turn up in the news due to deaths from drug overdoses (see Frahm & Puleo, 2000) or suicides, Americans ponder the incongruence of these afflictions with these students' advantages and promise.

Binge drinking fits within the performance of masculinity by focusing on self (the use of substances is self-indulgent), freedom (a way to escape stress and pressures and the constraints of success), fun (the use of substances is regarded as fun), and individuality or status (often males attempt to stand out by competing to see who can drink the most). It also has a covert other-oriented or relational aspect, as binge drinking is a way to conform with the other boys to the ideals of masculinity (contributing to high status, which helps get girls) and maintain group connections (bonding with peers).

Eating disorders, the use of performance drugs, and binge drinking represent gender-appropriate ways that students manifest stresses and pressures. Because the performance of femininity dictates that girls must care what others think and because of their emphasis on close personal relationships, much of the girls' stress and pressure comes from not disappointing others. They are allowed to openly demonstrate and acknowledge their pressures because showing weakness and caring what others think is part of their approved gender ideal. Further, the girls cope with the stresses by engaging in group stress-release activities, and some even abuse performance drugs or suffer from eating disorders because these fit within the prescribed behaviors for their gender.

On the other hand, because the performance of masculinity requires disregarding what others think and because of their emphasis on group connections, boys are often less affected by others' expectations. Furthermore, they must hide their pressures and stresses because their gender ideals forbid the show of weakness or caring what others think. Finally, the boys cope with their stress and pressure by engaging in solo stress-release activities or binge drinking because these behaviors fit the ideals of masculinity.

Throughout the students' discussions concerning their stresses and pressures, it is clear that in many ways they dislike the manner in which they are compelled to act. The girls talk disparagingly of the pressure they feel from others, they dislike the way they internalize and build up stress, and they admire the boys' ability to "let things slide" and "relax." The boys, on the other hand, reveal how they feel compelled to hide their stress, how hard they must work, and that they care about achieving.

:: FUN

As with excellence, the amount and kind of fun students engage in differ dramatically from individual to individual, but patterns also emerge in how the boys and girls negotiate activities that are considered "fun." Because the performance of femininity requires a focus on other and therefore caring what others think and controlling their behavior, the girls are allowed less freedom to engage in fun and have fewer expectations of fun. Boys, on the other hand, are expected, encouraged, and even pressured to have fun because the performance of masculinity requires that one not care about what others think and that one focus on self-pleasure. There is strong evidence that the boys and girls' desires and needs for fun are much more similar than is evident in their behavior and that they act according to what is "accepted" in order to present themselves in a gender-appropriate manner.

The types of fun the students engage in are widespread. They throw snowballs, make snowmen, sled, and skate in the wintertime. In the spring, they lie on blankets in the courtyard looking at magazines or strumming a guitar. They toss around a lacrosse ball or Frisbee, play "campus golf" (using a golf club to hit a tennis ball around campus), and skateboard in the library courtyard. They slide down a massive water slide on the back hills of the campus. They play tennis and other sports for fun, and there are sometimes faculty-versus-students athletic contests. They watch movies and TV, and the boys often describe being "hooked" on video or computer games. Despite the students' constant complaints that "there is nothing to do" and the frequent poor attendance at school-sponsored events, the school sponsors such events on campus and trips off campus on the weekends. These events range from form dances to roller skating, shows by hypnotists and mind readers, concerts, and instruction in sushi making. Other favorite events of the students are the annual Senior Lounge Disco, air bands contest, dances in the library courtyard, foam dances, talent show, Saturday night band series, and Mr. Bolton contest. The trips off campus include everything from excursions to distant cities for a day of food and shopping to local trips to movie theaters, Dunkin Donuts, or tag sales. In the winter the ski club spends Sundays skiing (or more often snowboarding) at ski resorts.

The type of fun the students discuss and care about most, however, is the illicit fun that occurs on campus, which consists primarily of sex and partying (which by their definition includes the use of drugs and alcohol). The number of students taken before the disciplinary committee each year and the students' own accounts indicate that a great deal of this type of fun takes place at Bolton.

This phenomenon is by no stretch of the imagination particular to Bolton students. One boy describes the use of illegal substances among American teenagers in general:

> Whenever we get together, you have to have alcohol or drugs. It is essential for any gathering. It's like, "Do you want to watch a movie?" "Yeah. Do you have a brew?" It's like we are conditioned that you can't have fun without it.

Crosier (1991) devotes an entire book to examining the "hidden curriculum" of preparatory schools. In his book, Crosier has collected accounts from past students at preparatory schools that expose the illicit activities that took place there involving drugs, alcohol, and sex.

Partying and Breaking the Rules

The girls list the most common types of rule breaking that take place at Bolton: being AWOL (going off their floor or off campus without permission), illegal intervisitation, drinking (what most people get caught for), and sex, in that order. The girls comment, "There is so much sex on this campus," "So much sex, it's unbelievable," or "Illegal intervis[ion] is *huge.*" Other types of rule breaking, although occurring less frequently, include drugs, smoking ("everybody smokes"), and use of Ritalin.

Being AWOL is the rule the girls will most often break because they will "run over" to other girls' dorms "just to talk." The girls in one dorm claim that the amount of boys and girls AWOL in the opposite-sex dorms is "pretty equal." One girl comments, "I know a lot of guys that do and a lot of girls that do." Another explains, "Yeah, 'cause they do off and on. You come here one night. I'll go there the next night." Others add that when boys or girls go to the opposite-sex dorm, they "come, like, in packs" and "there's usually at least two people."

The boys disagree on the most common type of rule breaking at Bolton. The boys list illegal intervisitation, drinking, skipping class, substance abuse, cheating, being awake after lights out, use of tobacco (in cigarettes or smokeless tobacco), being AWOL, and use of marijuana. In one dorm, the boys debate which occurs more, cheating or drinking, revealing how open the boys are regarding their own illicit activities. One boy claims that cheating is the most commonly broken rule: "Most people don't think, but cheating is really fucked up here." At this, another boy who contended that alcohol is the rule most broken counters, "Oh, come on!" The first boy insists, "There is *so* much." To which the second replies, "Not as much as alcohol." The first boy claims, "I cheat every day. That's more than I drink." The second retorts, "It is not more than you drink. I drink more than I fuckin' cheat." The first states mater-of-factly, "I cheat more than anything."

Gender Differences in Partying

Despite much evidence of these types of fun occurring on campus, rarely in our talks do the girls describe themselves or others in the room as engaging in illicit fun, especially the use of illegal substances. In a very rare case, one of the girls reports that she is not going to come back to Bolton the next year because she has been on probation since her sophomore year. She is open about her desire to party and states that she is leaving because "I deserve to party my senior year just like everybody else."

The girls describe the use of illegal substances by others, especially the boys, but the tone is almost always disapproving or, in the case of the boys, sometimes envious. One girl recounts how a girl used a number of different drugs before going to babysit a faculty member's children, saying, "I can't believe she would do that!"

The boys, on the other hand, are open and even boastful about their own use of illegal substances as well as that of others. The amount of partying that takes place at Bolton and stories of past escapades are a main part of the boys' discourse. The boys recount everything from past great moments in partying, such as when a past class president and prefect would wake underclassmen up at four in the morning to drink, to their own drunken escapades of the night before.

In one boys' dorm, which I have come to know well, the boys are open and recount a recent escapade. The roundabout manner in which the episode is slowly revealed both demonstrates the account's validity and provides insight into peer dynamics and the special issues of partying among these prep school students. At first the boys claim, "We don't have parties." But when they are describing the "definite" differences in the way boys and girls party, one boy, Cameron, explains almost overenthusiastically:

> Guys get buck drunk, take massive Glade rips [when I plead ignorance, they explain that Glade, an air freshener, is inhaled through a towel], and smoke anything they can get their hands on. And you just get as fucked up as you possibly can. And just piss in corners of annexways.

While he is saying this, some of the others snicker, and I'm not sure what is going on until one of the boys comments, "I can't believe he just said that," and others joke about how the dorm parent is going to get the tape and bust them. I then understand that this was an account of a recent incident.

One of the boys then explains that partying takes place "in rooms, late at night on Saturday nights, starting as soon as the security guard leaves the dorm, and we see his car pull away, bust out the whatever." At this, one of the other boys thinks he's told me too much and comments,

"We're toast right now! Watson dorm [their dorm] is done! Is this confidential?" After I assure them it is, they continue, "As soon as he leaves, you know no one is going to walk through, so you can just drink, smoke pot, cigarettes, sniff cocaine if anyone had any." Another boy adds:

> The teachers are not allowed to leave the dorms until 11:30 on weeknights and 12:00 on weekends and everyone knows when they're leaving. As soon as they leave nobody comes back through. As soon as they leave and the security guard comes through here.

The boys explain that since they are not allowed to go to other floors or be considered AWOL, most often they stay on their own floor. Sometimes they venture to other floors "because people around here just get so boring. After partying with them for like two hours, we'll go find new people."

At this point, the boys become open about the incident that took place the night before and about which they had been hinting. One states, "Yeah, last night we went to another floor." Cameron adds, "And pissed in the annexway." One boy comments, "I wish I hadn't passed out." One of the boys explains, "It's just like, 'You know what? I've been working my ass off all week and I've been stressing out and it's Saturday night. I can sleep in. I'm getting fucked up.'" This boy is new to the party scene, because one of the other boys says to him, "This just started for you last weekend." To which he responds, "Let's just say I've come a long way!"

At this point a boy who had not been present enters the common room, and the others tell him the topic of their conversation and that they are telling me about the partying they had done the night before. One of the boys states, "Chris just told how he passed out last night." The new boy exclaims, "You put that on tape?" Another adds, "She knows everything that happened last night." The new boy exclaims in an amused tone, "That's terrible! She's not supposed to know this." Cameron laughs, "We didn't tell her you puked, though." To which the new boy retorts, "Twice!" Other boys comment, "I puked too," "I didn't," "I did not puke. I did not puke but I couldn't walk." One African American boy claims that he was "tricked into" drinking by the others. The boy who tricked him confides, "I was like, 'Try this.' He said, 'Is it Coke?' 'Yes.' 'Ohhhh, that tastes good. I'll take more.'"

In general, the students view the boys as partying more heavily than the girls. The girls claim that the boys party more than they do because they "get away with it," they are shown more leniency by faculty and administrators, they have less supervision, and they can hide it better. The girls contend, "Everything goes on in the guys' dorms." A girl adds, "Guys bring kegs into the fucking dorm. Not one but *two*." When one of the girls says, "But [with] girls it's easier to, like, hide it," the others vehemently disagree, saying that "girls are big blabbermouths" and that their dorm parent is in their rooms "like all the time." The girls also think that the boys are more nonchalant about their drug use, while girls act like it is more of a "big deal." One girl comments:

> They also use more drugs and they don't think it's that big of a deal. Like, girls, if they do a major drug or something like that, they're like, "Oh my God, I can't believe I did that," whereas guys are like, "Oh yeah, I've done that."

The boys note about their partying, "Guys think about it more" and "Guys are more competitive about it. They're like, "Ha, I'm still standing and I've had this many more beers than you.'"

The boys sometimes claim it is the girls who party more often and use harder drugs. One boy contends, "I think at this school it's more girls than at home." Others suspect that girls simply "show it more" and are "more obvious." The boys assert that a group of girls "do worse" and do "more drugs" and "harder" drugs than the boys. One of the boys says, "Yeah, most of them don't have anything else. You know, about 75% of guys here are involved in sports that are important to them."

The students at Bolton believe that one of the reasons the boys party is because they face pressure and competition from others. "Guys feel pressure from each other for how much you drink," the girls explain. Although a few of the girls believe that the girls put similar pressure on each other and that the boys "always love the girl that can drink them under the table," they agree that the boys have more pressure and competition when it comes to partying. Most of the girls describe feeling pressure from boys *not* to party. They explain that guys "don't like girls who do anything, like, alcohol- or drugs-wise. They're like, 'You're retarded,' you know, like, 'Why are you doing that?'" A few of the girls contend that some boys do pressure girls to party: "Either they want one who doesn't do anything or they want one who does everything."

Feeling pressure to use substances, the boys often brag of personal use. A few dorms, whose residents are usually considered the social outcasts or as having low social status, are markedly different from the other dorms in their descriptions of little drug and alcohol use. In one such dorm, a popular African American boy, Adam, admits to low levels of use and makes the other boys admit to it as well. Although these students personally regard using substances negatively, they know that the majority of the students view using substances positively and their lack of use hurts their social status. Thus, to admit to not using substances is almost embarrassing. Although a few of the cooler students state that they use substances, others sheepishly describe little or no use. Adam asks the others, "Do you smoke trees? Trees is weed, if you don't know." The others answer negatively except for a few who say, "I have once" and "I have a couple of times, but I don't do it normally." He then asks them if they drink. One boy murmurs, "I don't drink," but most quietly and halfheartedly reply that they do. Adam asks, "What do you drink?" When one boy sheepishly responds, "Budweiser," Adam states flatly, "That doesn't count."

The performances of masculinity and femininity affect the teenage party scene both at Bolton and elsewhere. The students say that girls are more "social" drinkers, while the boys party to get "messed up." The girls claim that boys' partying is not about being social or going out "to have a good time" but rather about "going out to get, like, drunk, like, just so they're, like, messed up." One girl describes the boys' attitude as "I'm drinking 'cause I want to be drunk." The girls claim that the boys compete more about how much they can drink and "brag" about "being messed up all the time." Another girl adds, "When I go to a party, I'm going there to dance and to have a good time, not necessarily looking to hook up with somebody." The girls agree, "When guys party, they intend on getting drunk and, like, gettin' some," but some note that girls also sometimes go intending to "just get drunk."

How boys and girls approach the connection between partying and sex also differs. While the girls claim both genders are interested in "hooking up," the boys approach it as "get the girl drunk and get some," while the girls use alcohol as an excuse to deflect responsibility if they have sex. The girls also want sex but are apt to approach it as "Oh, let me get drunk" so that they are not responsible. Due to the double standard that the girls face, it is clear that they use alcohol as a means of having sex, but since they cannot be held responsible, they are less likely to be deemed a slut.

The boys say that the girls are more sedate and focused on the social aspects of partying than boys are. The boys contend, "Females are there just to have a good time. Males get them drunk so that they can have a good time." One boy explains, "You put a few drinks in her, then you put something else in her, you know, that's how it works." The boys add, "Girls just chill," and "And girls are like, 'We're just having fun.'" For boys, partying is "easier" because "girls have to worry about getting too drunk and getting used," pregnant, or "roofed."[2]

Although the boys agree with this gender difference in partying, they also make clear that how a student parties is largely individualistic. One boy reports, "I say it depends on the person because some girls are going out to get laid and do as many drugs as they can." Another agrees, "Girls *and* boys do that. More guys will do that than girls, but it generally just is different from person to person."

The performance of gender manifests itself when the boys and girls get drunk. The girls claim that "through drinking the girls try to show off" and give public displays of their inebriation such as "Woo, woo, look at me!" Others describe some girls' "idea of partying is to show off" and "to put on the show." Another says girls are like, "Oh, let me have two sips of beer and I'm gone." They agree that it is best if it is done "without puking."

The girls also play the role of needing to be taken care of at parties, with others (sometimes girls but often boys) playing the role of caretaker. The girls contend that "girls are dumb" and less responsible with their liquor, so boys must take care of them: "Guys are always the ones staying up all night and helping the girls up the stairs, into their beds, or sitting over the toilet with them." One girl adds, "Guys never get themselves to that state because it's an embarrassment to them, like, for everybody else." The girls conclude, "They seem to be, like, caretakers." This is because for boys being able to hold your liquor is expected and valued, whereas for girls "it's not a pride issue" and often even the opposite. One girl states that females "don't really care" how much each other can drink and "it's kind of, you know, to see who gets drunk first, so I can, you know, go . . . help her out."

The boys also note that girls often act drunk in what appears to be a way to confirm their femininity and weakness. The boys say that the girls are unable to hold their liquor, have "no tolerance for anything," and are "just stupid" about alcohol and drugs. One boy comments, "I think sometimes it's wicked annoying to be partying with girls and have them cocked off of two sips . . . hanging all over you and shit." Frequently the boys derogatorily say, "Women are two-beer queers, man." Others observe, "Yeah, but they fake it a lot of the time too." The boys repeatedly assert, "Chicks fake it."

The expectations for the boys, on the other hand, are exactly the opposite in that they get drunk but are not expected to show it and should be able to hold their liquor. The girls contend that boys do not use alcohol to show off; rather, "It's just the point of getting drunk or drinking as, you know, as much as they can and not puking" and "having contests" with "beer bongs and stuff." The boys' "job" is to have contests to show how much they can drink and to prove that they can hold their liquor. For boys it's "Let's see how much I can drink. Let's play the games. Let me be the man. Let's not throw up." These differences in behavior between the boys and girls demonstrate that they strategically modify and exaggerate their behavior in order to create the appropriate gendered image.

Partying Prep Style

Prep school partying is much different from teenage partying outside the bubble, especially in the types of illegal substances used. The girls claim the students primarily use the prescriptions drugs Ritalin and Adderall, alcohol, marijuana, and tobacco. Another drug that is mentioned is Ecstasy, but the girls report, "It's present but it's not an issue" except for the day students who purportedly use a lot of it. The only other drugs listed by the girls are LSD and other prescription drugs such as Prozac and painkillers.

In general, the girls report that there is more abuse of prescription drugs at Bolton than in their hometowns:

-Nobody would do Ritalin at home.

-If someone wanted to get the same effect as Ritalin at home, they'd take speed or coke . . .

-And get it ten times better.

-Seriously, Ritalin sucks!

Whether the amount of drugs used at Bolton is either less or more than in their hometowns depends on the student. While some of the students say that there are "more drugs here than at home" or they have "more exposure" to drugs at Bolton, others say there are fewer. Many of the girls report that "pot is *huge* here" but that "not many people here go beyond weed or alcohol" and "so many more" adolescents do hard drugs in their hometowns. Other drugs, such as Ecstasy and cocaine, are also listed as more common at Bolton than in many of the girls' hometowns.

The lack of availability of some substances and the fear of getting caught result in students abusing other substances. The girls explain that because "you have no access here . . . a lot of people will drink cough syrup to get drunk" and others "pop caffeine pills to get that wired feeling." At this, another girl (who later will be kicked out for drinking) emphatically acknowledges the access to illegal substances and explains:

> Granted it's easier to get alcohol and drugs at home, but if you
> know who to ask, if you ask your sketch friends, if you have sketch
> friends and you know where to get it, then you can. But it comes in
> waves. Like basically people will have, like, all this alcohol this one
> weekend, but then everyone will drink, like, so much, but then the
> next weekend there will be absolutely a drought on campus.

The illicit substances used at Bolton are different from what is used in the outside world due to availability, cost, different trends, and how easily substances can be detected. In general, the substances the boys at Bolton use most are alcohol, prescription drugs such as Ritalin, marijuana, tobacco, and then harder drugs such as Ecstasy, cocaine, crack, hallucinogenic mushrooms, Quaaludes, opium, and LSD. The boys explain that at Bolton, "You've got to find something that doesn't smell" and that drug use "comes in waves" due to availability. One boy notes, "It's like when they do it, everyone's got to do it." They discuss a recent wave of Ecstasy use, and one of the boys explains, "That's because, like, it usually comes in like a twenty-packet. It's all sold." The boys also use cold and cough medicines such as NyQuil and Robitussin in order to get buzzed.

The manner in which tobacco is used also differs at Bolton. Because of the strict expulsion rules for open flames in the dorms and the smell of cigarettes, cigarette smoking is restricted to certain places and there is much more use of smokeless tobacco. The boys contend, "Almost everyone dips. If they don't smoke on campus, then they dip" and "We could fill the headmaster's common room with dip spit." In one dorm the boys explain that the biggest difference in partying at Bolton and at home is "no butts" (cigarettes). Downplaying the differences in partying at Bolton, one boy says, "The only difference is that you can't smoke butts here." Instead of smoking in the rooms while they are partying, the students smoke in the woods or in places such as bathrooms where they can stand on chairs and the smoke will pass out of vents undetected.

Obtaining illegal substances is more complicated at Bolton than in society at large because the substances have to be sneaked onto campus. Many illegal substances are brought back to Bolton after breaks, and the amount of partying that takes place then is high. Day students and staff are sometimes suppliers.

Where and when the partying at Bolton takes place also differs from the outside world. Due to the lack of privacy and risk of detection, the places where students party are restricted to dorm rooms, dances, day students' houses, the woods, and prom. When partying takes place, it is "mostly on weekends," "late at night," and "either before you go out or, like, one or two in the morning. So you can go out and have fun. It's like, 'This concert really sucks but I'm having a blast.'"

The girls party more discreetly than the boys. In general, the girls describe their use of illegal drugs as restricted primarily to parties that are "off campus at, like, somebody's house . . . or wherever." They contend that the boys party both at off-campus locations as well as in their dorm rooms on campus, "wherever it's convenient" and "wherever they happen to be."

The special circumstances of boarding school alter the nature of partying for the students. The girls mention how unsocial and non-fun the partying is at Bolton because of the fear of getting caught. One girl contends, "All people do here is sit and drink. They don't go out dancing or go to a club, which is so much more fun than sitting around getting drunk." Others add, "They don't enjoy themselves . . . they just get trashed." One of the girls explains, "That's because everybody looks forward to Saturday night, but there's nothing to do, so let's just get fucked up and that's what everyone does."

The boys also party differently at Bolton due to the severe consequences of getting caught. The boys report, "Like, most shit done here is late at night" in "rooms on the weekends, Saturday nights." One boy contends, "Fuck that! Rooms during classes." Others assert that parties are often held at day students' houses.

The composition and the number of the groups that party together is also different because "there is no party scene" at Bolton in the sense of big parties on campus. The boys explain that students do not have parties but use substances in small groups:

> It's, like, in the [dorms], in one kid's room between three and four in the morning. . . . There's no, like, big parties. You can't have big

parties because they'd get busted immediately. If there's more than five people in a room, a teacher knows and goes in there.

Another boy points out, "There's less mixing of girls and guys. Here it's all guys."

In general, the students bemoan the lack of partying that takes place at Bolton and disagree with the contention made by some that the intensity and competitiveness evident in many areas of prep school life are also evident in the party scene (Cookson & Persell, 1985). Some of the girls remark: "What party scene?" "No, because we can't drink here," and "Girls don't do anything." Other girls contend that the intensity and competitiveness are not different than they are at home: "You just have to keep it hidden here" and "It's sneakier."

Many students do describe an intensity that they say is due to the special circumstances of boarding school, mainly that one can get kicked out. One girl reports, "It's more intense here because you have to hide it if you do. And when you do, it's a big deal." Another girl claims:

> Partying here is intense because it's, like, smoke as fast as you can, drink as fast as you can, fuck as fast as you can, because you're going to be caught if you take too much time. So it's quickness and quantity smushed up into a small amount of time. Like, people here don't just get tipsy. People here when they drink, they get fucking plastered, get fucking high, and it's because you have, like, a ten-minute period that you think you won't look sketchy for it. At home I would drink all night long. Here I would drink it all in ten minutes just to get plastered.

Whether or not the boys describe the party scene at prep schools as being more intense and competitive depends on if they are discussing actual parties or the amount of alcohol and drugs consumed. In general, the boys agree that although there are not large parties at Bolton, there is a great deal of substance use. Many of the boys cite stress and/or boredom as a reason that some students consume a large amount of illegal substances. In one dorm the boys agree that at Bolton the students do "party hard." One of the boys comments, "Damn straight, because there is nothing better to do." Another adds, "If they gave us something to do, we wouldn't be getting fucking retarded so much." In another dorm a boy believes that people use substances more at Bolton than at home "just because there's nothing else to do."

In an effort to avoid detection, the boys say, their use of substances is more intense: "Here you'll do stuff faster, stronger, and like you'll drink shit with Gatorade." Another adds, "Yeah, you don't see much beer drinking here." A third comments, "It's all about getting fucked up quick."

The amount of partying that boys do at Bolton compared to what they do at home is very individualistic. Boys who say they party more at Bolton claim, "The thing here is that you have the opportunity every night" and "Every night's a sleepover, you know. Every night's a party." Another adds, "If somebody wants to smoke pot they can do it every single day here. They have the opportunity to." Others disagree and contend, "It's probably easier to get away with at home." The boys conclude, "It depends who you are. It depends where you live."

Beating the System

In this structured world of school rules and intense adult supervision, much of the students' culture revolves around "beating the system" as a way to contrast themselves with adults (see Harris, 1995). For the boys, subversion of the rules at Bolton is part of the performance of masculinity, earning them status (see also Martino, 1999). For the girls, the issue is more complicated, as the desire to break the rules is at odds with their desire for perfection and relationships with adults. This is perhaps why almost all of the legends of rule breaking are about males.

The students are in agreement that it is "absolutely cool" to break the rules just for the sake of breaking the rules. The girls say that it feels good to get away with it and that "you're not cool until you've beat the system." The boys also say that it is cool to beat the system: "Hell yeah! It feels fucking great!" "Hell yes!" and "Absolutely!" One of the boys explains, " 'Cause when you break the rules, it's more fun." Another boy says that beating the system is "great! You feel powerful."

A few of the girls add that sometimes a feeling of paranoia lessens the elation. One student comments, "Sometimes it feels *really* good and sometimes you feel kind of sketchy afterwards. You're like, 'Who knows?'" The girls brag about beating the system but acknowledge that the boys brag more. The girls get caught more often because even though the boys brag more, they are "smarter about it" and "never brag about it beforehand or when they're doing it." Girls tend to "talk about it before, after, and during. Like, 'Hey, I'm drunk!'" Another adds, "And they squeal."

Many break the rules for the excitement of getting away with it. One girl exclaims, "That's why we break rules!" For others, rule breaking feels "like a rush and you get all this adrenaline." One girl explains that beating the system is "definitely" part of the draw:

> The excitement of breaking a rule, that's half the fun of it. That's why you get drunk on less alcohol on campus than you do off campus, because it's half that excitement and anticipation really, "Ohhhh, guess what I'm going to do? Heeheeheehee."

Another claims, "You need some sort of adventure in a place with so much routine. It's, like, over and over again, and it's, like, you know, doing little sneaky things to keep it exciting." Some girls claim that 80 or 90% of the times rules are broken, it is for the excitement or the challenge involved.

Many girls say that breaking rules and "doing stuff" is a rite of passage at boarding schools, and a girl explains:

> You can't go to a boarding school and, and not do it . . . you know, leave your senior year and never have done it. Like, what do you . . . you know, you can't go to college and . . . tell people, "Oh well, I went to a boarding school and I never . . . did this" . . . you know?

Other girls add that they break the rules "to tell your children that stuff."

Students who break the rules and get away with it earn respect from their peers, and the challenge is one of the reasons kids do it. In one dorm the boys all agree, "You get respect for it." Another claims, "Yeah, like if you break the rules and get away with it, you feel good about it." A boy then gives an example, "Like if a student can get stoned everyday and walk around and the teachers are oblivious to it, I think that is really cool." The boys reason, "If it wasn't cool to beat the system, we wouldn't talk about it so much."

The students do not agree to what degree the thrill of beating the system accounts for the number of times rules are broken. Some students claim that in most cases students break the rules because they want to have fun or to survive Bolton's demanding schedule.

Often the girls desire to break the rules but are afraid of the repercussions. In one dorm the girls mention that when the boys get away with something daring, they want to break the rules as well but are always too scared. One girl explains, "When the boys go streak, we all get, like, so riled up and, like, 'We're gonna do it today . . . we're gonna go toilet paper somebody's car' and we sit in the doorway and we're, like . . . "

At this, one of the other girls interjects, "Oh, what if we get in trouble?" The first girl concludes, "And we hear the security guard and then we, like, go to bed." The girls all agree and laugh.

Most of the boys say that beating the system is not why they break the rules, although they often say that it makes it more "fun" and "it makes you feel better." Boys break the rules "because they're sick of the system" and "because the rules are fucking ridiculous and they're sick of it." Others claim that "people don't get fucked up to break the rules, they get fucked up because they're bored and want to get fucked up."

Individual differences in partying are evident in one dorm where the boys claim that they break different rules for different reasons. Some boys party mostly as "a stress-relieving issue." One boy describes partying as "more like the whole stressed-out, end-of-the-week, 'I'm getting fucked up' thing." Other boys break rules just to beat the system. One says, "Beating the system would be like going outside. . . . A naked run would be awesome!" At this, the boys start to get worked up. One exclaims, "How many times did we suggest it?" Another adds, "No one has the balls to do one this year. Let's do one right now!" I'm starting to get a little worried that they are actually going to do it right then and there. Then one boy comments dejectedly, "You're toast if you do." Another adds, "It's too cold!" I am much relieved that they are starting to calm down. Another boy laughs, "You'd have to, like, extract your testicles from your lower intestine." The others laugh, and one says that in the cold weather their penises would not impress: "On the off chance you saw a girl she'd be like, 'Aaaghh!'" One of the boys then concludes:

> See, that's what's awesome about a naked run. Not only are you outside buck naked and you're running . . . but it's like, "Oh nice! We're doing this because we're not going to get caught.' It's just like the thrill of doing something . . . and that's like the ultimate.

The girls note a gender difference in how the students regard others breaking school rules. When a boy gets away with breaking the rules, his status increases and other boys herald the accomplishment and treat him as a hero. For the girls it is less acceptable, and girls often "rat each other out" because of the competition between them. Because rule breaking increases a boy's status more than it does a girl's and because boys are less often "ratted out" by other boys, the boys are more open and boastful about their rule breaking and "show it off" more than the girls. Conversely, when a girl breaks the rules, knowledge of it is kept more "inside" and she is more "secretive" about it.

Part of the culture of beating the system are the numerous legends of rule breaking passed on from class to class. The girls often add that these legends are "so cool" that "everyone has always wanted to do" it or wishes they had the "guts to do it." These include such things as a student who checked in on a Saturday night "and then just walked out the door and drove to, like, New York City," "big parties in the computer lab," "keeping cocaine in the tiles in the dining hall," "mass stealing at a mall . . . like, fifteen, twenty kids got caught for stealing," "the master key is passed on every year," "squash room keys are passed between the day students," and stories of "secret compartments" under rugs.

One of the most interesting accounts is of a tunnel connecting the male and female dorms on campus. A girl in one dorm shows the others where the tunnel is supposed to start: "Through that door, right there." Another then says, "Yeah, and, like, you have to, like, squeeze down this little thing and, like, there's this tunnel that runs under the entire [dorm] and it's, like, you have to, like, crawl the whole way." She adds, however, "Well, this is just what other people have told me. I haven't done it. That's disgusting. I wouldn't . . . but, like . . ." At this, one of the girls scoffs, "There's gotta be those bugs with eighty-five legs down there!" The first girl continues, "Yeah, exactly. He said . . . you can feel, like, spiders crawling on you and you just walk through spiderwebs, and, like, there's this much water and mud," at which she places her hands about six inches apart. She adds, "And you just climb through." Another girl adds that there are also rats in the tunnel. One of the girls exclaims, "Cool! Oh, I want to do it." The girls add that the boys recount going under the girls' dorm "and, like, scratch on the floorboards trying to freak people out."

The most frequently recounted and admired legend at Bolton is the story of one student who built a hot tub in his room. The girls explain, "He tapped into the hot water pipe. Like, somehow this kid is, like, brilliant, and he put it in his closet." They add, "And when he graduated he wrote a note to the headmaster that said, 'By the way, there's a hot tub in my room.'" The story usually ends with open admiration and a desire to duplicate the feat, such as "That'd be so cool. I want to do that . . . can we work on that in your room?" The boys recount these and other legends, treating the perpetrators as heroes: "That was bad-ass, man!"

Then there is the one about the cave:

-The dugout place down by the hockey rink where everybody went to smoke and drink.

-It was all underground. . . .

-It was, like, a huge cave. . . .

-And the dean of students found it. It was, like, his dog went down there, and he caught a whole bunch of students.

Another is the account of one boy who "lived in Brighton for like three years in a row and he drilled holes through several floors and walls and stuff to get a wire from the TV jack downstairs through a cable cutter up to his room to get cable TV." One legend is of "the kid who grew pot on the vine outside his window." The students recount yet another tale:

-The kids who lived in the triple. The roof was sagging from all their empty beer cans and stuff. They used to throw it up under the ceiling.

-I think there were two, like, Dumpsters full of alcohol bottles at the end of last year.

Still another legend is "the girl who gave 50 boys fellatio and then rang the victory bell . . . 'The Headmaster.' That's her nickname. Get it?"

One way the boys' talk differs from the girls' is the number of stories concerning the past or present leniency of faculty toward their partying. In one dorm, the boys remark that some faculty "turn a blind eye" to the partying that takes place unless it "gets out of hand." Some teachers "see but don't do anything, especially if it's, like, a four-year senior and they don't want to bust them." They describe that some of the teachers feel worse than the kids about busting them, adding that they have "an understanding" with their prefect: "He is never going to bust us."

This culture of beating the system arises despite the school's every effort to stop it. Although the school provides a challenging academic experience in an idyllic setting, establishes many rules to curb illicit activities, and hands out dire consequences to those who break the rules, ultimately it has little control over the culture the students themselves create.

Sex

Another type of fun that is central to the students' discourse is sex. Similar to partying, gender differences abound in how boys and girls approach sex at Bolton as well as in the ways sex differs at Bolton due to the special characteristics of boarding school. Again the association between a performance of masculinity focusing on self and a performance of femininity focusing on other results in gendered sexual behavior.

Prep Sex

Based on the number of students brought before the discipline committee for intervisitation violations and the students' discussions, sexual activity thrives on Bolton's campus. In the interviews, the students unanimously agree that Bolton students are "very" sexually active. The girls exclaim, "Oh Lord!" at the amount of sexual activity, or "booty shakin'," taking place.

Most of the girls report that the amount of sexual activity that occurs at Bolton is more than occurs in their hometowns. "It is so much more sexually active here," one girl asserts. One girl says, "There are more people here who have sex than at home," adding that for the amount of sex she has, "at home, I'm [considered] a slut but here not at all." Another adds, "I don't know if the act is more, but people talk about it more here. At home, it's more of a private thing, but here everybody knows."

A few of the girls claim there is more sex in their hometowns. In one dorm, when many of the girls say there is more sex at Bolton, several disagree and one states, "Are you kidding? My friends hook up with a different guy, like, every weekend."

Although the boys agree that sexual activity takes place on Bolton's campus, most contend that it is not as much as in the outside world (and not as much as they would like) because of the restrictions, dire consequences if they are caught, lack of places to go, or lack of coed parties with substances, or because the girls are "prudes." A few of the boys say that the amount of sexual activity is higher than at home because the Bolton girls are "whorish." Thus, the girls at Bolton are declared both whores and prudes at the same time.

Often the boys believe less sex takes place at Bolton due to the risk and consequences of getting caught. The boys in one dorm state that it is "so much easier to have sex at home" because there are fewer consequences. One of the boys explains, "Like if you get caught by your parents, it's like, 'Oh, just don't get her pregnant.'"

In another dorm the boys laugh and agree that the students at Bolton are "very" sexually active but "not as much" as at home because of the lack of privacy and places in which to have sex. One of the boys states, "If there was more chance they probably would be but . . . it's kind of hard. You get walked in on everywhere you go." Others explain, "At home when your parents go out, you have the whole house to yourselves, you get banging." He then adds in an unexcited tone, "Here it's like, 'Let's go to the football field.'" Another boy adds, "Yeah, like, 'I've got a key to this place. Let's go sneak in.'" Another states in fake excitement, "Let's go down to room F where there are cum stains all over the couches. That'll be romantic." One boy fantasizes about "conjugal visit rooms" on campus:

> I'm going to donate one when I'm alumni. . . . What I'd do is make, like, a student lounge and then make a room off of it that I only tell the students about . . . where they could go to fuck . . . it would have a disco ball, shag carpeting.

The boys also say there is less sex than at home due to the lack of coed parties where substances are used. One boy explains, "I think that substances have such an effect on teenage sexual activity that we're definitely not going to have as much sex because we don't have as much drugs and alcohol."

Some of the boys believe that the students at Bolton are "a lot more" sexually active than the adolescents in their hometowns. They cite the amount of casual sex at Bolton as well as the increased opportunities for frequent sex. One boy condemns the casual sex among the students at Bolton: "It's not normal just to hook up with random people." Another adds that there are more opportunities at a coed boarding school for "habitual" sex:

> At home it's easier to have sex with a girl because you have the chance of a bed and stuff. But here at school the people who do have sex have it all the time. Whereas at home it's not like that. Here at school every day's the same. There isn't like a special occasion. If you're going to have sex in the wood shop room, then you can do it every day.

One of the other boys adds, "It becomes a habit. It becomes a ritual."

Often the boys cannot agree whether or not there is more sexual activity at Bolton or in their hometowns, and it is dependent on where they are from. In one dorm a boy thinks students at Bolton are less sexually active than his friends at home. At this, another boy comments, "The Midwest is conservative. They are *definitely* more sexually active out here." At this, the first boy exclaims, "Oh God! Like every single girl is so prude compared to the girls at home." Others comment that a lot of sex occurs but that it takes place with only certain girls. One of the boys explains, "Like, girls that fuck do [it] a lot, and those that don't."

Due to the fear of detection and lack of privacy, the places where sex occurs at Bolton are often unconventional. The students describe the sexual activity as occurring "all over the place." Frequently mentioned sites include common rooms, the science building, bathrooms, dorm rooms, sports fields, the woods, squash courts, closets, classrooms (especially room F), laundry rooms, school vans, the chapel, the auditorium balcony, the dining room, and the girls' locker room. The students say, "You pick a place, people have had sex there" and "I don't think there's one place on campus that hasn't been desanctified." One girl complains that students are forced to have sex "in the most random, dirty, unromantic places that you could possibly have it." Another girl discloses, "Last year there were like six couples on the football field on Saturday night." A boy declares that sex takes place "anywhere you have a key to. If you have keys, you're golden. You have to find, buy, beg, borrow keys. Because everything is locked and everything can be unlocked." In one dorm, the boys say, "Room F. There's a certain couch in room F you just don't sit on." To which one boy adds, "Any couch at this school you don't sit on unless you know it's been cleaned recently." I am sitting on a couch and I look down at it suspiciously. The boys laugh and assure me that the one I am sitting on has just been cleaned. The boys continue to explain that the places of favor change: "It depends on the season. In the spring, it's always outside."

The girls say that students are "overly" sexually active because "people are bored" and "there's nothing else to do." One of the girls asserts, "Here, I think here you don't have that much to do in their free time so a lot of kids go and have sex."

The girls also contend that there is so much sexual activity at Bolton because people are much more "relaxed" about sex and sex is becoming "less of a big deal" everywhere, but especially at Bolton. One girl explains, "People are so much more open about it. It's not like we're hornballs. It's just more accepted here." Another adds, "Like here you're just more comfortable talking about it. Like if we were at home and we were talking about so-and-so who had sex, you'd think it was a big deal, but here it's kind of something you hear about a lot, so you get used to it."

Many of the girls say that the increased exposure to the opposite sex results in more sexual activity: "Because you're living with guys, you see them all the time, dinner, night, day" and so "you're more comfortable with them. So sex isn't so, like, foreign." Others say they "have more opportunity." Some of the girls contend that this increased exposure puts "more pressure on us because it's such a natural thing. People think it's just going to come naturally." The girls also claim, "There are a lot more random hookups" or sex without relationships at Bolton.

Many of the girls regard sex at Bolton as less meaningful due to the fear of detection, the pressures, and the strange places where people have sex. Some describe sex at Bolton as "dirtier here because people are doing it in fields. So it's, like, grosser here." The girls in one dorm debate whether or not sexual intercourse on campus can be meaningful due to the brevity and the unusual locations. One of the girls states that one cannot become sexually experienced on campus because "you don't have *sex*, you screw or you fuck on this campus because it's quick." At this, there is a chorus of nos from the other girls. The girl reiterates, "I can't see anyone, like, having sex on campus." Again there is a chorus of "No!" and "That is not true" and "No, no, no." The girls who disagree explain:

> -The other day during my free period I went out to the woods and I made love . . . . It is possible. It was great. And we weren't, like, screwing, we were like making love.

> -No. It's not just screwing on campus.

> -You can make love in the laundry room. Geez, I know, I've done it.

Girl Love/Boy Sex

It is part of the performance of femininity that girls care about relationships and love more than (or at least equal to) sex. When the girls admit to having sex without love, they often feel ashamed and give the excuse that they were drunk. Since being a "lightweight" and getting drunk easily are part of the performance of femininity, this lessens the severity of the unfeminine act of having sex without love and diminishes the harm such an act does to their status.

Commonly the girls attach love to the act of sex more than the boys do. In other words, "girls get more attached" and "boys just want sex." One girl complains, "Guys can be so detached. I don't understand it." The girls agree: "Guys think love is sex" and "Men love sex so they pretend they love the woman they're having it with." One group of girls angrily asserts that all boys look for in girls is "a body" and "don't care what the heck she sounds like or talks like" as long as it is someone with "a mouth like a Hoover [vacuum cleaner]. They want somebody to suck their dick."

Despite their public focus on relationships, several of the girls state that there are indeed boys with whom they would have sex but not date, and they name certain boys right off. In one dorm, many of the girls would have sex with a boy but not date him if they felt like sex and the male had sex appeal even if he was an "asshole." One of the girls present, a Muslim whose religion forbids premarital sex, is aghast. She questions the others in an unbelieving tone, "There are guys you would have sex with but would not go on a date with?" There is general agreement among the girls, and one explains, "Because there are some guys who have so much sex appeal, but you couldn't deal with them for the night because they're such assholes." The Muslim girl asks again in an unbelieving tone, "Then you would have sex with them?" Her incredulity is met with group laughter and agreement. One of the girls explains, "Yeah, 'cause you want sex." Another adds, "If I was drunk." They talk about one boy who they think would be "a good-ass hookup but I'd never want to date him" and "I want to bang him, but I'd never want to talk to him."

In the "rich bitch" dorm the girls debate sex for revenge, and I get the impression it has recently happened or one of them is contemplating it. One of the girls asks the others, "Would you have sex with someone just to piss off your friend?" The others respond:

-I definitely would.

-Depending on the situation.

-Depending on who the person was.

-If the friend was somebody that I'm thinking of, yeah.

-If the person was a bitch and ugly and had a really big forehead.

-Or had a butt for a chin.

Many girls who had sex but were not in a relationship contend that such hookups do not happen at boarding school as often as at home. The tone of these admissions is guilty and not boastful:

-Okay, I've truthfully had experiences where . . . this is so slutty, oh my God, but I've gone to parties and been completely wasted, completely blazed, and found a hot guy and ended up sleeping with him and barely known what's happening.

-I've had experiences like that when I haven't even known his first name.

Several of the other girls murmur agreement. The girls then contend that these types of experiences do not happen as often at boarding schools because they usually take place when substances are used. The use of substances offers at least partial protection from the derogatory labels given to girls who have indiscriminate sex. The girls contend:

-Being at a boarding school, things like that don't happen as much because we don't have the chances to go to raging parties . . . so it doesn't happen as often.

-Experiences happen like that when there are substances involved, I swear to God. 'Cause that's the only way people can let go of their inhibitions and not feel as slutty.

For boys, part of the performance of masculinity is to care about sex but not love. The boys emphatically agree that they separate love and sex more than the girls at Bolton do, commenting, "Guys don't give a shit," "Most guys, they're not about love. They just want to get some ass," and "They're more for love. We're just in it for sex."

Unsafe Sex

The students say that safe sex is not widely practiced at Bolton and attribute this to the belief that boarding school students are not at risk for AIDS or other STDs. This ties in with the students' beliefs in equality and inequality and about how they view themselves as different from (and arguably better or cleaner than) others.

Most students do not fear or protect themselves against STDs at Bolton because they believe that prep school students are "clean." One girl states, "I think the media sort of blows it out of proportion, to tell you the truth." Another girl adds, "Well, at boarding school . . . I think it, like, it isn't really an issue." The others agree that boarding school students are viewed as a "safe group." Others comment that unless "you go around sleeping with, like, people that get around" or "dirty people," then chances are you aren't going to get STDs. The few girls who disagree offer a glimpse of what very likely is the hidden reality. One girl asserts, "I think a lot of people have STDs on campus. I know three girls."

The boys also comment that safe sex is not practiced at Bolton because they do not think prep school students are at risk. Typical is one boy's contention that the threat of AIDS and STDs does not affect teenage sex, "not here" anyway. The others agree and make comments such as "Honestly, I don't know of anybody who has AIDS" and "No teenager." Another boy contends, "At these schools and stuff you really wouldn't think of anyone having it." The boys then contend that only "dirty girls" would have STDs and as long as they don't hook up with them, they are not worried. They add, "There's only one person here who might have it . . . Ashley . . . she was *pregnant* freshman year." One boy concludes, "Honestly, I like to think of people here as being clean, you know what I mean?"

Referring to "safe sex" to mean the use of birth control, the students say that pregnancy is their biggest fear. The students describe a general lack of condom use among the students except when used to prevent pregnancy. In one dorm, the girls ask rhetorically, "Do guys wear condoms?" and "Do they believe in them?" and then answer with a resounding "No!" In another dorm the girls say that there is "definitely . . . more a fear of pregnancy than anything else." A girl notes, "People are so careless. They don't consider it or they do post-sex, like, 'Oops, that was a little casual.'"

How the boys talk about sex depends on their personalities and the rank of their social cliques (e.g., nerds versus cool kids). The boys often compete to see how callous and insensitive they can be concerning sex, and the cool students compete the most. Ironically, the boys who perform insensitivity and callousness the best also describe having the most sex.

In one dorm where the boys say that pregnancy is their biggest worry, they agree that the threat of STDs has not altered teenage sex. One of the boys notes that there is more condom use, but not by him: "Yeah, more of them use rubbers, just not me. I fucking hate them!" A not-as-popular boy admits, "I'm more worried about getting a girl pregnant than anything." Many of the others agree and state that they if they did get a girl pregnant, they would want her to "abort it." The not-as-popular boy remains quiet while the cool boys banter:

-And if she doesn't, just hit her in the stomach . . .

-And if she has it, just don't talk to her, man.

-Give her a rusty coat hanger and say, "Just do what you got to do."

He then asserts, "My parents would kill me if they found out my girlfriend was pregnant. . . . My parents would go off on me, I'm serious." The other boys ask, "Who's your girlfriend?" When he reveals her name, someone shouts, "Who's Mariana? Somebody get a face book. I want to see this broad!" The boys proceed to look at the picture and groan, making lots of derogatory jokes and comments about her appearance.

In another dorm known for intellectual kids and music, the boys describe being worried about STDs and practicing safe sex. The boys are unanimous that the threat of STDs has altered teenage sex. One boy states, "Personally, [AIDS] scares the shit out of me." Others add: "Condom use and everything is way higher," "A lot less people will take that big risk now. They try to be a lot safer about it," and "Definitely safe sex is practiced." One boy comments, "Well, not everybody, but some people are more selective now. They'll talk to them before they fuck them." Another boy says, "AIDS, shit, I don't want to die, so I'm just not going to have sex . . . that and I can't get any."

Many boys contend that there has been an increase in oral sex at least partially due to the scare of STDs. The boys agree that oral sex has increased because of the unfounded belief that it is much safer than vaginal sex. One of the boys says, "I'd say a lot more people have oral sex instead of regular sex because of that." Others agree:

-You're right. Oral sex has increased, but the funny thing is you can still get AIDS from oral sex.

-You can get almost all STDs from oral sex.

-And many that are quite ugly.

The focus on self as core to the performance of masculinity is evident in their discussions concerning STDs. In one dorm many of the boys still contend that they do not practice safe sex, including a boy who has admitted to having herpes. When one boy says that the threat of STDs has affected teenage sexual practices "'cause now we all have to wear jimmy hats," the boy with herpes comments, "Frankly, it just makes me want to have more unprotected sex because I want to live on the wild side." The others react with "Apparently—you have herpes" and "Whaddaya mean? He's already got herpes. It's not going to get any worse." Another boy comments, "I think people don't really care about AIDS. I think anybody at this age now that got AIDS would just keep having sex 'cause you die anyway. Might as well keep having sex."

Because many of the STDs (including AIDS) can be transmitted by oral sex and due to the amount of casual oral sex that I was hearing about, I ask the students if boys ever wear condoms during oral sex. This question is always met with laughter and a loud chorus of nos. Typical is one girl's response: "Not in this area, only, like, in the ghetto."

The boys literally shout, "Why would you do that? That's the whole point!" They add, "It's an emphatic no."

The relatively large amount of oral sex without concern or protection seems to coincide with what is happening among other teens in America. Studies on oral sex among young adolescents reveal that there is a trend that teenagers are having more oral sex (Barrett, 2004), adolescents have oral sex earlier and with more partners than is the case with vaginal sex (Caristrom, 2005), they do not believe it is possible to get HIV from oral sex, and they do not use any barrier protection during oral sex (Boekeloo & Howard, 2002; Prinstein, Meade, & Cohen, 2003).

The responsibility for birth control and condoms for safe sex falls primarily on the girls. In general, the girls explain that they are the ones who will suffer most from pregnancy and that the boys are irresponsible and don't like to wear condoms. As one African American girl explains, "I take control of birth control because the bottom line is whether or not I get pregnant. And it's whether or not I get STDs." The girls generally agree that "girls all the time" take responsibility for birth control and condoms because males are "stupid," "pathetic," and "irresponsible" and "don't give a shit."

The girls reveal how the sexual double standard and the pressure on girls to maintain a good reputation adversely affect the girls protecting themselves by providing condoms. Debating which gender more readily has condoms available, some girls contend, "On average more guys have it," but others counter, "That is not true, for me it is always, always me." When one girl claims, "Like, I personally don't carry a condom around in my purse . . . but most guys carry a condom," the others agree but contend that this is largely due to the sexual double standard. One girl observes:

> But that goes back to the player-and-ho thing. If a girl carries around condoms, it's like, "Who are you going to sleep around with?" But if a guy carries around condoms, it's like, "Hey, he's going to get laid tonight."

The girls then conclude that no matter who has the condom, the female must take responsibility to see that it is used, "'cause otherwise they won't. They don't feel like doing it. It's a pain for them."

Although the health center on campus supplies free condoms, they are not easily accessible. The students must ask the nurses, some of whom are not perceived as friendly, and this inhibits most students. One of the girls says, "They offer the morning-after pill at the nurse's [office], but they still don't openly offer condoms." Another laughs, "Yeah, no guy has ever gone down and gotten one." In one group, when the girls discuss how uncommon condom use is at Bolton, one African American girl says about STDs, "There's a lot of them out there . . . you better watch it. At this one of the other students responds angrily:

> Which is why the health center is supposedly supposed to have condoms out, no questions asked. I have never seen a bowl of condoms. . . . I can't imagine asking Mrs. Heath for a condom. Oh my God! That woman tries to kill me if I ask for a Tylenol, swear to God!

The others agree, and one adds, "I think I'm going to ask her for a condom just for kicks. . . . I just want to see her reaction, that'll be awesome." Another adds, "That would be so funny."

The performance of masculinity includes a cavalier attitude and audacious insensitivity when discussing (and most likely when acting on) the responsibility for birth control and condom acquisition. The boys generally agree that the girls should provide the birth control. Although a few boys argue that they should help out and provide the condoms, most try to outdo each other in callousness. The boys state that "the chicks" always provide the birth control because it is "their body, their problem." One boy interjects, "I ain't paying for that shit. They're fucking expensive. I don't have no fucking money." Another agrees, "I'm providing the dick. She can provide the condom. It's just good manners."

∷ SENDING THEIR OWN KIDS

One final way to demonstrate gender differences in the meanings associated with excellence and fun is the students' response to whether or not they would send their own children to prep school. In general, most of the responses revolve around excellence and fun and differ greatly between the boys and girls. The vast majority of the girls would send their own children or would leave it up to them. Many make it clear that they would send them "only if they want to" because they themselves were forced to come.

The reasons the girls give for wanting to send their children center around issues of excellence, which include a focus on social excellence (the high class and prestige associated with attending boarding school) and relationships as well as the lower prevalence of partying than in public schools. For many, prep school is part of their life plan. One girl explains, "I have my whole life planned out. My kids will go to prep school after they travel to Europe." Others appreciate the relative safeness of boarding schools because the constraints placed on the students reduce the amount of partying on campus. While discussing the amount of temptations kids face, a girl says that she would send her own kids because "I think it's a safer place to be in general." Another concurs, "Yeah, it's a no-consequence environment." Others focus on the diversity of people they have met, saying, "I want my kids to experience that too."

The girls who would not send their own children, on the other hand, cite the amount of illegal drugs and sex at boarding school. One girl comments that she would not send them "because I'd be afraid of what they might do." Another agrees, "I wouldn't at all because I've seen what some people have done. No. It can change you a lot." One girl states, "I'd send them to a private day school or something 'cause then you get that good education but not all those . . . temptations."

The boys appear about evenly divided about whether or not they would send their own kids to prep school, but the reasons are often the exact opposite. Like the girls, those who would send their own children mostly cite "better sports," "better community," "better academics," "better education," and "good experiences," and a few refer to prep school as a rite of passage. They also would not force their kids to go to prep school because "there are a lot of kids here who are forced" and these kids "really resent it" and "hate it." A few of the students say that they want to put their own children "through the same hell I went through."

In contrast to the girls who would not send their kids away because there was too much fun at boarding school, the boys contend there is not enough fun and cite the lack of freedom and the sheltered environment. Some believe that the students are too sheltered because of the homogeneity of the Bolton population, Bolton's overwhelmingly affluent culture, its rural seclusion, and all the rules. One boy would not send his own children because "they'd have more fun being at home." Another agrees: "There are too many rules and you don't have as much freedom. . . . If you stay home, you can have a lot more fun." Another asserts, "There's no night life here, like on the weekends, and I kind of want my kids to enjoy that." One boy notes that he'll only send his children to boarding school "if I don't like my kids. If I like them, then I'll keep them home." Another states he'll send them "if they get out of control."

∷ FREEDOM AND CONSTRAINT

The balancing act of fun versus excellence is tied to freedom and constraint, powerful themes in the lives of the adolescent boys and girls at Bolton, and again the differences in how they manipulate them demonstrate the gendered paths to relationships and connections.

Constraint is symbolically associated with femininity. The girls are expected to constrain their urges and behaviors. Because of these associations, the girls are also under more cultural and institutional constraint. The girls do not desire to constrain their behavior, nor do they like being subject to more cultural and institutional constraint. They are indignant about the inequality of their constraint and express the desire for more freedoms. Despite their wishes, they constrain themselves in order to maintain bonds with others.

Freedom is symbolically associated with masculinity. Accordingly, boys expect more freedom, act more freely, and are given more cultural and institutional freedoms. Because of these associations, the fight for freedoms becomes paramount in the boys' concerns and behaviors. Despite this, the boys demonstrate a covert value for constraint so they can lead simpler and easier lives. It is also evident that in some ways the boys find security and reassurance in the existence of constraints.

Many forces coincide to make freedom a critical issue for these students. First, the larger American values of freedom, liberty, and democracy conflict with the amount of constraint the Bolton students face. Second, typical of American adolescents, they are struggling for freedom from their parents while at the same time living in a total institution that is regulated and structured. Constraint is more of a concern for the boys because they view conformity as curtailing their masculinity and their group bonds (such as being able to go hang out with friends). Because constraint is symbolic of femininity, the girls are not similarly threatened.

Constraint is a hallmark of most private schools. These schools restrict both student appearance and behavior in an attempt to mold students to a particular image or standard, and prep schools are no different. At preparatory school, students are told when to eat, study, and sleep. Strict rules govern how they must dress. Regulations dictate how they must decorate their rooms and keep them clean. They are allotted little time to socialize or to have fun, and it is a major violation of the rules to have any more contact with the opposite sex "than would be acceptable in public." The students' phone and Internet access is restricted. The school also sanctions everything from prom parties to senior pranks and senior skip day.

It becomes clear, however, that although administrators and teachers create a highly structured environment full of rules and demands devised to shape or guide the students into a desired mold (all designed to appeal to what parents want their children to become), the students also influence their environment. The students are not entirely constrained by static cultural scripts or binding socialization; rather, they consciously manipulate their actions and actively create their own culture, becoming co-creators of their environment.

Rogoff (1990b, 1998, 2003) describes how rather than development simply being influenced by culture or individuals influencing culture, development is an ongoing cultural process where people "develop as they participate in and contribute to cultural activities that themselves develop with the involvement of people in successive generations" (2003, p. 52). In this view, individuals and generations shape practices, traditions, and institutions at the same time as they build on what they inherit from previous generations. Similarly, Ortner (1996), expanding on the theories of Sahlins (1985), regards agency as both "a product and producer of society and history." As she points out:

> One of the central games of life in most cultures is the gender
> game, or more specifically the multiplicity of gender games available
> in that time and place. The effort to understand the making
> and unmaking of gender, as well as what gender makes, involves
> understanding the workings of these games as games, with their
> inclusions and exclusions, multiple positions, complex rules, forms
> of bodily activity, structures of feeling and desire, and stakes of
> winning, losing, or simply playing. (1996, p. 19)

The dichotomy between freedom and constraint is one of the primary battlefronts between the students and the school (and adults in general) and provides clear examples of how the students are actively involved in the processes of their own development. It also is a highly gendered opposition that lies at the heart of the students' performances of masculinity and femininity.

Overt Value of Freedom

Publicly almost all of students endorse freedom over constraint. While students' public appeals for constraint are rare, those for freedom are numerous. From chapel speeches to presidential platforms to newspaper articles, the students condemn the lack of freedoms at Bolton. Several students' chapel speeches describe how much they hate "all the rules" at Bolton and how glad they are to be leaving for greater freedom. One senior dedicates his entire speech to how much he hates "all the rules" while blatantly wearing his baseball cap in the chapel (which is against the rules). Many articles in the student newspaper also describe the complaints of students over the restrictions placed on them, such as one article entitled, "[Bolton] Changes the Rules: Limits on Phone and Internet Use Spark Student Complaints."

Covert Value of Constraint

Some of the students reveal a covert value of constraint. Mostly in their private writings, some desire "fewer choices and decisions" in order to increase the simplicity and ease of their lives and to decrease their pressures. Of those students surveyed, 36% of the boys and 59% of the girls state that they "sometimes wish to have fewer choices or decisions to make."

Wishing for fewer choices or decisions, the girls desire the increased "comfort" and security" that additional constraints will bring. One girl explains, "In some ways you . . . kind of want that sense of order that they put over you. Just for, like, comfort and security and to know that it's one less choice you have to make." Another girl writes, "I wish that I wasn't faced with any illegal substances and that my friends wouldn't be either." A girl writes that she wishes she had fewer choices or decisions to make "just so that life would be a lot easier and more enjoyable. There wouldn't be so much pressure to deal with all the time."

Similarly, one night after an interview in a girls' dorm when all the other girls have left, one of the girls, reflecting on all the difficult teenage issues we have just discussed, comments wistfully, "There is too much choice. We are all messed up." She imagines that in other cultures, where there are religious, familial, or economic restraints, it must be much easier. She concludes, "We have so much, yet they are happier within themselves." Thus, despite all the rhetoric about freedoms, she craves fewer freedoms and choices in order to simplify and add structure to her life.

Although fewer in number, some of the boys also privately write that they would welcome fewer choices or decisions. With more constraints and fewer pressures and responsibilities, these boys would enjoy a simpler, easier, and more fun life. Some of the boys view additional constraints as helping to protect them from making mistakes. In a dorm where most of the students do not desire fewer choices or decisions, one boy comments:

> I think more choices sometimes hurts us too. Like if my parents leave a decision up to me, I might make the wrong decision, and they knew it was wrong. I mean, they might advise me on it, but you have to go your way. But I think sometimes a parent knows better and it might not hurt to have them say, "Trust me."

A few boys in their private writings also describe their parents' "guidance" favorably. One writes that the issues he and his peers are dealing with are "sex, drugs, and alcohol" and that although his friends at home are also dealing with the same issues, "being away from home and away from my parents make these issues much tougher to deal with without their guidance."

Some of the boys wish they had fewer choices and decisions because of the peer pressure. One writes, "I wish we had fewer choices to make. Every choice you make isn't only for what you think but also a decision that will make you socially acceptable." Another writes that he wishes he had fewer choices because "that would make life so much simpler." He explains, "Decisions are the hardest things to make as adolescents. Drugs, alcohol, sex are all among them. Peer pressure makes it hard to choose the hard right over the easy wrong."

The amount of constraint the boys perceive in their lives varies greatly. Although some have too much choice in their lives, one boy has little choice yet describes this constraint positively. He states, "I think it's even different even in the different areas in the United States 'cause my path has been pretty narrow my whole life. I haven't had too many choices." This boy admits that he "kind of" finds the structure comforting: "It's good. I like it."

Constraint with Freedoms

Senior Pranks

As I am leaving a boys' dorm one night near graduation, Pete approaches wearing a black shirt with a black mask rolled up on his head. He whispers, "Are you coming to the senior pranks tonight? You might find them very interesting." Very quietly, so other students wouldn't hear, he tells me the students are meeting at 10:45 in the dining hall. Of course, I decide to attend.

When I sneak into the dining hall, I am surprised to see two faculty members, Mr. and Mrs. Anderson, who are the form deans. I am even more surprised when I discover that they are orchestrating the whole event. Some of the students have already turned the tables upside down and placed the flowers and napkins on the underside and the salt and pepper shakers on the legs. I don't see anything else that has been done, but Mrs. Anderson is not happy. In a loud, frazzled voice, she says, "You all have deviated from what we had planned." She adds, half angry, half pleading, "That has been done over and over. Can't you just stick to what's on the list?"

I ask and am told that the seniors at Bolton have to present their senior prank ideas to the administration for approval. Mrs. Anderson has the list of approved pranks and announces to the half-listening seniors, "This is what we are going to do." She then reads the items that have been approved. This includes stringing girls' underwear from trees, wrapping toilets in plastic, moving the dining room chairs, chaining closed the doors to the school buildings, and tying the headmaster's bike high in the air over the entrance of the building. The faculty members have purchased all the materials, including some chains and locks, and pass them out to the students.

As the students start taking the dining hall chairs outside and lining them up, I hear grumbling. One student mutters, "This is so stupid." Another asks, "What is the point of doing this?" Still another incredulously asks, "What are we doing?" His friend replies, "Don't even think about it, man." Another student sarcastically says, "Aren't we original."

After most of the chairs are taken out and lined up down the walkway, Mrs. Anderson yells, "We can divide into two groups. One group can go with Mr. Anderson and the other can go with Mrs. Anderson." She adds in an exasperated voice, "That is the only way we are doing it because the way you guys are acting, there needs to be an adult with each group." She pleads for them not to do anything that is not on the list, "especially involving animals," stating that she and her husband will get in trouble from the headmaster if things get out of hand. You can tell the students are itching to do more and that only their deep regard and friendship for their form deans keep them under control.

The students move to the main school building to block the entrance ways. They pile furniture up against the doors, but the deans make them remove it. They put paper towels up and down the stair banisters, but Mr. Anderson makes them take them down. They are allowed to chain shut all the doors and wrap the main entrance with cellophane for people to bump into unexpectedly. They hang yarn for people to trip over. There is excited talk and laughter about how school will not be able to start on time the next morning because people will not be able to get into the buildings. The seniors make plans to go out to breakfast with the deans until about nine, thinking that at that point things would be cleared up and they wouldn't be made to do any of the cleanup.

They call the night watchman, who opens the administration offices for them. They take the keyboards from the offices to hide them on the other side of campus. One student asks Mr. Anderson if they can write a note saying, "That's all right. That's okay. You're going to pump our gas one day." He says yes. The students want to move the school vans onto the front lawn. Mr. Anderson answers, "The only thing I'll go for is to block the front circle because otherwise you'll go on the grass and graduation is this week." Mr. and Mrs. Anderson are like hawks, making them stop or remove anything they don't approve of.

A number of students gather back in the dining hall. They take salad bowls and put them on the ground spelling out "Seniors rule" and then fill them with water. They proceed to take all the cups and bowls they can find (which were quite a few) and put them on the ground around the sign and fill them with water.

Things quiet down, and the students head back to their dorm. So I too start home. As I make my way across the campus lawn in the dark, two students approach me and ask, "Do you want to see a senior prank?" I reply yes, half hoping it is going to be something exciting and half hoping it is not. I am a little worried because Mr. and Mrs. Anderson do not seem to be involved. I feel some-what comforted because I know the girls, and they are both proctors and highly regarded by the faculty. We cross the street to where the freshmen dorms are. The girls explain that they are going to tie the freshmen into their rooms. They have string and say they have already done the freshmen boys' rooms but that the girls were still awake so they had to wait to do their rooms. As we approach the dorm and they tell me their plans, I whisper, "Has this been approved?" They reply, "We're not sure."

We take off our shoes outside the dorm and sneak in. I am nervous because this is the dorm of a stern and rigid faculty member and I dread being caught by him. The door to his apartment is open and his light is still on. We make it past *his door and up the stairs. The girls make quick work of tying the doors shut and then we are out again, much to my relief.*

The next morning I am very anxious to see how the school community deals with all of the obstacles to a normal day, and ready to enjoy the seniors' merriment over the chaos they have caused. By 7:20 the next morning, however, the campus looks almost back to normal. Most students never even see the senior pranks. The maintenance staff has already cut all the locks and taken down the yarn and cellophane that blocks entrances. The only evidence of the night's activities and all the seniors' work are the chairs outside the dining hall and the inside of the dining hall, where students go about getting their break-fasts around the turmoil. No delays. No chaos.

Although the students at Bolton focus primarily on their constraints, as adolescents in the United States they enjoy freedoms not available to adolescents in many other societies and they enjoy many freedoms not available at home. Thus, theirs is a dual reality of both constraint and freedom.

At Bolton, the students must abide by many rules. When accepted at Bolton, they receive a student handbook that lists all the school rules, the disciplinary system at Bolton, and the offenses and their likely consequences. "Major violations" include the possession or use of drugs and other contraband, being AWOL (defined as being "out of the dorm after check-in, off campus without permission, or travel violations"), stealing, lying, cheating, intervisitation violations (to enter a hallway or room of someone of the opposite sex, a student must have permission from a faculty member and when in the room the door must remain wide open), having an open flame in a school building (which includes candles, incense, and cigarettes), inappropriate sexual activity (defined as "anything not generally accepted in public"), and harmful actions. The use of tobacco is treated as a minor offense, but the use of marijuana calls for automatic expulsion.

The student handbook explains that the violation of a major rule ordinarily will result in a student being placed on disciplinary probation, and any student who is on probation and commits a major violation will likely be dismissed. However, any student caught using drugs, stealing, or having an open flame in a school building will likely be expelled even if it is a first violation.

The students at Bolton are required to dress according to certain guidelines (set forth in the student handbook) for classes, many meals, and other specified activities. The boys are required to wear "a coat and tie, or coat and turtleneck, and dress trousers." The girls are required to wear "dresses, skirts, or slacks with an appropriate blouse. A blazer must be worn with slacks or appropriate shorts." In addition, "pants and shorts with outside pockets, denim jackets, or sweaters may not be worn as part of class dress." It adds that students who are ill and visit the health center "must wear class dress until formally excused." The students are required to dress appropriately at all times, with the faculty as final arbiters of what is and what is not appropriate. During the period of this research, students were forbidden to wear pajamas to breakfast (including Sunday morning), tube tops, shirts that showed students' stomachs, and extremely short skirts or shorts.

There is mandatory study hall as well as specific check-in and lights-out times. Study hall is nightly at 8:00, and students must sign into their dorms. Often students are required to stay in their rooms with the doors open during study hall. In a few dorms, the students are required to sit at their desks and are not allowed to lie on their beds during study hall. Students in the lower grades who wish to leave the dorm must get a faculty signature. Radios and stereos must not be heard in the hall or adjoining rooms. The final curfew is 10:00 P.M., and all students are required to check into their dorms. Students not in their dorm, even if they are on another floor, are considered AWOL, a major offense. Underclassmen must turn off their lights at 10:35, while upperclassmen may leave them on until 12:00. These rules apply every night except on Saturday, when underformers may check in at 11:00 and upperformers at 11:30. The students may not leave their dorms before 6:00 in the morning.

There are rules concerning how students can decorate their dorm rooms. Any decoration depicting alcohol or drugs is not allowed. Also, pictures considered too revealing by the faculty are not allowed. Nails, tacks, staples, stickers, or tape must not be used on the dorm room walls, doors, or ceilings. Hot-air popcorn poppers and coffeepots are the only electrical appliances allowed. The furniture must be arranged so that the entire room is visible from the doorway and the entrance is not obstructed.

The boarding students are not allowed to have a car at school; day students, although they are allowed to drive themselves to school, are severely restricted in the use of their cars once there. The day students are not allowed to drive any boarding student or leave the campus during the day without permission.

Many types of student activities that are not curtailed at public high schools are severely restricted at Bolton. Senior skip day, senior pranks, and prom parties are all orchestrated and organized by faculty.

In order to get a chance to hear their parting thoughts about their experience at Bolton, I join the seniors on their senior skip day. Late one Wednesday afternoon in May I lug a huge bag of chips, candy, and cookies aboard a bus full of seniors bound for Maine. It is senior skip day and all seniors are required to attend this outing, which was voted upon by the class. In years past, classes have most often traveled to a large amusement park about an hour away. This year the class voted to go rafting in Maine. Not everyone is excited about it. There is some grumbling about how "skip days" are required and about how the money (about $150 per student) for the trip was automatically billed to their parents whether they wanted to go or not. There is also grumbling about the long drive. A few people are unhappy because they say they are sick but the dean of students has made them come anyway. Some kids are really excited, while some of the girls are nervous and not sure whether they are going to raft but might just stay at the bed-and-breakfast.

On the long bus ride, the kids watch movies, sleep, play card games, and chat. I offer food to anyone who will let me interview them about their parting thoughts as seniors.

All the way up on the bus, but especially as we near our destination, the girls keep asking with whom will they be rooming and with whom will they be rafting. There are some definite cliques among the girls, and it is apparent that they do not want to be rooming with the "wrong" girls. The girls are reassured that the leaders had foreseen this issue and assigned them rooms with other girls "they would have fun with." The boys do not seem to attach such dire importance to whom they will room with that night. A few of the boys remark, however, that they do not want to be with Ed, a boy they find annoying.

When we finally arrive at our destination, the buses drop the boys and male chaperones off at one bed-and-breakfast, and the girls, the female chaperones, and I continue about half a mile to another bed-and-breakfast. As we pile inside, find our rooms, and explore the bed-and-breakfast, many of the girls find the rustic but very comfortable Maine accommodations lacking. One girl sounds appalled when she exclaims, "I can't believe this place doesn't have a soda machine!" The girls gather for a movie around a fire in the living room. Some go outside for a bonfire. Others talk on the terraces. There are definite divisions, and the cliques keep to themselves. There is talking and giggling far into the night.

When we arrive at the rafting outfitter, we are made to wear wet suits because the water is so cold. Both the boys and girls seem uncomfortable with the tightness and revealing nature of the wetsuits, and several of the boys wear their baggy surfer-style swimsuits over their wet suits. The students are then told to divide themselves into groups of eight.

The students seem to enjoy the rafting, even the girls who had been ter-rified. Everyone is cold and, I think, glad to get back to shore and have a hot meal.

Give Me Liberty

The students view themselves as subject to a great many constraints from Bolton, society, and their parents. They also unanimously view boarding schools as being more restrictive and having more rules than public schools.

By far the most numerous complaints the girls have concern the restrictions at Bolton. One girl writes, "The dress code now sucks! I hate all the restrictions. It's the little annoying things like dress code and the point system that really piss me off." The issues one girl is facing include "the stupid, dumb, petty rules that [Bolton] has." An 18-year-old female complains, "I feel like I'm in lockdown at day care or something."

The boys also complain about the rules at Bolton. One male characterizes the intensity of faculty supervision at boarding school as "like buzzards on a dead carcass." Another boy writes that the hardest thing for me to understand will be

> how students who are technically adults who are 18 or 19 years old don't get the freedom they need. In the real world an 18- or 19-year-old can have a cigarette if they want. But if an 18- or 19-year-old has a cigarette here at [Bolton], they go to the disciplinary committee.

The students at Bolton also cite parents as a source of their constraint. One student reports that because her grades "aren't that great," her parents won't let her "have a boyfriend right now." Another girl writes:

> We think that the rules this year are way harsh and the school kind of sucks. Parents are only out to get us, same with teachers, sex is great, drugs and drinking are fun but only if you don't get caught.

One boy writes that he and his peers face "many problems with parents and the need to try to live on their own (and parents not wanting to let them)." Another boy writes, "I hate dealing with my parents, because they are always wondering what I'm up to and always want to talk."

One student describes not just the rules but also the lack of choices (such as in the classes they take and whether or not they do sports) as causing the students to "want to rebel." He blames the constraint in the students' lives for their low morale and apathetic attitude toward excellence: "People seem to do whatever it takes to squeeze by and just pass."

Unequal Restrictions

Because the performance of femininity includes having to act polite, having to control bodily functions, and having to control and deny one's sexuality, the students at Bolton agree that the girls are under greater constraint in the culture more generally as well as at Bolton. The girls perceive inequalities with regard to the rules at Bolton. These differences in the amount of constraint in the students' lives were evident to me, as many of the girls' dorm parents severely limited and restricted the amount of time the girls could participate in the interviews.

The girls complain regularly about the rules and regulations at Bolton. In one dorm a few girls complain about the rules against sexual contact on campus, but another girl atypically expresses the value of constraint. A girl with a serious boyfriend asserts, "I find [the rules against] illegal intervis *so* frustrating." Another girl, also with a serious boyfriend, agrees. At this, Elsa, an African American girl who is considered highly desirable by the boys, states, "Really? It doesn't bother me." One of the girls with the boyfriend rants:

> I don't understand why this school thinks they have any . . . [sighs in frustration]. It is so *frustrating.* I cannot be with my boyfriend intimately. I have to go and humiliate myself by going out to the field hockey field, by going to the [athletic building]. . . . It is so frustrating and humiliating. . . . I hate it! I hate it!

The girls then agree that there are no boarding schools that allow sexual activity. One girl adds, "'Cause we're minors." To which Elsa exclaims, "Exactly! We're not even supposed to be doing it."

The boys at Bolton recognize they have more cultural freedoms than the girls, but they complain about the amount of institutional constraint—the number and complexity of the rules at Bolton as well as the severity of the consequences. Personal control or control of one's self is not part of the performance of masculinity.

When I arrive to conduct an interview, Sean, obviously agitated, says that he has "some opinions" about the new one-chance rule for drugs (in an attempt to curb drug use the administration has mandated that now if kids are caught doing drugs, they are kicked out on their first rather than second offense). He launches into a tirade and gathers input from the other boys against the new rule. Sean argues that "experimentation with mind-altering substances" is inevitable and that the new severe punishment for use of all drugs will only result in the students using the harder, more dangerous, and more difficult-to-detect drugs. The other boys agree and help him explain. One interjects that students will experiment with "pill forms." Sean agrees, suggesting that students will turn to Ecstasy and opium. Others add cocaine and LSD to the list. Sean continues (with the others interjecting often):

> Heroin. It's all here, you know, and kids are going to want to, since it's our nature to experiment with drugs then, you know, they take away weed, which is pretty safe. You know, it's safer to smoke weed than to smoke cigarettes . . . as far as harming your body goes, and they push us towards harder, more addictive, more harmful . . . easier to hide, quieter if you will, substances, which I think is pretty dangerous.

After the boys criticize the school's fight against drugs as ineffective, Sean continues:

> See, they knew they had a problem. They knew that kids were smoking weed in the dorms and on campus too much, and they had a problem with it, you know, 'cause the word gets around, the fricking administration knows everything. So they say, "Oh, we have this problem with kids using drugs, so let's just say we'll kick them out," you know, 'cause that's the only thing that will scare us, you know. Like those drug counseling people come in, "Drugs are bad." You know, it doesn't do shit. . . . So we stop smoking weed and start to do other, more dangerous drugs, and they need to think about that.

The mixed benefits of freedom and constraint are revealed in one small dorm where the boys complain about how they are overly monitored while others in the larger dorms go wild. The boys contend about the larger dorms:

> -During study hall they walk into our rooms, like, every ten minutes. Over there, I went over there to study, nobody ever came to bother us.

-I've talked to kids in [Walton] and they say that after the first day of school, the dorm parent has never even been in the hallway, let alone in someone's room. Over here the dorm parents are always checking in, asking you what's going on and stuff.

One boy then admits that there are some advantages to the added constraints and supervision:

It can get really chaotic over in the [other dorms] and loud. Like if I had a paper I had to do and, like, I had to buckle down, I'd be so distracted. I'd be like, "Screw it," or I'd be so mad because so much was going on.

The other boys agree: "Yeah, you can get stuff done here, but it's not fun."

The students also complain about the restrictions the school places on rituals and traditions. Even sanctioned traditions, the students contend, are closely monitored and everything must be approved by the administration. The boys describe the sanctioned tradition of doing something "weird to the headmaster at graduation" such as giving him things as you approach to get your diploma, noting that they "have to get permission to do it" and they "definitely wouldn't be allowed to do what we want to do." They explain that they want to "take his bike and take it apart and each person give him a piece of the bike . . . and the last person give him a screwdriver or something like that." These boys add that at every boarding school graduation, the boys smoke cigars. They conclude, "It's one thing, like, 'God, smoking at school.'" These boys contend that sanctioned rituals or pranks "aren't any fun" and that "the whole point of a prank is to be *spontaneous*." They conclude, "That's the difference between public school and private school—you can't get kicked out of public school."

When I ask the seniors during the long bus ride to Maine whether or not they feel the control of senior skip day and senior pranks is an issue, many describe the amount of constraint negatively, but others describe it positively as something that is part of their upbringing and that puts them above others. One boy comments, "It really doesn't bother me. I'm used to it. I mean, you can't expect to, like, flip teachers' cars over and set bonfires, so . . ." Another comments, "I'm glad we show some restraint. It would be a public high school if we didn't show restraint, you know. We've sort of been conditioned that way, I guess."

Connections or Freedom

The way the students define close connections with their parents and teachers is a good example of their divergent focus on freedom and constraint. The girls focus on bonding and connections, while the boys say that freedom forms the basis for good relationships.

The girls define their closeness to their parents as dependent on their ability to communicate with them. For the girls, their ability to talk to their parents, their openness with each other, or their ability to have an "honest friendship kind of relationship" are the factors that designate a good or bad relationship. Not one girl mentions freedom or constraint issues directly when discussing her relationship with her parents. In describing a lukewarm relationship, one girl explains, "I don't really tell my parents stuff." Another girl contends, "I've been getting a lot closer to my mom. Like, when I was younger I never used to talk to her." Another girl's ability to talk to her mom is the most important aspect of their relationship:

> I think my mom's my best friend 'cause she's, like . . . she'll always talk to me and I'm not really afraid to talk to her 'cause she doesn't get mad if I tell her stuff. Like, she's just glad that I'm talking to her rather than, like, what it's about.

The girls even describe the struggle for independence, viewed as typical of adolescence in America, as revolving around relationships. One girl describes some pulling away but adds, "You still keep sort of a bond to your parents." Another explains, "You're pulling away at the same time that . . . you're starting to tell them about your life, or, you know, letting them know what you're doing."

When the boys describe their relationships with their parents and teachers, on the other hand, the quality of those relationships is based largely on the amount of freedoms they have. The boys base their judgment about whether their relationship with their parents is good primarily on the amount of trust and freedom their parents give to them. One boy says his relationship is good because "my mom trusts me." Another comments, "I know I have a good relationship with my mom 'cause she has a sense of trust. I have no curfew. I have a car. I have money, and she doesn't care what time I come back."

The boys agree that because they have gained certain freedoms at Bolton, they find the constraints their parents, especially their mothers, place on them unbearable when they return home. Typical is one boy's comments: "For some reason when I go home, I can only see her for so long now that I'm away. And I just get to the point where I can't take my mom."

One area where the girls focus on freedom and constraint is in their agreement that when they are home for a long period, such as during the summer, they don't get along nearly as well with their parents because of the constraints their parents place on them. Typically, when asked if their relationships with their parents deteriorate in the summer, the girls collectively groan in exasperation and shout: "I don't want to talk about it!" and "It's awful!" The girls attribute this deterioration to parental restrictions. One girl explains, "It's weird having to ask, tell your parents where you're going. Like, here you don't really have to." Others agree: "You just go."

Although the boys also say that their relationship with their parents has improved since they went away to boarding school, it is not because they talk more but rather because their parents now give them more freedom. One boy notes that his parents "now let me do whatever I want. They think it's cute if I drink." Others assert, "I can do whatever I want" and "I get nagged a lot less. Now when I'm home my mom just bakes me cookies and is just happy that I'm home." Others agree with one boy who comments, "My parents trust me a lot more . . . I get more freedom."

A few of the boys say that their relationship with their parents has worsened, basing this evaluation on the number of constraints they experience. Several explain that it is hard to return to living under their parents' rules. One boy states, "I got used to freedoms and it's hard to get used to readjust."

These differences in what the boys and girls view as the basis of a good relationship carry over to their relationships with teachers. The girls' relationships with the faculty at Bolton are based on whether the girls can talk to them and how open they can be. Some of the girls have found some of their "best friends in faculty here," claiming to be "more open about certain things to faculty" than to their parents. One girl explains, "Like, you're not going to tell your mom about that guy you hooked up with the other night, but, like, Miss Alexander, sure, we talk about it all the time." The girls add that there are definitely some teachers whom "you just want to tell to shut up" or who "drive you crazy," but that, unlike with parents, "you can be really choosy who you talk to."

Although not overt, the amount of the girls' freedom or constraint appears to have at least some influence on their relationships with the faculty. In dorms where the dorm parent is vigilant and restrictive, the girls often speak negatively of that individual and do not have close relationships with her. In one such dorm, the girls agree that "if you have a sucky dorm parent, life is hell."

In their relationships with the faculty, the boys cite communication and constraint as the measures of the quality of a relationship. In general, the boys say their relationship with the faculty is not very close because of the amount of constraints faculty place on them, the lack of trust, and their inability to talk to the faculty.

Many of the boys have positive relationships with some faculty and single out these teachers because of their ability to talk to the students and because of the freedoms they provide. These boys' close and open relationships with certain faculty are parent-like. One boy names his advisor as a faculty member he can "talk to about anything. She's my mother away from home." Another asserts, "There are certain faculty you can tell anything."

It is also possible for teachers to be too easy to talk to. The boys say one faculty member is close to many of the students and "has a lot of friends because he acts like us," but they regard this negatively, commenting, "He's an idiot" and "He's a kid who's never grown up. He's still in high school."

The two factors that influence student/faculty relationships are the type of individual the student is and the personality of the faculty member. This is demonstrated by the boys in one dorm as they debate the percentage of faculty who are "open and nice." The wide variation in the numbers that the boys cite proves that student closeness to the faculty is very personal and varies for different types of students. Although one boy who is a good student and highly regarded by the faculty cites the number at 55%, the others disagree vehemently with "What!" and "No way!" and contend, "That's just because you're a butt kisser." The other boys cite much lower numbers. One boy contends, "Maybe about 20% of the faculty you can talk to without them getting on your case about stuff." Others cite it lower still. One says 10%, while another contends that it is 3 or 4%. One boy lists it at 1% and explains, "There's only, like, two I feel like I could talk to." One student who focuses on fun and hockey instead of academics states that the figure is "0%. Mr. Brown [the hockey coach] is about the only one I would talk to if I had a really bad problem, but that's about it."

∷ REGRETS

During the senior skip day rafting trip, I ask some of the seniors whether, if they had to live their high school years over again, they would do anything differently. Although some of the students say that they would not do anything differently, most say that they would either study more or have more fun. Understanding the pressures they have undergone, it is not surprising to find that only boys regret not working harder while at Bolton. One boy admits that he would "work a little harder, a lot harder." Tyler comments, "I might do a little more work. I'd study for stuff and do homework. Maybe." Similarly, another boy says that the worst thing about his Bolton experience was "totally slacking off for all four years because then I'd have a totally different set of options for college. . . . I kind of regret not doing a little bit better. I know I could have."

Many of the seniors questioned, both boys and girls, say they would focus more on fun while at Bolton. Some of the girls, especially day students, regret how much time they spent achieving excellence. One states:

> At certain times I think I got too caught up in my work and I put too much time into it. . . . It got to the point that I was spending so much time on work that I forgot about, like, my friends and I became kind of secluded and stuff like that just because I got caught up in the process.

Rachel, a high-achieving day student, regrets "overchallenging" herself:

> I had a major burnout. Because I remember coming to Bolton and being, like, so excited to do work and all sorts of stuff like that, and now I'm just kind of like, "Whatever." And, like, when I got to Bolton I felt like I was smart and ready to conquer the world and I don't really feel that way anymore. And I think that has a lot to do with overchallenging myself and getting sucked into the competitive nature of the school . . . and wanting to be in, like, that recognized spot. So I think, like, overworking myself in some ways and stressing myself out is something that I regret.

A few boys say that they would "try to meet more people" and "focus on my social life."

The students make clear that they do not naturally fit the behavioral stereotypes for their respective genders but perform gendered behavior in order to establish bonds with their peers or the opposite sex. Lamenting that the boys are "allowed" to have fun, the girls reveal that much of the gendered behavior evident in partying, such as faking drunkenness, is a show. They make it clear that they would have more fun and sexual encounters if they did not have to worry so much about their reputations. They describe using being drunk as an excuse to have sex, and they describe not enjoying oral sex but performing it anyway because it is "expected." The boys reveal, especially in their private writings, how a focus on fun is expected and allowed, how much pressure they are under, and how much competition they face to drink, do drugs, and have sex in order to be cool. Many perform gender extremes not because of any natural need or desire but because of these pressures.

The ability to be self-reliant, feel no pressure, not care what others think, not work too hard, handle large amounts of alcohol or drugs, have sex, and behave in a callous manner appear to be the modern test of strength by which manhood is proven and status and rankings are established. Not surprisingly, the feminine ideal is weakness, whereby girls have breakdowns, fall to pieces, deny their sexuality, sacrifice, practice constraint, pretend to be drunk, blame their sexual escapades on being drunk, and appear caring and noncompetitive. This is how womanhood is proven.

7 ∷

Masculinity Wins the Day

Graduation day is sunny, just as the seniors prayed it would be. Rows of chairs and an elegantly decorated platform adorn the main green in front of the chapel. The campus looks its best, green and manicured with potted flowers in front of every building. The parents and other family members arrive on campus dressed in their finery for the occasion. The senior girls wear white dresses, which show off their spring tans, and all carry a single rose. The males wear khaki pants, white shirts, and blue blazers with the school emblem and tie. The ceremony begins with a brass quartet playing "Pomp and Circumstance." The seniors sit in the hot sun next to the faculty and their parents, listening to the headmaster, selected students, and an invited speaker talk about what an "idyllic setting" Bolton is, how special a class they are, and their opportunities and obligations as they go out into the world. A day boy is the class valedictorian, while a Korean girl is the second highest-ranking student. A day student who describes herself as "burned out" after four years of trying to stand out at Bolton receives the most prestigious award for "giving of herself" to the school. As their names are called, they cross the platform, shake the headmaster's hand, and receive their diploma. Each student gives him a piece to a puzzle that, when assembled, reveals a photograph of all the seniors hanging out of the windows of his house and waving. Several of the students (and their parents) look relieved that they have finally graduated. When it is all over, there are goodbye hugs and tears from friends and faculty. Many of the boys smoke cigars.

The seniors, who spent the morning packing their belongings into their parents' cars, have until 5:00 P.M. to leave campus. After their last good-byes, the seniors depart. Some head home with their parents. Others celebrate at senior parties. Although a few senior parties are local, especially the night after graduation, others are in all parts of the country, from Boston, Dallas, and Washington, D.C., to New York City and California. Some seniors spend their summer traveling the country to attend these parties to celebrate the end of their prep school rite of passage. For these Bolton graduates, whether they become stockbrokers in New York or lawyers in Boston, whether they'll be working the political arena in Washington or strolling the beaches of Naples, Florida, they will have instant connections not just with individuals who attended Bolton Academy but also with those from any other New England prep school. These privileged adolescents and potential future leaders have shared academic, artistic, athletic, and social challenges, yet foremost among the things they have learned is how to play the game of gender. Although they lost friends along the way, they have made it. They are now alumni and "part of a club."

This study of the everyday lives of prep school students reveals how privilege and social hierarchies are perpetuated through cultural traditions and institutions such as schools. Attending preparatory school, the Bolton students must enact, negotiate, or resist the larger cultural values and power structures, the practices and traditions of the school, the pressures and expectations of their parents, and the inner workings of their peer groups and in doing so create their world. As Ortner (1996) points out, understanding the multiplicity of gender games at a particular time and place involves investigating "how gender games themselves collide with, encompass, or are bent to the service of other games, for gender is never, as they say, the only game in town" (p. 19).

Having grown up in a patriarchal society with traditions of female subordination and attending a prep school where success and competition are the rule, both the male and female students incorporate the values of men and masculine characteristics into their self-esteem and self-concept. Both the boys and the girls at Bolton value the masculine characteristics of self-focused lives, individuality, fun, and freedom while devaluing the feminine characteristics of other-focused lives, lack of fun, conformity, and constraint. The unequal gender status in society increases a belief in gender dichotomy, and the students perform extremes in gendered behavior in order to conform to these beliefs. In doing so, the girls perform femininity at the same time that they devalue it with negative consequences to their self-esteem.

A close examination of their lives reveals that the path to acceptance for these students is based on excelling at gender. The boys and girls have similar needs for status and desires for human bonds but direct their sociality differently because it is by excelling at gender that the students are best able to fulfill both of these needs. Because of a complex system of symbolic oppositions, the behaviors that the students associate with one gender are shunned by the members of the other, encouraging and reproducing extremes in gendered behavior. Thus, when facing the pressures of fitting in, the boys and girls find that ultimately it is by excelling at gender-specific self- and other-oriented behavior that they are able to rise above others and achieve status and power, yet also achieve human bonds through popularity. They clearly perceive that the connections built at prep school will last, and that merely having gone to the same prep school at different times nonetheless creates a bond that they desire. For instance, when a female student commented on how going to prep school will help her in her life past college, she said, "I just went to a wedding and my aunt was marrying this guy . . . and all his friends from Andover and Harvard were there . . . and they were wearing their Andover ties and . . . it was the cutest thing I have ever seen. . . . I was, like, that's how I want it to be for me."

Many different forces work together to reproduce the extreme gender performances. The importance of success, excellence, and appearances among the upper class (which includes most of these students' parents and acquaintances) encourage extremes in gendered behavior. When fathers make fun of their daughters' (or mothers') weight, when mothers see nothing wrong with their daughters not eating, when parents expect them to be perfect, or when families do not associate with anyone "ugly" or over a size eight, they are reproducing these extremes. When parents call the hockey coach at all hours of the night demanding to know why their son is not playing more, when they expect their sons to get into the family alma mater and to be the captain of every team, pressure them to go to the gym, and ignore or even encourage delinquent behaviors because "boys will be boys," they are reproducing these differences.

Through their disciplinary systems, supervision, policies, dress codes, social events, sports, academic competitions, social hierarchies, academic curricula, gendered subjects, and selective admissions, prep schools such as Bolton also sustain the value of gendered behaviors. When the girls' dorms are more closely supervised or the girls receive harsher punishments, when boys are not believed when they are sick, or when boys' sports teams are given better equipment or fields, institutions reproduce gendered behaviors.

The students themselves through their peer culture reproduce extremes in gendered behavior. When the boys tell the girls how great they look even though they are anorexic or have starved themselves for a week, when they tell girls that they would look like "models" if they spent an hour straightening their hair, or when their public lists of the prettiest girls or the ones they would most like to have sex with are made up of "size zero," "silent," and "dumb" girls, their actions reinforce extreme feminine behavior. When they discuss the ways they are going to torture their own sons so they will excel at sports, they reveal how important this attribute is for male status and how these values are reproduced generation after generation. Similarly, when the girls talk despairingly about sexually inexperienced boys, make fun of what they consider small penises, talk about marrying for money, use smart boys and then ditch them, or date "bad-asses" and "jerks" rather than "nice" boys, they are reinforcing extreme masculine behavior.

The interplay of gender, class, sexuality, and race/ethnicity structures and hierarchies result in multiple and often opposing masculinities and femininities (see also Bettie, 2003). The "very preppy" boys rest their masculinity on their wealth and appearance. The hockey players champion their "bad-ass" attitude, muscularity, and athleticism. The African American boys take pride in their muscularity, athleticism, and appearance. For all of these boys, not being "gay" or "feminine" defines their masculinity (see also Connell, 1995; Martino, 1999), and their effort to distance themselves from homosexuality and femininity often results in extreme gendered behavior. "Subordinate" masculinities and femininities (including homosexuals) are marginalized and picked on mercilessly. During the time of this study, no students at Bolton are openly gay.

The girls base their femininity on good looks and sexual propriety but differ in their focus on appearance, being perfect, and controlling their behavior. They establish their femininity in opposition to masculinity. Their desire for perfection and excellence often results in extreme gendered behavior. Many girls internalize the "voices" (L. M. Brown, 1998) of the patriarchal society in which they live, devaluing women, female traits, and their own lives.

The students at Bolton also perform class and ethnicity/race. Most students "totally" change their behavior, appearance, language, or accent at Bolton in order to fit into the preppy mold, only to revert to their old ways at home. The only two wealthy African Americans girls at Bolton prioritize their wealth over their ethnic bonds. The poorer girls inflict reverse classism on the wealthy students by making fun of Tiffany bracelets or Ugg boots even though some harbor a yearning for these badges of femininity and wealth.

The Bolton students present themselves as fitting the gender ideals because this is how they are best able to achieve their desire for self-interest through status and power as well as develop bonds with others. Gendered behaviors become exaggerated because the boys and girls attempt to outdo each other in their focus on self or other in order to gain as much status and as many connections as possible. Despite "fear" of doing so, a few fight to resist the prescribed ideals in order not to "violate [their] principles."

The students pay a price for their performances. The Bolton girls generally compete to see who can be the most other-focused and thus the most feminine. They eat only salads, starve themselves, binge and purge, overexercise, abuse performance drugs, and take diet supplements until they pass out in attempts to reach bodily perfection and to be the girl who can fit into a size two. They use study hall time to do their hair and spend an hour each morning straightening it. A girl has to bandage her arm because her friend burned her while trying to iron her hair straight. They spend all day trying on makeup and go shopping for hair color during exams. They wear short skirts in arctic temperatures to show off their bare legs as well as wear flip-flops in the snow to display their "cute" toenails. The girls try to outdo each other in their sympathy and devastation when a friend is expelled. They see who "gets drunk the fastest" and then who will care the most and come quickly to her aid. They have breakdowns, stress out, and fall apart during exams, trying to see who can achieve perfection and therefore please everyone.

The boys, on the other hand, generally compete to see who can be the most self-focused and thus the most masculine. The boys compete to be the captain of every team. When possible, they spend all day lifting in the weight room and take protein supplements to be the strongest and to have the lowest body fat percentage. All the boys in one dorm conspire to sit in the common room with their shirts off when they know girls will be coming by to sell pizza for a field hockey fund-raiser. They compete to see who can be the most cruel and insensitive ("just punch her in the stomach, man"), who can be the most rude and "bad-ass" (the boys often would see who could fart the loudest into the microphone), and who can care the least about their appearance and academics. They compete over who has the most sex. The coolest boys brag about having sex twenty-four times in a four-day period and belittle the less sexually experienced to the point of driving them out of the room. They decorate their rooms with beer posters even if they don't like beer. They compete to see who can drink the most or do the most drugs as signs of strength and manliness, and they regard those who do not join the competition as social outcasts.

The students of both genders often do not desire to conform to the prescribed standards of gender-specific behavior (or at least the most extreme ones), but most do so anyway. Under the public gendered performances, there are regrets and personal compromise. The girls are open and vocal in their complaints about having to care what others think about their appearance and behavior. They feel constrained by the gender ideals and "scared to do" what they would like because of the repercussions of deviating from the prescribed focus on other. They hide their "true" selves and wear "a mask" in front of others. They describe "dying to be free, wrenching, and waiting for" liberation from the need to conform to these ideals. Conformity retards their "growth and very existence" as well as "restricts" their education and inhibits their talent. They care "too much" and are "afraid of what other people think."

Although the boys infrequently discuss wanting to break away from gender stereotypes, they write about feeling lonely and bemoan their inability to show and share emotions. They describe disguising their desires and weaknesses because they don't want to do anything that makes them "look like less of a bad-ass" or "fucks" with their image. They feel they cannot follow their passions because they "worry about the masculine thing to do." They hide from their friends that they care about academics and "the amount of work they have to do" because they fear being labeled a "nerd" or "geek."

Notwithstanding the prescribed cultural ideals, the girls demonstrate covert male traits of individuality and autonomy through their "cruelty," "backstabbing," being "two-faced," "ratting," and intense competition among themselves. They envy the relatively easygoing, "straightforward," and "less competitive" nature of the boys' relationships. They demonstrate self-focused needs in their desire to have more fun, to be more "carefree," and to be "able to let things slide." They lament their own pressure to "please everyone" and desire to act more like boys, who are allowed to be "more relaxed and laid back." They "fake" being drunk and "put on a show" of drunkenness in order to conform to the expected behaviors. They want sex but pretend to be drunk so as not to face the punishment of being deemed a slut. They enjoy being with opposite-sex friends because they can act on these desires and behave in a more self-focused manner. They disparage females and their stereotypical behaviors of sensitivity, emotionality, and caring. Valuing the male characteristics of power, freedom, and ease in their lives, many would prefer to be male.

Similarly, the boys demonstrate female traits in their desire for relationships and closeness. They write about their need to fit in and their desire for closer friendships and to be a member of a team. They say they would act less self-oriented if they did not have to worry about their image and being cool. Many prefer girls as friends so that they can behave more as they would like to by sharing emotions, tears, sympathy, and understanding.

Although the students perform gender to differing degrees, most students adhere to the prescribed gender roles despite opposing wishes or desires because of numerous and intense cultural rewards and punishments. Conforming to the accepted gendered performances is rewarded with social success, while deviating from them results in social ostracism or chastisement. These gendered performances are enforced in subtle and not-so-subtle ways in students' everyday lives by their parents, the school, their peers, and their own ideas of gender-appropriate behaviors.

The girls who conform to the ideals of femininity, especially those whose appearance fits the ideal of straight blond hair, blue eyes, and thinness and who do not appear "too smart," receive many social and thus status rewards. Not only are they accepted into the right clique, but they are also highly sought after by the boys, make the boys' lists of the best-looking girls, receive flowers on Valentine's Day, and get a date for prom. The tomboy or serious academic who is almost the antithesis of the ideal woman, on the other hand, complains about not being able to get a boyfriend. It is no wonder an athletic girl wishes she did not do sports but rather participated in dance or drama in order to be seen as "more feminine."

The rewards and punishments the boys receive for performing a focus on self are clear. A "bad-ass" boy is viewed as sexually appealing due to his complete disregard of others and his "I don't give a fuck" attitude, while the girls label boys who demonstrate "too much" concern over their appearance as "sick" and contend that their focus on what others think diminishes their sexual appeal. The plight of the two freshman dorms, one considered cool and the other not, is clear evidence of the costs of coolness in regards to the squelching of sensitivity and caring and its rewards in peer acceptance and success with the opposite sex.

The boys label other male students who demonstrate too much of an interest or focus on their appearance as "the pink team." The boys call a male who admits that he cares whether or not he is on the girls' lists of the best-looking male students a "self-conscious bitch." One boy is not valued by his peers or girls because his interest in computers and not sports is not regarded as cool, whereas a gifted athlete and tri-captain of sports teams has so many sexual encounters that some girls label him a "male slut." The boys constantly attempt to outdo each other in their sexual prowess and experience, and those that deviate from the ideals of masculinity are habitually called "gay" or "fag." Conforming to the ideals of sexuality is important to the students. Proving their hetero-sexuality is a paramount concern for the males. Not being deemed a slut is paramount for the females.

Because conformity to these gender ideals correlates to popularity, the ultimate reward is relationships and bonds. Often the most popular girls demonstrate an almost complete focus on other. They seem pri-marily interested in their appearance, focusing on makeup, clothes, and hair or eating very little in an effort to lose weight. The "best" prefect is the one who gives out goody bags at Halloween. The girls who are knowledgeable about clothes and makeup become the center of prom preparations. The girls who focus on athletics or academics and could be considered more self-focused are less concerned with fitting the ideal in appearance. Often these girls are less popular and long to be "more feminine."

Frequently the popular male athletes conform most to the ideal of "self." They often outdo the others in their sexual prowess, experience, and callousness. They are said to date only attractive girls. They stand in sharp contrast to the unpopular "nerds" who appear able to resist the pressures to conform perhaps either because they cannot achieve the gender ideals or because they have less to lose. The "nerds" are apt to demonstrate concern or caring for others and the desire to be sensitive or to have closer relationships.

When individuals do not perform in the prescribed manner for their gender, other students chastise, ridicule, or (worst of all) leave them out. Girls are condemned as being "shallow," while boys are mocked as being "so sensitive." The students make derogatory jokes about both boys and girls who in some way fail to meet expectations. When they insult a male, they attack his masculinity and question his strength or sexual power or accuse him of being "gay." When they insult a girl, they attack her looks or her sexual constraint.

Although both genders police gender-specific behavior, it is same-sex peers who tend to enforce them the most strictly, often through humor and ridicule. It is the other girls who are most apt to start rumors about a girl, make fun of her clothes, and be the first to condemn her as a slut.

It is the boys who are most likely to ridicule other boys who do not drink, are sexually inexperienced, cry, study "too much," cannot "get with" girls, or have "ugly" girlfriends; boys are also more likely to spread rumors that other boys are "gay." This fits with the historical trend that when a particular cultural tradition is viewed as harmful by the general society or outsiders, such as male or female circumcision, female infibulation, or virginity testing, it is often the members of the same sex that are the strongest supporters of the traditions (see LaFraniere, 2005).

Although seemingly contradictory, the only way these students are able to achieve both self-interest and human bonds is by performing the extremes of self- or other-oriented behavior. The boys develop more relationships and connections with both girls and other boys by focusing on themselves (self). The girls develop their self-interest and status through the relationships they form with others. That each gender must achieve both self-interest and connections with others by focusing exclusively on self or other can help explain the large gender divisions in how they present themselves to others. Since the students' ability or willingness to perform gender according to the ascribed gender ideals dictates whether they will be popular and sought-after or seen as a "loser" and left out, it is only logical that they present themselves to others as having as much of the gender-appropriate qualities as possible. The benefits of being popular seem for most students to outweigh the costs to their well-being and to their true selves.

:: THE MALLEABILITY OF GENDER

Class, regional, sexual, ethnic, and individual differences also reveal the importance of context and agency in development. The wealthiest girls appear curtailed by an extreme focus on pleasing others.[1] They consistently place the most importance on appearance, thinness, and prestige and feel more pressure from boys to be "perfect" and to constrain their behavior. In an effort to stand out as excelling in these areas, the wealthy girls judge others on their appearance or the quality, cost, or labels of their clothing. The less wealthy girls, day girls (who are frequently more academically motivated), and serious athletes on scholarship appear less focused on others and act more in their own self-interest.

Among the boys, the wealthy care what others think of their appearance (especially the quality of their clothing) but in other regards appear equally self-focused as the less wealthy boys. The less wealthy athletes on scholarship often appear most boastful and callous about sexual exploits, whereas the wealthy boys are boastful and callous about wealth and privilege.

With regard to race and ethnicity, the African American students speak differently about issues of self and other than do most of the other students. The African American girls often have a strong sense of self. Many of them are outspoken and make jokes about being "too much to handle." They are more focused on careers, and many want to be lawyers. They also demonstrate less willingness to perform oral sex and are more apt to condemn male promiscuity.

Although the African American and white boys share a similar focus on self, the African American girls are apt to hold black boys accountable for their self-focused behavior. In one case, the African American girls call a black boy a "ho" because he "hooked up" with a large number of white girls. In another instance, a black boy who came to Bolton worrying about his reputation is dating many white girls at the end of the year and no longer seems concerned about his reputation.

The African American students of both genders also appear to have more pressure placed on them to care about others.[2] They describe having to represent their race while at Bolton, and they tell of the sacrifices their parents and sometimes entire families make for them to come to prep school. Once they "make it," they are expected to give back to others less fortunate. On Martin Luther King Jr. Day, the guest speaker tells the African American students that they are expected not to forget where they came from and should return to their communities to help the people there.

International students, especially those from Asian countries, differ from the American students in their value of independence and focus on self and fun. The Asian students of both genders are unusually focused on their academic work and describe closer family ties and a greater sense of duty toward others. No doubt many of these students do not fit this stereotype or change once they come to Bolton. This became clear after I spent hours talking with two Asian boys, one who had a drug problem and another who was wrestling with the dilemma of his father's wish that he become a doctor and his own desire to become an artist.

Individual and group differences in focus on self and other reveal the malleability of gendered behavior. Biology does not dictate gender differences in behavior. Instead, the differences between the members of different groups demonstrate the interconnection between culture and development. The differences between individuals highlight the power of human agency.

:: EDUCATED IN EXCELLENCE

At Bolton the students learn to value and expect success and accept the pressures and stresses that accompany the endless pursuit of excellence in academics, athletics, and arts that the school works so hard to instill. Almost all, however, learn to appreciate and strive for the material trappings, advantages, and importance of wealth as well as the gender ideals of the upper class. Among the peer groups at Bolton, the girls learn to strive for perfection and wealth (the latter primarily through a wealthy husband), while boys learn to strive to be the best and to be wealthy above all else. These values are reinforced by the upper-class students and imparted to the less wealthy students through direct instruction ("Some girls are out for the money" and "People who say money isn't everything in the world don't have any") and the obvious advantages of wealth and prestige. In general, the wealthiest students desire money the most and place the most emphasis on accumulating wealth in the future.

There are undeniably academic advantages to this focus on excellence. The plight of women in higher education, where a high-pressure peer system encourages them to focus on relationships with men rather than on getting good grades, has been widely recognized and dubbed as being "educated in romance" (Holland & Eisenhart, 1990). In most cases, the girls at Bolton are at least as focused on academic excellence as the boys because their pursuit of perfection includes acceptance at a prestigious college. Although some girls spend study hall borrowing clothes or fixing their hair for the next day, others work hard and excel in the classroom. Some are interested in careers, while others know that only by gaining admission to the "right" college will they be able to meet a man of the "right" social group with the "right" school tie. Many are intent on being perfect and drive themselves hard to achieve this goal. So at least while at Bolton, the girls appear no more likely to be derelict to their studies, and they often are the top scholars. Driven to be the best, many boys also push themselves hard in order to excel academically and achieve status and wealth. The high grade point averages of these students, however, often come with a heavy price.

There are also consequences of privilege that limit the potential of the wealthy students. I noticed and heard faculty and administrators at various prep schools comment that these wealthy students feel entitled, are unaware of their advantages, are disinterested in and disengaged from the plight and problems of the real world, often have low self-esteem, are impatient (they are not used to having to wait for things) and easily bored, question their own worth while at the same time having a false sense of their own worth because of their wealth, and are unusually "stuff-hungry" and materialistic. These characteristics adversely affect not only the privileged adolescents' education but also their humanity.

It is a Tuesday night and a guest speaker, a professor of archaeology from Boston University, has come to Bolton to give a talk on the excavations and new discoveries taking place near the pyramids in Egypt. Freshman world history students are required to attend. In the very back of the auditorium, two rows of girls giggle throughout his presentation, needing to be told several times by the faculty members to be quiet and pay attention. At the end of his talk, he calls for questions. When a girl with glasses sitting up front and very interested in his talk asks a complicated question, the girls in the back row all burst into muffled giggles and nudge each other.

The gendered performances of the students are costly and inhibit their learning, their academic success, and ultimately their potential. These hindrances affect their behavior in the classroom as well as their ability or motivation to focus on homework. The boys think they "look cool by not caring" about their grades. They brag in front of others about not doing their work. Their focus on being cool, not working too hard, having fun, and not caring has its price. The boys, not the girls, regret not working hard enough at Bolton, and both genders often claim that the girls work harder than the boys. Many boys think that the girls have more academic advantages and focus. They believe that if they were girls, "more would be expected" of them academically, they would be "favored in the academic setting," and they would be "smarter and more disciplined." One boy believes that if he were a girl, his "grades would improve because guys tend to follow their friends who do not work." Another describes "feeling like an outsider" at Bolton because he is "a motivated person":

> So many kids that go here do not see life twenty years down the line. They are overprivileged and only see the here and now. I work hard to reach my goals and here the other students almost condemn such an approach. They don't understand pain before pleasure. Work hard and life will be enjoyable. They just want to slack off and chill.

The girls, however, also seem inhibited in the classroom. One freshman girl registers surprise at "how silent girls are in class." She used to go to an all-girls school, "so I was used to girls being very forward, and then I noticed that girls were a lot more passive than the guys were. That was the first thing I noticed." Many girls, especially the younger girls, feel the need to "dummy down" in the presence of others and not to be too smart or a "nerd." The girls explain that "boys don't like girls who are too outgoing or talk too much" and that boys want "silent dolls on their arm." The girls often describe pressure to be quiet in class, especially if they have a male teacher or there is a cute boy in their class. One girl mentions that in a class where she likes a boy, she doesn't say a thing "because I might say something stupid." The scorn of other girls also seems to silence girls; one cannot be too smart and still part of the popular cliques.

Sitting in on a few classes, I observe how being "too smart" is not viewed as a positive trait in either gender. Those who show their intelligence are often literally shunned by the other students. I witness boys who are smart enough to ace tests sit in class not contributing. I see a senior girl's behavior change when she develops a romantic relationship with a boy in the class. She changes from participating actively and showing enthusiasm to almost complete silence. Several experienced teachers say how the presence of "just one strong boy in the class" causes the girls to be much quieter.

Similarly, teachers relate that an understanding of the gender performances involving self and other can explain the frequent gendered behaviors that take place in their classrooms, such as boys being more talkative, impulsive, excited about open competition, playing the class clown, and being less intimidated by others. After reading this study, a teacher who had worked in prep schools for over a decade commented, "I saw all these behaviors but I couldn't understand where they were coming from and why the students would act this way. Now I think I understand."

A recent trend in education occurring in America is that girls are outperforming boys in school. The divergence between how the genders perform in school has caught national attention, with a *Newsweek* cover story reporting that twelfth-grade girls score on average 24 points higher than boys on standardized writing tests and 16% higher on reading tests and are 36% more likely to take advanced placement or honors biology in high school; 22% more girls than boys are planning to go to college (Tyre, 2006). At Bolton, the girls now consistently earn higher

grades than the boys. Although biological differences such as brain mat-
uration and lateralization are possible contributors to gender differences
in academic performance, these variables have not changed over time.
Something is changing in American adolescent culture to create these
new trends.

The root of this disparity in academic success lies in the feminiza-
tion of academic focus and hard work, coupled with the masculinization
of illicit fun among America's youth. At Bolton, the girls slightly but
consistently outperform the boys in their GPAs, with the most difference
occurring their sophomore and junior years, just when both genders
describe the most pressure to fit the gender stereotypes. There is little
doubt that performing extreme gendered behavior affects the learning
of both boys and girls.

∷ MASCULINITY OVER FEMININITY

Through sociocultural contexts and power relations, individuals develop
and construct gender (Leaper, 2000). The cultural segregation of boys and
girls combined with living in a patriarchal society affects their development because they incorporate its values and language into their self-
esteem and daily interactions (L. M. Brown, 1998; Henley & Kramarae,
1991). Research in Western countries has consistently shown that children rate males and male attributes more highly than females and female
attributes (Antill, Cotton, Russell, & Goodnow, 1993; Archer & Macrae,
1991; Thorne, 1993; Lobel, Bempechat, Gewirtz, Shoken-Topaz, & Bashe,
1993; Lockheed, Harris, & Nemceff, 1983).

By middle childhood, children in the United States are aware that
women and "feminine" activities are devalued and that women face
more discrimination and restrictions than men (Intons-Peterson, 1988).
By early adolescence, boys rate themselves more highly than girls, and
masculinity is associated with a higher sense of general well-being
(Cate & Sugawara, 1986). The divergence between how satisfied boys
and girls are with their gender is reported to increase until adolescence, with 13-year-old girls being the most dissatisfied (Antill, Cotton,
Russell, & Goodnow, 1993). Beginning at adolescence, girls' self-esteem
is lower than boys' (American Association of University Women, 1992).
They also have more appearance and weight concerns than boys, suffer
more from depression (Angold et al., 2002; Klerman & Weissman 1989),
and have lower self-confidence and fewer expectations for success.

The students at Bolton value the self-focus of masculinity over the other-focus of femininity, and most value male lives over female ones. The students' extreme performances involving self and other add to the gender dissatisfaction among the girls. The girls at Bolton are aware of their subordinate status. Most accept the devalued status of females but try to distance their "true selves" from women and things feminine. The girls frequently disparage female traits and the stereotypical behavior of other women and girls. They distance themselves from this devalued status by describing their gendered behavior as being the result of performances rather than true inclinations or tendencies. Facing intense pressures to conform to the ideals of femininity, they have hidden (and often leave unrealized) desires to resist and redefine these gendered parameters. Because other and femininity are so devalued, the girls desire to act more self-focused but continue to be trapped in the performances of orientation toward other.

The boys are also well aware of the subordinate status of women and things feminine. They feel pressured to act in sexist, misogynist, and homophobic ways in order to distance themselves from women and deny in themselves any "feminine" (nurturing, caring, or sensitive) characteristics. Although boys at coed preparatory schools were found to have more egalitarian views toward women and homosexuals than boys at single-sex schools (Addelston, 1996), the atmosphere remains decidedly negative. The self-concepts and social anxiety of the boys also suffer from the gendered ideals they are expected to uphold (see also Reichert & Kuriloff, 2004).

Both genders believe their lives would be completely altered if they were the opposite sex, viewing gender as affecting their thoughts, actions, feelings, emotions, ideas, choices, perspectives, interests, and futures. Although the girls believe that being of the opposite sex would make a large difference to their lives in regard to their goals, interests, and how they are treated, they do not think that they *themselves* would be different. The boys believe being female would make a bigger difference and frequently comment that as a female "I wouldn't be me" and "I wouldn't have the same opinion of self."

Both the boys and girls believe boys' lives are "easier" and "less stressful." They view the girls as having more pressure to look good, pressure to act appropriately (including sexually), self-induced stress and pressure because they worry, pressure to please others, and stress about grades. The students believe the boys have more athletic pressure, pressure to act cool or "like an asshole," and sexual pressure (to "get some play," to be experienced, and to have a large penis). In addition, the boys view themselves as having more academic pressure as well as pressure to be successful and wealthy so they can provide for their families. Overall the students view the girls as having much harder lives.

∷ TO BE FEMALE OR MALE?

Similar to studies on gender preference (see Hollos & Leis, 1989) among adolescents in other cultures, the boys and girls at Bolton differ markedly in their gender satisfaction. The boys are unanimous and enthusiastic in their preference to be male. While some of the girls prefer to be female, many say that if given the choice they would prefer to be male. The girls who would like to remain female are much less certain about their choice than are the boys.

The girls demonstrate a wide variety of gender satisfaction. Some of the girls respond, "I'm happy being a girl" or "I'd rather be a woman. Definitely!" and cite women as being more "open," "emotional," and "supportive" and that they "get to buy clothes and makeup" and have "more clothing options." Although almost all of the girls describe the female biological role negatively ("I hate going through periods" and "I don't want to have to go through giving birth and the whole nine-month thing"), a few of the girls who like being female are eager to have kids. "It's all so amazing," one girl gushes, revealing that she and her friend sometimes "wear our backpacks backward and pretend that we're pregnant." Some girls are happy not to have the stress of having to work or be successful. One girl comments that, as a woman, she "can stay home, raise the kids, and just go to luncheons and play tennis. Why would I want to change that?"

Others are not sure whether or not they would prefer to be male or female: "There are so many differences, you can't really compare" and "It's like comparing a pro hockey player and a pro basketball player. You can't say who's better."

Just over one-third of the girls I interviewed in the six girls' dorms (approximately 90 girls), mostly the older students, are emphatic that they would prefer to be male. Their primary reasons center around their dissatisfaction with bodily functions, the sexism prevalent in society, and their negative view of stereotypical female behavior. They believe that "guys can get away with being ugly much easier than a girl can" and "guys seem to have so much more fun than we do." Most contend,

"Priorities usually go towards men." One girl confesses, "Sometimes I want to be a man just because I feel that girls are so emotional, like every single day there seems to be a problem." The negative side to female relationships is repeatedly emphasized. The girls assert that they are more "vicious," "conniving and backstabbing," and "fake" and that males "are more straightforward" and "trustworthy."

The viewpoints of the younger girls differ from those of the older girls. In both the freshman and sophomore dorms, the girls are much more content being female than are the older girls. In the freshman dorm, despite their contention that it is harder, the girls unanimously want to be women and the discourse is extremely pro-female. They say women are cleaner, smarter, and more emotional.

The same is true in the sophomore dorm. One girl states, "I love being a woman," and the others agree. Their reasons center on what they view as women's sensitivity and emotions and the female focus on other, the very factors the older girls condemn and give as reasons for wanting to be male. These girls view women as "nicer," "more sensitive," and getting to show more feelings and emotions. Perhaps the reason the younger girls differ so markedly from the upperclassmen is because they are relatively new to the system and have not yet been hardened to the realties of inequality their older counterparts have faced or they have not yet come to accept society's devaluation of "other."

The boys I interview in all nine dorms (approximately 120 boys) are unanimous that they would want to be male. There is no debate. Not one boy said he would want to be female. The boys often laugh when I ask the question, as if the answer is obvious, and shout: "A man!" (with the tone of "How could it be otherwise?"), "Oh God!" (said as though it would be *terrible* to be a woman), "I would *hate* being a woman!" "Most definitely!" and "It's a given!" that they would prefer to be male.

The boys' reasons center around the unpleasantness and pain of female bodily functions and biological role, sexual discrimination, sexual double standards, the pressure women feel to look good, the scrutiny and criticism women receive from men, the sexual advances and remarks women receive from men, rape, control and freedom, that men have more power, the pressure women face to act appropriately, and that it is more fun to be a man. Some of the boys comment that if they were a woman, they would "not have to work" or feel pressured to be successful. As one boy explains, "If I was a woman, I wouldn't have to be successful and wealthy or fail at life." They quickly decide, however, that the good things about being male still far outweigh the bad.

The clear enthusiasm the boys demonstrate for being their own sex is telling. Typically, after a very loud and unanimous response that they would want to be male, they elaborate by citing advantages: "Better jobs," "Easier," "More money," "Not as much sexism," "You're expected to mess up. Like, if you're a son, if you get into trouble in high school, you don't have to be perfect," "It's more fun to be a guy," and "From all that I've experienced, being a man is better."

Although most of the girls at Bolton perform a focus on other, they generally do not value it. Instead, both the boys and the girls value a focus on self and other masculine characteristics. This is at least partly due to the students' incorporation of the American values of independence, individuality, and freedom in their lives. For the boys, these larger cultural values combine with the male gender ideals to exert pressure on them to hide their natural needs and desires. For the girls, what they value is in direct contradiction to how they are pressured to act, so they not only hide their true needs and desires but also have low self-esteem and gender dissatisfaction. Living in the context of a patriarchal society, the girls seem to accept society's view of their inferiority.

Some research suggests that despite their socially inferior status, adolescent girls protect their self-esteem by reevaluating feminine characteristics as positive (Alfieri, Ruble, & Higging, 1996). Among the students at Bolton, however, only the youngest girls view female characteristics positively, and in general both the boys and girls value male characteristics more highly and male lives over female ones.

:: SECOND BEST

The students, the institution of preparatory school, and American society as a whole value the qualities of self over other, individuality over conformity, and freedom over constraint. In general, the symbols associated with being female and femininity are devalued, while those associated with being male and masculinity are more highly prized. That the boys and girls describe the girls' focus on other unfavorably and that the girls are not proud to possess sensitivity, caring, and compassion demonstrate that their values are often contradictory to their prescribed gender ideals. Because the reality of these girls' lives differs from their ideals, they often experience low self-esteem and gender dissatisfaction.

The reality of the boys' lives also does not meet their values and ideals. Because demonstrating a lack of self-esteem is the antithesis of masculinity, the boys are much less open about their feelings of inadequacy. It is unlikely that the boys are much better than girls at meeting the ideals of their gender, in the boys' case self-reliance, strength, ability to provide, and being "the best at everything." The boys also face much pressure to attain academic, athletic, social, and monetary success in life. They feel pressure to surpass or at least uphold the expectations of their wealthy and successful parents. Often they suffer problems with self-esteem but do a better job of hiding it.

Race, religion, sexual orientation, class, and not fitting society's ideals do not in themselves affect a person's self-concept, but rather society's negative reactions cause low self-esteem (Rosenberg, 1979; G. H. Mead, 1934; Tajfel, 1978a, 1978b, 1987; Goffman, 1963).[3] Thus, the messages others send concerning the degree to which an individual meets cultural ideals determine to a large degree the student's self-esteem and self-identity. Because of the high institutional and class standards of excellence, few individuals actually meet the ideals expected of them. Although they are in the vast majority, individuals of both genders who do not fit both theirs and others' ideals of being perfect or the best at everything often describe suffering from low self-esteem. The girls are viewed by both themselves and the boys as "inferior" in status. The degree to which these girls accept their lower status varies, but it appears that most accept society's devaluation of women and femininity.

Devalued or "stigmatized" minorities have the choice of either accepting or rejecting their inferior status (Tajfel, 1978a, 1978b, 1987; Goffman, 1963).[4] If they reject their status as inferior, they can either assimilate and demand equality, redefine their "inferior" characteristics positively, redefine the ideals they are trying to achieve by creating new dimensions for comparison, attempt to achieve success in areas usually considered beyond their reach, or view their condition as a blessing in disguise.

Some students are adept at either redefining the negative characteristics (such as viewing sensitivity, emotionality, or a healthy body size positively) or creating new dimensions for comparison (new ideals of femininity and masculinity that do not revolve around the self/other dichotomy). These students resist and rebel against gender expectations. Some boys talk about the need to cry and to have close relationships. They date nice girls whom others call "ugly." Some girls refuse to focus on their appearance above all else, to give blow jobs when they don't want to, or to violate their principles by conforming to stereotypical behaviors. They shock others with their acceptance of and confidence in their bodies. This self-empowerment appears to be the key ingredient for positive self-esteem for these students (see also Coates, 1986), and hope lies in these acts of resistance to challenge the arbitrary limitations based on ideas about gender.

:: BROADER IMPLICATIONS

Some of the issues that the Bolton students face may be distinct to pre-paratory schools due to the institutional emphasis on individuality and excellence, but others are undoubtedly the same for other American adolescents. The issues distinct to boarding school may include the intense stress, pressure, and fatigue associated with the perceived need to be perfect and the pressure for excellence; guilt about their privilege or cost of their schooling; intense parental pressure to be successful in all areas of their lives including academics, athletics, and appearance; institutional pressure; pressure to equal or surpass their parents' wealth and social standing; nearly unlimited resources; and heightened gender differences due to the pressure to excel at gender. The consequences of these unique circumstances and pressures often exacerbate the issues other American teens face, including eating disorders and body image dissatisfaction, the abuse of performance drugs, sleep deprivation, use and dealing of illicit drugs, stress-related breakdowns, binge drinking, cheating, suicide, and teenage sex.

Unlike the claim of representativeness inherent in traditional com-munity studies, the problem orientation approach used in this study does not make the claim that the microcosm equals the macrocosm of American culture.[5] Instead, this work deals only with this group of elite adolescents. This study does have implications on a larger scale, how-ever, as it reveals certain processes, cores of important symbols, and pat-terns of behavior and language use that have meaning not only for other similar groups but also for the American dialogue as a whole.

Power structures shape the nature of human development (Leaper, 2000; Garcia Coll et al., 1996) within which individuals construct and develop their sense of gender in a sociocultural context by means of social interactions. This study of adolescent peer cultures reveals the relation-ship between agency and context and demonstrates the dynamic inter-play of culture and development. Often individual differences between adolescents of the same gender arise due to class, race/ethnicity, sexual orientation, or individual psyche as they accept, resist, or try to change gender ideals. The differences in gendered behavior mask the relative similarities between the needs and desires of the boys and girls.

This research reveals the power of cultural scripts as well as how individuals act strategically to create and recreate gender in their every-day social interactions. I hypothesize that a juxtaposition between gender ideals obscures similarities among American adolescents and that they employ similar performance strategies in order to conform. Although this group of elite teenagers is in many ways unique, the patterns revealed in this work speak to the lives of other American adolescents in different degrees. Ultimately, this work reveals how a slice of adolescent life at a New England boarding school sheds light on the perpetuation of power in America and the cultural dialogue concerning gender, class, race, ethnicity, sexual orientation, and social inequality.

:: THE POWER OF KNOWLEDGE

After I completed my research, I presented my findings to the school community, and the students unanimously validated my findings. Several students noted the importance and value of understanding the performative aspects of gender and the self/other dichotomy. One girl said:

> It's important for everybody to know these things because some guys don't know they're putting pressure on girls and vice versa and I think it would be really beneficial to let everyone know of your findings.

Another girl noted,

> Learning about the self and other mentalities make it easier for males and females to have a clearer comprehension of why we react the way we do, and visa versa . . . by seeing it mapped out, one could see the motivation for certain behavior.

A boy approached me after the presentation and asked if I wrote my findings down because "I think what you said is important and I'd like to have a copy so I can periodically refer to it so I don't forget."

The hope for extending beyond these extreme gendered performances to a more humanistic existence lies in awareness and in creating new dimensions for comparison. By becoming aware of the pressures each gender faces and the motivations behind such extreme behaviors, adolescents themselves, their parents, and educators can recognize the folly and waste resulting from these straitjackets on behavior. One girl notes the power of individual resistance to cultural scripts and expectations:

> I feel both sorrow, relief, and epiphany. . . . I am a jumble after that presentation as I feel embarrassed that I fit parts of the girl stereotype, angry and a little envious of the male generalization, but overall informed and ready to shift my state of mind. Throughout high school I have been so afraid. I was never a conformist because I was too proud, so I stayed shy and hid my true self even though I've never violated my principles. This year as a senior, more than ever, my silence and insecurity have encumbered me and I've been struggling to realize what you made us aware of tonight. Fear holds me back. But I feel that the perspective I have gained from tonight and other incidents is helping me move in the right, stable direction. Thank you for being interested in a topic which many refuse to confront, and thank you for promoting such a complex but needed cause. I truly respect what you did.

Researchers have advocated programs and materials that increase boys and girls' knowledge and understanding about gender and "bring to light for examination and discussion, the gender dimension in social life and education" (Connell, 2000, p. 168). The ultimate goal is to enable boys and girls to "see the world from standpoints they normally regard as other," including those of the opposite sex and other masculinities or femininities (Connell, 2000, p. 169), and to "learn to be the opposite sex" (Sapon-Shevin & Goodman, 1992).

Simply talking together about the issues and pressures they face can help adolescents cope and resist. The students at Bolton clearly enjoyed our discussions and described "getting a lot" out of them. The year after the research was completed two of the girls who had been particularly involved in my research started a group on campus to get together and discuss the pressures and issues of gender. Although the group was primarily for girls, boys were also welcome. The girls told me that their idea for this group had come from our talks together. They had gained so much from sharing with other girls about these issues that they did not want to stop.

As it is often same-sex peers who most actively police gendered behavior, it is in reality the boys who are limiting themselves and the girls who are limiting themselves. Thus, to make the biggest impact the primary goal should be to change not the attitudes of the opposite sex but rather those of one's own sex.

Aware parents and educators can also work to help adolescents break out of the bonds of gender extremes. The awareness and involvement of fathers in this process appears to be particularly important, as children tend to view them as the "custodians of gender role norms" (Katz & Walsh, 1991). The modeling and attitudes of fathers have been found to be especially influential in the creation of gendered behavior and attitudes in their children (Turner & Gervai, 1995) and the amount of gender satisfaction their children feel (Burns & Homel, 1986). Men also have been more successful than women in eliciting counterstereotypical behavior in children, especially in boys (Katz & Walsh, 1991).

A fuller understanding of the causes of gendered behavior can help parents and educators work in the direction of less restrictive gender ideals and more fulfilling and meaningful lives. By understanding the importance of agency in gendered behavior and the underlying similarities between males and females, parents and teachers can work toward reducing their differential expectations. Understanding the power of expectations and their substantial effects on gendered behavior, the divergent pressures boys and girls feel, and the importance of the peer group in solidifying gendered behaviors allows parents and educators to take these factors into account. They can model and encourage non-stereotypical behaviors, emphasize the importance of traits other than looking cute or being cool, expect and accept both the need for relationships and connections and the need for autonomy and status from both genders, make sure policies and rules are as equal as possible, and not tolerate "boys will be boys" behavior or expect perfection in girls.

This study suggests that just as economic strategies largely determine gender stratification in whole cultures, so might differences in available resources among the different classes in one society.[6] Among the upper class, the surplus of available resources means women tend to fill different roles than do women of other social classes. It is possible that the especially sharp divisions between masculinity and femininity evident as the Bolton students perform extremes in gendered behavior are connected to a relatively larger imbalance in the contribution of resources and a more defined separation between the public and domestic sphere among the upper class. The upper-class woman can afford to stay at home, and her participating in volunteer organizations, spending the time at the gym to stay thin, shopping for the right clothes, taking care of the large house and social functions, and attending to her beauty bring status to the husband and family. The upper-class male, also caught up in the powerful oppositions between masculinity and femininity, must provide at all costs. The Bolton students generally believe that it is not necessarily important for a man to be working or contributing to society; he just needs to be wealthy and provide plentiful resources to his family. Not to be successful and wealthy is to "fail in life." Money and its trappings are an essential part of the upper-class definition of masculinity and femininity and appear to be directly linked to the extremes and uniqueness of their gendered behavior.

The values, issues, and pressures evident in the lives of these upper-class adolescents add to our understanding of how class, ethnic/racial, and sexual difference is often constructed and performed in relation to gender. Understanding these interconnections reveals how membership in hierarchical social categories affects development. Knowing the importance of historical, social, and situational contexts, parents, teachers, and adolescents themselves can better navigate the gendered oppositions that adolescents manipulate and negotiate as they play the game of gender.

Notes ▪▪

CHAPTER 1

1. The names of all schools have been changed. All individuals depicted in this book are composite characters. Any resemblance to any actual person of that name is purely coincidental. The pictures in the book are of students at a different prep school, and none of the individuals pictured was involved in the research. Descriptions of the physical aspects of the school itself are also a composite.

2. *Culture* is defined here as "a system of inherited conceptions expressed in symbolic form" whereby humans "communicate, perpetuate and develop their knowledge about and attitudes towards life" (Geertz, 1973, p. 89). It is the pattern according to which individuals in a particular place must construct their lives; thus it is something they cannot escape (Varenne, 1986). Symbols encode meanings whose significance emerges in social interactions.

3. This research examines the daily lives and peer culture of one group of adolescents in America. Adolescence, the period of physical and psychological development between the onset of puberty and maturity, is pivotal for many reasons. This stage of development between childhood and adulthood is a time of change in social status as well as a period of training for adulthood that often includes new experiences, responsibilities, obligations, and pressures. This research views adolescence as a period of identity formation with special interests and concerns, during which individuals develop a concept of self and personhood and are particularly concerned with how they appear to others and belonging to their peer group (Erickson, 1963).

4. Anthropologists have discredited the popular concept of race—physical types or groupings based on perceived genetic similarity—and instead contend that physical differences occur on a continuum such that no distinct divisions between groups can be made. The *idea* of race, however, continues to influence these students' lives, as do its social, historical, and political consequences.

Instead of race, it is ethnicity, or cultural associations, that is of importance in regard to behavior. In this book I use the term "race" when referring to the consequences of a group of people being socially constructed as a race, and the term "ethnicity" when describing a common culture based on a shared identity and history. I use the conjunction of the two, "race/ethnicity," when referring to a conglomeration of the two concepts.

5. In his classic work *Childhood and Society* (1963), Erikson identifies eight stages of psychological development and contends that adolescence is characterized by a crisis between identity and role confusion. He states that during the stage of adolescence, youths are primarily concerned with "what they appear in the eyes of others as compared with what they feel they are" (p. 261).

6. Classic works in the study of gender include Brod, 1987; Chodorow, 1971, 1974; Ortner, 1974; Ortner & Whitehead, 1981; Rosaldo & Lamphere, 1974; and Sanday & Goodenough, 1990.

7. Symbolic interactionism incorporates theories of strategic interaction and the presentation of self. This approach stresses the importance of symbols and can be defined as "the mutual orientation of persons, one to another, such that the acts of one both respond to and influence the acts of the other" (Hewitt, 1976, p. 12). Symbolic interactionism takes everyday life as the human reality from which it derives, ordering concepts and forms of reasoning. The basic principles of symbolic interactionism are that (1) "human beings act toward things on the basis of meanings that things have for them," (2) "the meanings of such things is derived from, or arises out of, the social interaction one has with one's fellows," and (3) "these meanings are handled in, and modified through, an interpretive process used by the person in dealing with the things he encounters" (Blumer, 1969, p. 2).

8. As Thorne (1993) contends, individuals "play" gender in their daily interactions through "social relations, the organization and meanings of social institutions, [and] collective practices" (p. 4). This social orientation, coupled with the power of cultural scripts or norms to shape behavior and that of individual "agency" or strategy to negotiate and resist these forces, factors into how individuals manipulate gender identities.

9. Although adolescent issues in the United States remain addressed primarily by journalists, sociologists, researchers of women's studies and child development, and psychologists, in recent years anthropologists have examined adolescence (see Suarez-Orozco & Suarez-Orozco, 1995; Rosenfield, 1971; Moffatt, 1989; Canaan, 1986; Brown, Larson, & Saraswathi, 2002). The primary difference between anthropology and the other approaches is anthropology's emphasis on the use of participant observation. The works in other disciplines are complementary, and the value of multiple approaches is undeniable.

10. Sherif (1979) criticizes the narrow view of traditional psychology research used to examine sex differences and contends that it examines behavior in contrived and carefully controlled laboratory settings and deals only with "selectively chosen data" and thus is usually unrepresentative of daily life (p. 108). Parlee (1979) describes findings on sex differences as misleading and invalid because the research typically occurs in artificial contexts. Other researchers have advanced similar criticisms (see Eagly, 1987; Bernard, 1974; Block, 1976).

Some have questioned the relevance of childhood socialization theories to understanding the factors that maintain sex differences among adults or adolescents (Eagly, 1987).

CHAPTER 2

1. Mills (1959) in his study of the "power elite" maintains that prep schools are essential for the preservation of privilege.

2. Boarding schools fit Van Gennep's (1960) definition and description of a rite of passage, which includes distinct stages of "separation," "transition," and "incorporation" and can be compared to rites of passage cross-culturally (Mahdi, Foster, & Little, 1987; Eliade, 1958).

3. Ostrander (1979) contends the ideal upper-class woman is a society lady or a Lady Bountiful rather than a career-minded achiever, and her volunteerism furthers the family's class and status far more than would a paid job.

4. The preparatory school life described in several works fits Goffman's characteristics (Rae, 1983; Prescott, 1970; Lambert, 1974; Wakeford, 1969), and researchers argue that Goffman's theories of total institutions apply directly to preparatory schools (Cookson & Persell, 1985; Crosier, 1991).

5. A few works provide descriptive accounts of boarding school life from former headmasters (Wakeford, 1969; Prescott, 1970) or students of color (Cary, 1991; Anson, 1987).

6. The feeling of separateness and the importance of their experience is demonstrated in part by the amount of time prep school students devote to remaining in contact with the other students and providing financial aid to their alma mater. Alumni and parents of alumni give millions of dollars annually to the schools' campaigns.

CHAPTER 3

1. This work employs the analytic theories of symbolic anthropology and symbolic interactionism. Symbolic anthropology, as I use the term, is the study of symbols and meanings in the tradition of Geertz (1972, 1973, 1983), V. Turner (1974), Spindler and Spindler (1977, 1987), Schneider (1968), and Varenne (1977, 1986). The proponents of a symbolic approach believe there is an American *something*—be it cultural style, concepts about the world, ideas concerning relationships, or cultural dialogue—that Americans share, and that this commonality is based on the sharing of common symbols.

2. Anthropologists and psychologists debate the dichotomy of two different types of self-concepts among societies as a whole, with some cultures placing primary importance on the individual and others more highly valuing the community or larger group. In the United States and other large Western societies, self-determinacy or the relationship of self and personhood in relation to society is viewed as individualistic or independent. However, in other societies, largely Asian, African, and Latin countries, self-determinacy is viewed as interdependent or relational. Researchers describe individuals of Western countries as more apt to have an "independent" concept of self, whereby they

view themselves in terms of their own abilities, accomplishments, traits, and values. Individuals from countries that nurture an "interdependent" concept of self, on the other hand, are more likely to view themselves in terms of their relationships with others and their social roles (Tonnies, 1957; Riesman, 1950; Bellah, Madsen, Sullivan, Swidler, & Tipton, 1985; F. L. K. Hsu, 1953; Shweder & Bourne, 1984; Markus & Kitayama, 1991; Triandis, 1996).

3. Baumeister and Leary (1995) describe the need to belong or "maintain at least a minimum quantity of interpersonal relationships" as "innately prepared and thus nearly universal" among humans. They view human beings as "naturally driven toward establishing and sustaining belongingness" and point out how "the desire to form social bonds would have both survival and reproductive benefits" (p. 499). Similarly, Mascolo and Li (2004) contend that all individuals need and are concerned with individuality and relatedness, but because they live in particular cultural and historical climates, individuals "construct ways of representing individual selves within social relationships in relation to each other" (p. 3).

Gabriel and Gardner (1999) expand on Baumeister and Sommer's theories and also argue against theories that portray women as "highly relational" compared to men. Based on evidence from laboratory tests, they assert that when interdependence is defined as not just close relationships but also connections to a group, men are as social as women. Men view collectives (in contrast to relationships) as important. Although females demonstrate self-construals that are more relational in affect, motivation, and cognition, males demonstrate collective self-construals that are group-oriented. Thus, both genders are equally focused on connections, but at different levels. They conclude, "We found consistent evidence that implied that men and women differ not in a focus on independence versus interdependence per se but rather in the aspect of interdependence that is focused on" (p. 651).

Similarly, the argument that the pursuit of power is the counterpart to love, as both involve an attempt to escape loneliness and isolation (Morgenthau, 1962), suggests that males' quest for power, instead of being evidence of male desire for autonomy (Cross & Madson, 1997), is more likely due to their desire for connections.

4. Other researchers have noted the strong loyalties and group identification that males develop. The Robbers Cave study (Sherif, Harvey, White, Hood, & Sherif, 1961), in which boys were randomly assigned to different groups, reveals how intense and lasting bonds quickly develop between males. Kashima and colleagues (1995) demonstrate that men's friendship groups are more cohesive than women's because women's friends tend not to be friends with each other while men's do.

5. Shields (2002) proposes that the "key link" between gender and emotion is that gender performance serves to verify the authenticity of the self by displaying emotions appropriately. A broad network of social influences operate interdependently to influence gender conceptions and roles (Bussey & Bandura, 1999). Parents strongly believe that boys and girls have different attributes and skills (McGuire, 1988), which results in different expectations for their opposite-sex children and ultimately differences in the performance and

self-perception of the children themselves (Eccles et al., 1993). Parents accept more anger from their sons and fear from their daughters (Birnbaum & Croll, 1984), actively encourage their children to participate in gender-stereotypical activities (Lytton & Romney, 1991; Fisher-Thompson, 1993), and speak and discuss emotions differently with their boys and girls (Leaper, Anderson, & Sanders, 1998; Fivush, 1989). All of these divergences in expectations and treatment have an impact on children's behavior, personality, and learning (Pellett & Ignico, 1993; Klebanov & Brooks-Gunn, 1992; Eccles & Jacobs, 1986).

Similar differential treatment and expectations in schools further encourage gender-stereotypical behavior. Teachers hold stereotyped beliefs about boys and girls' skills (Shepardson & Pizzini, 1992). They often respond negatively toward counter-gender-stereotypical behavior, and their responses have been shown to change children's behavior over time (Kramer, 1991). School structures and practices also encourage the differentiation between boys and girls (Thorne, 1993; Meece, 1987). Boys and girls choose different courses and view their capabilities differently regardless of any differences in ability (Halpern, 1992).

Peer group norms among boys as traditionally emphasize dominance, competition, and interdependence, while those among girls emphasize the closeness of relationships and sensitivity to others. Also, in girls' peer groups nonconfrontational interactions are encouraged, while in boys' groups confrontational, assertive interactions are encouraged (see Leaper & Damon, 1994). Deaux and Major (1987) argue that the expectations of the perceivers, self-systems of the actor, and situational cues combine to guide gender performance and are seen as integral to the performances.

6. Underwood's (2003) contention that women's anger is very real but has different subtleties, such as emotional expression, relationship with the target of her anger, and alternative types of social responses, is confirmed in this work.

7. Erving Goffman's (1974) principle of "frame" describes the perceptual mechanism whereby the nature and purpose of behaviors can be recognized by the participants as "play," or not functional or literal. Thus, the audience has both an effect on behaviors and a role in altering and defining the meanings of them.

8. The *New York Times Almanac* of 2003 ranks *Glamour* as the 31st most popular magazine in the United States (for 2001) with a circulation of 2,170,476, behind *Cosmopolitan* (ranked 20th with a circulation of 2,701,167), *Seventeen* (ranked 28th with a circulation of 2,351,570), and *YM* (ranked 30th with a circulation of 2,241,509).

9. *Maxim* is becoming increasingly popular. Although it did not rank in the top 100 magazines in the United States by circulation in the 2000 *New York Times Almanac* (for 1998), it ranked 26th with a circulation of 2,533,521 in the 2003 edition (for 2001), behind *Playboy* (ranked 17th with a circulation of 3,154,560).

10. In Csikszentmihalyi and Rochberg-Halton's (1981) study of Chicago homes, the authors describe gender differences similar to those found at Bolton in the ways boys and girls relate to objects. In their study the males place higher importance on TVs, stereo sets, sports equipment, vehicles, and trophies, while the females value photographs, sculpture, plants, plates, glass, and textiles.

The authors point out that the pattern of the males is similar to that of children, while that of the females is similar to the pattern demonstrated by grandparents.

CHAPTER 4

1. L. M. Brown (1998) also describes a difference between working-class and middle-class girls' versions of femininity. Working-class girls resist white middle-class versions distancing themselves from women and femininity because of the association with relational treachery and vulnerability. Middle-class girls are more caught up in the struggle of coming to terms with the contradictions between "good" and "bad" girls central to middle-class version of femininity.

2. My knowledge of the wealth of the students is by no means exact. Who was at Bolton on scholarship and who was not usually became apparent during the interviews. In almost all cases, the wealth of the students labeled "wealthy" was revealed to me during the course of the research, either by themselves or other students.

3. The use of foods such as whipped cream, chicken nuggets, and french fries as sex aids, as described in a study by Canaan (1986), is used to define "kinky" sex.

4. When one partner licks the other's anus.

5. Canaan (1986) describes a sexual liberalism due to lack of a sexual double standard (although she was able to interview only female students) except in regard to kinky sex, as well as slight value placed on virginity.

CHAPTER 6

1. Research on actual sex differences in emotion has found few differences with the exception of a slightly greater amount of anxiety in females (Feingold, 1994; Meece, Wigfield, & Eccles, 1990). Rather, researchers believe that both boys and girls learn to hide non-gender-appropriate emotions. Although young children demonstrate similar emotions, during elementary school boys start hiding emotions such as anxiety, fear, and sadness, while girls begin to hide anger and other similar emotions (Eisenberg, Martin, & Fabes, 1996). Underwood's (2003) work revealing that the genders share similar emotions but hide the ones not deemed gender-appropriate is reinforced by research that indicates that in some cases anxiety (such as test anxiety) is more prominent among boys but their hesitancy to admit their anxiety results in girls being viewed as more anxious (Lord, Eccles, & McCarthy, 1994).

2. Rohypnol, or "roofies," is a date rape drug that causes unconsciousness and/or amnesia.

CHAPTER 7

1. This is a pattern also found by Brown and Gilligan (1992), and L. M. Brown cites these differences as the reason she looks to middle- and lower-class girls to find the resistance to cultural ideals she documents in her 1998 work *Raising*

Their Voices. Similarly, Brown describes how many of the working-class girls in her study are not "deluded by, passive to or easily indoctrinated with cultural prescriptions." Instead, many girls resist, adapt, and appropriate the language of the powerful to suit their own needs.

2. Stack (1974) describes a culture of extensive sharing and altruistic behavior among African American families in a ghetto community, revealing how the scarcity of resources encourages a focus on others in order to build alliances and ensure survival. It is possible that decades of discrimination have resulted in similar elements being retained among the African American students at Bolton.

3. According to Rosenberg, the conversion of society's negative attitude toward one's group, and thus oneself, into the individual's attitude toward himself is probable only if certain assumptions are accepted. These assumptions include (1) that the individual knows how the broader society feels about him, (2) that he accepts the social view of his group, (3) that he believes the societal view of his group applies to him, and (4) that he is concerned with majority attitudes.

4. If members of a devalued group accept their inferior status in order to maintain a positive self-image, they can either compare themselves with others in a similar situation, attempt to become part of the "in" group, or try to change or eliminate the stigmatized element. It appears that these coping strategies may be why so many of the students compare themselves to others (which might explain the intense competition described between the female students as well as the vying for status among the males) or go to extreme lengths to lose weight or become "buff" in order to fit ideals of appearance. Despite these efforts, it is clear that many of these adolescents accept the view of themselves as inferior, and consequently their self-esteem suffers.

5. This work and other context-limited studies are derived from this idea of an American symbolic system, yet they attempt to deal effectively with the issue of diversity. These studies approach American culture by examining in detail one small group and then contending that they say something about the American dialogue as a whole. The advantage these studies have over the symbolic studies discussed above is that although the authors agree that there is some sort of American dialogue, they do not contend that there is one symbolic system or that the symbols mean the same things to all Americans. They focus on one particular group and describe what the symbols mean to them, and these meanings then become part of the diverse American dialogue (see Greenhouse, 1983, 1986a, 1986b; Myeroff, 1978; Stack, 1974; Carbaugh, 1988; Spradley & Mann, 1975; G. L. Hicks, 1976; Moffatt, 1989; Beeman, 1986b).

6. The relative power of men and women in a society as well as the divergence between masculinity and femininity differ greatly from one culture to the next. Cross-cultural studies have revealed a correlation between how much each gender contributes to the household and the degree to which women are relegated to a separate domestic sphere with the degree of gender stratification (Sanday, 1974; Draper, 1975). The amount of gender stratification found in a society correlates with the degree to which maleness and femaleness are viewed as separate and different and the degree to which the traits of the

opposite gender are avoided. Among many tribes in Papua New Guinea, for example, where patrilineal and patrilocal societies have developed because of extensive warfare over scarce resources, gender stratification is large. In these societies, men fear contact (even sex) with women and see everything feminine as dangerous and polluting. Similarly, among hunters and gatherers such as the Inuit where men contribute most of the food due to the lack of resources other than meat and women stay home while the men go off and hunt, gender stratification is much greater than among most hunter-gatherer groups, where both genders wander about and women provide the majority of food through gathering.

Bibliography ∷

Ablard, K. E., & Lipschultz, R. E. (1998). Self-regulated learning in high achieving students: Relations to advanced reasoning, achievement goals, and gender. *Journal of Educational Psychology*, 90(1), 94–101.

Addelston, J. (1996). Exploring masculinities: Gender enactments in preparatory high schools. *Dissertation Abstracts International: Section B: The Sciences and Engineering*, 57(5-B), 3450.

Adler, P. A., & Adler, P. (1998). *Peer power: Preadolescent culture and identity.* New Brunswick, NJ: Rutgers University Press.

Adler, P. A., Kless, S. J., & Adler, P. (1992). Socialization to gender roles: Popularity among elementary school boys and girls. *Sociology of Education*, 65, 169–187.

Albrecht, S. L., Bahr, H. M., & Goodman, K. L. (1983). Divorce and remarriage: Problems, adaptations, and adjustments. Westport, CT: Greenwood Press.

Alfieri, A., Ruble, D. N., & Higging, E. T. (1996). Gender stereotypes during adolescence: Developmental changes and the transition to junior high. *Developmental Psychology*, 32, 1129–1137.

American Anthropological Association. (1989). *Code of ethics of the American Anthropological Association.* Retrieved from aaanet.org/committees/ethics/ethcode.htm.

American Association of University Women. (1992). *How schools are shortchanging girls: The AAUW Report: A study of major findings on girls and education.* Washington, DC: American Association of University Women Educational Foundation.

Andersen, A. E., & DiDomenico, L. (1992). Diet vs. shape content of popular male and female magazines: A dose-response relationship to the incidence of eating disorders? *International Journal of Eating Disorders*, 11, 283–287.

Angold, A., Erkanli, A., Silberg, J., Eaves, L., & Costelo, E. J. (2002). Depression scale scores in 8–17-year-olds: Effects of age and gender. *Journal of Child Psychiatry and Psychiatry*, 43, 1052–1063.

Anson, R. (1987). *Best Intentions.* New York: Random House.

Antill, J. K., Cotton, S., Russell, G., & Goodnow, J. J. (1993). Measures of children's sex typing in middle childhood: II. *Australian Journal of Psychology,* 45 (1), 25–33.

Archer, J., & Lloyd, B. (1982). *Sex and gender.* Cambridge, England: Cambridge University Press.

Archer J., & Macrae, M. (1991). Gender-perceptions of school subjects among 10–11-year-olds. *British Journal of Educational Psychology,* 61, 99–103.

Ashmore, R. D. (1990). Sex, gender and the individual. In L. A. Pervin (Ed.), *Handbook of personality: Theory and research* (pp. 486–526). New York: Guilford Press.

Baltzell, E. D. (1964). *The Protestant establishment.* New York: Random House.

Bandura, A. (1989). Social cognitive theory. *Annals of Child Development,* 6, 1–60.

Barrett, A. (2004). Oral sex and teenagers: A sexual health educator's perspective. *Canadian Journal of Human Sexuality,* 13(3–4), 197–200.

Baumeister, R. F., & Leary, M. R. (1995). The need to belong: Desire for interpersonal attachments as a fundamental human motivation. *Psychological Bulletin,* 117, 497–529.

Baumeister, R. F., & Sommer, K. L. (1997). What do men want? Gender differences and two spheres of belongingness: Comment on Cross and Madson (1997). *Psychological Bulletin,* 122, 38–44.

Beeman, W. O. (1986a). *Language, status and power in Iran.* Bloomington: Indiana University Press.

Beeman, W. O. (1986b). Freedom to choose. In H. Varenne (Ed.), *Symbolizing America.* Lincoln: University of Nebraska Press.

Belenky, M., Clinchy, B., Goldberger, N., & Tarule, J. (1986). *Women's ways of knowing: The development of self, voice and mind.* New York: Basic Books.

Bellah, R. N., Madsen, R., Sullivan, W. M., Swidler, A., & Tipton, S. M. (1985). *Habits of the heart: Individualism and commitment in American life.* Berkeley: University of California Press.

Belle, D. (1989). Gender differences in children's social networks and supports. In D. Belle (Ed.), *Children's Social Networks and Social Supports* (pp. 173–188). New York: Wiley.

Benenson, J. F., Apostoleris, N. H., & Parnass, J. (1997). Age and sex differences in dyadic and group interaction. *Developmental Psychology,* 33, 538–543.

Bernard, J. (1974). *Sex differences: An overview (Module 26).* New York: MSS Modular Publications.

Berndt, T. J., & Hoyle, S. G. (1985). Stability and change in childhood and adolescent friendships. *Developmental Psychology,* 21, 1007–1015.

Best, R. (1983). *We've all got scars: What boys and girls learn in elementary school.* Bloomington: Indiana University Press.

Bettie, J. (2003). *Women without class: Girls, race, and identity.* Berkeley: University of California Press.

Binion, V. J. (1990). Psychological androgyny: A black female perspective. *Sex Roles,* 22, 487–507.

Birch, L. L. (1987). Children's food preferences: Developmental patterns and environmental influences. *Annals of Child Development,* 4, 171–208.

Birnbach, L. (1980). *The official preppy handbook.* New York: Workman.

Birnbaum, D. W., & Croll, W. L. (1984). The etiology of children's stereotypes about sex differences in emotionality. *Sex Roles,* 10, 677–691.

Bjorkqvist, K. (1994). Sex differences in physical, verbal, and indirect aggression: A review of resent research. *Sex Roles,* 30, 177–188.

Block, J. H. (1976). Issues, problems, and pitfalls in assessing sex differences: A critical review of "The psychology of sex differences." *Merrill-Palmer Quarterly,* 22, 283–308.

Blumer, H. (1969). *Symbolic interactionism.* Englewood Cliffs, NJ: Prentice Hall.

Blumer, H. (1972). Action vs. interaction. *Society,* April 1972, 50–53.

Boekeloo, B., & Howard, D. E. (2002). Oral sex experiences among young adolescents receiving general health examinations. *American Journal of Health Behavior,* 26(4), 306–314.

Bourgois, P. (1985). Crack in Spanish Harlem: Culture and economy in the inner city. *Anthropology Today,* 5(4), 6–11.

Bradbard, M. R., Martin, C. L., Endsley, R. C., & Halverson, C. F. (1986). Influence of sex stereotypes on children's exploration and memory: A competence verses performance distinction. *Developmental Psychology,* 22, 481–486.

Briggs, J. (1998). *Inuit morality play: The emotional education of a three-year-old.* New Haven, CT: Yale University Press.

Brod, H. (Ed.) (1987). *The making of masculinities.* Boston: Allen & Unwin.

Bronfenbrenner, U. (1979). *The ecology of human development.* Cambridge, MA: Harvard University Press.

Brown, B. B. (1990). Peer groups and peer cultures. In S. S. Feldman & G. R. Elliot (Eds.), *At the threshold* (pp. 171–196). Cambridge, MA: Harvard University Press.

Brown, B. B., & Clasen, D. R. (1986). Developmental changes in adolescents' conceptions of peer groups. Paper presented at the biennial meeting of the Society for Research in Adolescence, Madison, WI.

Brown, B. B., Larson, R. W., & Saraswathi, T. S. (2002). *The world's youth: Adolescence in eight regions of the globe.* Cambridge, England: Cambridge University Press.

Brown, L. M. (1998). "Voice and ventriloquation in girls' development." In K. Henwood, C. Griffin, and A. Phoenix (Eds.), *Standpoints and differences: Essays in the practice of feminist psychology.* London: SAGE Publications.

Brown, L. M. (2003). *Girlfighting: Betrayal and rejection among girls.* New York: New York University Press.

Brown, L. M., & Gilligan, C. (1992). *Meeting at the crossroads.* Cambridge, MA: Harvard University Press.

Bruch, H. (1973). *Eating disorders.* New York: Basic Books.

Bruch, H. (1978). *The golden cage.* New York: Vintage Books.

Brumberg, J. J. (1997). *The body project.* New York: Random House.

Buchanan, C. M., Eccles, J. S., & Becker, J. B. (1992). Are adolescents the victims of raging hormones: Evidence for activational effects of hormones on moods and behaviors at adolescence. *Psychological Bulletin,* 111(11), 62–107.

Bugental, D. B., & Goodnow, J. J. (1998). Socialization process. In W. Damon (Series Ed.) & N. Eisenberg (Vol. Ed.), *Handbook of child psychology: Vol. 3.*

Social, emotional and personality development (5th ed., pp. 389–462). New York: Wiley.

Buhrmester, D. (1990). Intimacy of friendship, interpersonal competence and adjustment during preadolescence and adolescence. *Child Development*, 61, 1101–1111.

Buhrmester, D. (1996). Need fulfillment, interpersonal competence and the developmental contexts of friendship. In W. M. Bukowski, A. F. Newcomb, & W. W. Hartup (Eds.), *The company they keep: Friendship during childhood and adolescence* (pp. 158–185). New York: Cambridge University Press.

Burns, A., & Homel, R. (1986). Sex role satisfaction among Australian children: Same sex, age, and cultural group comparisons. *Psychology of Women Quarterly*, 10, 285–296.

Buss, D. M. (1995). Psychological sex differences: Origins through sexual selection. *American Psychologist*, 3, 164–168.

Buss, D. M., & Schmitt, D. P. (1993). Sexual strategies theory: An evolutionary perspective on human mating. *Psychological Review*, 100, 204–232.

Bussey, K., & Bandura, A. (1992). Self-regulatory mechanisms governing gender development. *Child Development*, 63, 1236–1250.

Bussey, K., & Bandura, A. (1999). Social cognitive theory of gender development and differentiation. *Psychological Review*, 106, 676–713.

Butler, J. (1990). *Gender trouble: Feminism and the subversion of identity*. New York: Routledge.

Canaan, J. (1986). Why a 'slut' is a 'slut': Cautionary tales of middle-class teenage girls' morality. In H. Varenne (Ed.), *Symbolizing America*. Lincoln: University of Nebraska Press.

Carbaugh, D. (1988). *Talking American*. Norwood, NJ: Ablex.

Caristrom, L. K. (2005). Oral sex and vaginal intercourse in late adolescence: Gender differences in attitudes, norms, and intentions. *Dissertation Abstracts International: Section B: The Sciences and Engineering*, 66(2-B), 1217.

Cary, L. (1991). *Black Ice*. New York: Random House.

Cate, R., & Sugawara, A. I. (1986). Sex role orientation and dimensions of self-esteem among middle adolescents. *Sex Roles*, 15, 145–158.

Caughey, J. (1986). On the anthropology of America. In H. Varenne (Ed.), *Symbolizing America*. Lincoln: University of Nebraska Press.

Cawley, J., Joyner, K., & Sobal, J. (2006). Size matters. *Rationality and Society*, 18, 67–94.

Chapman, R. L. (1986). *New dictionary of American slang*. New York: Harper & Row.

Chandos, J. (1984). *Boys together: English public schools, 1800–1864*. New Haven, CT: Yale University Press.

Chodorow, N. (1971). Being and doing: A cross-cultural examination of the socialization of males and females. In V. Gornick & B. K. Moran (Eds.), *Woman in sexist society*. New York: Basic Books.

Chodorow, N. (1974). Family structure and feminine personality. In M. Z. Rosaldo & L. Lamphere (Eds.), *Woman, culture and society*. Stanford, CA: Stanford University Press.

Chodorow, N. (1978). *The reproduction of mothering*. Berkeley: University of California Press.

Chodorow, N. (1999). *The power of feelings*. New Haven, CT: Yale University Press.

Chu, J. Y. (2000). Learning what boys know: An observational and interview study with six four year old boys. Unpublished doctoral dissertation. Graduate School of Education, Harvard University.

Chu, J. Y. (2004). A relational perspective on adolescent boys' identity development. In N. Way & J. Y. Chu (Eds.), *Adolescent boys: Exploring diverse cultures of boyhood*. New York: New York University Press.

Coates, J. (1986). *Women, men and language*. London: Longman.

Coates, J. (1996). *Women talk: Conversation between women friends*. Oxford, England: Blackwell.

Coates, J. (2003). *Men talk: Stories in the making of masculinities*. Malden, MA: Blackwell.

Coie, J. D., & Dodge, K. (1998). Aggression and antisocial behavior. In W. Damon (Series Ed.) & N. Eisenberg (Vol. Ed.), *Handbook of child psychology: Vol. 3. Social, emotional and personality development* (5th ed., pp. 779–862). New York: Wiley.

Cole, M. (1985). The zone of proximal development: Where culture and cognition create each other. In J. V. Wertsch (Ed.), *Culture, communication, and cognition: Vygotskian perspectives* (pp. 146–161). Cambridge, England: Cambridge University Press.

Coles, R. (1977). *Children of privilege*. Boston: Little, Brown.

Collins, W. A., & Luebker, C. (1994). Parent and adolescent expectancies: Individual and relational significance. In J. F. Smetana (Ed.), *Beliefs about parenting: Origins and developmental consequences*, 65–80. San Francisco: Jossey-Bass.

Cookson, P. W. Jr. (1985). Boarding schools and the moral community. *Journal of Educational Thought* 16 (Aug.): 89–97.

Cookson, P. W. Jr., & Persell, C. H. (1983). *Preparing for power: America's elite boarding schools*. New York: Basic Books.

Cooper, M. L. (1994). Motivations for alcohol use among adolescents: Development and validation of a four-factor model. *Psychological Assessment, 6*, 117–128.

Connell, R. W. (1995). *Masculinities*. Berkeley: University of California Press.

Connell, R. W. (2000). *The men and the boys*. Berkeley: University of California Press.

Cornelisen, A. (1976). *Women of the shadows*. New York: Vintage Books.

Counsell, C., & Wolf, L. (2001). *Performance analysis*. New York: Routledge.

Crick, N. R., Bigbee, M. A., & Howes, C. (1996). Gender differences in children's normative beliefs about aggression: How do I hurt thee? Let me count the ways. *Child Development, 66*, 710–722.

Crick, N. R., & Grotpeter, J. K. (1995). Relational aggression, gender, and social-psychological adjustment. *Child Development, 67*, 1003–1014.

Crick, N. R., Wellman, N. E., Casas, J. F., O'Brien, M. A., Nelson, D. A., Grotpeter, J. K., et al. (1999). Childhood aggression and gender: A new look at an old problem. In D. Bernstein (Ed.), *Nebraska symposium on motivation* (pp. 75–140). Lincoln: University of Nebraska Press.

Croll, J. (2003). Nutrient intake, physical activity, unhealthy weight control behaviors, and related psychosocial factors among adolescents involved in weight-related and power team sports. *Dissertation Abstracts International: Section B: The Sciences and Engineering*, 64(6-B), 2600.

Crosier, L. M. (1991). *Casualties of privilege.* Washington, DC: Avocus.

Cross, S. E., & Madson, L. (1997). Models of the self: Self-construals and gender. *Psychological Bulletin*, 122, 5–37.

Csikszentmihalyi, M., & Larson R. (1984). *Being adolescent.* New York: Basic Books.

Csikszentmihalyi, M., & Rochberg-Halton, E. (1981). *The meaning of things: Domestic symbols and the self.* Cambridge, England: Cambridge University Press.

Csikszentmihalyi, M., & Schneider, B. (2000). *Becoming adult: How teenagers prepare for the world of work.* New York: Basic Books.

Cunningham, M. (2001). African American males. In J. Lerner & R. Lerner (Eds.), *Adolescence in America: An encyclopedia* (pp. 32–34). Santa Barbara, CA: ABC-CLIO.

Cunningham, M., & Meunier, L. N. (2004). The influence of peer experiences on bravado attitudes among African American males. In N. Way & J. Y. Chu (Eds.), *Adolescent boys.* New York: New York University Press.

Currie, D. H. (1999). *Girl talk: Adolescent magazines and their readers.* Toronto: University of Toronto Press.

Davis, M. H., Luce, C., & Kraus, S. J. (1994). The heritability of characteristics associated with dispositional empathy. *Journal of Personality*, 62, 369–391.

De Beauvoir, S. (1953). *The second sex.* New York: Vintage Books.

Deaux, K., & Major, B. (1987). Putting gender into context: An interactive model of gender related behavior. *Psychological Review*, 102, 458–489.

Deutsch, M., & Gerard, H. B. (1955). A study of normative and informative social influence upon individual judgment. *Journal of Abnormal and Social Psychology*, 51, 629–636.

Dittmar, H., Lloyd, B., Dugan, S., Halliwell, E., Jacobs, N., & Cramer, H. (2000). The "body beautiful": English adolescents' images of ideal. *Sex Roles*, 42, 9–10.

Domhoff, W. (2002). *Who rules America?: Power and politics.* Boston: McGraw-Hill.

Draper, P. (1975). !Kung women: Contrasts in sexual egalitarianism in foraging and sedentary contexts. In R. Reiter (Ed.), *Toward an anthropology of women* (pp. 77–109). New York: Monthly Review Press.

Dugger, K. (1985). Social location and gender-role attitudes: A comparison of black and white women. *Gender & Society*, 2, 425–448.

Dye, T. R. (1995). *Who's running America?: The Clinton years.* Englewood Cliffs, NJ: Prentice Hall.

Eagly, A. H. (1987). *Sex differences in social behavior: A social-role interpretation.* Hillsdale, NJ: Erlbaum.

Eagly, A. H., Wood, W., & Fishbaugh. L. (1981). Differences in conformity: Surveillance by the group as a determinant of male nonconformity. *Journal of Personality and Social Psychology*, 40(2), 384–394.

Eccles, J. S., & Jacobs, J. E. (1986). Social forces shape math attitudes and performance. *Signs, 11*, 367–389.

Eccles, J. S., Jacobs, J., Harold, R., Yoon, K. S., Arbeton, A., & Freedman-Doan, C. (1993). Parents' and gender-role socialization during middle childhood and adolescence. In S. Oskamp & M. Costanzo (Eds.), *Gender issues in contemporary society* (pp. 59–83). Newbury Park, CA: Sage.

Eckert, P. (1989). *Jocks and burnouts: Social categories and identity in the high school.* New York: Teachers College Press.

Eckert, P. (2004). Symbols of category membership. In C. Delaney (Ed.), *Investigating culture.* Malden, MA: Blackwell.

Eder, D. (1995). *School talk: Gender and adolescent culture.* New Brunswick, NJ: Rutgers University Press.

Eisenberg, N., & Fabes, R. A. (1998). Prosocial development. In W. Damon (Series Ed.) & N. Eisenberg (Vol. Ed.), *Handbook of child psychology: Vol. 3. Social, emotional and personality development* (5th ed., pp. 701–778). New York: Wiley.

Eisenberg, N., Martin, C. L., & Fabes, R. A. (1996). Gender development and gender effects. In D. C. Berliner & R. C. Calfee (Eds.), *The handbook of educational psychology* (pp. 358–396). New York: Simon & Schuster.

Eliade, M. (1958). *Rites and symbols of initiation.* Woodstock, CT: Spring.

Engfer, A., Walper, S., & Rutter, M. (1994). Individual characteristics as a force in development. In M. L. Rutter & D. F. Hay (Eds.), *Development principles and clinical issues in psychology and psychiatry.* Oxford, England: Blackwell.

Erikson, E. H. (1963). *Childhood and society.* New York: W. W. Norton.

Erikson, E. H. (1968). *Identity: Youth in crisis.* New York: W. W. Norton.

Errington, F., & Gewertz, D. (1987). *Cultural alternatives and a feminist anthropology: An analysis of cultural constructed gender interests in Papua New Guinea.* New York: Cambridge University Press.

Etcoff, N. (1999). *Survival of the prettiest: The science of beauty.* New York: Doubleday.

Fagot, B. I. (1985). Beyond the reinforcement principle: Another step toward understanding sex roles. *Developmental Psychology, 21*, 1097–1104.

Feingold, A. (1994). Gender differences in personality: A meta-analysis. *Psychological Bulletin, 116*, 429–456.

Feldman, S. S., Rosenthal, D. R., Brown, N. L., & Canning, R. D. (1995). Predicting sexual experience in adolescent boys from peer rejection and acceptance during childhood. *Journal of Research on Adolescence, 5*, 387–411.

Ferguson, A. (2000). *Bad boys: Public schools in the making of black masculinities.* Ann Arbor: University of Michigan Press.

Festinger, L., Schachter, S., & Black, K. (1950). *Social pressures in informal groups: A study of a housing community.* Palo Alto, CA: Stanford University Press.

Fine, M. (2004). Witnessing whiteness/gathering intelligence. In M. Fine, L. Weis, L. Powell Pruitt, & A. Burns (Eds.), *Off white: Readings on power, privilege, and resistance* (pp. 245–256). New York: Routledge.

Fine, M., Weis, L., Powell Pruitt, L., & Burns, A. (Eds.), (2004). *Off white: Readings on power, privilege, and resistance.* New York: Routledge.

Finegan, J. K., Niccols, G. A., & Sitarenios, G. (1992). Relations between prenatal testosterone levels and cognitive abilities at 4 years. *Developmental Psychology*, 28(6), 1075–1089.

Fisher-Thompson, D. (1993). Adult toy purchases for children: Factors affecting sex-typed toy selection. *Journal of Applied Developmental Psychology*, 14, 385–406.

Fivush, R. (1989). Exploring sex differences in the emotional content of mother-child conversations about the past. *Sex Roles*, 20, 675–691.

Foucault, M. (1978). *The history of sexuality*. New York: Pantheon.

Frahm, R. A., & Puleo, T. (2000). Days so bright, then 'a night gone wrong': Full of both promise and drugs, Trinity seniors hit a dead end. *Hartford Courant*, Apr. 2.

Freeman, D. (1983). Margaret Mead and Samoa: The making and unmaking of an anthropological myth. Cambridge, MA: Harvard University Press.

Freedman, R. (1986). *Beauty bound*. Lexington, MA: Lexington Books.

Freud, S. (1934). *General introduction to psychoanalysis*. New York: Washington Square.

Freud, S. (1959). Some psychological consequences of the anatomical distinction between the sexes. In S. Freud, *Collected papers* (pp. 186–197). New York: Basic Books.

Freud, S. (1962). *Three essays on the theory of sexuality*. New York: Avon. (Original work published 1905)

Furman, W., & Buhrmester, D. (1992). Age and sex differences in perceptions of networks and personal relationships. *Child Development*, 63, 103–115.

Gabriel, S., & Gardner, W. L. (1999). Are there "his" and "her" types of interdependence? The implications of gender differences in collective versus relational interdependence for affect, behavior, and cognition. *Journal of Personality and Social Psychology*, 77(3), 642–655.

Galen, B. R., & Underwood, M. K. (1997). A developmental investigation of social aggression among children. *Developmental Psychology*, 33, 589–600.

Garcia Coll, C., Lamberty, G., Jenkins, R., McAdoo, H., Crnic, K., Wasik, B. H., et al. (1996). An interactive model for the study of developmental competencies in minority children. *Child Development*, 67, 1891–1914.

Garcia Coll, C., & Marks, A. (In press). *Children of immigrants: Academic attitudes and pathways during middle childhood*. New York: Oxford University Press.

Garfinkel, H. (1967). *Studies in ethnomethodology*. Cambridge: Polity.

Garner, D. M., Garfinkel, P. E., Schwartz, D., & Thompson, M. (1980). Cultural expectations of thinness in women. *Psychological Reports*, 47, 483–491.

Gavin, L. A., & Furman, W. (1989). Age differences in adolescents' perceptions of their peer groups. *Developmental Psychology*, 25, 827–834.

Geertz, C. (1972). Deep play: Notes on the Balinese cockfight. *Daedalus*, 101(1), 1–37.

Geertz, C. (1973). *The interpretation of cultures*. New York: Basic Books.

Geertz, C. (1983). *Local knowledge*. New York: Basic Books.

Gilligan, C. (1982). *In a different voice*. Cambridge, MA: Harvard University Press.

Gilligan, C., Lyons, N. P., & Hanmer, T. J. (Eds.) (1990). *Making connections: The relational worlds of adolescent girls at Emma Willard School.* Cambridge, MA: Harvard University Press.

Gilmore, D. D. (1990). *Manhood in the making: Cultural concepts of masculinity.* New Haven, CT: Yale University Press.

Goffman, E. (1959). *The presentation of self in everyday life.* Edinburgh: University of Edinburgh Press.

Goffman, E. (1961). *Asylums.* Garden City: Anchor Books.

Goffman, E. (1963). *Stigma.* Englewood Cliffs, NJ: Prentice Hall.

Goffman, E. (1967). *Interaction ritual.* Garden City: Anchor Books.

Goffman, E. (1969). *Strategic interaction.* Philadelphia: University of Pennsylvania Press.

Goffman, E. (1974). *Frame analysis.* Cambridge, MA: Harvard University Press.

Goodwin, M. H. (1990). *He-said-she-said: Talk as social organization among black children.* Bloomington: Indiana University Press.

Goodwin, M. H. (2006). *The hidden life of girls: Games of stance, status, and exclusion.* Malden, MA: Blackwell.

Gordon, R. A. (1990). *Anorexia and bulimia.* Cambridge: Blackwell.

Grabill, K. M., Lasane, T. P., Povitsky, W. T., Saxe, P., Munro, G. D., Phelps, L. M., et al. (2005). Gender and study behavior: How social perception, social norm adherence, and structured academic behavior are predicted by gender. *North American Journal of Psychology, 7*(1), 7–24.

Gray, J. (1992). *Men are from Mars, women are from Venus.* New York: Harper-Collins.

Greenhouse, C. (1983). Being and doing: Competing concepts of elite status in an American suburb. In G. Marcus (Ed.), *Elites.* Albuquerque: University of New Mexico Press.

Greenhouse, C. (1986a). *Praying for justice.* Ithaca: Cornell University Press.

Greenhouse, C. (1986b). History, faith and avoidance. In H. Varenne (Ed.), *Symbolizing America.* Lincoln: University of Nebraska Press.

Gregg, J. L. (2003). *Virtually virgins: Sexual strategies and cervical cancer in Recife, Brazil.* Stanford, CA: Stanford University Press.

Halpern, D. (1992). *Sex differences in cognitive abilities* (2nd ed.). Hillsdale, NJ: Erlbaum.

Harkness, S. (2001). Culture and social development. In D. Gilbert, A. Fiske, & G. Lindzey (Eds.), *The Handbook of Social Psychology: Vol. 2.* New York: McGraw-Hill.

Harris, J, R. (1995). Where is the child's environment? A group socialization theory of development. *Psychological Review, 102,* 458–489.

Harrison, L. (2005). *The clique: The invasion of the boy snatchers.* New York: Little, Brown.

Healy, P. (2001). Responding to suicides, MIT expands mental health care. *Boston Globe,* Aug. 29.

Henley, N. M. (1995). Ethnicity and gender issues in language. In H. Landrine (Ed.), *Bringing cultural diversity to feminist psychology: Theory, research, and practice* (pp. 361–395). Washington, DC: American Psychological Association.

Henley, N. M., & Kramarae, C. (1991). Gender, power, and miscommunication. In N. Coupland & H. Giles (Eds.), *"Miscommunication" and problematic talk* (pp. 18–43). Thousand Oaks, CA: Sage.

Heward, C. (1988). *Making a man of him: Parents and their sons' education at an English public school 1929–1950.* London: Routledge.

Hewitt, J. P. (1976). *Self and society.* Needham Heights, MA: Allyn & Bacon.

Hicks, D. V. (1996). The strange fate of the American boarding school. *American Scholar,* 65(4), 523–535.

Hicks, G. L. (1976). *Appalachian valley.* New York: Holt, Rinehart & Winston.

Hollan, D. (1992). Cross cultural differences in the self. *Journal of Anthropological Research,* 48, 283–300.

Holland, A., & Andre, T. (1994). Athletic participation and the social status of adolescent males and females. *Youth and Society,* 25(3), 388–407.

Holland, D., & Kipnis, A. (1994). Metaphors for embarrassment and stories of exposure: The not-so-egocentric self in American culture. *Ethos,* 22, 316–342.

Holland, D. C., & Eisenhart, M. A. (1990). *Educated in romance: Women, achievement, and college culture.* Chicago: University of Chicago Press.

Hollos, M., & Leis, P. E. (1989). *Becoming Nigerian in Ijo society.* New Brunswick, NJ: Rutgers University Press.

Hollos, M., & Leis, P. E. (2002). Remodeling concepts of the self: An Ijo example. *Ethos,* 29(3), 371–387.

Hsu, F. L. K. (1953). *Americans and Chinese: Two ways of life.* New York: Henry Schuman.

Hsu, L. K. G. (1987). Are eating disorders becoming more common in blacks? *International Journal of Eating Disorders,* 6, 113–124.

Hymes, D. (Ed.) (1972). *Reinventing anthropology.* New York: Pantheon.

Intons-Peterson, M. J. (1988). *Gender concepts of Swedish and American youth.* Hillsdale, NJ: Erlbaum.

Jackson, L. A. (1992). *Physical appearance and gender.* Albany: State University of New York Press.

Jankowaik, W. R. (1993). *Sex, death, and hierarchy in a Chinese city: An anthropological account.* New York: Columbia University Press.

Jefferson, M. (2000). Freud aside, what do women want of their bodies? *New York Times,* May 15.

Jessor, R., Colby, A., & Shweder, R. (Eds.). (1996). *Ethnography and human development: Context and meaning in social inquiry.* Chicago: University of Chicago Press.

Johnston, L. D., O'Malley, P. M., & Bachman, J. G. (1999). *National survey results on drug use from The Monitoring the Future Study (1975–1997): Volume 1. Secondary school students.* Rockville, MD: National Institute on Drug Abuse.

Jones, A., & Miley, M. (2007). *Restless virgins: Love, sex and survival at a New England prep school.* New York: William Morrow.

Jordan, J., Kaplan, A. G., Miller, J. B., Stiver, I. P., & Surrey, J. L. (1991). *Women's growth in connection: Writings from the Strone Center.* New York: Guilford.

Jordan, J. V., & Surrey, J. L. (1986). The self-in-relation: Empathy and the mother-daughter relationship. In T. Bernay & D. W. Cantor (Eds.), *The psychology of today's woman.* Cambridge, MA: Harvard University Press.

Kashima, Y., Uichol, K., Gelfand, M. J., Yamaguchi, S., Choi, S., & Yuki, M. (1995). Culture, gender, and self: A perspective from individualism-collectivism research. *Journal of Personality and Social Psychology*, 69, 925–937.

Katz, P. A., & Walsh, V. (1991). Modification of children's gender-stereotyped behavior. *Child Development*, 62, 338–351.

Klebanov, P. K., & Brooks-Gunn, J. (1992). Impact of maternal attitudes, girl's adjustment, and cognitive skills upon academic performance in middle and high school. *Journal of Research on Adolescence*, 2, 81–102.

Klerman, G. L., & Weissman, M. M. (1989). Increasing rates of depression. *Journal of the American Medical Association*, 261 (April 21).

Killen, M., & Wainryb, C. (2000). Independence and interdependence in diverse cultural contexts. In S. Harkness, C. Raeff, & C. Super (Eds.), *Variability in the social construction of the child: Directions for child and adolescent development* (pp. 5–21). San Francisco: Jossey-Bass.

Kinderman, T. A., McCollom, T. L., & Gibson, E. Jr. (1996). Peer networks and students' classroom engagement during childhood and adolescence. In K. Wentzel & J. Juvonen (Eds.), *Social motivation: Understanding children's school adjustment*. New York: Cambridge University Press.

Kohlberg, L. (1976). Moral stages and moralization. In T. Lickona (Ed.), *Moral development and behavior*. New York: Holt, Rinehart & Winston.

Kramer L. R. (1991). The social construction of ability perception: An ethnographic study of gifted adolescent girls. *Journal of Early Adolescence*, 11, 340–362.

Kring, A. M. (2000). Gender and anger. In A. H. Fisher (Ed.), *Gender and Emotion: Social psychological perspectives* (pp. 211–231). Cambridge, England: Cambridge University Press.

Kuczynski, L. (1997). Accommodation/negotiation: A model of compliance within relationships. Paper presented at the annual meeting of the Society for Research on Child Development, Washington, DC.

Kuriloff, P., & Reichert, M. (2003). Boys of class, boys of color: Negotiating the academic and social geography of an elite independent school. *Journal of Social Issues*, 59, 751–769.

Kuwayama, T. (1992). The reference other orientation. In N. R. Rosenberger (Ed.), *Japanese sense of self* (pp. 121–151). Cambridge, England: Cambridge University Press.

Labov, W. (1964). *The social stratification of English in New York City*. Washington, DC: Center for Applied Linguistics.

Labov, W. (1972). *Language in the inner city: Studies in the black English vernacular*. Philadelphia: University of Pennsylvania Press.

LaFraniere, S. (2005). Women's rights laws and African custom clash. *New York Times*, Dec. 30.

Lakoff, R. T. (1975). *Language and woman's place*. New York: Harper & Row.

Lakoff, R. T. (1990). *Talking power: The politics of language*. New York: Harper & Row.

Lambert, R. (1968). *The hothouse society*. London: Weidenfeld & Nicolson.

Larkin, R. W. (1979). *Suburban youth in cultural crisis*. New York: Oxford University Press.

Lasane, T. P., Sweigard, P. N., Czopp, A. M., Howard, W. L., & Burns, M. J. (1999). The effects of student academic presentation on perceptions of gender and sociability. *North American Journal of Personal and Social Psychology, 67*, 664–673.

Leaper, C. (2000). The social construction and socialization of gender In P. H. Miller & E. K. Scholnick (Eds.), *Towards a feminist developmental psychology* (pp. 127–152). New York: Routledge.

Leaper, C., Anderson, K. L., & Sanders, P. (1998). Moderators of gender effects on parents' talk to their children: A metaanalysis. *Developmental Psychology, 34*, 3–27.

Leaper, C., & Damon, W. (1994). Childhood gender segregation: Causes and consequences. *New Directions for Child Development, 65*, 67–86.

Lebra, T. S. (1976). *Japanese patterns of behavior.* Honolulu: University of Hawaii Press.

Lévi-Strauss, C. (1969a). *The elementary structures of kinship.* Boston: Beacon. (Original work published 1949)

Lévi-Strauss, C. (1969b). *The raw and the cooked.* New York: Harper & Row. (Original work published 1964)

Lobel, T. E., Bempechat, J., Gewirtz, J., Shoken-Topaz, T., & Bashe, E. (1993). *The* role of gender-related information and self endorsement of traits in pre-adolescents' inferences and judgments. *Child Development, 64*, 1285–1294.

Lockheed, M. E., Harris, A. M., & Nemceff, W. P. (1983). Sex and social influence: Does sex function as a status characteristic in mixed-sex groups of children? *Journal of Educational Psychology, 75*, 877–888.

Lord, S., Eccles, J. S., & McCarthy, K. (1994). Risk and protective factors in the transition to junior high school. *Journal of Early Adolescence, 14*, 162–199.

Lorene, C. (1991). *Black ice.* New York: Knopf.

Low, B. S. (2000). *Why sex matters: A Darwinian look at human behavior.* Princeton, NJ: Princeton University Press.

Luthar, S. S. (2003). The culture of affluence: Psychological costs of material wealth. *Child Development, 74*, 1581–1593.

Luthar, S. S., & D'Avanzo, K. (1999). Contextual factors in substance use: A study of suburban and inner-city adolescents. *Development and Psychopathology, 11*, 845–867.

Lykes, B. M. (1985). Gender and individualistic vs. collectivist bases for notions about self. *Journal of Personality, 53*, 356–383.

Lytton, H. (1990). Child and parent effects on boys' conduct disorder: A reinterpretation. *Developmental Psychology, 26*, 683–697.

Lytton, H., & Romney, D. M. (1991). Parents' differential socialization of boys and girls: A meta-analysis. *Psychological Bulletin, 109*, 267–296.

Maccoby, E. E. (1998). *The two sexes: Growing up apart, coming together.* Cambridge, MA: Belknap Press.

Maccoby, E. E., & Jacklin, C. N. (1974). *The psychology of sex differences.* Stanford, CA: Stanford University Press.

Mahdi, L. C., Foster, S., & Little, M. (1987). *Betwixt and between: Patterns of masculine and feminine initiation.* Chicago: Open Court.

Maine, M. (1991). *Father hunger: Fathers, daughters and food.* Carlsbad, CA: Gurze.

Marcus, G. E., & Hall, P. D. (1992). *Lives in trust*. Boulder, CO: Westview.

Marcus, J. (2002). The ultimate guide to New England's private schools. *Boston Magazine*, Oct., 75.

Markus, H., & Kitayama, S. (1991). Culture and the self: Implications for cognition, emotion and motivation. *Psychological Review*, 98, 224–253.

Markus, H., & Oyserman, D. (1989). Gender and thought: The role of the self-concept. In M. Crawford & M. Gentry (Eds.), *Gender and thought: Psychological perspectives*. New York: Springer-Verlag.

Martin, C. L., Ruble, D. N., & Szkrybalo, J. (2002). Cognitive theories of early gender development. *Psychological Bulletin*, 128, 903–933.

Martino, W. (1999). "Cool boys," "party animals," "squids," and "poofters": Interrogating the dynamics and politics of adolescent masculinities in school. *British Journal of Sociology of Education*, 20, 239–263.

Martino, W., & Meyenn, B. (Eds.). (2001). *What about the boys? Issues of masculinity in schools*. Buckingham, England: Open University Press.

Mascolo, M. F., & Li, J. (2004). *Culture and developing selves: Beyond dichotomization*. San Francisco: Jossey-Bass.

McGuire, J. (1988). Gender stereotypes of parents with two-year-olds and beliefs about gender differences in behavior. *Sex Roles*, 19, 233–240.

McGuire, W. J., & McGuire, C. V. (1982). Significant others in self space: Sex differences and developmental trends in social self. In J. Suls (Ed.), *Psychological perspectives on the self: Vol. 1* (pp. 71–96). Hillsdale, NJ: Erlbaum.

McIntosh, P. (2003). White privilege: Unpacking the invisible knapsack. In A. Podolefsky & P. J. Brown (Eds.), *Applying anthropology: An introductory reader* (pp. 212–215). New York: McGraw-Hill.

McLaren, L. (2002). Neighborhood level vs. individual level correlates with body dissatisfaction. *Journal of Epidemiology and Community Health*, 56, 193–199.

Mead, G. H. (1934). *Mind, self, and society*. Chicago: University of Chicago Press.

Mead, M. (1928). *Coming of age in Samoa: A psychological study of primitive youth for Western civilisation*. New York: Morrow.

Mead, M. (1935). *Sex and temperament in three primitive societies*. London: Routledge.

Mead, M. (1949). *Male and female: A study of the sexes in a changing world*. New York: Morrow.

Meece, J. L. (1987). The influence of school experiences on the development of gender schemata. *New Directions for Child Development*, 38, 57–73.

Meece, J. L., Wigfield, A., & Eccles, J. S. (1990). Predictors of math anxiety and its influence on young adolescent's course enrollment intentions and performance in mathematics. *Journal of Educational Psychology*, 82, 60–70.

Messerschmidt, D. ed. (1981). *Anthropologists at home in North America*. Cambridge, England: Cambridge University Press.

Miller, J. B. (1976). *Toward a new psychology of women*. Boston: Beacon.

Miller, K. E., Melnick, M. J., Barnes, G. M., Farrell, M. P., & Sabo, D. (2005). Untangling the links among athletic involvement, gender, race, and adolescent academic outcomes. *Sociology of Sport Journal*, 22, 178–193.

Mills, C. W. (1959). *The power elite*. London: Oxford University Press.

Moffatt, M. (1989). *Coming of age in New Jersey*. New Brunswick, NJ: Rutgers University Press.

Moller, L., Hymel, S., & Rubin, K. H. (1992). Sex typing in play and popularity in middle childhood. *Sex Roles, 26,* 331–353.

Morgan, M. B. (2004). Sports participation in the lives of adolescent females: Who is playing and what is the relationship with body mass index, weight concerns, self-esteem and depression? *Dissertation Abstracts International: Section B: The Sciences and Engineering, 65*(4-B), 2105.

Morgenthau, H. (1962). Love and power. *Commentary, 33,* 247–251.

Munro, P. (1990). *Slang U*. New York: Harmony.

Myeroff, B. (1978). *Number our days*. New York: Simon & Schuster.

Nahemow, L., & Lawton, M. P. (1975). Similarity and propinquity in friendship formation. *Journal of Personality and Social Psychology, 32,* 203–213.

Nagell, K., Olguin, R. S., & Tomasello, M. (1993). Processes of social learning in the tool use of chimpanzees (*Pan troglodytes*) and human children (*Homo sapiens*). *Journal of Comparative Psychology, 107,* 174–186.

Nemeroff, C. J., Stein, R. I., Diehl, N. S., & Smilack, K. M. (1994). From the Cleavers to the Clintons: Role choices and body orientation as reflected in magazine article content. *International Journal of Eating Disorders, 16,* 167–176.

Newton, E. (1979). *Mother camp: Female impersonators in America*. Chicago: University of Chicago Press.

Novick, E. R. (1999). A comparison of self-esteem, gender role orientation, and body image in adolescent female athletes and nonathletes. *Dissertation Abstracts International: Section B: The Sciences and Engineering, 59*(9-B), 5150.

Ogbu, J. U. (1981). Origins of human competence: A cultural-ecological perspective. *Child Development, 52,* 413–429.

Ogden, J., & Thomas, D. (1999). The role of family values in understanding the impact of social class on weight concern. *International Journal of Eating Disorders, 25,* 273–279.

Ortner, S. (1974). Is female to male as nature is to culture? In Michele Z. Rosaldo and Louise Lamphere (Eds.), *Women, culture and society* (pp. 67–88). Stanford, CA: Stanford University Press.

Ortner, S. (1991). Reading America: Preliminary notes on class and culture. In R. Fox (Ed.), *Recapturing anthropology: Working in the present*. Santa Fe: School of American Research Press.

Ortner, S. (1996). *Making gender: The politics and erotics of culture*. Boston: Beacon.

Ortner, S. (2003). *New Jersey dreaming: Capital, culture, and the class of '58*. Durham, NC: Duke University Press.

Ortner, S., & Whitehead, H. (Eds.). (1981). *Sexual meanings: The cultural construction of gender and sexuality*. Cambridge, England: Cambridge University Press.

Osgerby, B. (2001). *Playboys in paradise: Masculinity, youth and leisure-style in modern America*. New York: Berg.

Ostrander, S. A. (1979). Class consciousness as conduct and meaning: The case of the upper class woman. *Insurgent Sociologist, 9,* 38–50.

Ostrander, S. A. (1984). *Women of the upper class*. Philadelphia: Temple University Press.

Packer, M. J. (1993). Away from internalization. In E. A. Forman, N. Minick, & C. A. Stone (Eds.), *Contexts for Learning* (pp. 254–265). New York: Oxford University Press.

Parlee, M. B. (1979). Psychology of women. *Signs: Journal of Women in Culture and Society, 5*, 121–133.

Pellett, T. L., & Ignico, A. A. (1993). Relationship between children's and parents' stereotyping of physical activities. *Perceptual and Motor Skills, 77*, 1283–1289.

Peshkin, A. (2001). *Permissible advantage?: The moral consequences of elite schooling.* Mahwah, NJ: Erlbaum.

Petrie, T. A., et al. (1996). Sociocultural expectations of attractiveness for males. *Sex Roles, 35*, 581–590.

Piaget, J. (1972). Intellectual development from adolescence to adulthood. *Human Development, 15*, 1–12.

Pipher, M. (1994). *Reviving Ophelia.* New York: G. P. Putnam's Sons.

Pittman, F. S. (1985). Children of the rich. *Family Process, 24*, 461–472.

Plumwood, V. (1993). *Feminism and the mastery of nature.* New York: Routledge.

Prescott, P. S. (1970). *World of our own.* New York: Coward-McCann.

Prinstein, M. J., Meade, C. S., & Cohen, G. L. (2003). Adolescent oral sex, peer popularity, and perceptions of best friends' sexual behavior. *Journal of Pediatric Psychology, 28*(4), 243–249.

Radke-Yarrow, M., & Kochanska, G. (1990). Anger in young children. In N. L. Stein, B. Leventhal, & T. Trabasso (Eds.), *Psychological and Biological Approaches to Emotion*, 297–310. Hillsdale, NJ: Erlbaum.

Rae, D. (1983). *A world apart.* Guildford, England: Lutterworth.

Reichert, M., & Kuriloff, P. (2004). The glare of the looking glass: The constitution of boys' sense of self in schools. *Teachers College Record*, 554–572.

Resnick, M. D. (1999). Cited in PBS Online, The lost children of Rockdale Country. Is it isolated, or is it everywhere? Experts who work with teens and families offer their perspectives on this FRONTLINE report. Retrieved December 22, 2002, from http://www.pbs.org/wgbh/pages/frontline/shows/georgia/isolated.

Riesman, D. (1950). *The lonely crowd: A study of the changing American character.* New Haven, CT: Yale University Press.

Rogoff, B. (1990a). The joint socialization of development by young children and adults. In M. Lewis & S. Feinman (Eds.), *Social influences and socialization in infancy: Vol. 6. Genesis of behavior* (pp. 253–280). New York: Plenum.

Rogoff, B. (1990b). *Apprenticeship in thinking: Cognitive development in social context.* New York: Oxford University Press.

Rogoff, B. (1998). Cognition as a collaborative process. In W. Damon (Series Ed.) & D. Kuhn & R. S. Siegler (Vol. Eds.), *Handbook of child psychology: Vol. 2. Cognition, perception and language* (5th ed.). New York: Wiley.

Rogoff, B. (2003). *The cultural nature of human development.* New York: Oxford University Press.

Rosaldo, M., & Lamphere, L. (Eds.). (1974). *Women, culture, and society.* Stanford, CA: Stanford University Press.

Rosen, L. W., Shafer, C. L., Dummer, G. M., Cross, L. K., Deuman, G. W., & Malmberg, S. R. (1988). Prevalence of pathogenic weight-control behaviors among Native American women and girls. *International Journal of Eating Disorders, 7*, 807–811.

Rosenberg, M. (1979). *Conceiving the self*. New York: Basic Books.

Rosenberg, N. R. (1992). Introduction. In N. R. Rosenberger (Ed.), *Japanese sense of self* (pp. 1–20). Cambridge, England: Cambridge University Press.

Rosenfield, G. (1971)."*Shut those thick lips": A study of slum school failure.* New York: Holt, Rinehart & Winston.

Rubenstein, R. P. (1995). *Dress codes: Meanings and messages in American culture.* Boulder, CO: Westview.

Rubin, K. H., Bukowski, W., & Parker, J. G. (1998). Peer interactions, relationships and groups. In W. Damon (Series Ed.) & N. Eisenberg (Vol. Ed.), *Handbook of child psychology: Vol. 3. Social, emotional and personality development* (5th ed., pp. 619–700). New York: Wiley.

Rubin, Z, Peplau, L. A., & Hill, C. (1981). Loving and leaving: Sex differences in romantic attachments. *Sex Roles, 7*, 821–835.

Sahlins, M. (1985). *Islands of history*. Chicago: University of Chicago Press.

Sahlins, M. (1976). *Culture and practical reason*. Chicago: University of Chicago Press.

Sampson, E. E. (1988). The debate on individualism: Indigenous psychologies of the individual and their role in personal and societal functioning. *American Psychologist, 43*, 15–22.

Sanday, P. (1974). Female status in the public domain. In M. Z. Rosaldo & L. Lamphere (Eds.), *Women, culture, and society* (pp. 189–206). Stanford, CA: Stanford University Press.

Sanday, P. R., & Goodenough, R. G. (1990). *Beyond the second sex: New directions in the anthropology of gender*. Philadelphia: University of Pennsylvania Press.

Sapon-Shevin, M., & Goodman, J. (1992). Learning to be the opposite sex: Sexuality education and sexual scripting in early adolescence. In J. T. Sears (Ed.), *Sexuality and the curriculum*. New York: Teachers College Press.

Saussure, F. (1959). *Course in general linguistics*. New York: Philosophical Library.

Schemo, D. J. (2001). Suit says assaults are routine at an exclusive prep school. *New York Times*, Aug. 30.

Schneider, D. (1968). *American kinship*. Englewood Cliffs, NJ: Prentice Hall.

Schwartz, D. M., Thompson, M. G., & Johnson, C. L. (1982). Anorexia nervosa and bulimia: The socio-cultural context. *International Journal of Eating Disorders, 1*, 20–36.

Shaywitz. B. A., Shaywitz, S. E., Pugh, K. R., & Constable, R. T. (1995). Sex differences in the functional organization of the brain for language. *Nature, 373*, 607–609.

Shepardson, D. P., & Pizzini, E. L. (1992). Gender bias in female elementary school teachers' perceptions of the scientific ability of students. *Science Education, 76*(2), 147–153.

Sherif, C. W. (1979). Bias in psychology. In J. A. Sherman & E. T. Beck (Eds.), *The prism of sex: Essays in the sociology of knowledge* (93–133). Madison: University of Wisconsin Press.

Sherif, M., Harvey, O. H., White, B. J., Hood, W. R., & Sherif, C. W. (1961). *Robbers Cave experiment: Intergroup conflict and cooperation.* Middletown, CT: Wesleyan University Press. (Original work published 1961)

Shields, S. (2002). *Speaking from the heart: Gender and the social meaning of emotion.* Cambridge, England: Cambridge University Press.

Shweder, R. A. (1990). Cultural psychology: What is it? In J. W. Stigler, R. A. Shweder, & G. Herdt (Eds.), *Cultural psychology* (pp. 1–46). Cambridge, England: Cambridge University Press.

Shweder, R. A., & Bourne, E. J. (1984). "Does the concept of the person vary cross-culturally?" In R. A. Shweder & R. A. Levine (Eds.), *Culture theory: Essays on mind, self and emotion* (pp. 158–199). Cambridge, England: Cambridge University Press.

Silverstein, B., Perdue, L., Peterson, B., & Kelly, E. (1986). The role of the mass media in promoting a thin standard of bodily attractiveness for women. *Sex Roles, 14,* 519–532.

Silverstein, B., Peterson, B., & Perdue, L. (1986). Some correlates of the thin standard of bodily attractiveness for women. *International Journal of Eating Disorders, 5,* 895–905.

Simmons, R. (2002). *Odd girl out: The hidden culture of aggression in girls.* San Diego, CA: Harcourt.

Simmons, R., & Florance, R. (1975). Sex, sex roles, and self image. *Journal of Youth and Adolescence, 4*(3), 229–258.

Sittenfeld, C. (2005). *Prep: A novel.* New York: Random House.

Smith, P. A., & Midlarsky, E. (1985). Empirically derived conceptions of femaleness and maleness: A current view. *Sex Roles, 12,* 313–328.

Spencer, M. B., Cunningham, M., & Swanson, D. P. (1995). Identity as coping: Adolescent African American males' adaptive responses to high-risk environments. In H. W. Harris, H. C. Blue, & E. H. Griffith (Eds.), *Racial and ethnic identity: Psychological development and creative expression* (pp. 31–52). New York: Routledge.

Spencer, M. B., & Dornbush, S. (1990). *American minority adolescents.* In S. S. Feldman & G. R. (Eds.), *At the threshold: The developing adolescent* (pp. 123–146). Cambridge, MA: Harvard University Press.

Spindler, G., & Spindler, L. (1977). Change and continuity in American core values: An anthropological perspective. In G. D. DeRenzo (Ed.), *We the People.* Westport, CT: Greenwood.

Spindler, G., & Spindler, L. (1982). Anthropologists view American culture. *Annual Review of Anthropology, 12,* 49–79.

Spindler, G., & Spindler, L. (1987). Schonhausen revisited and the rediscovery of culture. In G. Spindler & L. Spindler (Eds.), *Interpretive ethnography of education: At home and abroad* (pp. 137–170). Hillsdale, NJ: Erlbaum.

Spiro, M. E. (1993). Is the Western conception of the self "peculiar" within the context of the world cultures? *Ethos, 2,* 107–153.

Spradley, J. P., & Mann, B. J. (1975). *The cocktail waitress: Woman's work in a man's world.* New York: McGraw-Hill.

Stack, C. (1974). *All our kin.* New York: Harper & Row.

Stanback, M. H. (1985). Language and black woman's place: Evidence from the black middle class. In P. A. Treichler, C. Kramarae, & B. Stafford (Eds.), *For Alma Mater: Theory and practice in feminist scholarship* (pp. 177–193). Urbana: University of Illinois Press.

Steedman, C. (1987). *Landscape for a good woman: A story of two lives.* New Brunswick, NJ: Rutgers University Press.

Steele, J. R., & Brown, J. D. (1995). Adolescent room culture: Studying media in the context of everyday life. *Journal of Youth and Adolescence, 24,* 551–576.

Steiner, H., McQuivey, R. W., Pavelski, R., Pitts, T., & Kraemer, H. (2000). Adolescents and sports: Risk or benefit? *Clinical Pediatrics, 39*(3), 161–166.

Sterk, C. E. (2000). *Tricking and tripping: Prostitution in the era of AIDS.* Putnam Valley, NY: Social Change.

Stewart, A. J., & Lykes, M. B. (1985). Conceptualizing gender in personality theory and research. In A. J. Stewart & M. B. Lykes (Eds.), *Gender and personality: Current perspectives on theory and research.* Durham: Duke University.

Stice, E., Schupak-Neuberg, E., Shaw, H. E., & Stein, R. L. (1994). Relation of media exposure to eating disorder symptomatology. *Journal of Abnormal Psychology, 103,* 836–840.

Stice, E., & Shaw, H. E. (1994). Adverse effects of the media portrayed thin-ideal on women and linkages to bulimic symptomatology. *Journal of Social and Clinical Psychology, 13,* 288–308.

Stokes, J., & Levin, I. (1986). Gender differences in predicting loneliness from social network characteristics. *Journal of Personality and Social Psychology, 51,* 1069–1074.

Strauss, C. (2000). The culture concept and the individualism/collectivism debate: Dominant and alternative attributions for class in the United States. In L. Nucci, G. Saxe, & E. Turiel (Eds.), *Culture, thought, and development* (pp. 85–114). Mahwah, NJ: Erlbaum.

Striegel-Moore, R. H., Silberstein, L. R., & Rodin, J. (1986). Toward an understanding of risk factors for bulimia. *American Psychologist, 41,* 246–263.

Suarez-Orozco, C., & Suarez-Orozco, M. (1995). *Transformations.* Stanford, CA: Stanford University Press.

Sutton, L. A. (1995). Bitches and skankly hobags: The place of women in contemporary slang. In K. Hall & M. Bucholtz (Eds.), *Gender articulated: Language and the socially constructed self* (pp. 279–296). New York: Routledge.

Tajfel, H. (1978a). *The social psychology of minorities.* London: Minority Rights Group.

Tajfel, H. (Ed.) (1978b). *Differentiation between social groups: Studies in social psychology of intergroup relations.* New York: Academic Press.

Tajfel, H. (1981). *Groups and social categories: Studies in social psychology.* Cambridge, England: Cambridge University Press.

Tajfel, H. (1987). Social categorization, social identity and social comparison. In H. Tajfel (Ed.), *Differentiation between social groups: Studies in the social psychology of intergroup relations* (pp. 61–76). London: Academic Press.

Tannen, D. (1990). *You just don't understand: Women and men in conversation.* New York: Ballantine.

Tannen, D. (Ed.). (1993). *Gender and conversational interaction.* New York: Oxford University Press.

Tannen, D. (1994). *Gender & discourse.* New York: Oxford University Press.

Thomas, V. G., & James, M. D. (1988). Body image, dieting techniques and sex role traits in urban black women. *American Journal of Orthodontics, 76,* 84–94.

Thorne, B. (1993). *Gender play: Girls and boys in school.* New Brunswick, NJ: Rutgers University Press.

Tobin, J. J., Wu, D. Y. H., & Davidson, D. H. (1989). *Preschool in three cultures: Japan, China, and the United States.* New Haven, CT: Yale University Press.

Tocqueville, A. (1945). *Democracy in America.* New York: Appleton. (Original work published 1835)

Tolman, D. L., Spencer, R., Harmon, T., Rosen-Reynoso, M., & Striep, M. (2004). Getting close, staying cool: Early adolescent boys' experiences with romantic relationships. In N. Way & J. Y. Chu (Eds.), *Adolescent boys: Exploring diverse cultures of boyhood* (pp. 235–255). New York: New York University Press.

Tonnies, F. (1957). *Community and society* (C. P. Loomis, ed. & trans.). New York: Harper & Row. (Original work published 1887)

Trautner, M. N. (2005). Doing gender, doing class: The performance of sexuality in exotic dance clubs. *Gender & Society, 19,* 771–788.

Triandis, H. C. (1996). *Individualism and collectivism.* Boulder: Westview.

Turner, J. C., Hogg, M. A., Oaks, P. J., Reicher, S. D., & Wetherell, M. S. (1987). *Rediscovering the social group: A self-categorization theory.* Oxford, England: Basil Blackwell.

Turner, P. J., & Gervai, J. (1995). A multidimensional study of gender typing in preschool children and their parents: Personality, attitudes, preferences, behavior, and cultural differences. *Developmental Psychology, 31,* 759–772.

Turner, V. (1974). *Drama, fields, and metaphors.* Ithaca, NY: Cornell University Press.

Tyre, P. (2006). The trouble with boys. *Newsweek,* Jan. 30.

Underwood, M. K. (2003). *Social aggression among girls.* New York: Guilford.

Unger, R. H. (1993). Alternative conceptions of sex (and sex differences). In M. Haug, R. E. Whalen, C. Aron, & K. L. Olsen (Eds.), *The development of sex differences and similarities in behaviors* (pp. 457–476). London: Academic Press.

Useem, M. (1984). *The inner circle: Large corporations and the rise of business political activity in the U.S. & U.K.* New York: Oxford University Press.

van Gennep, A. (1960). *The rites of passage.* Chicago: University of Chicago Press. (Original work published 1909)

Varenne, H. (1977). *Americans together.* New York: Teachers College Press.

Varenne, H. (1986). *Symbolizing America.* Lincoln: University of Nebraska Press.

Wakeford, J. (1969 *The cloistered elite.* New York: Praeger.

Wang, M. C., & Taylor, R. D. (2000). *Resilience across contexts: Family, work, culture, and community.* Mahwah: Erlbaun.

Way, N. (1998). *Everyday courage.* New York: New York University Press.

Way, N., & Chu, J. (2004). *Adolescent boys: Exploring diverse cultures of boyhood.* New York: New York University Press.

Way, N. Stauber, H. Y., Nakkula, M. J., & London, P. (1994). Depression and substance use in two divergent high school cultures: A quantitative and qualitative analysis. *Journal of Youth and Adolescence, 23,* 331–357.

Weinberg, I. (1968). Some methodological and field problems of social research in elite secondary schools. *Sociology of Education, 41,* 141–55.

Weisfeld, G. (1999). *Evolutionary principles of human adolescence.* New York: Basic Books.

Weisner, T. S., Gallimore, R., & Jordan, C. (1988). Unpacking cultural effects on classroom learning: Native Hawaiian peer assistance and child-generated activity. *Anthropology and Education Quarterly, 19,* 327–351.

West, C., & Fenstermaker, S. (1995). Doing difference. *Gender and Society, 9,* 8–37.

West, C., & Zimmerman, D. H. (1987). Doing gender. *Gender and Society, 1,* 125–151.

Whiting, B. B., & Edwards, C. P. (1988). *Children of different worlds: The formation of social behavior.* Cambridge, MA: Harvard University Press.

Wilder, D. A. (1986). Cognitive factors affecting the success of intergroup contact. In S. Worchel & W. G. Austin (Eds.), *Intergroup relations* (pp. 49–66). Chicago: Nelson-Hall.

Wilder, D. A., & Thompson, J. E. (1980). Intergroup contact with independent manipulations of in-group and out-group interaction. *Journal of Personality and Social Psychology, 38,* 589–603.

Williams, J. E., & Best, D. L. (1982). *Measuring sex stereotypes: A thirty-nation study.* Beverly Hills, CA: Sage.

Wolfe, A. (1991). *America at century's end.* Berkeley: University of California Press.

Zernike, K. (2000). Ease up, top colleges tell stressed applicants. *New York Times,* Dec. 7.

Zweigenhaft, R. L., & Domhoff, G. W. (2003). *Blacks in the white elite: Will the progress continue?* Lanham, MD: Rowman & Littlefield.

Index ⁍

athletics (*continued*)
  pressure of performance, 224
  self-esteem and, 136
  steroid use and, 137–138
  valuation by females, 114
  wealth and, 91
autonomy and status, 38, 40–41, 43

"bad-ass" attitude of boys, 3, 36, 45, 91, 105, 235, 294
binge drinking. *See also* drugs/drug use; eating disorders
  eating disorders and, 240
  masculinity and, 241
  pressure/stress/burnout and, 19, 21, 307
  of upper class males, 18, 241
bitch squad (girls), 62, 103–104, 107–111, 183–197. *See also* high-class club
bonding, 8, 49
  and binge drinking, 241
  of girls, 283
  of males, 49, 65, 72–73
  socioeconomic *vs.* ethnic, 99
  in sports teams, 73
  and status, 40–42, 99, 190
boys. *See* males

class
  consequences of, 298–299
  and ethnicity/race, 107–111
  price of, 17–18
  and student view of masculinity/femininity, 2
class, lower
  refusal to sell-out by, 166
  sticking together by, 190
class, middle
  resistance to upper class, 99
  sexuality of, 138
  togetherness of, 190
  and working class boys, 99
  and working class girls, 90
class, upper. *See also* bitch squad
  and eating disorders, 18, 240
  emphasis on appearance, 17, 94, 196, 240, 290

gender ideals of, 8
  ideal of purity of females, 139
  importance of volunteerism, 75
  male as provider, 311
  and male binge drinking, 18, 241
  prep schools as entrance to, 27–28
  whites, and boarding schools, 14
  women's focus on social status, 17, 75, 310
class, upper-middle, eating disorders, 18, 240
The Clique television series, 14
cliques, 206–211. *See also* bitch squad (girls); high-class club (boys); nerds
  crowds *vs.*, 164
  defined, 164
  in dining hall, 31, 49, 62, 211–212
  importance of, to students, 165
  of wealthy boys, 127, 189
  of wealthy girls, 48, 51, 62, 103, 127, 191
clothing. *See also* appearance
  judgements based on, 296
  magazine portrayal, 80
  non-preppy style, 178
  and performing class, 94
  preppy style, 94–100
  socioeconomics of, 199–200, 303
college(s), 79, 84, 228–232. *See also* Ivy League colleges
  and admissions, 15, 17
  and boys, 230
  and girls, 229–230, 298
  and right college, 217, 298
  and stress/burnout, 19, 223–224, 228–232
  and student goals, 56, 75, 178, 182, 201, 222–223, 225
community service, 74–76
competition, 16, 27, 185, 204, 209. *See also* athletics; sports teams
  and relationships, 51
condoms, 264–268
conformity, 161–163. *See also* individuality
  and boys, 270
  covert value of, 93–161

and race/ethnicity, 90–91
satisfaction with, 301, 303–305
and social class, 90–91
stereotypes of, 90, 287, 293, 301, 309
gender development, 5
and cognitive processes, 6
and peer groups, 9
psychoanalytic basis for, 5
gender differences, 2–3, 16
and academic performance, 3
biological perspective, 8
and evolutionary theorists, 6
and needs, 39
and social linguistics, 61–63
gender ideals, 5, 11–12, 43, 118–119
gender performance, 7, 40, 60
girl talk/boy talk, 61–65
girls. *See* females
Glamour, 77–78, 80–81
goals
connections as ultimate, 203
and drive to succeed, 298–299
grade priority, 56
male *vs.* female, 9
and priorities, 55–61
stress/pressure of, 27
Gossip Girl television series, 13
groups. *See* peer groups

happiness/unhappiness, 17–18, 241
hazing, 27, 204
amongst Korean students, 182–183
Bolton's policy against, 27, 45
as rite of passage, 204–205
high-class club (boys), 96, 108,
183–197. *See also* bitch squad
hockey, 45, 56, 85, 184, 208, 228. *See
also* masculinity
"bad-ass" player attitude, 291
cliquishness of, 208
and gender identity, 100
importance to boys, 45, 56, 73, 85,
96, 137–138, 208, 225
pressure from parents, 290
pressure to be good, 228
homosexuality, 131, 139, 291. *See also*
sexuality

and boys, 160–161
and girls, 158–160
human development
complexity/diversity of, 4
paradigm shift in, 4
and research methodologies, 9–10
traditional theories of, 3–4
Hustler, 80

ideal man, 119–122, 125–127
ideal woman, 122–125
ideals of self, 39
identity
bravado/macho, African American
males, 90
and clothing, 94–95
formation, women, 5, 6
and nonconformity, 89, 98
individuality, 89–100, 161–163
vs. collectivism, 38
vs. conformity, 38, 89–93
inequality, 166–170, 203–206,
215–216
international students, 1, 180–184, 297
issues and pressures, 45–46
Ivy League colleges, 15, 28, 228–232.
See also college(s)

J. Crew, 96–97

kicked out (of school), 49–50, 201
kinky sex, 141, 145–146
Korea, 182–184

language, 61–65. *See also* student
terminology
Lauren, Ralph, 95–96
legends, 257–258
Lilly, 95–96
love, 262–264
lower-class. *See also* upper-class
refusal to sell-out by, 166
sticking together by, 190

Mademoiselle, 77–78
magazine culture, 76–81
of African American girls, 78

pressures. *See also* stress
  binge drinking from, 19, 21, 307
  concerns of African American
    students, 227, 229
  of conformity, 91–92
  of looking good, girls, 111–113
  of looking good, males, 113–114
  about masculinity, 223, 235, 242
  other-focused, of females, 139
  by parents, on children, 18, 19,
    26–27, 111, 113, 135, 197, 202,
    228, 307
  of performance, of females, 89–90,
    222, 235
  sexual, 139–143, 143–150
private education, demographics
  of, 15
prom, 64–72
  the dance, 71–72
  getting fit for, 67–69
  getting ready, boys, 71
  getting ready, girls, 69–71
  prom shopping, 65–66
  tuxedo rental, 66–67
prom rituals, 65–73
  choice of dates, 68–69
  dancing, male *vs.* female
    perspectives, 71–73
  female appearance concerns, 65–66,
    69–71
  male appearance concerns, 66–67, 71
  preliminary eating behavior, 67
public highs schools *vs.* preparatory
  schools, 21–22

race/ethnicity, 11, 190–191
  and divergent masculinities/
    femininities, 90, 291
  and eating disorders, 136, 240
  and gender, 90–91
  and girls, 121, 191
  and peer groups, 165
  and race relations, 170–181
  and student appearance, 109–111
racial stereotypes, 177, 186–187, 194
ranking systems, 114–117
regrets, 219–220, 286–287

relationships, 46–51, 76. *See also*
  bonding; opposite-sex friends;
  romance; sexuality
  and conformity, 295
  desire to secure, by boys, 294
  desire to secure, by girls, 227
  difficulties/complications, 51–52
  as domain of females, 43
  and eating disorders, 240, 241
  and girl love/boy sex, 262–264
  importance of fitting in, 40
  lack of time for, of males, 18
  and magazine culture, 76
  and male self-directedness, 46
  opposite-sex friends, 52–54
  and performing gender/class/
    ethnicity, 164
  romances, 54–55
  and sex, 262
  and women, 38, 44
revenge sex, 263
Ritalin, 26, 239–240, 250–251. *See also*
  stimulants
rites of passage, 16
  for girls, 255
  and hazing, 204–205
  and seniors, 289
  and summer travel, 289
  for upper classes, 14, 16, 21
  for wealthy Americans, 2
rituals, 7, 24, 72–73. *See also* prom
  rituals
  and cultures, 12
  female, 65–73, 205
  male, 205–206
  school restriction of, 282
  and sexual activity, 260
  of sports teams, 73
  Topless Tuesday, 104
  and traditions, 204–206
  and values, 20
romance, 54–57
rules/rule-breaking, 243–258,
  276–277, 279–282

scholarship students, 25, 183–184,
  195–196, 215, 227